A PART OF NO TRIBE

MY LIFE THROUGH ONE THOUSAND SINGLES

VOLUME TWO - THE EIGHTIES

IAN MOSS

EMPIRE PUBLICATIONS
1 Newton St., Manchester M1 1HW

Contents

Preface

This is a magnificent, erudite and authoritative reference guide to music released in the 1980s. It consists of an eloquent description and evaluation of 1,000 tracks - counting down from 100 -1 for each year – as chosen by Manchester musical maverick, Ian "Moët" Moss.

Ian joins the dots between music released in each year of the eighties with reminders of the socio-political turmoil under Margaret Thatcher's Conservative government and the marvellous music that stemmed from this troubled, chaotic and colourful decade. A seminal figure on the Manchester music scene since the 1970s, Ian was one of a handful of people who actually *did* attend the legendary Sex Pistols gig at the city's Lesser Free Trade Hall in June 1976 leading him, like just about everyone else, to want to form a band. According to Ian in Volume 1 of this series (1970s), the three Sex Pistols gigs he attended in 1976 "changed my life and changed my perception of what could be done with music; and this in turn made me reassess my whole existence and thought processes". He subsequently immersed himself in the vibrant and evolving music scenes in the city and draws on his experiences as both punter and singer-songwriter of punk band The Hamsters and uses this perspective to make incisive and witty commentaries on the releases described in *A Part of No Tribe*. Not only did The Hamsters play with such Manchester luminaries as Joy Division and The Fall, Ian's claims to fame – as related in this book – include declining an offer to audition for a role that was subsequently filled by Tim Roth for the TV drama *Made In Britain*, being in a supergroup that included drummer Mike Joyce (while he was still in The Smiths) and ex-Fall guitarist (now radio DJ) Marc Riley, and being punched in the face by the Bay City Rollers' guitarist!

The result of these experiences is a book that is so much more than the 'Top 1,000 Tracks of the 1980s' I expected when Ian asked me to help him edit it. It brings together singles – released in seven- and twelve-inch format – that are not only unexpected and subjectively selected but placed side-by-side in novel combinations. The rules of Ian's game are that they were all enjoyed (and mostly owned) by him during his wild forays into the magical maze of Manchester's gigs and club nights, such as the those hosted at the Cyprus Tavern, Haçienda, Boardwalk, Gallery, Rafters and The Ritz. Each entry includes the tracks on both sides of the single, the record label under which it was released and the highest UK chart entry. Given that there were multiple versions of most of these singles, the ones listed here are mostly those which Ian has owned himself. Clearly the ones selected by Ian to be closest to number one in each year are records especially close to his heart and ones for which he would want you to feel similar love. But let's not get too uptight about the order in each year because – as listening to a playlist of these tracks will prove – Ian has deliberately, and very skilfully juxtaposed the popular with the obscure, the Australian punk with the Detroit house, the minimalist electro with the alt-country rock. Being as he is part of no tribe, Ian has lovingly crafted an alternative to the standard 'top tracks of the eighties' list. Here, for instance, The Mekons sit proudly next to Madonna in adjacent entries, Melvins with Manatronix, The Slits with Spoonie Gee, Suicide with S-Express, Pixies with Prince, Martha and The Muffins with Michael Prophet. Unfettered as it is by musical snobbery (downwards or upwards), sales (some sold millions, others just a handful), genre, or indeed radio shows, being part of no tribe is the ingredient which makes this such an essential musical reference guide to the eighties, one which negates the stereotyped view of that decade - as Ian himself puts it - as one of "tastelessness and artificiality [...] pastel-coloured knitwear, shiny tracksuits, Noel Edmonds and Phil Collins".

The decision to make this a compendium of singles from the eighties - ignoring album tracks that made no appearance on singles - is highly significant, because successful single sales could make or break musical artistes in the eighties. They were a gateway to national radio play or an appearance on chart dominated programmes such as *Top of the Pops*, *The Tube*, *The Old Grey Whistle Test* or *The Oxford Road Show*, and as such wielded an influence for DIY music artistes well beyond anything today's fragmented streaming culture can offer. The consolidation of the popularity of the twelve-inch single, which gave space for longer versions of tracks that could not be played on the radio, grew hand-in-hand with the influence of DJ culture and the various underground, often anti-establishment scenes that emerged in the eighties. In the pre-internet age, buying the single was the only sure-fire guarantee that you could hear the music you love on tap, without the vocal interference of hysterical radio DJs babbling over the intros and outros. The one exception was John Peel's late-night Radio 1 programme where you could hear (and therefore successfully record) tracks uninterrupted in their entirety. Peel showcased many of the bands that appear in this book and from which much of my own music education stemmed. But what I have learnt from editing this book and listening to just about every song it describes, is that many of us Peel acolytes unwittingly exhibited the kind of tribal behaviour that we claimed to reject, clinging to the music genres and artistes presented in that two-hour show as if all outside it was a complete vacuum.

So the assemblage of records in this book is, like its writer, as 'punk' as it gets. Not punk as in just three-chord, two-minute-long, guitar-thrash, shouty-wordy punk (the best kind of which Ian is himself a skilful practitioner) but punk as experimentation, as accepting no boundaries, as not pandering to the whims of music executives or cynically leeching off trends for a quick buck. Most of all Ian appreciates the wealth of new genres from their roots in post-punk, disco, reggae and soul and their transformation into rap, Chicago & Detroit house, acid, techno, Italo-disco, hi-NRG, trance, grunge, electro-minimalism, proto-Britpop and a bewilderingly array of other sub-genres I wouldn't dare try to categorise. Ian's continuing involvement with a wealth of local musicians from all walks of life and his nurturing of new talent in the 2020s, as collaborator, gig-organiser and record label owner of German Shepherd Records, ensures that tribalism will never flourish in his presence.

Editing this book has been an education and a complete joy. It has completely reinvigorated my somewhat tired and narrowed view of what I thought constituted eighties music. Providing a unique and thorough perspective on some of the best music of that decade, this is both an essential reference book and an important historical document.

Matt Davies
Bass guitarist, Factory Acts

Foreword

The twist from the dark introspection of late '70s post-punk, the bleeding canyons of goth, the thrash of the emergent American alternative, to the garish hyperbole of the '80s often seems seismic. As if, in an energy flash, in came Kajagoogoo and leg-warmers. And, make no mistake, the eighties would become the most derided of musical eras. It's not hard to see why. What other era would allow this writer - 24 at the start of the decade - to prance about unchallenged in a yellow leather motorcycle jacket, scarlet corduroy jeans, indeed, woollen leg warmers and bright orange suede shoes. Not to mention the hair, which had evolved into a Ziggy-inspired wonky mullet.

And this in Stockport!

Was this an indication of the new age of liberalism or, indeed, a sugary wash of colour and hype? And let's be honest, there is a strand of eighties culture that really did seem like the second wave of glam. This and the mid-term horrors of Band/Live Aid, where bolshy worthiness battled with the bitchy edge of pop. Personally, I never forgave the insulting song-title 'Do They Know It's Christmas?' but that's just me.

All this... and Shakin' Stevens!

Well, that's one way of glimpsing the decade but as this, Ian Moss's second exploration of a ten-year musical journey (following his unveiling of the seventies) perceptively highlights, the eighties actually provided a depth and scope of musical tastes and stylistic advances that remain beyond comparison. It dawned on me recently that I spent much of the decade listening to Miles Davis (who enjoyed a captivating renaissance), Tom Waits and Motown. Odd choices, perhaps but that didn't mean that I lived in some retrospective dream.

Like most people I arrived home from work every Friday evening and immediately tuned in to *The Tube* on Channel Four. Eighties weekends truly began with The Jam, rushing onto that Newcastle stage and I would watch rapt as I devoured an exotic vegetable lasagna.

I loved it all. The beauteous and the plain daft. Pastel-coloured trousers and floppy hats. In Manchester we were unholy and wholly fortunate. In May 1982 The Hacienda opened, initially to unleash a varied cocktail of music onto that maple dance-floor: old Motown, fun and reggae, chunks of goth and Eurobeat. In 1983 I accompanied New Order during the latter days of their American tour and was exposed to hip-hop, electro, Chicago house… and this funny little English band, soaking in these diverse and street-inspired sounds while struggling with their embryonic electronic devices, would be inspired to make the greatest music of their lives.

Personally, for what it's worth, a part of me will forever be driving through North Wales, listening to ABC's *Lexicon of Love*… and Dexy's, Fun Boy Three and The Bunnymen's unearthly Liverpool album, *Ocean Rain*.

I skim the surface here but on these pages Ian digs as deep as a Mansfield miner. His writing is devoid of hipness and pose and stylistic overplay, which is ironic in a book on the eighties. He was an outsider artist back then and remains so today. He is outside looking in… or perhaps inside looking out? I don't think there is a music writer in England right now who is blessed with such a broad vantage point and depth of musical knowledge. Ian understands that the narrowness that seems to define this fascinating decade is an illusion which continues through re-runs of *Top of the Pops* and, yes, memories of the aforementioned *The Tube*, *The Oxford Road Show* and *Loose Talk*. We eagerly anticipated these television shows and captured them on our new VCRs. What freedom, to be able to watch and re-watch!

Yet Ian has always had the ability to pull back from the perceived view and present a wider truth. It is the story of a fabulous reality, much of which has languished in the shadowy fringes. Ian can take you there…

Mick Middles
March 2023

Introduction

I was aged 22 as we shuffled out of the seventies into the eighties. I suppose I expected things to pretty much carry on the same way they had been going - in a relatively predictable trajectory - but I was wrong. Huge changes would occur politically, technologically, sociologically, and above all artistically, notably in music. Here in the UK, the Conservative Party - under the leadership of Margaret Thatcher - laid siege to the working classes. They attacked the unions and the welfare state, preaching a culture of 'greed is good', and caused a schism in society, a clear dividing line between the haves and have nots. They dragged the country into an avoidable war in the Falkland Islands, provoking an outbreak of nationalistic pride and jingoism on one side and abhorrence and shame on the other.

In 1980 the US elected as its 40th president one Ronald Reagan, a right wing bigot and former b-movie actor. He was a dangerous buffoon whose finger seemed itching to press the nuclear war button against a visibly-weakening Soviets. Despite this, muscles were being flexed behind the so-called 'Iron Curtain', as the Soviets were clearly up for a fight that may well have triggered Armageddon. Thatcher, of course, loved Reagan and the feeling was mutual and together they created an axis of evil. US military bases with missiles aimed at the USSR were welcomed on British soil while relations with our European neighbours were strained to breaking point by Thatcher's 'us and them' attitude. All of this would have a huge influence on the arts, as the field became highly politicised. And in film, theatre and music, voices of dissent challenged the brutalist, heartless policies of our leaders.

An avalanche of technological advances influenced further developments in musical instruments and recording studios. The pace of change was such that one model supplanted the previous new thing at amazing speed. Prices became affordable, opening up routes for a new breed savvy enough to seize the possibilities of what was achievable with synthesisers, drum machines, samplers and imagination. The synth-pop explosion at the beginning of the decade was followed by the hip-hop, house and techno scenes, built on the synergy of humans and machines to create something fresh, exciting and new - music that looked to the future rather than rehashing the past. This co-existed with the still vibrant underground of artists using conventional instrumentation in unconventional ways to underpin their desire for self-expression. In the UK, punk - without ever dying completely - was supplanted by so-called 'Indie', a term used to describe a fey, jangly, twee confection much loved by music journalists at the (by now appalling) *New Musical Express*. America produced music with more intelligence and grit, ranging from hardcore through to industrial and country music-tinged sounds offering vibrant expression and human connection. The dominant figures of the seventies declined markedly in influence. David Bowie, Stevie Wonder and The Bee Gees lost their sparkle, while Bob Marley sadly lost his life. New stars emerged in the shape of Prince and Madonna while lesser-known figures such as Juan Atkins and Afrika Bambaataa dramatically reshaped music, taking it from the margins into the mainstream.

I will attempt to lead you through the music that sound-tracked my 1980s. As the book title suggests, I was part of no tribe, immersing myself in all forms of music. I hung out at all manner of clubs, frequented tiny gigs with a handful of punters and lost myself among the thousands in huge arena-sized shows. Keeping an open mind preserved the joy of these experiences.

The aim of this book is not to create a definitive guide of the best music of the era but a reflection of my tastes at the time. My opinions are no more valid than yours.

From the Factory and the Funhouse at the start of the decade, through the years of The Boardwalk, The Haçienda and beyond. Step back in time with me into the era of body-popping, break-dancing and jacking; into the era of synth-pop, acid house, no wave and grunge; into the era that saw a change from the seven to the twelve inch single before the invention of CDs created space for longer tracks and multiple mixes of the same song.

Treat this book as a voyage through sound with me as your navigator.

As Frankie said, "Welcome to the Pleasuredome!"

Ian Moss, March 2023

1980

Manchester in 1980 was my playground. I was fairly well-known, being the singer in a band called The Hamsters who gigged regularly in major venues that catered for the vibrant Manchester musical underground. The Funhouse at the Mayflower Club in Gorton was the venue with which we were most associated but we also played at the legendary Factory, AKA The Russell Club in Hulme; the Cyprus Tavern on Princess Street where I also DJed in the Cellar Bar, sometimes run as The Can Club by The Fall and Manchester Polytechnic's Cavendish House. Then there was The Squat, Rafters and Ardri Ballroom - music coursed through the city as it did my veins.

Along with its football teams, music was the heartbeat of Manchester. Andy Zero ran the *City Fun* magazine which assembled the disparate strands, creating a semblance of order and unification. It allowed hitherto unconnected artists to forge alliances, acting as a barometer of taste by promoting acts it deemed most worthy of patronage. Its importance cannot be understated.

Newly released records were largely purchased at Discount Records, a stall in the underground market. Here, I was afforded a generous discount and topical banter owing to my role in the cultural milieu *and* the fact it was run by nice, friendly people. Second-hand vinyl was hoovered up at John Hillell's shop in Ashton-under-Lyne where I passionately sought out rare soul sounds Record labels had sprung up. Rabid, Object and TJM released music by local bands, somewhat overshadowed by Buzzcocks-sponsored New Hormones who hosted the Beach Club at Oozits on Shudehill where art-house cinema and excellent bands competed for attention and, of course, Factory Records. Factory were often regarded with disdain and suspicion owing to a perceived elitism and their high-profile media links. 'Fat Tory' became their alternative title! Attitudes softened in the wake of Ian Curtis's tragic death. Genuine sorrow and pain swept through the community. I spent an evening in the Millstone pub with the remaining members of Joy Division and their manager Rob

Gretton just a week or so after Ian had died. Still in a state of shock, they seemed resolved to carry on. It was difficult to see how they could possibly put their will into practice, yet remarkably seven weeks later they played a low-key and very dignified set at the Beach Club as New Order. It was poignant, signifying an end to one chapter and the opening of a new one. A brand new decade and a regeneration for them, the city and the UK post punk scene.

The wider musical world was also on the cusp of change and another horrible death came to signify that the innocence of the 1960s and 70s was over. In December I woke to the news that John Lennon had been murdered.

The dream was well and truly over and a new reality was upon us.

EVENTS

In Saudi Arabia 63 insurgents are beheaded for their part in a siege at the Great Mosque in Mecca.

The existence of Janus, a moon of Saturn, is established.

There is a mass boycott by 82 western nations of the Moscow Olympics in protest at the Russian invasion of Afghanistan but not the United Kingdom who attend over the wishes of the UK government.

A mass exodus of people dissatisfied with life in Cuba becomes known as The Mariel Boatlift.

There is rioting in Saint Paul's, Bristol instigated by racist policing.

Zimbabwe gains independence from the UK. Robert Mugabe is elected as prime minister.

Six Iranian terrorists take control of the Iranian embassy in London holding staff hostage. A six-day siege is ended when the SAS storm the building killing five terrorists. The BBC interupts coverage of the World Snooker Championship final to show live coverage of the end of the siege.

Yugoslavian leader Josip Broz Tito dies.

Lech Walesa leads strikes in the shipyard of Gdansk in Poland leading to the formation of the first free trade union in the Soviet block. It is named *Solidarność* (Solidarity).

The Gotthard tunnel in Switzerland is opened - the world's longest highway tunnel at 10.1 miles.

Iraq initiates war with neighbouring Iran.

Riots in Tallinn, Estonia are crushed by the occupying Soviet forces.

Manchester United sign Ray Wilkins from Chelsea for £750,000 and finish second in the league in the 1979/80 season. Under manager Dave Sexton, the playing style is boring to watch. Joe Jordan is top scorer with a paltry 13 goals. Liverpool win the league, Nottingham Forest the European Cup and West Ham the FA Cup. English fans riot at that year's European Championship as the hooligan problem grows.

NOTABLE BIRTHS

Jenson Button; Xavi; Ronaldinho; Russell Howard; Jay Reatard; Venus Williams; Macaulay Culkin; Ben Whishaw; Jake Gyllenhaal; Luke Chadwick; Carl Kirton.

NOTABLE DEATHS

Cecil Beaton; Professor Longhair; Jimmy Durante; Bon Scott; Dixie Dean; Jesse Owens; Jean-Paul Sartre; Alfred Hitchcock; Ian Curtis; Billy Butlin; Peter Sellers; Yootha Joyce; John Bonham; Hattie Jacques; Steve Peregrine Took; Steve McQueen; Mae West; Darby Crash; Oswald Mosley; John Lennon; Tim Hardin; Tito

NOTABLE BOOKS PUBLISHED

A Confederacy of Dunces - John Kennedy Toole

Midnight's Children - Salman Rushdie

No One Here Gets Out Alive - Danny Sugerman

Earthly Powers - Anthony Burgess

Rites of Passage - William Golding

Waiting for the Barbarians - J M Coetzee

The Name of the Rose – Umberto Eco

NOTABLE FILM RELEASES

Airplane; The Coal Miner's Daughter; The Elephant Man; The Empire Strikes Back; Heaven's Gate; Raging Bull; The Shining; Breaker Morant; The Big Red One.

AUTHOR'S NOTE

Before I start, a special mention must go to a version of Syd Barrett's wonderful song 'Gigolo Aunt' by Vibrators front man Knox Carnochan. It really should be included because it is a great record but though its omission was an oversight, I cannot bring myself to delete another choice to shoehorn it into position.

100
ELVIS COSTELLO
AND THE ATTRACTIONS
New Amsterdam
Dr Luther's Assistant/Ghost Train/
Just a Memory
36
F-Beat Records

On the back of his success with the single 'Oliver's Army' and album *Armed Forces*, Elvis Costello booked himself into a cheap recording studio in Pimlico where he recorded dozens of new songs in demo form playing all the instruments himself. 'New Amsterdam' was one of those songs. It was attempted using his band The Attractions but none of their attempts matched the fluidity and charm of the demo and so ultimately that was the version used for a public release.

The song portrays somebody landing in New York and finding themselves bewildered by the pace of things and lack of warmth. That sense of bafflement is perfectly captured in the clever word play which tumbles from Costello's tongue. And this is complimented by a superb snaking melody that rolls and tumbles in time with the vocal creating a compelling, near mesmerising, whole.

99
PYLON
Cool/Cool Dub
NO CHART PLACING
DB Records

Pylon emerged from Athens, Georgia, playing a nervy yet melodic brand of quick stepping art-pop. Drums are disciplined and rigid whilst the guitar is used in bursts like a ray gun. They are at once playful but also deadly serious and, in singer Vanessa Briscoe Hay, had a vocalist who delivered powerfully with a distinct oddball style. 'Cool' is a song about people *acting* cool rather than doing the things they really want to do. It is a denunciation of self-denial over artistic self-expression.

98
JOHN CALE
Mercenaries (Ready for War)
Rosegarden Funeral of Sores
NO CHART PLACING
Spy Records

John Cale rarely released singles. The fact that this was specially recorded for that specific purpose suggests it was considered special by its creator. 'Mercenaries' is a vicious sounding rocker with crashing drums, slashing guitars and pounded piano to the fore. None of those instruments though match Cale's primal, disturbing and uncomfortable vocal as he inhabits the persona of a killer going into combat only for the money. Not a sliver of conscience is offered up in this deeply dark, cynical and highly-charged portrayal which is also something of a thriller. The B-side, 'Rosegarden Funeral of Sores' was covered later in the year by Bauhaus on the 12" release of their version of T-Rex's 'Telegram Sam'.

97
THE MOB
Witch Hunt/Shuffling Souls
NO CHART PLACING
All the Madmen Records

The Mob were a band from Yeovil. Each member was an individual friend of mine, and as The Mob they and my band The Hamsters played many times together around the time of this release. Opening with a harrowing scream, The Mob's individualistic sound startles as Mark Wilson's almost skeletal guitars mesh rhythmically with Graham Fallows' crisp drums and the superlative melodic bass-playing of Curtis Youe pulses, acting as the heartbeat of the song. Mark begins to sing in a totally unconventional style - nakedly raw, sounding spooked as paranoia about a gathering storm of oppression is sniffed out. Just over the horizon are dark forces intent on a crackdown. Just over the horizon is the coming of the Witch Hunt...

96
ROBERT WYATT
At Last I am Free/Strange Fruit
NO CHART PLACING
Rough Trade

In 1978 Chic had released their second album, *C'est Chic*. Its centrepiece had been 'At Last I am Free', seven minutes of gorgeous, smooth, ice cool contemplation wrapped in a song about a romantic parting that also signified the hope of renewal. Two years later English counter-culture figure Robert Wyatt reshaped the song in his own style. Gone is the luminous sheen and wide-screen approach of Chic's original. Replaced by a slimmed down to four minutes flesh and blood version, Wyatt locates the agonised soul of the song atop a shuffling track of piano, organ and percussion. At his plaintive best, Wyatt pulls on the heartstrings revealing the pain in letting go of a love, even as he accepts it is an action he must take.

95
FAD GADGET
Fireside Favourite/Insecticides
NO CHART PLACING
Mute Records

Frank Tovey was Fad Gadget. This, his second single, was also the second release from Mute Records following The Normal's 'Warm Leatherette'. Fad Gadget's sound at this point is best described as a futuristic primitivism. He utilised modern technology - synthesisers and drum machines - combining them with found objects and playing with them as if they were children's toys, coaxing sounds that would have surprised the manufacturers. Add a lyric comparing sexual conquest with nuclear war, sung in a disarmingly jaunty, naïve nursery rhyme style and the result was inventive and highly-=memorable.

94
KURTIS BLOW
The Breaks/Instrumental/
Do It Yourself
47
Mercury Records

This became the first hip-hop single to sell 500,000 copies and earn a gold disc. It was unusual in the genre because instead of samples, a crack live band were assembled to lay down the funky groove over which Kurtis Blow rapped about 'the breaks'. These were the misfortunes in life that must be traversed and overcome. Repetition of the word 'break' indicates when a lyric ends, followed by the musical breakdown over which the break-dancers from Harlem to Harpurhey could do their energetic thing with style.

93
ECHO AND THE BUNNYMEN
Rescue/Simple Stuff/Pride
62
Korova Records

The Bunnymen's second single was a confident, sure-footed gem for such an inexperienced band. Singer Ian McCulloch cuts a lovelorn figure, poetic and sensitive, pleading to the object of his desire to rescue him over an upbeat melody. Will Sergeant's guitar flourishes add colour to the beat provided by bassist Les Pattinson and the flesh and blood drummer, Pete de Freitas, who had replaced 'Echo', the band's drum machine. Towards the end of the song, the rhetorical question in the refrain 'Is this the blues I'm singing?' is a stroke of lyrical genius.

92
ALAN VEGA
Jukebox Babe / Lonely
NO CHART PLACING
Celluloid Records

With Suicide on hold, Alan Vega launched his solo career with this delicious, warped neo-rockabilly track, accompanied by Phil Hawk on minimalistic guitar. Playing an unchanging riff alongside a pulsing electronic rhythm, Vega hiccups his way through the track akin to Elvis Presley *in extremis*. All the momentum of the track comes from the increasingly frenetic vocal. Vega's breathing is laboured and desperate. A brief snatch of mouth harp further enervates, and the track is wrapped up in under three minutes. 'Jukebox Babe' was painterly in an impressionistic style and an exciting artistic diversion for Suicide's devotees to digest .

91
BLUE ANGEL
I'm Gonna be Strong/Anna Blue
NO CHART PLACING
Polydor

Composed by writing team Barry Mann and Cynthia Weil, 'I'm Gonna Be Strong' was first recorded by Frankie Lane in 1963. A year later Gene Pitney took a hyper-dramatic and emotional reading into the charts. Now came Blue Angel, fronted by Cyndi Lauper, who used the Pitney version as a template and magnified every shred of emotion until it becomes an anguished tour de force of soul-shredding power. A song without choruses, it builds from relative calm to its final agonised cry and silence. Lauper transforms it into a burning showcase for the incandescent purity of her voice, capable of reducing listeners to either awed silence or sorrowful tears brought about by a beautiful performance that conveys such deep despair.

90
SPOONIE GEE
MEETS THE SEQUENCE
Monster Jam
Monster Jam Instrumental
NO CHART PLACING
Sugar Hill Records

Spoonie Gee was an early rapper and the person credited with coining the phrase 'hip-hop'. He had appeared as part of The Treacherous Three on the single 'New Rap Language'. 'Monster Jam' was his first release on signing to Sugar Hill Records. Backed by female rap trio The Sequence, the sound here follows the highly funky template laid down by previous Sugar Hill singles such as 'Rappers Delight'. The thinking presumably was 'if it ain't broke it don't fix it', and this indeed still sounded very fresh and crisp indeed.

89
THE POP GROUP/THE SLITS
Where There's a Will There's a Way
In the Beginning There was Rhythm
NO CHART PLACING
Rough Trade

Sharing a drummer in Bruce Smith as well as an artistic sensibility and an uncompromising approach, it made much sense for The Pop Group and The Slits to join together to release this shared single. Both bands use funk rhythms as a starting point to launch their aural manifestos. They were both blessed with an utterly startling vocalist who heeded no conventions. Mark Stewart brings a whiff of cordite into his performance as he defiantly states we should "join the undefeated!" Equally arresting, Ari Up sing-speaks her way through the cheerful James Brown influenced riffing and attests that "silence is a rhythm too". Both sides of this single are touched by magic.

88
THE SOFT BOYS
I Wanna Destroy/Old Pervert
NO CHART PLACING
Armageddon Records

The Soft Boys, fronted by Robin Hitchcock, are usually equated with an eccentric brand of particularly English psychedelic whimsy. But here on 'I Wanna Destroy You' they bare teeth and flex muscles delivering an anti-fascist anthem decrying the media's role in whipping up jingoistic pride that leads to war. Musically, it's a series of guitar-heavy surges that all lead to the gleefully sung, twisted pop choruses of "I Wanna Destroy You"!

87
MARTHA AND THE MUFFINS
Echo Beach/Teddy the Dink
10
Dindisc

Martha and the Muffins hailed from Toronto and were signed to Virgin Records' supposedly all-electronic Dindisc label. 'Echo Beach' was only the third song ever written by guitarist Mark Gane, who was inspired to write the lyric when engaged in a mind-numbing job examining rolls of wallpaper for faults. Aligned to a distinctive guitar pattern, the song positively sparkles. Keyboards and saxophone parts add a warm, dreamy texture and layers of emotional depth as the singer yearns for the mythical Echo Beach, a sepia-drenched memory of a better time and place.

86
MICHAEL PROPHET
Gunman/Gunman Version
NO CHART PLACING
Volcano

Michael Haynes was renamed and initially championed by Vivian 'Yabby You' Jackson who gave him musical direction and his production techniques to extract the best from Michael's incredible crying tenor vocal style. Here though, he teamed up with ghetto producer 'Junjo' Lawes to record the autobiographical 'Gunman' about an armed robbery at his home. Over a dramatic horn riff and hypnotic bass-line, the tale of waking to find intruders with guns and bayonets standing over him is recounted. The fear and tension are palpable and though the rhythm makes the urge to dance irrepressible, the vocal is one of reality and dread.

85
YELLOW MAGIC ORCHESTRA
Computer Games (Theme from the Invaders)/ Firecracker
17
A&M Records

Blending Asian melodies with American R&B rhythms alongside computerised sound effects simulating arcade games, this release was irresistible and hugely influential among the fledgling hip-hop community. De La Soul, Afrika Bambaataa and Mantronix where amongst those who later sampled it.

84
THE UNDERTONES
Wednesday Week/I Told You So
11
Sire Records

Undertones song-writing guitarist John O'Neill had emerged as a credible rival to Buzzcocks' Pete Shelley, as creator of pop-punk nuggets that lodged in the memory and the hit parade. In 1980 they had already released the excellent 'My Perfect Cousin', but easily topped that gem with this stylistic departure. Their usual approach displayed the strong influence of The Ramones but with this single they adopted a slower, gentler and altogether richer sound, akin to sixties acts such as Honeybus or Simon Dupree's Big Sound. It was a tale of bemused hurt at a callous romantic rejection and extracted a brilliant singing performance from Feargal Sharkey.

83
LOOSE JOINTS
Is It All Over My Face? (Female Vocal)/
Is It All Over My Face? (Male Vocal)
NO CHART PLACING
West End Records

Written and produced by Arthur Russell and made a dance-floor smash at New York's Paradise Garage by DJ Larry Levan, this was dance music as high art - a sophisticated and subtle mix of Latin percussion, flute and guitar. Voices sit quite low in the mix but audible enough for the impact of the sexually graphic lyric to be heard and felt, it was akin to a re-enactment of 'The Last Days Of Sodom' set beneath the lasers and mirror balls of the discotheque.

82
WAS NOT WAS
Wheel Me Out/
Hello Operator… I Mean Dad… I Mean Police… I Can't Even Remember Who I Am
NO CHART PLACING
Ze Records

Detroit natives David Weiss and Don Fagenson formed Was Not Was in 1979 and were a perfect fit for Mutant Disco label Ze. Their first release was 'Wheel Me Out', an outré dance track voiced with great panache by David's mother Elisabeth Elkin Weiss who was a former radio pioneer and actress. Containing an utterly relentless, killer groove and a wonderfully melodic hook, it was underpinned by a puzzling lyric imbued with gravitas by Mrs Weiss, and a gospel style chorus. 'Wheel Me Out' was a quite wonderful introduction into the strange sonic world of the newly christened Don and David Was.

81
KANO
It's a War/Ahija
NO CHART PLACING
Emergency Records

Kano were an Italo-Disco project put together in Milan. They created music heavy on funky R&B rhythms, incorporating hand-claps, synthesiser pulses, and effects-laden vocals that sounded like the future had arrived on those club dance-floors intent on pushing the musical envelope rather than playing safe. I first heard this at Manchester gay club, Bernard's Bar. It sounded monumental and exciting back then and retains some of that atmospheric quality in the present too.

80
JOHN FOXX
Underpass/Film One
31
Virgin Metal Beat

'Underpass' was the first release by John Foxx after he left Ultravox. It was a chillingly cold piece of robotic music played entirely on synthesisers displaying a strong dystopian vision that reflected the feelings of the time

- people forced to live in horrible brutalist architecture, a corrupt and violent police force and an uncaring, callously cruel government. Foxx perfectly captured the experiences of a night-time drive through empty, ugly, urban landscapes.

79
JOSEF K
It's Kinda Funny/Final Request
NO CHART PLACING
Postcard Records

Edinburgh's Josef K were a band who rejected the rock 'n' roll look and lifestyle in search of something purer and more cerebral. They were be-suited, teetotal and serious, determined to pursue their own agenda in their own style. They sounded superficially similar to their label mates, Orange Juice, sharing similar tastes in American soul and English post punk bands. They were, however, much more sombre and dark-hued. Claims have been made that 'It's Kinda funny' is about the death of Ian Curtis and is carried on a bass line clearly borrowed from Joy Division. However, singer-songwriter Paul Haig told *Uncut* magazine in September 2014 that it is a "song about the human condition", based on falling for a girl who's he'd arranged to meet but who didn't fathom the depths of his emotion. "So the first part is a very normal unrequited love thing. Then it goes off into the existential chewy stuff". Either way reading through the cryptic lyrics the ambiguity and delivery provides a compelling grace and distinct charm.

78
THE RAMONES
Baby I Love You
High Risk Insurance
8
Sire Records

Teaming up with Phil Spector in the hope that the liaison would signal a change of fortune and provide The Ramones with hits, the relationship between band and producer was apparently fraught and failed in its objective commercially and artistically. The one exception was a remake of Spector's own 'Baby I Love You', originally a hit for The Ronettes in 1963. Sung exquisitely by the group's great romantic figure, Joey Ramone, the rest of the band are practically smothered in the sweeping string arrangement. Although the record was a surprising but deserved hit, it did little in the way of providing lasting popularity for the band. It simply didn't sound like them.

77
THE TEARDROP EXPLODES
Treason (It's Just a Story)
Read It in Books
NO CHART PLACING
(Reissued 1981 - 18)
Zoo Records

Fizzing, superior pop with swirling Doors-influenced organ adding a psychedelic tinge marked The Teardrop Explodes final independently released single. Produced by ex-Big In Japan man Clive Langer, along with Alan Winstanley, it packed a mighty punch. Also of note was B-side 'Read It in Books' jointly written by Teardrop's frontman Julian Cope and Ian McCulloch when they were allies. It had previously been recorded and released on Echo and The Bunnymen's first single

76
SPANDAU BALLET
To Cut a Long Story Short
To Cut a Long Story Short (Instrumental)
5
Chrysalis Records

Emerging from London's Blitz Club and soon to be dubbed 'New Romantics', Spandau Ballet arrived with this striking piece of electro pop. A jagged synth-line embedded in an up-tempo funk style atop glitter beat drums is the platform for lyrics about an ex-soldier traumatised by war, sitting alone on a park bench thinking of the boy he once was and lamenting what he has suffered. Far exceeding my expectations and counteracting my prejudices, I happily conceded it really was excellent.

75
YOUNG MARBLE GIANTS
Final Day/Radio Silents/ Cakewalking/Colossal Youth
NO CHART PLACING
Rough Trade

The Welsh trio of Alison Statton and brothers Stuart and Philip Moxham combined to make strikingly modest yet highly original music. Their minimalistic simplicity - including an absence of drums - made them a unique proposition, and Stuart Moxham's song-writing was consistently melodic and intriguing. The four tracks here provide a vivid snapshot of Young Marble Giants' distinctiveness. Philip's nimble bass playing, Stuart's scratchy guitar and ear-worm organ figures, and the clarity of Alison's restrained and quiet singing. Young Marble Giants carried warmth, intelligence and an adventurous spirit in their songs.

74
GO BETWEENS
I Need Two Heads
Stop Before You Say It
NO CHART PLACING
Postcard Records

The core duo of Robert Forster and Grant McLennan had travelled from Australia to the UK to kick-start a musical odyssey that produced many jewels. Signed to Glasgow label Postcard, they entered the studio with Steven Daly of Orange Juice on drums and Alternative TV and future Psychic TV guitarist Alex Ferguson producing.

'I Need Two Heads' had been written by Forster in response to the seemingly inexhaustible amount of tasks that needed attention as the pair acclimated to life in the UK. With a deliciously funny lyric and a chiming guitar accompaniment, their opening statement was a joyous and resounding success.

73
THE SPECIALS
Do Nothing/Maggie's Farm
4
Two-Tone Records

With their previous single 'Stereotypes', The Specials had moved on from their ska/punk beginnings and were shaping up to be something more satisfying and interesting. The single version is given a spacey lounge atmosphere, with the addition of 'ice rink string sounds' by Jerry Dammers. Rico Rodriguez was also allowed more room to display his creativity and coaxed incredible sounds from the trombone whilst the lugubrious vocals of Terry Hall were a perfect match for this new direction. Lynval Golding's lyrics allude to a sense of frustration at a prevailing societal apathy, set to a disarmingly cheerful and ironic melody. The flip side was a dirge-like take on Bob Dylan's classic song – transformed into a two-fingered salute to our horrible prime minister in residence.

72
JAMES BLOOD ULMER
Are You Glad to be in America? TV Blues
NO CHART PLACING
Rough Trade

Following a career that featured stints with such luminaries as Ornette Coleman and Larry Young, guitarist James Blood Ulmer was no secret to the jazz world where his fractious style of bloodily unleashing shards of thrilling notes was highly appreciated. A deal with Rough Trade brought him to a wider audience of jazz virgins who found themselves equally astonished by the man's fire and skill. 'Are You Glad to be in America?' was an avant-garde jam on a funky theme, with Ulmer's vocal rich and soulful - a vital ingredient as he jives and winds through a fragmented lyric. Resplendent with thought and expression, thick with doubt among flashes of anger, the answer to the question seemed to be a fairly emphatic no.

71
LOLEATTA HOLLOWAY
Love Sensation
Short End of the Stick
NO CHART PLACING
Gold Mind Records

Written and produced by Dan Hartman, 'Love Sensation' was not originally intended for Loleatta Hathaway but Bette Midler or Patti Labelle. His mind was changed when he witnessed a Holloway club performance, which he tried to recreate in the studio after multiple takes. The high-intensity result lights up the recording as she strains agonisingly over the energetic track. The single was a dance chart hit in the US and enjoyed an afterlife as a dance single staple, sampled multiple times most notably for the Black Box hit 'Ride On Time'.

70
ORANGE JUICE
Blue Boy/Love Sick
NO CHART PLACING
Postcard Records

On the Postcard era singles, the young Orange Juice rattled and jangled inelegantly whilst Edwin Collins crooned in a most un-rock like manner. The effect was curiously charming, for beneath the limited instrumental prowess and air of arrogance, the band carried a heart bursting with fabulous pop melodies and funny, clever wordplay. They were quite irresistible though irritating too, as I discovered when my group The Hamsters shared a bill with them on their first foray south of the border from their native Glasgow to Manchester.

However 'Blue Boy' was a fabulous single, a remnant of the set played by the pre-Orange Juice band The Nu Sonics. Fronted by songsmith Collins it is something of an homage to Buzzcocks' Pete Shelley with echoes of that band's style in its construction. 'Lovesick' was equally strong and perhaps more individualistic.

69
BUZZCOCKS
Strange Thing/Airwaves Dream
NO CHART PLACING
United Artists

It was clear even then that time was running out for Buzzcocks. Their third and best album, *A Different Kind of Tension,* flopped, as did two magnificent singles taken from it. The tour arranged to support it had seen half-empty venues and reviews had been more interested in support act, Joy Division, than Buzzcocks themselves. Compounding things, Pete Shelley was dealing with the stress and depression that ensued by self-medicating, using LSD as an escape. With three double A-side singles planned, this was the second and one of Buzzcocks' best ever. With excellent production from Martin Hannett, Shelley's 'Strange Thing' was a dark scab-scratching exercise in a repetitive style, somewhere between Wire and Can. Steve Diggle's 'Airwaves Dream' was also fine, similar to Joy Division's more up-tempo recordings, riding on a propulsive but melodic bass line from Steve Garvey with an urgent vocal from Diggle.

68
MATERIAL
Discourse/Slow Murder
NO CHART PLACING
Red Records

Material were led by highly-regarded bassist Bill Laswell, and pursued an avant-funk direction displayed here on their first release. The bass is, of course, to the fore and provides what melody is on offer as the drums chatter and atmospheric blocks of sound are dropped into the mix while a vocal is chanted with a large degree of venom, not dissimilar to the sound of The Pop Group, undoubtedly a good thing.

67
COATI MUNDI
Que Pasa/Me No Pop I
32
ZE Records

Sugar-coated Andy Hernandez - otherwise known as Coati Mundi - was the vibraphone and marimba player as well as musical director for Kid Creole And The Coconuts, and this single constituted his first foray into solo work. The tracks are light, happy-go-lucky excursions into Latin jazz. Coati Mundi plays a larger than life character in the vein of pre-war band-leaders such as Cab Calloway or Spike Jones and his irrepressible good-humoured charm and style shines through on this jewel of a single.

66
THROBBING GRISTLE
Adrenalin
Distant Dreams (Part two)
NO CHART PLACING
Industrial Records

Two missives from the death factory were issued on the same day in the form of a pair of Throbbing Gristle singles, 'Subhuman'/'Something Came Over Me', and 'Adrenalin'/'Distant Dreams (Part Two)'. The latter seems to have stemmed primarily from the Chris Carter and Cosey Fanni Tutti axis within the unit. Both tracks take almost pretty, synthesised melodies with gentle rhythms that retain a subversive edge. 'Adrenalin' is manipulated - sped up over an increasingly agitated sounding Genesis P-Orridge chanting "paper thin adrenalin". 'Distant Dreams (Part Two)' is more conventional and yet more disturbing. Maintaining a steady pace, it is at once beguiling and chilling in its cynical sweetness that slowly reveals its sinister heart.

65
THE FEELIES
Fa Ce-La/Crazy Rhythm
NO CHART PLACING
Stiff Records

The Feelies came from Hoboken, New Jersey, just the other side of the Hudson River from the bright lights of Manhattan and played regularly at local venue Maxwells. They count amongst bands with that 'so near yet so far' quality i.e., undervalued by most yet influencing the likes of R.E.M. and Weezer.

'Fa Ce-La' had been released by Rough Trade a year before Stiff released it again in the hope of igniting interest in the group's debut album *Crazy Rhythms*. As a sales ploy it didn't succeed. What people were missing out on was a band who mirrored the twin guitar approach of Television married to the motorik beat of Neu, understood and utilised the repetitive approach of Steve Reich and had some of the melodic gifts associated with The Beatles or Velvet Underground. Those strengths are here on the two sides of this single that should never have remained a secret known only to a privileged few.

64
THE CRAMPS
Drug Train/Love Me
I Can't Hardly Stand It
NO CHART PLACING
Illegal Records

'Drug Train' is the sound of The Cramps having listened to the James Brown dance classic 'Night Train', deciding to record a kind of homage in their own inimitable and seditious style. It pops, shakes and rattles, and at times almost leaves the tracks. It's a wild ride, and over the rocking rhythm Lux Interior howls, croons and stutters until the train pulls into the station.

63
DEVO
Whip It /Snowball/Gates of Steel
51
Virgin Records

Here Devo satirise the optimistic notion that problems can be dealt with by simply whipping them into shape using a phrase that many people will presume also refers to Sadomasochistic practices. 'Whip It' takes Roy Orbison's 'Oh Pretty Woman' as a musical template and adds a prominent rigid drum beat combined with synthesised whiplash sounds to create something arresting, stimulating and hugely entertaining.

62
VISAGE
Fade to Grey/The Steps
8
Polydor

Visage were assembled with the aim of showcasing Steve Strange, the flamboyant face at the forefront of a movement springing up at Billy's club and The Blitz. These places needed new electronic music for DJ Rusty Egan to play and hence evolved a band of sorts comprising Strange on vocals, with guests Midge Ure, Billy Currie (Ultravox), Dave Formula and John McGeoch (Magazine). Ure and Currie wrote their second single, 'Fade to Grey', and Gary Numan band members Chris Payne and Cedric Sharpley assisted with the programmed rhythms. It was heavily atmospheric and featured lyrics sung in English by Strange and spoken in French by Egan's girlfriend Brigitte Arens which lent an air of sophistication and modernity. It was also blessed with a gorgeous melody and a state-of-the-art Godley and Creme video which helped secure its success both artistically and commercially.

61
THE ASSOCIATES
The Affectionate Punch
You Were Young
NO CHART PLACING
Fiction Records

Mixing harsh, abrasive textures with the refined and sumptuous, The Associates worked with no musical safety net. Indeed they operated at the extremes to create a music that felt distinctly European in flavour. 'The Affectionate Punch' has an incessant Motown-style pounding piano as its base, contributing to its dance-ability. A hint of Weimar-era cabaret adds a decadent twist, and the cherry on top of Alan Rankine's tasty confection is the incredible vocal by Billy Mackenzie which here is powerful, playful and as always, crystalline.

60
ADAM AND THE ANTS
Kings of the Wild Frontier
Press Darlings
48 (1981- 2)
CBS

Having failed in all his endeavours to achieve the fame and success he so desperately desired, Adam Ant turned to Svengali figure Malcolm McLaren to mastermind his breakthrough. The duplicitous shopkeeper instead betrayed his eager young charge, stole his ideas and then persuaded his band to leave him to form Bow Wow Wow. A forlorn Adam had been 'kippered' but his self-belief pulled him through, forming a new band with two drummers to provide a Burundi beat. He found a perfect song-writing foil in ex-Rema Rema guitar player Marco Pirroni, who introduced a spaghetti western sound into the exciting, exotic mix. The result was the thunderous, brilliant pop anthem 'Kings of The Wild Frontier'. It was hated by the old audience who craved more of the Ants' creepy sexual perversions, but Adam and his new Ants were embraced by a fresher-faced crowd who hailed them for their dash and panache. It was a real life fairy tale with Adam Ant as Prince Charming.

59
THE SELECTER
ON MY RADIO
TOO MUCH PRESSURE
8
Two-Tone Records

The Selecter - named after the term used for the DJ at reggae sound systems - were a multi-racial band from Coventry. They ploughed a similarly ska-influenced musical furrow as label mates The Specials, sharing their first release, the song 'The Selector' with The Specials' classic debut 'Gangsters' on a double A-sided 1979 single which became the best-selling independent single of that year. Follow-up 'On my Radio', written by guitarist Neol Davies, was a provocative critique of bland and conformist radio playlisting, which ironically was ignored or misunderstood by the jocks who played the single incessantly and helped make it a hit. Sung in a falsetto by Pauline Black and complemented by a sparkling organ break, it was a fine record. B-side 'Too Much Pressure' was a highly successful hybrid of speedy punk meets ska - a splendid track in its own right.

58
THE BROTHERS JOHNSON
Stomp/Let's Swing
6
A&M Records

'Stomp' is an irrepressible, hedonistic disco anthem. Strings, synths and bass combine to create an incessant groove powered by a hand-clapping and foot-stomping, friendly rhythm that leads to a surging celebratory chorus. Designed for the dance floor, The Brothers Johnson executed this single to perfection.

57
THE BEAT
Mirror in the Bathroom
Jackpot
4
Go-Feet Records

The Beat soon transcended their ska-punk leanings and their third single, propelled by David Steele's audacious bass line in 2/2 time, is sonically a world away from the sound of sixties Jamaica. Lyrically The Beat were streets ahead of their contemporaries, with imaginative and unpredictable subject matter. In 'Mirror in the Bathroom', Dave Wakeling examines the nature of narcissism through an array of reflective surfaces. It is bold, bright, sharp and quick-witted.

56
COLIN NEWMAN
B / Classic Remains
Alone on Piano
NO CHART POSITION
Beggars Banquet

The temporary split of Wire allowed Colin Newman to record material under his own name. From his debut album *A to Z* came the minimalistic-titled single 'B'. It is magnificently skewed pop, not dissimilar to Wire's releases but less regimented. It's looser and more extreme nature features a wordless, half-screamed vocal over what could pass for a children's rampage through the musical section of a toy shop.

55
ADAM AND THE ANTS
Ant Music/Fall In
2
CBS

Sandwiched between this single and 'Kings of The Wild Frontier' (see No. 60 above) was single 'Dog Eat Dog' which had put the Ants in the hit parade top ten for the first time and created a hunger for more among the band's swelling tribe of followers. 'Ant Music' did not disappoint. It was the best single yet: cocky, cheeky and catchy, it possessed a killer chorus advising one and all to "unplug the jukebox and do us all a favour, that music's lost its taste so try another flavour - ant music!" Adam's new found confidence couldn't be displayed any more explicitly than that.

54
BLONDIE
Call Me
Call Me (Instrumental)
1
Chrysalis

Charged with providing the theme song for the movie *American Gigolo*, Giorgio Moroder was thwarted by contract issues from collaborating with first choice Stevie Nicks. He turned instead to Blondie singer Debbie Harry and asked her to write a lyric to a demo he had recorded titled 'Man Machine'. She performed that task effortlessly, writing from the perspective of the film's main character, a male prostitute. There is no awkwardness in the melding of Moroder's machined dance-floor rhythms and the band's conventional instrumentation. Harry's cool and street-edged voice is the perfect conduit for her subtly provocative lyric.

53
CRIME
Gangster Funk/Maserati
NO CHART PLACING
B-Square Records

San Francisco's Crime, who had released the incendiary 'Hot Wire To My Heart' in 1976, came to my attention once again with this release. They play a muscular punk-funk hybrid full of raw vitality. James Brown, Iggy Pop, King Kong and Jesus Christ get name checks too!

52
THE TREACHEROUS THREE
A New Rap Language/Love Rap
[BY SPOONIE G]
NO CHART PLACING
Enjoy Records

The Treacherous Three had featured Spoonie G as part of the front-line of the crew's original incarnation. He remained an affiliate after his departure and used his influence to get a Treacherous Three recording included as the B-side of his 'Love Rap' single. 'A New Rap Language' was the chosen track and demonstrated the Three's fast style which was achieved by dubbed speed rapping. It was dizzying and mesmeric and indeed a great leap forward in terms of rap style. The minimal bass and percussion funk track it rode across was all that was required, such was the rhythmic power of the interwoven voices with their syllables and rhymes crammed within.

51
GRANDMASTER FLASH AND THE FURIOUS 5
Freedom/Freedom (Instrumental)
NO CHART PLACING
Sugar Hill Records

After releasing their debut single on Enjoy Records, Grandmaster Flash and the Furious 5 moved to Sugar Hill Records for the follow up, providing they could record over a particular track – 'Get Up And Dance' by a group called Freedom who provided this single with its title. With its bass in your face and horns absolutely scorching, the five rappers simply lined up behind microphones and cut the track live, creating a funking hypnotic party anthem and early hip-hop classic.

50
DIANA ROSS
I'm Coming Out/Give Up
13
Motown

After commissioning Bernard Edwards and Nile Rogers to write and produce her final album for Motown, Diana Ross was extremely unhappy with the results. She had initially loved 'I'm Coming Out' - interpreting it as being about her emerging from the control of the Motown machine but when a friend pointed out the song's overtly gay connotations apparently she broke down in tears, suspecting sabotage to ruin her career. The record was a fabulous sassy piece of disco pop with a seriously impressive groove and even contained a jazz trombone solo but she had nothing good to say about it. Her opinion was no doubt reversed when the song became a huge hit and its adoption as an anthem by the LBGT community added substantial numbers to her audience.

49
ULTRAVOX
Vienna/Passionate Reply
2
Chrysalis

With new vocalist Midge Ure replacing John Foxx, Ultravox enjoyed a dramatic change in fortunes with the release of 'Vienna'. It's a long, slow, brooding piece with a drum pattern resembling a heartbeat at its base and neo-classical grand piano at the fore. A violin solo enhances the sense of tainted grandeur. Ure - unsure in which direction to take the track - declared "this means nothing to me" and was told by producer Conny Plank to sing that then! It became the iconic chorus of what is an iconic single.

48
CRASS/POISON GIRLS
Bloody Revolutions/
Persons Unknown
NO CHART PLACING
Crass Records

A double A-sided single from the two bands at the forefront of what would become known as 'anarcho-punk'. This was a fundraising benefit to pay for the opening of The Wapping Autonomy Centre (also known as the Anarchist Centre). Crass were clearly a caring, compassionate and highly-principled group of individuals. However, I always thought they were somewhat out of touch with the struggles of much of the working class. What they *were* good at was presenting ideas with the power to make people think and 'Bloody Revolutions' is a powerful and considered diatribe against the politics of power. Poison Girls were no less serious and yet their work was somehow warmer and more humane. Their records didn't take the sledgehammer approach of Crass but were just as angry about injustices and persecution. They were more reasoned and much more inclusive as demonstrated on the excellent 'Persons Unknown'.

47
DEXYS MIDNIGHT RUNNERS
Geno/Breakin' Down the Walls of Heartache
1
Late Night Feelings

Signed by EMI and given their own vanity label to release music on the powers that be were reluctant to release 'Geno' as a single, preferring the Johnny Johnson and the Bandwagon cover version, 'Breaking Down the Walls of Heartache'. The band dug their heels in and won that battle. Their follow-up to the independent release 'Dance Stance', 'Geno' was written by Kevin Archer and Kevin Rowland and relates a concert by Geno Washington that Rowland attended in his mid-teens. He comprehends that the performer he so idolised was in truth quite mediocre and has no magic to impart. It paints a picture of the scene and captures the moment of realisation that motivates Rowland to always try harder, to never allow himself to become so tame. With its chanted intro and outro, a running-on-the-spot rhythm and lumbering horns, this was an ungainly record but it contained a sincere intensity and a bitter-sweet atmosphere that was compelling.

46
B52s
Give Me Back My Man
Give Me Back My Man (Version)
61
Island Records

Over a cyclical riff embellished by hand claps, an emotional sounding Cindy Wilson sings solo. And there's a glockenspiel solo from Fred Schneider taking a back seat from lead vocals. It's a riveting soundtrack to a tale of a broken-hearted girl pleading with her love rival to give her back her man, promising in return to give up the fish and candy in her hand. It's slightly disturbing and surreal while being hugely entertaining, as only the B52s could be.

45
PAUL McCARTNEY
Temporary Secretary
Secret Friend
NO CHART PLACING
Parlophone

Wings had a good run but ended up sounding tired, dull and absolutely predictable. To refresh his jaded muse Paul McCartney holed up alone with some synthesisers and allowed his imagination free reign, resulting in the creation of his best music in years. 'Temporary Secretary' was issued as a limited edition 12-inch single. It was quite extraordinarily funky and fresh and also extremely eccentric as, over a chattering incessant rhythm, wonky sounding synths bubble and pop while McCartney sings from the point of view of a creepy businessman phoning an employment agency looking to recruit a temporary secretary for dubious purposes.

44
KATE BUSH
Army Dreamers/Delius/
Passing Through Air
16
EMI

The tune is plucked out sadly in waltz time as Kate Bush narrates from a grieving mother's perspective the tale of her soldier boy son's corpse being returned from overseas where he has been killed in an accident. She thinks of the choices denied to him for lack of money and a good education, leading him to join the army. The mother reflects on her self-perceived failings as a mother and how she must carry on despite her grief. Deemed seditious by the UK government and banned from receiving airplay during the first Gulf War, 'Army Dreamers' is not in the slightest bit accusatory but a sad reflection on wasted lives and loss.

43
THE CURE
A Forest/Another Journey by Train
31
Fiction Records

Robert Smith's guitar was heavily laden with effects to create a cavernous, swirling sound into which the naked vulnerable voice intones what appears to be a bad dream of being lured into the trees and becoming lost. This was the record where The Cure discovered their signature Gothic sound of minor keys and heavy atmospherics enhanced by the addition of Matthieu Hartley's keyboards. It would serve them well and 'A Forest' was a startling record. The B-side incidentally was an instrumental version of the group's previous single, 'Jumping Someone Else's Train'.

42
BLONDIE
Atomic/Die Young Stay Pretty
1
Chrysalis

Pulling together influences as varied as the nursery rhyme 'Three Blind Mice' to the Northern soul classic 'I'm on My Way', 'Atomic' was an amalgam of different elements. Keyboard player and the song's composer Jimmy Destri confessed he was trying to write something in the style of previous hit 'Heart Of Glass', but went with the spaghetti western theme that emerged. Debbie Harry recalls making the lyric up as the band rehearsed and using the word 'Atomic' as a signifier of power and futurism rather than in any literal sense. The band were possessed with the magic touch at this time and no matter how diverse the elements of the song, by the time it was recorded they had conjured up a highly cohesive work. Its urgent, distinct, mutated-disco core of entwined guitar and synthesiser was a perfect counterpoint to Harry's cold and slightly disinterested vocal. The 12-inch version of the record contained a commendable live cover of David Bowie's 'Heroes' featuring Robert Fripp on guitar.

41
MAGAZINE
A Song From Under the Floor-boards/Twenty Years Ago
NO CHART PLACING
Virgin

"I am angry, I am ill and I am as ugly as sin" sings Howard Devoto. It's a stunning opening to a song full of vivid, lyrical imagery, matched by music that is both elegant and dissonant. It contains not only Dave Formula's grand neo-classical keyboard fills but a pulverising funky bass part from Barry Adamson matched by John Doyle's crisp drumming. John McGeoch's guitar is typically inventive, extracting barely believable noise from the instrument. Devoto continues in a self-loathing tone as he distils Dostoevsky *Notes from The Underground* into four minutes of superb pop music on this exceptional single.

40
SIOUXSIE
AND THE BANSHEES
Happy House/
Drop Dead – Celebration
17
Polydor

Here came Banshees Phase 2. Having recruited guitarist John McGeoch from Magazine, the band became much more musically expressive and expansive. McGeoch is hugely impressive on this record, adding swathes of colour where previously all was grey. Even more impressive is drummer Budgie whose African-style rhythm was a bold stroke and adds exaggerated bounce. The sarcastic lyrics – "this is the happy house, we're happy here, in our happy house, oh it's such fun…" - displays a knowing too-good-to-be-true cheerfulness to the point that no matter how much happiness is being displayed, we are fully aware that there are dark secrets behind the smiles ending on an unconvincing denial of the existence of "hell".

39
THE FALL
How I Wrote Elastic Man
City Hobgoblins
NO CHART PLACING
Rough Trade

Brilliant satire from Mark Smith based on US comic book writer and Plastic Man creator Jack Cole, who killed himself aged forty-three. The persona adopted by Smith in the song is hounded by press and fans, much like artists across all areas of popular culture are trapped by public fascination. Changing 'Plastic Man' to 'Elastic Man' was a ploy to ensure DC Comics didn't sue him. The lyric was used to top a loping, repetitive, almost country and western (country and northern?)-style guitar groove while new fifteen-year-old drummer, Paul Hanley clatters gleefully away behind them. Meanwhile flip side 'City Hobgoblins', painted a picture of the Fred Perry clad feral youths who were a blight upon city centre Manchester.

38
THE FALL
Fiery Jack/2nd Dark Age/
Psykick Dancehall #2
NO CHART PLACING
Step Forward Records

The Riley-Scanlon-Hanley musical axis of this exciting Fall line-up provided a high-octane rockabilly piece perfectly suited for Mark Smith to extemporise over. 'Fiery Jack' was probably inspired by The Cramps and Tav Falco's Panther Burns who the band were fans of and played gigs with. Smith rampages over it in entertaining fashion, painting a word portrait of a heavy drinking, amphetamine-fuelled forty-five year-old hard case. The eponymous first-person narrator has an unswerving, no-nonsense world-view, at odds with the younger people Mark was dismissive of, particularly those in the music scene. It is remarkable that Mark was still in his early twenties and yet describes and idealises the pub-dwelling, humorous and curmudgeonly character he himself later became!

37
DRINKING ELECTRICITY
Cruising Missiles
Shaking All Over (Dub)
NO CHART PLACING
Pop Aural

Drinking Electricity were a male-female synth pop duo whose first two singles had been rather uninspired - covers of The Flamin' Groovies 'Shake Some Action' and Johnny Kidd and the Pirates' 'Shaking All Over'. This, their follow-up, tore up the script completely and was a self-composed classic. 'Cruising Missiles' was a moody, minimal, instrumental piece of imaginative electronica, the like of which I'd never heard before.

36
SIMPLE MINDS
I Travel/New Warm Skin
NO CHART PLACING
Arista Records

The young Simple Minds here mix up their influences of *Low*-era Bowie, Giorgio Moroder and punk, to create a chilly but very tasty disco rock concoction. 'I Travel' has a compelling nervous energy in its machine-like rhythm and attached to it is the distinct flavour of a decadent old Europe.

35
PRINCE
When You Were Mine/
Gotta Broken Heart Again/Uptown
NO CHART PLACING
Warner Bros. Records

Only released as a 12-inch promo single, this was nonetheless an incredible record - up-tempo and slight with acoustic guitars as a base and a catchy killer keyboard motif used to punctuate the verses. Prince is lyrically ambiguous as we don't know if he is adopting a male or a female persona. He could be portraying a masochistic cuckold reduced to pained voyeurism or the viewpoint of a female friend who has been supplanted by a male lover and is left feeling alone and degraded.

34
CHANGE
Searching/Angel in my Pocket
11
WEA

Change were an Italian-American disco act with an unusual modus operandi. The tracks were written in Italy and the backings recorded in Italian studios by Italian musicians before being shipped to America where, in New York's Power Plant studio, vocals would be added. The relatively unknown Luther Vandross had been a very busy backing vocalist and singer of television adverts for products such as Kentucky Fried Chicken. On 'Searching', he seizes the opportunity to significantly build his reputation. Over a backing that was unmistakably influenced by

Chic, Vandross, who came to be known as the voice of his generation, adds his smooth as velvet tenor to create a classy dance floor sound of enduring quality.

33
THE BIRTHDAY PARTY
Mr Clarinet/Happy Birthday
NO CHART PLACING
4AD

The Boys Next Door were a run-of-the-mill Australian new wave band. They morphed into The Birthday Party who were a deeply disturbing, unclassifiable Australian band of darkly beautiful brilliance. Mr Clarinet is a lyrically slight song of longing by Nick Cave that is performed with spit-in-your-eye belligerence, Cave howling out his desire akin to some crazed backwoodsman full of moonshine and haunted by loneliness. The rest of the band are not to be outdone by his outré performance, creating a frightful stomping racket that Captain Beefheart would have been proud to lay claim to.

32
GRACE JONES
Private Life/She's Lost Control
17
Island Records

Moving away from the disco sound that had defined her early career, Grace Jones was now surrounded by a team of crack musicians. This included rhythm masters Sly and Robbie who created an artful and fluid reggae-rock hybrid that was astonishing even before the addition of Jones' extraordinary voice and unique phrasing. Here, they take a Chrissie Hynde song she had recorded with The Pretenders in 1979, reassemble it, reboot it and await the inevitable acclaim this audacious music deserved and duly received. Roxy Music's 'Love is the Drug', was given a similar makeover and on the B-side here, Joy Division's most iconic early song is gleefully manipulated to fit this new design.

31
TALKING HEADS
I Zimbra/Air
NO CHART PLACING
Sire

David Byrne's fascination with African musical forms steered Talking Heads onto a journey of musical discovery that started with 'I Zimbra'. This snaking rhythmic collision of two cultures was aided by a veritable team of African percussion players along with guests Brian Eno adding electronic treatments and Robert Fripp with hot guitar licks. Over this was chanted a lyric taken from German poet Hugo Ball's nonsense Dada poem, 'Gadji Beri Bimba': "Gadji beri bimba clandridi, Lauli lonni cadori gadjam, A bim beri glassala glandride, E glassala tuffm I zimbra" – which is untranslatable!

30
KATE BUSH
Babooshka/Ran Tan Waltz
5
EMI

'Babooshka' is the tale of a paranoid wife who tests her husband's devotion and fidelity by adopting a pseudonym and writing him love letters. He is responsive because he is reminded of his wife in happier times. She becomes more embittered and paranoid and the relationship is ruined as signified by the sound of breaking glass. The tale is set to a musical backdrop played in an Eastern European folk style, while the inimitable Kate Bush relays the tale with evident relish.

29
ABBA
The Winner Takes It All
Elaine
1
Epic

Written, as always, by Benny Andersson and Bjorn Ulvaeus and with the lead vocal provided by Agnetha Faltskog, 'The Winner Takes It All' was in many ways art imitating real life. The lyrics relate the experience of a divorce as written by Bjorn in a drunken emotional state that, although not a *literal* telling of his own situation, nevertheless contained many true feelings that his wife Agnetha then had to sing. Little wonder that this single, beautiful though it is, seems infected by pain and devastation at its bruised heart.

28
THE CLASH
Bankrobber/Rockers Galore…
12
CBS

This was lightweight, fun stuff, even with the inclusion of a myth-building rebel lyric that Joe Strummer quite simply could never resist. A more accurate "daddy was a Foreign Office secretary" didn't scan as well! The Clash, from the start, were poseurs at heart. Even if their hearts were basically in the right place, their political affiliations and manifestos made them a hugely contradictory outfit. I learned to take their propaganda with a pinch of salt and simply enjoy the music, because if you could do that, the music was very good and often capable of stirring emotions.

'Bankrobber' isn't one of their famed rabble rousers but a gentle lilting cod-reggae piece. With a debt to Bob Dylan's 'Knocking On Heaven's Door' in its DNA, it somehow comes together as a piece of great sing-along pop in the manner of Mungo Jerry's 'In The Summertime' from one era or Culture Club's, 'Karma Chameleon' from another.

27
DIANA ROSS
Upside Down/Friend to Friend
2
Motown

Another single from the Chic song-writing and production team that Diana Ross reputedly hated, 'Upside Down' gave Ross her biggest hit in a decade. It was an irrepressible piece of funky pop, absolutely laden with musical and vocal hooks that sounded amazing coming from a transistor radio or from a state of the art sound system. It was Chic at their absolute peak, aligning with the iconic figure of Diana Ross, using her distinctive voice to create glorious celebratory records that were such a joy that even her sourness towards the project failed to dampen the listeners' pleasure.

26
FIRE ENGINES
Get Up and Use Me
Everything's Roses
NO CHART PLACING
Codex Communications

This was jagged, brutalist guitar funk where the guitarists used no chords and the drummer eschewed cymbals and hi-hats, simply attacking skins with much venom. The vocal was an excited, tuneless whine. The recording cost £46 and the end result was a thrilling amphetamine rush of a single that made me squeal with animalistic pleasure. Whenever I got a chance to DJ, this record was on the turntable.

25
THE GAP BAND
Burn Rubber on Me
(Why You Wanna Hurt Me)
Nothin' Comes to Sleepers
NO CHART PLACING
Mercury

'Burn Rubber on Me' was a huge club record that gained no traction from radio programmers despite being obvious hit material. It was hugely funky, with the bass and synth lines providing a deadly groove alongside a frenzied questioning vocal and exasperated cry to a lover who has taken all that was available before deserting him.

24
TV SMITH'S EXPLORERS
Tomahawk Cruise/See Europe
NO CHART PLACING
Big Beat Records

After The Adverts split following the crashing commercial failure of their excellent second album, *Cast Of Thousands*, TV Smith formed The Explorers, a more expansive and musically adept grouping. The first fruit of their labours was this piece of intelligent protest against the UK government allowing American Cruise missiles, aimed at Russia, to be placed on British soil. Lyrically the song draws on folk traditions and asks highly pertinent questions, whilst musically it is a pulsing, dramatic piece with elements of both a muscular punk style at its base and a keyboard adorned prog rock sheen on the surface.

23
TWINKLE BROTHERS
Never Get Burn
Jah Kingdon Come
NO CHART PLACING
Front Line

The Front Line label set up by Virgin Records had released lots of magnificent music from Jamaica in its three year run, but none of it had made even the slightest dent on the mainstream so inevitably 1980 saw it closed down but not before this glorious anthem was issued. Its majestic, even-paced rhythm, with grooving horns, is overlaid with Norman Grant's heartfelt and yearning vocal which pulls at the emotional heart strings and touches the soul with his conviction, as he relays a series of biblical scenes that attest to the protective love of Jah.

22
STEVIE WONDER
Masterblaster (Jammin')
Masterblaster (Dub)
2
Motown

Stevie had toured with Bob Marley as his opening act and developed a deep respect and love of the man's music and principles. 'Masterblaster' is the musical manifestation of Stevie's feelings and a tribute to Marley who is name-checked in the song. The song also mentions that "peace has come to Zimbabwe", referring to a conflict that Marley had been deeply disturbed by. Musically, Stevie serves up a full tilt funk-reggae hybrid of immense power. Combined with an irresistible groove he then adds one of his incredible vocals, full of passion and unrestrained love and joy.

21
DEUTSCH -AMERIKANISCHE-FREUNDSCHAFT
Kebabträume/Gewalt
NO CHART PLACING
Mute

D-A-F moved to London from Germany and signed to Mute records at which point they had slimmed into a three-piece unit (later a duo of core members Robert Gorl and Gabi Delgado-Lopez). This, their first single, combines childlike and sinister qualities. It marries a militaristic beat to a nursery rhyme style tune. Dissonant and disturbing, instruments hiss and scream. Vocals are in native German, but even though I don't understand the language, the intonation makes evident they contain provocations and a defiant oppositional viewpoint. Despite these seemingly off-putting component parts the record does not repel the listener. It's a new form of dance music – hypnotic, exciting and compelling.

20
THE SPECIALS
Stereotype
International Jet Set
6
Two Tone

The world of the Specials had darkened considerably inside twelve months. There were internal problems as members resented what they perceived as Jerry Dammers' autocratic control. Problems too with drugs and alcohol. Add physical attacks by racists, one of which left

Lynval Golding seriously injured, and you get an idea of the turbulence within and around the group. These problems bled into the music.

In 'Stereotype' we are treated to what sounds like a spooked fairground ride of slightly off-key Wurlitzer organ while Terry Hall dead-pans the story of a Jack-the-lad character who blames his girlfriend when he contracts a venereal disease. At the end of his treatment, he celebrates by getting drunk, causing a fight, and is pursued by police before wrapping himself around a lamp post in a crash. A deeply unsettling and thought-provoking single where The Specials sniped at the lifestyles of a large part of their constituent audience.

19
DAVID BOWIE
Fashion/Scream Like a Baby
5
RCA

'Fashion' had a funk-reggae rhythm not completely unrelated to Bowie's earlier 'Golden Years'. Robert Fripp layered a mechanical and grating guitar riff over the main rhythm, while Bowie pokes fun at the gullibility of fashion victims in his caustic lyrics: "Fashion - turn to the left, Fashion - turn to the right" he croons mockingly in the direction of the New Romantics, the Mod revivalists, the skinheads, punks and myriad tribes seeking a uniform to hide behind.

18
QUEEN
Another One Bites the Dust
Dragon Attack
7
EMI

Every single track that Queen had ever recorded at this point in time had a variable degree of pomposity to it. They took themselves terribly seriously and sound-wise, they were a veritable cliché. And then bassist John Deacon took to hanging out with Chic, re-jigged their bass line from, 'Good Times', and set to work on creating a Queen record that would groove. Taylor and May were unenthusiastic but Freddie Mercury saw a world of possibilities in this change of musical direction and threw his unstinting support into getting the record made. Lots of work went into creating the sound, utilising sound effects put through a harmoniser and various multi-speed techniques. It sounded incredible but it's true strength was at its heart in Deacon's bass riff combined with a magnificent vocal by Mercury. Encouraged to release it as a single by Queen fan Michael Jackson, they did just that and reaped long term rewards from this artistic reinvention.

17
THE JAM
Start/Liza Radley
1
Polydor

This is written by Paul Weller and George Harrison, although the former Beatle wasn't credited despite the main guitar part and bass riff being exact copies from Harrison's Beatles song, 'Taxman'. 'Start' nonetheless showed The Jam in an extremely favourable light. It was smart and snappy and displayed a wondrous light touch while Weller's lyric was thoughtful and wise, delivered in machine gun fire, staccato bursts.

16
CRISTINA
Is That all There Is?/Jungle Love
NO CHART PLACING
Ze Records

Released and then rapidly withdrawn due to the demands of songwriters Lieber and Stoller who were upset with the artistic licence being used on their work, 'Is That All There Is?' had been a Randy Newman-arranged US hit for Peggy Lee in 1969 and that version was a smart satire on high expectations. The song was an ironic take on disillusionment, delivered good-naturedly enough to be non-threatening. With the aid of producer August Darnell Cristina sing-speaks and twists the song into a hellish Mandrax and champagne-laced update of Brecht and Weill style realism. It is bleak and unsentimental, and here the protagonist positively relishes the pain and decadence. It is also quite brilliant!

15
JOY DIVISION
Atmosphere/She's Lost Control
NO CHART PLACING (1988 -34)
Factory

Originally released only in France, by the *Sordide Sentimental* label in March, the song was given a British release two months later following the death of Ian Curtis. 'Atmosphere' is a daring, gossamer-thin piece of music that contains power in its turbulent undercurrents. All the instruments are used with great subtlety and restraint except for a glistening synth line that adds a shaft of light to penetrate the sombre gloom. Martin Hannett's production is superbly nuanced, providing a perfect platform for Ian Curtis to deliver a performance that is rich and moving.

14
SIOUXSIE
AND THE BANSHEES
Christine
Eve White Eve Black
22
Polydor

'Christine' is a song about Christine Sizemore, a woman who struggled with multiple personality disorder, having twenty-two distinct identities to cope with. Steve Severin read the book *I'm Eve* - written by Sizemore and her cousin - and took inspiration to write the lyric for 'Christine'. It refers to two of her personalities, 'The Strawberry Girl' and 'Banana Split Lady'. The single was a bold departure in style for the Banshees. A more expansive construct with a lighter than usual touch, John McGeoch performs wonders with a distinctive acoustic guitar riff and a prominent electric organ solo. The b-side, 'Eve White Eve Black' continues the story by relating two of Christine's most dominant personalities in conflict with each other.

13
THE JIM CARROLL BAND
People Who Died
I Want the Angel
NO CHART PLACING
ATCO Records

Jim Carroll was a writer/poet who was a hustler and rent boy as a teenager (at 53rd and 3rd as was Dee Dee Ramone). He picked up a heroin addiction too. His *Basketball Diaries* which documented these times was published in 1978 and later became a Hollywood feature film. At that point Carroll quit the temptations of New York to start anew in California.

Encouraged by ex-girlfriend Patti Smith to form a band he recorded an album, *Catholic Boy*, from which came 'People Who Died'. It is a jolting, highly-charged single delivered with huge intensity, detailing the way in which many of Carroll's friends had met their end. It is unrelenting, merciless and powerfully emotional. Although it did not fare well on release, it was used by Steven Spielberg in his film *E.T.* and since then several other films have used it as part of the soundtrack. A host of cover versions have been released, signalling its classic status.

12
SPLIT ENZ
I Got You/Double Happy
12
A&M Records

When Split Enz emerged from New Zealand in the mid-70s they looked incredible and carried a whiff of the exotic. Linked to Roxy Music, being produced by Phil Manzanera, I was intrigued enough to purchase their first UK album. It disappointed me, seeming lightweight and lacking conviction and they dropped off my radar. What a pleasant surprise it was then when I heard 'I Got You', a fully focused near-perfect piece of pop brilliance combining throbbing bass and rhythm guitar with a pulsating electric organ riff. A fantastic conversational vocal from Neil Finn and choruses that simply build to an excited crescendo expressing doubt and pain whilst sounding euphoric.

11
MICHAEL JACKSON
Rock With You
Working Day and Night
7
Epic

Michael Jackson effortlessly lets the song do the work here. And because the song is so good he can serve up an unadorned performance, free of histrionics and the vocal ticks that were by now a trademark. This is a sweetly soulful record, and over smooth strings a buoyant Michael sounds free of baggage and very happy. Reminiscent of the best of Smokey Robinson's best solo work, 'Rock With You' is a sheer delight..

10
THE FALL
Totally Wired
Putta Block
NO CHART PLACING
Rough Trade

Defiantly lo-fi, the drums are lead instruments, the bass thunders, and guitars sting like angry wasps. This was The Fall displaying a belligerent disregard for convention, taking a song that had the potential to be a real pop hit and using it to demonstrate to the music industry that this group did not compromise. A song about hypocrisy perhaps? And most certainly a song celebrating amphetamine use. Ornette Coleman and Captain Beefheart are cryptically included within the lyric as oblique reference points but no more. For this is The Fall at their most obnoxious, pugnacious and boldest best.

9
MOTÖRHEAD
Ace of Spades
Dirty Love
15 (2016 -13)
Bronze

As dark and dangerous as a panther, as rapid as machine gun fire and as brutal an invading Mongol horde 'Ace of Spades' is a rampage committed to vinyl. It shakes, rattles and thunders from the bass and drum axis while the guitar is akin to the scorching of a flame thrower. Over this glorious racket Lemmy fires out gambling metaphors in a throaty growl. This transcended the metal genre it was bracketed in and tapped into the primal heartbeat of untamed rock 'n' roll.

8
DEXYS MIDNIGHT RUNNERS
There There My Dear
The Horse
7
Late Night Feelings

'There There My Dear' was written as an open letter to somebody called Robin who epitomises the pseudo-intellectual poseurs Kevin Rowland encounters in the music industry but can't abide. It's a coruscating assault upon the integrity of his target, who is ridiculed for his insincerity in the way he adopts fashions in clothing, music and literature that will be discarded when no longer viewed as cool. This superficiality irks the accuser who issues challenges and finally concludes that he himself must "search for the young soul rebels" who signify a purity and honesty he requires as a cleansing antidote in his life. Rowland spits out the lyric in a torrent of indignation with a passion that burns. There are no choruses. The song simply screams, close to chaos and bordering on manic. The instrumentation is the equal of the vocal, matching its fervour, as horns punch out a jack-hammer riff and the piston-like drums are augmented at times by rapid stabs from rhythmic guitars and Hammond organ.

7
TALKING HEADS
Once in a Lifetime
Seen and Not Seen
14
Sire

This was a full-on collaboration between Talking Heads and Brian Eno who not only produced and co-wrote the song but played on it and contributed much to its unusual flavours and textures. The song came together from long improvised jams where the best bits were selected to be played and played again. Essentially they were looping and sampling their own sounds without using machines. Rhythm and percussion was inspired by Afro-beat, in particular Felá Kuti from whom Eno borrowed extensively. The exaggerated differing rhythms affect the song's balance and alter its sense of gravity. David Byrne delivers the lyrics in the style of a preacher addressing a congregation. He ruminates on his accumulated possessions, realising he has no recollection of where they came from or indeed what value he truly attaches to his beautiful car, his beautiful house, his beautiful wife. He concludes he lives in only a half-conscious state. It is a frightening eye-opener.

6
YELLO
Bimbo
I.T Splash
NO CHART PLACING
Do It Records / Ralph Records

Yello's first single, 'Bimbo', was the staggering. Its disco themes are stretched and squeezed into different shapes before being reassembled to create a wildly different original form. Over this, voices playfully combine to offer an abstract critique of the superficiality and inherent smugness of self-delusional types who perceive themselves as special. Aimed simultaneously at the feet and the mind, 'Bimbo' was the most stimulating fun around.

5
PETER GABRIEL
Biko
Shosholoza/Jetzt Kommt Die Flut
38
Charisma

Every time I listen to this record I am inevitably reduced to a sobbing, wretched state of sorrow and anger over man's inhumanity to his brothers and sisters. The song details in plain language the murder of anti-apartheid activist Steve Biko who was beaten to death by South African policemen while being detained in custody. It is musically sparse - just a simple beat played on a Brazilian drum, some distorted guitar and the harrowing sound of a bagpipe lament. It is bookended by two recordings of African songs played at Steve Biko's funeral. Peter Gabriel sacrifices himself to the song and its message. There is no show-boating in the delivery of the words, but one feels his angry indignation as he warns the oppressive regime that "the eyes of the world are watching now, watching now" Just writing this down has brought me to tears again. Gabriel has gathered the sadness and created a work of beauty that is a lasting tribute to Steve Biko and others like him who struggle against injustice.

1980

4
JOY DIVISION
Love Will Tear Us Apart
These Days
13
Factory

Recorded at Pennine Studios in Oldham in January 1980 but with the end result deemed not good enough, the version that was released was cut at Stockport's Strawberry Studios in March. The song is brisk but elegant and warmly produced, expanding on the band's sound by featuring a twelve string Eko guitar part played by Bernard Sumner while Ian Curtis was encouraged to adopt a Frank Sinatra style croon during the song. Lyrically, the song concerns the breakdown of Ian Curtis's marriage as well as his suffering with epilepsy and the pressures of everyday life weighing heavily on him. It was, and is, something of a masterpiece and displays a confidence growing within the band that would surely have seen them unafraid to experiment with and develop their sound. Sadly, that was not to be. On 18th May 1980, Ian Curtis took his own life. 'Love Will Tear Us Apart' was released in June and became his epitaph as well as being a true classic record.

3
DAVID BOWIE
Ashes to Ashes
Move On
1
RCA

'Ashes to Ashes' seemed to me to be where David Bowie reflected on his life changes over the previous decade, by playing the Major Tom figure from his 1969 hit 'Space Oddity' who has survived despite continuing to drift in space, losing his hair and becoming a junky. Is he reflecting on his years as a vampiric figure strung out in Los Angeles with this allusion? I rather think so, although nothing is obvious or clear within the lyric or its performance which falls somewhere between that of a hymn and a nursery rhyme.

As befits the complexity of the song its studio-created sound is equally well thought out and executed. It is richly textured conveying a mood of being trapped in a tiny sterile space with its off-kilter rhythms suggesting malfunctions in the essential equipment. The sound created by the synth guitar played by Chuck Hammer is a key ingredient in the dramatic atmosphere of the piece, while the mathematical approach of bassist George Murray and Drummer Dennis Davis offer a jarring counterpoint. The most vital aspect to the success of 'Ashes to Ashes' though was Bowie's vocal performance which is assured and commanding whilst remaining natural and conversational as he offers forth his ruminations on the turbulence of the decade he is leaving behind.

2
PETER GABRIEL
Games Without Frontiers
The Start/I Don't Remember
4
Charisma

There was a long running pan-European television game show titled *Jeux Sans Frontiers*. It was run as a tournament/competition and each country's representatives were dressed in ridiculous parodies of national costume. Ostensibly it was all fun but often it would get a little too competitive and over serious. It's British title was *It's a Knockout* - a microcosm of war, or as the title states 'Games without Frontiers', a weekly battle to conquer foreign opponents.

In the song's lyric, the participants are all children and have names such as Adolph and Enrico that tie them to specific nations. All the children have flags to fly from hilltops except for 'Lin Tai Yu'. Presumably she represents Tibet under Chinese occupation? Kate Bush lends her voice on backing vocals. The tune and rhythm are sickly-sweet and creepy with a dark tinge. The whistled section is plain disturbing. One imagines pistol shots and hears door hinges creaking and then being banged shut while Gabriel narrates the tale deadpan lest anyone should mistake the song for anything less than a deadly series observation.

1980

1
BOB MARLEY AND THE WAILERS
Redemption Song
Redemption Sing (Band Version)
NO CHART PLACING
Island Records

Written by Bob Marley in 1979 when he had received the prognosis for cancer that would eventually kill him, 'Redemption Song' was his defining song, one that will live through the ages. Played on unadorned acoustic guitar without a hint of a reggae rhythm, the song is a spiritual lamentation on pain inflicted upon a soul, whereby the only survival course is to find the mental strength to conquer fear. He is addressing universal suffering but without doubt simultaneously addressing his own mortality. It is deeply moving. Key phrases in the lyric are lifted from a speech made by Marcus Garvey in Nova Scotia in 1937 and woven into Marley's equally powerful and evocative words. The B-side is a full band version of the track as performed by the Wailers in concert and as magnificent as that is, it loses much of the power in the version where Bob Marley sings reflective and alone, with just his acoustic guitar as accompaniment.

A lunchtime pint or three in The Nelson, Didsbury 1981

1981

Early eighties Manchester was in a state of flux in tandem with the rapidly evolving music scene. 'The Factory' at the Russell Club closed. The New Hormones-sponsored Beach Club opened its doors for the last time and its home at Oozits on Shudehill burned down. Andy Zero ceased promoting his 'Funhouse' at the Mayflower club and, though the venue continued to host bands they tended to be from the wave of unimaginative and testosterone-fuelled 'Punk's not Dead' revivalists. Rafters continued to flourish and The Gallery on Peter Street was occasionally interesting. Other venues of note were De Ville's, and briefly The Illuminated 666 club on Fennel St – "behind the Cathedral" as the old Granada TV used to announce! I had to quit my position as singer in The Hamsters and joined forces with Graham Ellis, once of a fine band called Elti Fits. He recruited two associates - superb bass player Tim Oliver and a powerhouse drummer called Greg from Banbury Cross. We called ourselves 'The Do Dos' and listened to lots of James Brown records which informed our direction. As luck would have it, Graham held the keys to the spacious cellars beneath the War On Want offices on Oxford Street. We could rehearse free of charge there, opening the space later as pubs closed as a not-even-vaguely-legal venue christened 'The White Noise Club' which attracted an audience from the growing number of young people housed in the failed social experiment that was Hulme's Crescents which proved to be completely unsuitable for the families they had been designed to house. Here, the enterprising Adam Lesser had converted his premises into a recording studio that could be hired cheaply and get good results. It was an invaluable resource. I had fallen into a thriving, supportive scene that stimulated creativity and yet hardly registered among those not privy to its delights.

In contrast there was turbulence aplenty at the top table of the city's music makers in 1981. Buzzcocks' time was up. Magazine burst apart. New Order had yet to see movement beyond their Joy Division legacy. It was not easy to see who would fill the void. Apart from The Fall, who didn't court mass appeal, the city had lost all its main standard bearers and from the outside at least Manchester appeared a spent force. Emerging talent in Sheffield, Bristol, Liverpool and

Glasgow seemed to give them the creative edge. But wheels within wheels were spinning, people took stock, and soon the city would rise Phoenix-like rise from the ashes.

NOTABLE EVENTS

The Yorkshire Ripper, Peter Sutcliffe, is finally arrested after a police operation of enormous scale and huge ineptitude, the first Ripper murder had been in 1975 and he first came to the attention of police in 1969 .

Irish Politician Bernadette Devlin and her husband are shot by a UDA assassination squad in front of their children. British soldiers watching the house fail to intervene. It is suspected the British Conservative government were colluding with the loyalist terrorists who committed the crime.

Iran releases 52 American hostages minutes after Ronald Reagan's presidential inauguration, to end what became known as the Iran hostage crisis, lasting 14 months.

The first DeLorean sports car comes off the production line in Dunmurry, Northern Ireland.

Jiang Quing (madame Mao) is sentenced to death in China.

Abstentionist 27-year-old MP Bobbly Sands, and a member of the Provisional IRA, begins a hunger strike at Maze prison on March 1st in a protest to demand political status. Dying in May, he is the first of 10 hunger strikers to end their life in prison.

The first London Marathon takes place with 7,500 runners.

Ronald Reagan is shot by John Hinckley in a failed assassination attempt.

There are riots in Brixton as the community rise against racist policing.

Pope John Paul II is wounded in an assassination attempt by Mehmet Ali Agca in Vatican City.

The entire Italian government is forced to resign when links to the Fascist Masonic order 'Propaganda Due' are exposed.

President Ziaur Rahman of Bangladesh is assassinated.

The first five cases of AIDS are recorded in Los Angeles.

Toxteth in Liverpool, Chapeltown in Leeds, Handsworth in Birmingham, Moss Side in Manchester and St Paul's in Bristol are amongst the British urban ghettos that see riots flare in opposition to the police.

Israel bombs Beirut destroying apartment blocks and killing 300 civilians.

MTV is launched with the playing of 'Video Killed The Radio Star' by Buggles.

The first episodes of *Only Fools and Horses*' and *Postman Pat* are aired by the BBC.

France abolishes capital punishment.

Egyptian president Anwar Sadat is assassinated by army figures opposed to his negotiations with Israel. He is succeeded a week later by Hosni Mubarak.

President Ronald Reagan signs a top-secret agreement for the United States to support the rebel Contra group in Nicaragua through the CIA in their war against the democratically elected Sandinista government.

Muhammad Ali loses his last boxing bout to Trevor Berbick.

The first use of crack cocaine is reported in the USA and the Caribbean.

Pepsi Cola enters China which becomes the first country with a population recorded of over one billion people.

In sport, cricketer Ian Botham single-handedly wins England the Ashes while middle distance runners Steve Ovett and Seb Coe exchange mile world records three times in nine days in September.

Manchester United finish the 1980-81 season in eighth place. They are boring to watch and draw 18 games. They make a club record signing, paying £1m for Gary Birtles, a prolific goalscorer for Nottingham Forest. He is not up to scratch and scores just one goal in 28 appearances. At the end of the season, the quietly dignified but dull Dave Sexton is sacked as manager and replaced by the brash and tacky perma-tanned Ron Atkinson. Aston Villa win the league and Tottenham the FA Cup beating Manchester City 3-2 in a replay.

NOTABLE BIRTHS

Alicia Keys; Justin Timberlake; Elijah Wood; Park Ji-Sung; Craig David; Roger Federer; Nico Muhly; Serena Williams; Patrice Evra; Zlatan Ibrahimović; Nemanja Vidic; Britney Spears.

NOTABLE DEATHS

Bill Haley; Joe Louis; Nelson Algren; Bob Marley; Anya Phillips; Albert Speer; Bill Shankly; Lotte Lenya; Natalie Wood; Cornelius Cardew; Hoagy Carmichael.

NOTABLE FILMS

Das Boot; Raiders of the Lost Ark; Thief; Time Bandits; Lola; Chariots of Fire ; The French Lieutenant's Woman; An American Werewolf in London; My Bloody Valentine; Shivers; Southern Comfort.

NOTABLE BOOKS

The Hotel New Hampshire- John Irving
Midnight's Children - Salman Rushdie
Chronicle of a Death Foretold - Gabriel Garcia Marquez
The Heart of a Woman - Maya Angelou
Bliss - Peter Carey
The Meeting at Telgte - Gunter Grass
Cities of the Red Night - William Burroughs
Elvis - Albert Goldman
Bodily Harm - Margaret Atwood

100
ABBA
One of Us/ Should I Laugh or Cry
3
Epic

Abba's first single from their last album The Visitors showed that even though the marriages and interpersonal relationships between them had broken down, their professionalism in pursuit of pop perfection lost no focus. They were still growing musically and constantly improving, but the lyrical subject matter showed they were also growing apart. This record is full of pain and sorrow but beautiful nevertheless. It must have been harrowing for all involved in the recording studio. Its melancholia is evident and sometimes tough to bear.

99
BLONDIE
Rapture/Walk Like Me
5
Charisma Records

Blondie displayed their versatility and the fact that their success hadn't separated them from the sounds of the street. 'Rapture' begins as a beguiling piece of soft funk that leads into a tribute to the early rap scene. As the beat grows tighter and Tom Scott blows an atmospheric saxophone part, Debbie Harry goes into an extended rap coda, partly a surreal stream-of-consciousness jive about a man from Mars eating cars, but also taking time out to name-check early hip-hop pioneers Grandmaster Flash and Fab 5 Freddie. Neat!

98
THE ASSOCIATES
White Car in Germany / The Associate
NO CHART PLACING
Situation Two

The Associates were flexing their muscles and pushing their experimental ethos hard. Machines hiss and pulse here but at the song's core is the beating bloody heart of the human and Billy McKenzie's fabulous expressive voice. Here, sounding more sombre and magisterial than ever, he imparts a fractured, cryptic Dadaist lyric.

97
FREEEZE
Southern Freeeze/
Instrumental Version
8
Beggars Banquet

British funk was coming of age and losing its inferiority complex towards its American cousin. 'Southern Freeeze' was cool and confident with an easy grooving feel, augmented by Latin percussion and a synth melody. Sung with panache and nonchalance by guest singer Ingrid Mansfield Allman, the lyric attests to a dance move popular with clubbers at the Royalty in Southgate where during plays of Rodney Franklin's popular 'The Groove' at a point where the music drops out for a bar, the dancers would 'freeze' their movement and strike a statuesque pose.

96
ORANGE JUICE
Poor Old Soul/
Poor Old Soul Pt. 2
NO CHART PLACING
Postcard Records

A push and pull takes place in this charming but shambling piece of music as the twin influences of The Velvet Underground and Chic do battle for the song's soul. Subway Sect Vic Godard's 'we oppose all Rock and Roll' manifesto is referenced at the midpoint as Edwyn Collins cries 'no more Rock and Roll for you'. This is sung with a smile while riding the bass and drum rhythm, before a guitar flourish signals a rising crescendo of modest proportions to end a joyous few moments of pure pop pleasure.

95
PYLON
Crazy/M Train
NO CHART PLACING
DB Records

Stylistically treading a ground not musically dissimilar to the B52s, who were highly supportive of Pylon, the crucial difference between the two bands was that Pylon were a darker-hued proposition. Even though their sound was energetic and danceable there was a weight within their music and a sense of hurt. Add to that the depth that singer Vanessa Briscoe summoned up in her performance and one can perhaps understand that this was a band who - as is evident on this fine single - were a little too disturbing and real to be allowed easy access into the mainstream.

94
GRACE JONES
Walking in the Rain
Peanut Butter
NO CHART PLACING
Island Records

Recorded in 1978 by Australian outfit Flash and the Pan, the song was turned by Grace Jones into an anthem of fierce independence and invincibility as this woman strides unflinchingly through a harsh urban landscape casting glances of displeasure and disdain at the dull depression of the place. She progresses purposefully, where even nature's attempts to stop her with a storm fail dismally. She is indomitable, strong and fearless and 'Walking in the Rain' is a perfectly nuanced performance of restraint and power. It is magnificent!

93
THE GUN CLUB
Sex Beat/Ghost on the Highway
NO CHART PLACING
Beggars Banquet

Hank Williams, Robert Johnson and Iggy Pop at their wildest and most blood-spattered collide to stage a giant shindig inside the fertile mind of Jeffrey Lee Pierce who founded the Gun Club. He led their rampage through the swamplands playing a wild and alternate take on this punk rock thing that incorporates neglected blues and country idioms and substantial roots flavours. Here he yelps and moans a tale of sex, drugs and the devil over a polka beat, the like of which we hadn't heard before. It was spooky and fine.

92
FRANK ZAPPA
You Are What You Is
Pink Napkins
NO CHART PLACING
Barking Pumpkin Records

Frank at his most snarky and sarcastic takes aim at two foolish characters. One is comfortable and middle class but seeks to enhance his masculinity and alter people's perceptions of him by feigning hardship and singing the blues. The other is a black man determined to appear Caucasian to the point of dropping his own culture and even substituting his diet for one that will be deemed white. Played out over a wickedly quick guitar lick, this was Frank attacking the fakes and poseurs he encountered whilst using humour as a weapon and offering sound advice - we are what we is and we ain't what we're not!

91
BC GILBERT AND G LEWIS
Ends With the Sea
Hung Up To Dry Whilst Building An Arch
NO CHART PLACING
4AD

Wire were shut down and placed into cold storage but Bruce Gilbert - who considered the Wire a flesh and blood art installation rather than a band - and bassist Graham Lewis, formed several short-lived collaborative units together that explored the counterbalance between the melodic sensibilities of Gilbert with the churning menace inherent in the playing style and vocals of Lewis. Here, on 'Ends With The Sea', they tiptoe between sharp edges of guitar through an eerie studio-created landscape of intriguing possibilities. And while they lead us to no particular location, we undoubtedly benefit enormously from undertaking the journey with them.

90
TELEVISION PERSONALITIES
I Know Where Syd Barrett Lives
Arthur the Gardener
NO CHART PLACING
Overground Records

Pink Floyd's founding father Syd Barrett had disappeared from public view and scrutiny a decade before this single appeared. A legend grew about this strange and most secretive recluse. As is often the case, the truth was more prosaic, and Barrett wasn't a recluse at all. He had simply been damaged by the pop star life, withdrawing from that aspect of his life by living quietly but unhidden in Cambridge.

Here, TVP main man Dan Treacy sings a fragile sweet homage to Syd. He echoes the repetitive drones Barrett had incorporated in his own music and a picture emerges of the two picnicking together eating sausage rolls as the river dreamily rolls by and birds sing. It is incredibly twee but suffused with such sincere affection for the song's inspirational character that it succeeds as a moving tribute.

89
PAPA MICHIGAN
AND GENERAL SMILEY
Diseases
Little John
NO CHART PLACING
Greensleeves Records

Jamaican dancehall style was upon us and Michigan and Smiley were at the forefront of the trend. 'Diseases' borrows the lick from 'Mad Mad' by Alton Ellis, and the pair then gleefully perform a lyric that is almost perversely surreal, seeming to suggest that Jah will strike down women who wear trousers with hideous diseases such as elephantiasis. They tread a fine line between being humorous and objectionable but they surmount the problem with an effervescence and energy that ultimately charms.

88
"D" TRAIN
You're the One for Me
Instrumental
30 (1982)
Prelude Records

Emerging from out New York's jazz underworld, the principal pair of singer James D Train Williams on vocals and musician Hubert Eaves put together "D" Train to enable the release of 'You're The One For Me'. With this release they captured a feeling of what was coming, creating a bridge between the more organic soul funk offerings of the late 70s and the electro funk that would follow. Indeed, with Williams' gospel style singing and the cutting edge use of juddering synth rhythms, 'You're The One For Me' can be seen as a huge precursor and influence on the early house music scene.

87
THE ROLLING STONES
Start Me Up
No Use Crying
7
Rolling Stones Records

It might be tempting and convenient to write The Rolling Stones out of 80s history. After all, following the fire and brimstone of the 60s, they'd pretty much slumbered through the 70s doing just enough to keep the lucrative enterprise afloat whilst Jagger and Richards aimed bitching asides at one another. What a surprise then that 'Start Me Up' was a titanic return to form that seriously kicked. All the classic ingredients were once more aligned: a brilliant choppy riff, the guitars of Richards and Ronnie Wood weaving around each other; Charlie Watts nailing the rhythm; Bill Wyman underpinning it with nimble fingered bass and Jagger sings it like an elderly delinquent!

86
THE SLITS
Earthbeat
Begin Again Rhythm
NO CHART PLACING
CBS

Eco-aware, feminist funk with an Arabic flavour, mixed together in Slits style where rules do not apply and barriers are pushed against. In 'Earthbeat' they create gentle music that is totally unconventional, but the mix of voices and percussion in combination with the simple glistening guitar sound combine to make this single eerily beautiful.

85
SPROUT HEAD UPRISING
Throw Some Water in
Nothing to Sing (part 2)
NO CHART PLACING
Stiff Records

Sprout Head Uprising were the brainchild of Michael 'Wadada' Ward of Suns of Arqa fame. 'Throw Some Water In' was a Lee Perry song which compares motor car maintenance with looking after the human body. This version sees it transformed from its grooving reggae origins into an amphetamine-flavoured Bluegrass stomp and it is fabulous! A few years later, passing a bikers pub called The Globe in Ashton under Lyne, I was astonished to read on a chalkboard "Tonight on stage, Sprout Head Uprising". I entered the premises and joined a sparse crowd watching the band who I found charming. The motorcycle boys were less impressed and with the band's bassist being of Asian origin the stain of racism inevitably soured things further. Threats were issued toward the band and I was compelled to act tough and intercede. I steered the band out of the venue and discovered Mr. Ward was an Ashton native. We chatted as we strolled to his abode where he presented me with Sprout Head vinyl which I still enjoy immensely.

84
THE CRAMPS
Goo Goo Muck / She Said
NO CHART PLACING
I.R.S. Records

Kid Congo Powers had replaced Bryan Gregory on guitar but that made no discernible difference to the loose-limbed, swampy, gonzo-style rockabilly that oozed out of The Cramps' creaking amplification. With 'Goo Goo Muck', they tackle a track cut in 1962 by Ronnie Cook and the Gaylads which they effortlessly make their own. The song is played straight, with a lovely clean guitar sound to the fore. No hammy showbiz tricks to enhance the natural strangeness and absence of affectation that lay within The Cramps. They throb rather than groove, and singer Lux simmers and smoulders. Many tried to appropriate what The Cramps created but none came close.

83
SIOUXSIE
AND THE BANSHEES
Spellbound
Follow the Sun
22
Polydor

With guitar player extraordinaire, John McGeoch, fully integrated into the band, Siouxsie and The Banshees unleashed their full sonic force without eroding any subtlety or indeed any loss of the deep mystery which was such a crucial part of their makeup. 'Spellbound' positively thundered along with no concession to commercial considerations. It is akin to riding a lightning bolt, subtly-woven guitars crackle with energy but are clever rather than crude. Siouxsie rides the wave of sound as Boadicea rode her chariot, bold and magnificent, channelling her voice by pushing and pulling it into abstract shapes equally as challenging to prevailing pop orthodoxy as this band of extraordinary musicians.

82
DELTA 5
Shadow
Leaving
NO CHART PLACING
PRE Records

Delta 5 comprised three women and two men based around Leeds University Arts Department that spawned Gang Of Four and The Mekons. After a run of critically-acclaimed raw singles that mirrored their live sound they had money to spend on studio time, having signed to Charisma Record's offshoot PRE. They attempt and succeed in producing something more flavoursome and expansive. 'Shadow' contains the band's trademark spidery funk sensibility combined with a dub echo and even a hint of very English baroque pop. Carried off with much gusto, it was sadly the beginning of the end rather than a new beginning for Delta 5 who split before the end of the year.

81
LINX
Intuition
Together We Can Shine
7
Chrysalis

David Grant's light-as-a-feather vocal sits atop a distinctive Caribbean steel band feel, swooping Spanish guitar runs, a rock solid rhythm combination, and saxophone and keyboards used as tasteful flavours. These enticing ingredients made 'Intuition' a refreshing take on funk that was sharp as a tack, displaying a lively freshness at odds with generic slow and low grooving. Indeed, with no American influence discernible, Linx displayed undeniable pop savvy, individuality and a touch of genuine class.

80
THE MOB
No Doves Fly Here
I Hear you Laughing
NO CHART PLACING
Crass Records

The fear of a cataclysmic war was very real. We looked at the super powers and shuddered. Who could trust the monsters in The White House and Kremlin? Only fools. Some chose to dance and celebrate life as a riposte and coping strategy. The Mob chose to present an unpalatable vision of what a post-apocalyptic future might feel like if one of these lunatics with the capacity to destroy pushed the button and plunged the world into darkness. 'No Doves Fly Here' is an anguished waltz through the aftermath - a guided tour of the devastation wreaked upon the planet and the population. The earth is screaming in agony and the spirits from the corpses strewn over its surface weep. Funeral-paced but naggingly insistent, here was a record that was no fun at all. It was, though, a record that was making a statement. A record needing to be heard.

79
SCRITTI POLITTI
The "Sweetest Girl"
Lions After Slumber
64
Rough Trade Records

Scritti Politti had been a joyless bunch of Marxist-theorising pseuds and hippies who were the leading lights in the self-righteous ghetto of DIY music making, where political posturing was deemed more important than being even vaguely listenable. And then onstage in Brighton, singer Green Gartside collapsed. He was whisked away to his family home in South Wales for a period of nine months convalescence. During this time, Gartside pondered his motivations and musical direction, and concluded that it was time to abandon doctrine in favour of embracing a more thoughtful approach, stripping away the sanctimony from his songs.

'The "Sweetest Girl"' was the first we heard of the recalibrated Scritti Politti and it was sensational. Featuring Robert Wyatt on keyboards, playing in his inimitable style, here was a record of aching beauty, intriguing lyrics sung with purpose and clarity over a lilting groove that hinted at reggae. It sounded like sunshine streaming through an open window - bright, illuminating and warm.

78
VIVIEN GOLDMAN
Launderette
Private Armies
NO CHART PLACING
Window

Vivien Goldman was a music press journalist who had been Bob Marley's UK press officer. She lived in Paris for a spell and was a member of a post-punk duo called Chantage. An EP was released by New York label 99 Records under her own name and then with little fanfare these two tracks were extracted from it, gaining a British release. F

Featuring contributions from Public Image Ltd's Keith Levine, noted experimental musician Steve Beresford, Raincoats violinist Vicky Aspinall, and shared production between Levine and John Lydon ('Launderette'), and Adrian Sherwood on Private Armies, these were wonderful excursions into experiments with sound. A rolling dub reggae bass line provided by Aswad's George 'Levi' Oban collides with the left-field thought, and Vivien Goldman presides over the results, adding sing song vocals that express a feeling of alienation and frustration. "If you can't get a hard on, get a gun" she taunts at one point - an uncompromising statement contained on a brilliantly uncompromising single.

77
BROOKLYN EXPRESS
Sixty-nine
Change Position (88)
NO CHART PLACING
One Way Records

Utilising a once-heard, never-forgotten sample from 'Spank' by Jimmy Bo Horne, this absolute disco monster was created by Brooklyn Express. Infectious and struttingly rhythmic, at around the four-minute mark of its nine-minute duration, the track explodes into a futuristic funk section that hits like a freight train before resuming in a more measured but assuredly non-predictable fashion. This was a euphoric and contagious sound that set pulses racing.

76
23 SKIDOO
Ethics / Another Baby's Face
NO CHART PLACING
Pineapple Products

This was the debut single by 23 Skidoo and this line-up (for line-up changes were a constant feature in the group's history) produced what was perhaps their most orthodox release in terms of sound and structure. All things are relative though, and this was still a long way from trad rock. The guitar is as scratchy as porcupine quills. The drums and bass are busy and insistent, the vocal equally so. The whole piece has a nervous energy that erupts into a volley of noise at its conclusion.

75
VIRGIN PRUNES
Twenty Tens (I've Been Smoking All Night)/ Revenge/
The Children Are Crying/
...Greylight
NO CHART PLACING
Baby Records

Virgin Prunes were absolutely unmissable. They looked like nothing on earth and sounded like aliens. They took a blank canvas and splattered it artfully with their sometimes harrowing, sometimes beautiful, sometimes subtle and sometimes brutal, music. They were vivid and visceral, always challenging and often funny. They were extreme in all they did and in every emotion they expressed. This was their first release, and it is fully formed and switched on. There is no hint of the tentative, no playing safe. It was hugely inspiring and liberating to catch the Virgin Prunes in all their magnificent glory and each track here is astonishing. After this single they signed to Rough Trade and this same year issued a slew of singles and EPs in myriad formats that were often as baffling as they were brilliant.

74
SPANDAU BALLET
Chant No. 1 (I Don't Need This Pressure On)
3
Reformation Publishing Co. Ltd

Their previous single - the entertaining, slightly homoerotic and hugely idiosyncratic 'Musclebound' - had given Spandau Ballet their third hit in a row. Their momentum seemed unstoppable, but they took a chance by abandoning the glossy synth sound that had brought success, for something dirtier and harder. 'Chant No. 1' was a Was Not Was-inspired funk reset that featured the blistering horn section of Beggar & Co. The song is lyrically slim, a celebration of hedonistic and adventurous night-life. The lyric in truth matters little. Verses are merely interludes between the choruses which deliver a slogan perfectly designed to reflect the increasingly hard times brought about by Margaret Thatcher's socio-economic reign of terror. The horn riffs are thrilling and the electronic drums that power the song ever-forward are crisp as they propel the message onto hot sweaty dance floors. "I Don't Need This Pressure On! I Don't Need This Pressure On!".

73
MADNESS
Grey Day
Memories
4
Stiff Records

With an ominous and menacing sound matching a miserably bleak lyric concerning the daily struggle endured by the protagonist of this all too familiar vignette of everyday life, this was a world away from the cheeky ska playing chappies of yore. Surprising then that 'Grey Day' was written by keyboardist Mike Barson and featured in pre-Madness sets as far back as 1978 when the band were called The North London Invaders. Despite its downbeat theme, the song managed to be catchy and appealing. In execution and feel, 'Grey Day' echoed the melancholy dramas such as 'Dead End Street' and 'Waterloo Sunset' that had made the Kinks so venerated. Indeed with their uncanny high quality, hit-writing knack and Everyman sensibility, Madness shared many traits with Ray Davies and co.

72
THE BIRTHDAY PARTY
Release the Bats
Blast Off
NO CHART PLACING
4AD

Although The Birthday Party were surely caricaturing themselves and their associations with an image of Gothic horror and vampires, the use of heavy irony and self-parody as a creative tool produced spectacular results. 'Release The Bats' transcends its origins and reveals itself as an edgy and abrasive maelstrom, a capturing of the soul of this insanely exciting band of volatile talents onto wax. Here the bass churns, the drums suggest a voodoo dance, while the twin guitars are distorted beyond recognition. And in the midst of this cacophony, Nick Cave shrieks about "bat horror vampire sex" and at other points simply unleashes guttural incomprehensible noises that build on the atmosphere of dissolute chaos.

71
SMOKEY ROBINSON
Being With You / What's In Your Life For Me
1
Motown

Written specifically for Kim Carnes by Smokey Robinson, he was instead persuaded by producer George Tobin, who had severed ties with Carnes, to record it himself. For the first time in his solo career, Smokey allowed himself to be produced by somebody else and placed himself in Tobin's hands. The producer selected a pool of musicians from the cream of West Coast session players who had appeared on numerous disco hits and created a luscious and rich bed of sound over which Smokey's honey-toned declarations of love and fidelity soothed and seduced. Never breaking pace, this was elegant and cool. It would be a much imitated sound in the coming years.

70
FRANTIC ELEVATORS
Searching for the Only One
Hunchback of Notre Dame
NO CHART PLACING
Crackin' Up

The Frantic Elevators were a band formed by my brother Neil with his friend Mick Hucknall as singer. They were Beatles obsessives and developed a quirkily melodic writing style born of that influence. Managed at this point by Roger Eagle, the esteemed musicologist and inventor of what became the Northern Soul scene when he opened The Twisted Wheel club in Manchester, the band based themselves in Liverpool where Roger had run the equally influential Eric's club that helped launch the likes of The Teardrop Explodes and Echo and the Bunnymen. They seemed on the cusp of a breakthrough with the release of this single. Two excellent songs, one a tuneful and well-crafted song about seeking love and the other a collision of art noise and existential crisis. Well written and performed, splendid production, a singer with a special voice. Surely it would achieve something? Alas not.

69
HÜSKER DÜ
Statues
Amusement
NO CHART PLACING
Reflex Records

Hüsker Dü hailed from Minneapolis but the influence of Manchester's Joy Division is apparent on 'Amusement'. They employ a similar sounding 'Sturm und Drang' with muted dynamics, whilst Bob Mould's vocal intonations are remarkably similar to those of Ian Curtis. Stylistic similarities to PIL are also apparent in 'Statues'. And yet there is more to the songs and their performances than these influences. They exhibit an inherent power, intelligence and seriousness of intent that signified the emergence of a truly incredible band.

68
THE TEARDROP EXPLODES
Reward
Strange House in the Snow
6
Mercury

Julian Cope was cock-a-hoop at the success that The Teardrop Explodes were having. "Bless my cotton socks I'm in the news" he proclaimed on the opening line of 'Reward'. And at that point he probably believed it was his destiny to become a cultural figure somewhere between Elvis Presley and Jim Morrison. 'Reward' bottled up all Julian's excitement and then shook it up until it fizzed, bubbled and ultimately cascaded in an unstoppable torrent. The bass is a pummelling Northern Soul approximation, the drums thump hard and the rest is a speeding frenzy of trumpets, keyboards and huge choruses.

67
WIRE
Our Swimmer
Midnight Bahnhof Café
NO CHART PLACING
Rough Trade

Wire had been released by *Harvest Records* as a result of underwhelming sales figures and the realisation that this most uncompromising outfit were unlikely to ever conform and make more marketable product. 'Our Swimmer' was recorded in 1979 and needed a home and so a one-off deal was struck with *Rough Trade.* By the time the single was released, Wire had ceased to exist. *Rough Trade* had no promotional budget and so the record slipped between the cracks, barely heard. The shame of that was that 'Our Swimmer' was absolutely classic Wire. As intriguingly obscure as ever lyrically, the voice and the rhythm absolutely insistent, fragments of funk bass and guitar in the breakdowns, it had a momentum that pushed and pulled and smelled as fresh as a daisy.

66
JOSEF K
Sorry For Laughing
Révélation
NO CHART PLACING
Les Disques Du Crépuscule

Inspired by American funk and disco along with Penguin classic editions of Camus and Kafka, fuelled by no stimulants stronger than caffeine and rejecting all rock music clichés such as encores (viewed as being patronising), it is fair to say Josef K took themselves very seriously and that is reflected in their music. On 'Sorry For Laughing', despite its jaunty if prickly rhythms, there is an intensity attached to every word delivered by Paul Haig, equally each note seems considered and analysed before being played. They inhabit a suffocating place but the purity of their emotions positively gleams through the murk.

65
FIRE ENGINES
Candyskin
Meat Whiplash
NO CHART PLACING
Pop Aural

Fire Engines became much more influential once they'd ceased to exist than they ever were in their natural lifespan. Sometimes the world needs time to catch up. This was their finest and most successful single and by rights should have hogged daytime radio play and become a *bona fide* hit. 'Candyskin' was a rich irresistible dish - one part T. Rex, one part The Supremes, colliding in a roller disco. It was pop music nirvana. Meanwhile, 'Meat Whiplash' married the sound of Captain Beefheart to that of Gene Krupa on surf boards.

64
THE BLUE ORCHIDS
Disney Boys /The Flood
NO CHART PLACING
Rough Trade Records

Former Fall founder members Una Baines and Martin Bramah formed The Blue Orchids and recruited another ex Fall member Eric McGann as bassist, John Cooper Clark provided the band name and this was their first release.

Combiingd a hallucinatory quality mixed with a take-no-prisoners attitude, 'Disney Boys' attempts to combine a tale of a street rip off with the nasty underbelly that lies beneath the artificiality of Donald Duck and Micky Mouse as American cultural icons , whilst 'The Flood' is a rush of fiery psychedelia, Una's keyboard work along with Bramah's guitar and strained singing voice were highly distinctive and helped make this a very satisfying statement of intent.

63
CRASS
Nagasaki Nightmare
Big 'A' Little 'A'
NO CHART PLACING
Crass Records

The fact that the stance here is resolutely humanist, rather than political, adds huge power to this record that details the horror of the second nuclear bomb to be dropped on a city full of people. While tensions escalated as Russia and America manufactured increasing amounts of weapons of mass destruction, this historical retrospective was a timely and poignant reminder of the potential consequence of these weapons. Crass go for subtlety rather than a sledgehammer to deliver this song. It is light but urgent musically and voiced compassionately by the female members of the band rather than being spat out aggressively by Steve Ignorant.

62
BEGGAR & CO
(Somebody) Help Me Out
Rising Sun
15
Ensign

Emerging from the ranks of early Brit funk act, Light Of The World, the horn heavy Beggar & Co were a more direct and vibrant proposition.

This was their first single and features a vocal chanted in unison, where from a downtrodden position the aspiration is to climb and feel respect. The bass line is an approximation of a wriggling worm and gives the track a groove. Synth lines snake through it and the horns are uplifting and celebratory. This was the sound of young black Britain expressing itself... loud, proud and with joy.

61
IMAGINATION
Flashback
Burnin' Up
16
R & B Records

Their risqué and ridiculous image as scantily clad, conspicuously oiled, Roman centurions certainly drew attention, but probably undermined the quality of their music in many people's eyes. In 1981 'Flashback' was one of three hit singles they enjoyed of the highest quality. It is elegant, unhurried and memorable. The 'Flashback' single also has the incredible piano-led B-side, 'Burnin' Up', which is a prototype for the embryonic Chicago house sound and surely a reference point for Marshall Jefferson's early anthems. 'Imagination' traded in what can only be described as 'post-disco'. There was an appreciation of space in their recordings which, whilst elegant and sophisticated, lacked nothing in adventurousness.

60
VIC GODARD
& THE SUBWAY SECT
Stop That Girl/
Instrumentally Scared/
Vertical Integration
NO CHART PLACING
Rough Trade/Oddball Productions

On 'Stop That Girl' Vic is supported by the uncredited Black Arabs on this delightfully un-rock 'n' roll accordion-led tale of a Sapphic rival stealing the lovelorn narrator's girlfriend away. Vic's vocal is as wavering and anti-heroic as any male lead vocalist has ever dared be. The Black Arabs add a fifties-style cooing accompaniment to create a piece that is unconventional and non-classifiable.

59
PRINCE
Do It All Night
Head
NO CHART PLACING
Warner Bros. Records

Prince certainly wasn't aiming to charm daytime radio playlisters, and therefore mainstream audiences, by releasing singles as blatantly sexual as 'Do It All Night' which helped promote a rebellious outsider image and gave him a fascinating exotic (and erotic) appeal. That needed to be backed up by talent and the undoubted quality of the record. It opens with a captivating, though simple, keyboard motif before drums, rhythm guitar and bass kick in and provide a supple, raunchy platform for Prince to coo salaciously about what he wants to do all night. The B-side was his controversial and delightful ode to oral sex… 'Head'!

58
INNER LIFE
Ain't No Mountain High Enough
Ain't No Mountain High Enough (The Garage Version)
NO CHART PLACING
Salsoul Records

Inner Life were a studio-based production team aiming, and succeeding, in creating music to fill nightclub dance floors. 'Ain't No Mountain High Enough' features the powerfully voiced Jocelyn Brown who delivers an energetic and passionate version of the Diana Ross *Motown* classic. It dispenses with the original's structure and melody completely, as it mutates into a symphonic clash between strings and synthesisers that compete over a pulsating rhythm.

57
MAXIMUM JOY
Stretch/Silent Street/Silent Dub
NO CHART PLACING
Y Records

Bristol is not a big city and perhaps because of that there appeared to be a thriving, close-knit musical community where mutually supportive alliances could flourish. Maximum Joy came together in the wake of both The Pop Group and Glaxo Babies reaching the end of the road. Members from both those groups joined forces in the new group, alongside singer/violinist/clarinettist Janine Rainforth.

'Stretch', their first release, reflects the cultural melting pot the band inhabited, with elements of dub and jazz embedded in its scratchy, funky framework. It is adventurous, frenzied and complimented by an artless natural vocal from Rainforth who sings, shouts and screams a lyric about positivity and possibilities. Picked up by *99 Records* for an American release where it became a club hit in New York, its ripples are still felt.

56
E.S.G
You're No Good/U.F.O./Moody
NO CHART PLACING
Factory

E.S.G - short for Emerald, Sapphire and Gold - formed in New York in 1978 and comprised sisters Renee, Valerie, Deborah and Marie Scroggins. In 1981, Tony Wilson approached them after seeing them perform at Hurrah, and three days later they were recording these tracks with producer Martin Hannett. The band play a skeletal funk-punk hybrid with a Latin flavour. The vocals are bitter-sweet and haunted whilst the rhythms convey a dark edge.

The three tracks are strikingly original and of high quality. 'U.F.O.' - which was recorded in the last 20 minutes of studio time left over - particularly caught the attention of the hip-hop community and is one of the most sampled tracks ever.

55
PIGBAG
Papa's Got A Brand New Pigbag
The Backside
NO CHART PLACING
(reached no 3 when reissued 1982)
Y Records

Formed in Cheltenham and using the name Us Corporation, the nascent band jammed in parks and at bus stops before deciding to take themselves more seriously. On hearing The Pop Group had split up, a deputation hitch-hiked to Bristol to persuade bass player Simon Underwood to join them. They knocked on his door and popped the question. Remarkably he accepted their invitation and brought along his tenor sax playing chum Ollie Moore. 'Papa's got a brand New Pigbag' was the inspiration of founder member Chris Hamlin. It was performed as a 20-minute piece at the band's first gig, supporting The Slits in Bristol.

Slits manager and Y Records boss, Dick O'Dell, was impressed and asked them to record the track. Trimmed to under four minutes, this instrumental record was absolutely explosive. Every component part is straining towards the extreme. Underwood's bass is monstrous and unforgiving and the horn riffs are hard and unforgettable. It was a riot of funk, jazz, punk and world music rolled into a ball of gleeful excess… uncontainable and unforgettable.

54
ABC
Tears Are Not Enough
Alphabet Soup
19
Neutron Records

Evolving out of Sheffield synthesiser band Vice Versa, the re-imagination that took place as they became ABC was radical and bold. 'Tears Are Not Enough' was the new group's first single and acted as a manifesto for their future intentions. It was funky with a glossy sheen of exaggerated sophistication and singer Martin Fry added a pristine croon pitched somewhere between Bryan Ferry and Englebert Humperdinck. A previous generation would have sneered at a lack of authenticity but at this point it no longer mattered. What *did* matter was the release of a classy and clever record whose sound looked forward. Soon, producer Trevor Horn would begin working with the band and their creations would become ever more luxurious, lavish and enchanting.

53
DEFUNKT
The Razor's Edge
Stranglin' Me With Your Love (Revisited)
NO CHART PLACING
Hannibal Records

Many musicians were mixing up their rock roots with soul and jazz influences but for Defunkt, the roles were reversed as revered jazz trombonist Joe Bowie gathered this ensemble from the remnants of James

White and the Blacks and created a feverish, highly intense fusion of jazz, funk and punk. Think Miles Davis with Sonic Youth and James Brown. This was the group's opening salvo - nine minutes plus of energetic playing. It is an instrumental except for sharp half-spoken street jive that culminates in chanted interjections of "I gave up a lot, but I won't give in". It jerks and spasms, wriggles and writhes. The bass pummels and the horns alternate between wailing and hammering home a titanic riff that act as the song's hook, while the drums and rhythm guitar anchor the track and propel it towards the dance floor.

52
MAGAZINE
About the Weather
In the Dark
NO CHART PLACING
Virgin

Guitarist John McGeoch left Magazine in the middle of 1980. His replacement – ex-Ultravox Robin Simon - followed suit six months later. So for Magazine's last album of the era, Howard Devoto's friend Ben Mandleson stepped into the ranks. The changes seemed to have stripped away the belief remaining members had in the band, and the final album was a lacklustre affair in general. One bright spot was 'About the Weather' where Dave Formula serves up an up-tempo piano led Motown pastiche that positively sparkles. Here Devoto rouses himself and sings his enigmatic lyric, about being unable to control changes, with assurance and vim.

51
NEW ORDER
Ceremony
In a Lonely Place
34
Factory

'Ceremony' was New Order's first post-Joy Division release and came in two versions. The first was issued in January, featuring Bernard Sumner, Peter Hook and Stephen Morris and came as a 7" in a gold sleeve and a green-sleeved 12" with a longer version of 'In a Lonely Place'. The second appeared in September, on 12" only, a re-recording which added new member, Gillian Gilbert, on guitar and a remixed version of the B-side. 'Ceremony' was one of the last written by Joy Division with a lyric by Ian Curtis and a version was recorded just three days prior to his death. The sound is therefore unsurprisingly very close to that of a Joy Division record with Bernard Sumner's vocal heavily influenced by Curtis. The song itself is mid-tempo and flows effortlessly, utilising loud and quiet passages alternately to display its dynamics whilst Martin Hannett's production adds atmospherics and a palpable tension.

50
JOHN LENNON/YOKO ONO
Watching the Wheels
Yes I'm Your Angel
30
Geffen Records

John Lennon's death had touched a collective nerve that sent a succession of releases to number one spot in the UK charts. But by the time 'Watching the Wheels' was released as the third single from the *Double Fantasy* album, the collective grief had been sated. And so this record slipped through the cracks to some extent. 'Watching The Wheels' was, in fact, Lennon close to his best, offering his own perspective and answering the negative comments concerning his five-year absence from the music scene as he became a house husband caring for his infant son. His writing is spare and to the point. While his delivery on the whole is conciliatory, it still contains hints at defiant indignation and is far from saccharine. Musically too the song is pretty much unadorned beyond a combined piano and dulcimer accompaniment. As for the B-side, Yoko's touch deserts her on this occasion, with 'Yes I'm Your Angel' being completely inconsequential mush, irremediably dressed up as a roaring twenties style flapper.

49
R.E.M.
Radio Free Europe
Sitting Still
NO CHART PLACING
Hib-Tone Records

A synthesiser-played figure signals the opening of this debut single from R.E.M. before the band kick in. The playing is brisk and taut but equally light and unclichéd. Its guitar melodies intertwine on top of a driving beat, and singer Michael Stipe babbles excitedly but unintelligibly through the verses and choruses save for the phrase "Radio Free Europe" which is delivered with great urgency. This was baffling and somewhat mysterious, and yet undeniably these unknowns from Athens, Georgia had something special contained in their sound.

48
ADAM AND THE ANTS
Stand and Deliver
Beat My Guest
1
CBS

'Stand and Deliver' was brash and flash, mixing punk and glam with spaghetti western guitars. Riding hot on the heels of 'Ant Music', the track was the band's first chart number one, entering the hit parade at that position on the week of its release. The lyric was utterly preposterous and silly, concerning itself with looking good and the adventures of a "dandy highwayman". It was, without doubt, very silly indeed but it was also exciting and expansive.

Unafraid of ridicule, it was perfect pop existing in a glamorous fantasy. On the B-side was another reworking of an original 1977 Ants song. 'Beat My Guest' that had been played at the band's first ever gig showing that silliness was nothing new and the original set of songs had been even sillier than the new ones!

47
DAVID BOWIE
Scary Monsters and Super Creeps
Because You're Young
20
RCA

As the title track and third single taken from the previous year's album, most people were already familiar with this song which was the understandable reason for its muted reception and modest sales. It is still a magnificent song, about a woman driven mad by a man which is delivered from his perspective. Bowie adopts his 'Cockney voice' to deliver the sinister tale, imbuing it with a taste of the lower class criminal being portrayed. Robert Fripp plays volcanic guitar whilst synthesised drums provide a modernist counterpoint.

46
GIL SCOTT HERON
"B" Movie/Is That Jazz?
NO CHART PLACING
Arista Records

Beginning with the immortal line "the first thing I wanna say is mandate my ass", '"B" Movie' - in its 12 minutes plus form - is Gil Scott Heron's masterpiece. Quite possibly the greatest American poem of the 20th century: it tears up the notion that the American dream is alive; it accuses the country of being frightened of the future and instead wallowing in a Hollywood manufactured version of the past; it damns the country for wanting John Wayne as president but in his absence settling for Ronald Reagan and turning life into a B-movie.

The single version is edited down to five minutes 18 seconds of calm, reasoned vitriol, and though not a match for the full form epic, it is nonetheless magnificent and essential listening.

45
JAPAN
Visions of China
Taking Islands in Africa (Remix)
32
Virgin

With a prominent and distinctive bass line as the centrepiece of the song, it is layered with instrumentation displaying an eastern flavour. Drums and percussion play a martial beat and singer David Sylvain gives a trademark cool, crooning performance on what remains a memorable piece of hypnotic art-tinged pop.

44
QUEEN AND DAVID BOWIE
Under pressure/Soul Brother
1
EMI

David Bowie was living in Switzerland and his record contract with RCA was at an end. Queen were coincidentally recording in

Switzerland so Bowie called into the studio to pick their brains about the size of advances record companies were offering as he surveyed his career options. They jammed together, playing songs by Cream and Mott the Hoople, took drugs, drank a lot of wine and decided to create something new. John Deacon had a bass line, Bowie altered it slightly and it was a killer. Queen wanted structure, but Bowie encouraged them to trust their instincts and proceed with no road map. By the end of the day the basic track was complete along with snatches of lyrics and sections of Freddie Mercury's expressive scat singing. The next morning, Bowie appeared with a complete, very dramatic, lyric and took control.

Recording complete, Bowie and Mercury clashed about the mixing of the track, resulting in a compromise. 'Under Pressure' was issued as a single with neither Queen or Bowie caring enough to promote it. The public loved it though, recognising its magic; the mix of the funky groove, Queen's rock pomp, Bowie's soulful style and Freddie Mercury's theatrical power somehow came together to create a wondrous cohesive whole rather than a jarring clash of too many egos.

43
CYBOTRON
Alleys Of Your Mind
Cosmic Raindance
NO CHART PLACING
Deep Space Records

Formed in Detroit, Cybotron consisted of Juan Atkins, Richard 3070 Davis and John "Jon 5" Housley. Their reference points included Kraftwerk, Funkadelic, Yellow Magic Orchestra and Futurist literature. They married their influences into a sound designed to mirror their surroundings and in particular reflect the dying auto industry on which Detroit's economy was so reliant. Released on Atkins own Deep Space Records label, 'Alleys Of Your Mind', with its crisp programmed beats, funk rhythm and machine treated vocals, created an image of future decay and empty production lines... a bleak future. The song pointed towards a musical future too; here were the first stirrings of Techno…

42
FUN BOY THREE
The Lunatics (Have Taken Over The Asylum)
Faith, Hope and Charity
20
Chrysalis

Written while still members of The Specials, Terry Hall, Lynval Golding and Neville Staples took the song with them following the acrimonious split that saw them form Fun Boy Three. 'The Lunatics' is a song of political satire lampooning Reagan and

Thatcher as mad people who have seized power. It has an exceedingly Spartan sound with a simple drum beat and snake charmer's pipe that leaves plenty of room for the three voices to combine and create a distinct atmospheric sound.

Incidentally, when a reformed version of The Specials recorded a new album 38 years after this record's release 'Lunatics' was revived and included. This time it targeted the insane and incapable leadership provided by the bigot Donald Trump and the hapless Theresa May.

41
BUSH TETRAS
Things That Go Boom In The Night/Das Ah Riot
NO CHART PLACING
Fetish Records

I had a memory of seeing Bush Tetras at The Haçienda, but as that club was yet to be built, I did some research and concluded I saw Bush Tetras at Rafters! What is absolutely certain though is I thought they were wonderful. They were rhythmic and bass-centred and their music shared the sensibility, but not the sound, of Dub reggae. It was wild and unique. At the first opportunity I purchased the only Bush Tetras record available in the UK – 'Things That Go Boom In The Night'. It exceeded my already high expectations. Its unhurried drum and bass rhythm is cut by frenetic guitar noise, and the female vocals are enunciated with eerie precision from the very midst of the rising, increasingly urgently played musical maelstrom.

40
DAVID BYRNE & BRIAN ENO
The Jezebel Spirit/Regiment
NO CHART PLACING
Polydor

The twin doyens of art rock teamed up to make the album *My Life In The Bush Of Ghosts*, where the combination of found sounds mixed with live instrumentation and doing away with conventional vocals was, for the time, a radical departure and critically well-received. The exception was the track 'The Jezebel Spirit' which was selected to be a single. Here, the 'found sound' is a recording of an exorcism, performed on a seemingly fallen woman, hence the insulting label 'Jezebel' which is associated with prostitution. Some critics - presumably affected by their own Catholic guilt - accused the pair of exploitation and sensationalism. They were off the mark in my estimation as this excellent track combines the kind of African rhythms utilised by Byrne's Talking Heads with the excited voice of the preacher involved in the exorcism to create a startling piece of music.

39
YOU'VE GOT FOETUS ON YOUR BREATH
Wash It All Off/333
NO CHART PLACING
Self Immolation

Jim Thirwell's recorded debut came with this 'limited to 1,000 copies' single. I luckily picked up a copy out of curiosity at what an act named You've Got Foetus On Your Breath might sound like! Placing the disc on the turntable, I found they sounded like a riot or an explosion of provocative statements – "Why kill time when you can kill yourself?" being a choice example. These were seamlessly married to a barrage of sounds, including nursery rhyme rhythms and electro-powered rockabilly. It was snotty, cheap and nasty and no doubt highly offensive to the easily offended. I thought it was sparkling, fresh and quite brilliant.

38
KIM WILDE
Cambodia/Watching for Shapes
12
RAK

Kim Wilde had burst into the national consciousness with her fizzing hook-laden single 'Kids In America' at the start of the year. Two more hits followed, all written and produced by her brother Ricky and father Marty who had been one of Larry Parnes' stable of tame British rockers in the early 60s. Having proved that they could craft effervescent pop and Kim could deliver it, they decided to aim for more depth and maturity with the fourth single.

Usually this well-meaning move signals disaster, but here they got it right. With a chilly Eastern-flavoured synthesiser backing and haunting melody, Kim recounts a tale concerning the US bombing raids on Cambodia. She portrays the wife of a pilot sent to drop bombs horrified by what he has to do. He ultimately flies a mission he does not return from, leaving his wife with memories of his sadness. Sung with empathy and restraint 'Cambodia' was extremely good, thoughtful pop.

37
ODYSSEY
Going Back To My Roots
Baba Awa
4
RCA

At this point of their career hit followed hit for Odyssey, and whilst not the biggest of those hits, this has proved to be extremely durable and iconic. This a cover version of the 1977 original, written and performed by Lamont Dozier, and is a call to embrace self-identity that touches on the importance of family and a striving for fulfilment. Performed in a disco style with gritty exuberance, 'Going Back To My Roots' was anthemic good time music that filled dance-floors. It was also thought provoking in its punchy uplifting message; it was in short, disco perfection.

36
MATERIAL
Bustin' Out/Over & Over
NO CHART PLACING
Ze Records

Material were a heavyweight proposition featuring superb musicianship. On 'Bustin' Out' they add the stellar talent of ex-Labelle singer Nona Hendryx, as they moved away from their experimental jazz roots towards funkier sounds aimed at the clubbing crowd. What they produced was what came to be described as an absolute banger. It truly was dynamic. Up-tempo synths pumped, the bass-line is incessant and fluid and guest guitarist Ronnie Drayton serves up an extended guitar solo that is sensational. Nona Hendryx is utterly captivating as she nails a vocal full of conviction.

35
IAN DURY
Spasticus Autisticus
Spasticus Autisticus (Version)
NO CHART PLACING
Polydor

Ian had become disabled as a child after contracting polio. As 1981 had been designated by the UN as 'International Year of Disabled Persons', Ian sensed how sickening and patronising the representation of disabled people would be and recorded 'Spasticus Autisticus'. Written in cahoots with long-term musical foil Chas Jankel, it was a very pointed riposte, provocative in the extreme and painfully honest. Ian was refusing to be invisible to those uncomfortable with bodies that didn't conform to a vision of aesthetic beauty. Nor was he humbly proffering gratitude to people sticking a few shillings in a collection box to make themselves feel good. 'Spasticus Autisticus' was a true tour de force. It is one of the greatest lyrics this brilliant lyricist penned and one of the finest performances of his career displaying a range of emotions from playful to vicious. The lyric dictates a repeated refrain of "I'm Spasticus!" from Ian and band members which echoes the famous scene in the cinematic epic *Spartacus*. A superb jittery funk backing gives Ian a wonderful platform for this brilliantly conceived single that was banned as being offensive by the BBC and suppressed by Ian's own record label.

34
TONI BASIL
Mickey/Hanging Around
2
Radialchoice

Toni Basil appeared seemingly out of nowhere with this infectious single. She was however something of a veteran, being a dancer-choreographer of high repute. She had danced with Davy Jones in The Monkees' film *Head* and appeared as part of the dance troupe The Lockers alongside acts as disparate as Frank Sinatra and Funkadelic. She also choreographed David Bowie's 1974 *Diamond Dogs* tour and as far back as 1966 had released her first single. 'Mickey' was the 15-years-later follow up. The song had originally been recorded by British band Racey in 1979 as 'Kitty'. Toni Basil changed the gender of the titular character, added a memorable chanted section to the song, filled it with fizz, sang it with total exuberance, shook it up and watched it explode! It was irrepressible and inescapably catchy, with enough infectious energy to light up a room.

33
PRINCE
Controversy/When You Were Mine
NO CHART PLACING
(1993 - No 5)
Warner Bros. Records

Addressing rumours concerning his sexuality and his race and then incorporating a chanted Lord's Prayer into the midst of the song encouraging accusations of blasphemy, this was Prince at his most challenging and liberal baiting. It was also a moment of pop genius. His sound has become more skeletal but also more loose-limbed and supple, allowing a true appreciation of his playful falsetto vocal and the intricacies of the instrumentation to produce the mouthwatering groove that is as breathtaking as waves rolling in from the sea.

32
DEXYS MIDNIGHT RUNNERS
Plan B/Soul Finger
58
EMI

The original Dexys split, with members going on to form The Bureau and Blue Ox Babies, leaving only Kevin Rowland and trombonist "Big Jim" Patterson in place. A new band was put together – a new look of boxing boots and hooded tops to emphasise a purity through physical cleansing was adopted, and 'Plan B' was released as a single. There was no dramatic shift in the musical approach with horns still featuring prominently. However, the band did seem energised, faster on their feet and more muscular than ever.

'Plan B' lyrically takes the form of Rowland addressing somebody and urging them to believe in him. It maybe Rowland imagining himself speaking to Patterson, though more likely he is voicing the dialogue from inside his own head. He sings of "whispers more than loud enough, try to make you feel not good enough", possibly about the departed ex-band members, but more likely acknowledging his own doubts and lack of self-belief. Bill Withers is referenced, and his song 'Lean On Me' cited as inspirational and uplifting.

'Plan B' was a remarkable single and a glimpse into the heart, troubled soul and mind of its writer and singer .

31
THE JACKSONS
Can You Feel It/Wondering Who
6
Epic

Written by brothers Michael and Jackie Jackson as a unifying call for the people of the world to come together and be as one, it's lofty theme was matched by the magisterial power of the music and the repeated questioning vocal refrain of the song's title. With a fantastically emotional lead vocal from Michael, a relentless funky disco beat and the addition of a choir, 'Can You Feel It' was one of the finest ever records to emerge from the Jackson household.

30
PERE UBU
Not Happy/Lonesome Cowboy Dave
NO CHART PLACING
Rough Trade

Nothing obscure or hidden on this single. The band play a cheerful tune that chimes in the manner of playful children, whilst David Thomas carries this approach into his singing, at times sounding like a seven-year-old. The lyrics speak of happy bees buzzing in harmony and equally happy oddball birds in South America, and asks can we be as happy as they are? Curiously, none of this sounds too twee. In DJ sets I often used to give this record a spin in clubs where even the most jaded of cool hipsters were forced to smile and shake a leg.

29
THE BONGOS
Bulrushes/Automatic Doors
NO CHART PLACING
Fetish Records

I was vacationing in New York towards the end of this decade, and friends took me to see some bands at The Knitting Factory. I was introduced to several people, shook hands, exchanged pleasantries and then an introduction was made: "Rob, he used to be in a band called The Bongos" … "What! I love The Bongos", I gushed. The Bongos' bass player, Rob Norris, seemed to think I was merely being polite and exaggerating my feelings. "Why would some English guy know or care about us?" could well have been his reasoning. I persisted and spoke about the Bongos album *Drums Along the Hudson*. I enthused about the 'Mambo Sun' single. But the record I love most, I told him, is 'Bulrushes'. I clearly knew my stuff and my sincerity was no longer in doubt. It was nice to show my appreciation for all the pleasure I'd received listening to his band.

'Bulrushes' is one of those records that touches the soul. If it was better known it would be regarded as a classic. It is the sort of guitar pop that groups like Badfinger and Big Star played and a song either of those seminal bands would have killed to have written. It has a warm, rippling groove and a chiming guitar that is perfect, the whole thing moves purposefully with grace while singer Richard Barone passionately emotes a succinct but mysterious lyric eluding to a search for the baby Moses that fascinates me to this day .

28
EARTH, WIND & FIRE
Let's Groove
Let's Groove (Instrumental)
3
CBS

Harshly dismissed by George Clinton as "Hot Air No Fire", while Earth, Wind & Fire may not have had Clinton's maverick spirit, they were superb craftsmen. During their decade-straddling golden period, they delivered a stream of radio-friendly, floor-filling singles of the highest quality. 'Let's Groove' was a highlight of the run which was nearing its end. Here Earth, Wind & Fire tailor the sound for a new era and, though the track is bass heavy and has a monumental horn riff courtesy of the Brecker Brothers, also prominent is synthesiser, electric guitar and a robotic voice run through a vocoder. It's up-tempo and uplifting, with lyrics suggesting that spiritual enlightenment exists within the groove and may be located on the dance floor.

27
TALKING HEADS
Houses in Motion
50
Sire

The jittery funk style of Talking Heads is here fused with an approximation of African 'highlife' style. While David Byrne further dissects the incongruous strangeness within suburban living, avant-garde trombonist Jon Hassell adds an air of strangeness and an off kilter solo that helps emphasise the precarious nature of life itself.

26
SOFT CELL
Bedsitter/Facility Girls
4
Some Bizzare

'Bedsitter' is a kitchen sink drama voiced immaculately by Marc Almond over an evocative futuristic soundtrack by Dave Ball. It details the dark and damaging underbelly of the clubbing scene - the pretence, the loneliness, the drink and drugs. It is like a modernist take on the descent into Dante's Inferno with a big sing-along chorus.

25
PATRICK COWLEY
Menergy
I Wanna Take You Home
NO CHART PLACING
Fusion Records

Patrick Cowley's work with Sylvester, as well as his epic mix of Donna Summer's 'I Feel Love', provided him with the platform to begin a solo career. He grabbed the chance with both hands and here, with Menergy, delivered a complete classic with an unapologetic gay theme. Opening with a grand lush electronic sweep, the track lifts off with the introduction of a pulsating electronic riff, ascending higher as a mix of natural and machine-treated vocals deliver a lyric full of sexual energy - or has Cowley has it, 'Menergy'. As the (m)energy gets higher and higher, Cowley introduces drops in the music, signifying sexual release, before building up yet more energy and tension. Sadly, a year later (aged 32), Cowley became an early victim of the little known AIDS virus that raged through his native San Francisco.

24
J WALTER NEGRO
& THE LOOSE JOINTZ
Shoot The Pump (Parts 1 & 2)
Shoot The Pump (Instrumental)
NO CHART PLACING
Island Records

Marc André Edmonds was a graffiti artist in New York going by the name Ali. His works were political and satirical. He coined the phrase 'Zoo York' and used it as the title of a comic orientated magazine he founded and published. As hip-hop emerged, Ali formed a band. Giving himself a new alter ego for the project, he became J Walter Negro. Meanwhile, The Loose Jointz were a tight-as-a-nut live band who played a smoking Latin-tinged funk. On 'Shoot The Pump' Ali regales us with a tale of using a monkey wrench to open up a water hydrant and spray passers-by, which is to "shoot the pump". The police arrive, mistake the wrench for a gun, and shoot him, that is, they "shoot the punk"! Miraculously he survives because he's wearing a bullet proof vest. He opens up the hydrant again to once more' Shoot The Pump'. It's no work of Shakespearean literary merit, but it is an action-packed, cartoon-style, urban adventure that is brilliantly conceived and executed.

23
D.A.F
Der Mussolini
Der Räuber Und Der Prinz
NO CHART PLACING
Virgin

D.A.F. were extreme. They were confrontational. In terms of attitude they resembled New York art terrorists Suicide. Their sound was stripped-to-the-bone brutalist techno. They set out to pulverise the listener on 'Der Mussolini'. The electronic rhythms are rough-edged and jagged. Nothing is smooth; they jar and crunch. But do not imagine though that they were humourless, for here the listener is invited to alternately "dance the Mussolini" and "dance the Adolph Hitler" as they mock two of the 20th Century's most feared dictators for their ridiculous appropriation of uptight stiffness in everything from speech patterns to salutes and the ludicrous goose-stepping march. They are reduced to objects of laughable inadequacy and the inspiration of a novelty dance craze.

22
THE HUMAN LEAGUE
Don't You Want Me
Seconds
1
Virgin

The lack of commercial success for the original Human League brought simmering conflicts to the surface and resulted in the two seemingly most talented members leaving to form Heaven 17. Bequeathed the group name along with its substantial debts - and inescapable tour commitments in 10 days' time - singer Phil Oakey and visuals facilitator Philip Adrian Wright fetched in synthesiser player Ian Burden and a pair of still at school female backing singers, Susan Sulley and Joanne Catherall, and hit the road. Audiences hated the new line up and the girls in particular faced abusive catcalls. Oakey, Wright and Burden recorded a single, 'Boys and Girls', which surprisingly sold better than previous Human League records, and because of it the record label decided to fund an album. Martin Rushent was chosen as producer and ex-Rezillo Jo Callis added to the line-up.

Three singles from the album *Dare* were released preceding 'Don't You Want Me'. Each was an enormous success. Oakey was furious when 'Don't You Want Me' was chosen to be released as a single too. He detested it, thought of it as a cheap novelty track that was too poppy. The public disagreed! They loved it. Loved its drama, as vocals from different viewpoints by Oakey and Sulley were exchanged. They loved the gritty reality of sexual power plays being vividly enacted. But mostly they loved the chorus. The chorus was gigantic. The chorus was unforgettable. The chorus was contagious and demanded to be sung along to. The record was fabulous and was the biggest seller of the year, making the Human League household names.

21
EURYTHMICS
Never Gonna Cry Again
Le Sinistre
63
RCA

This was Eurythmics' first single and even though they went on to a run of high quality hits, this arguably was the finest single of their career. Produced artfully by Conny Plank, it is a claustrophobic song. Annie Lennox's vocals are mixed much lower than they would be on subsequent releases where her powerful, pristine voice was used as a selling point. Here the treatment is much more subtle. With Can members Jaki Liebzeit on drums and Holger Czukay providing a French horn solo and footsteps alongside the flute and synthesiser parts of Annie Lennox, and a thumping bass part from Dave Stewart, this is a record with a serious groove of genius proportions.

20
THE FALL
Lie Dream Of A Casino Soul
Fantastic Life
NO CHART PLACING
Kamera Records

So picture this. I've been roped into DJing a Christmas function at a local pub. Everyone is dressed up and well scrubbed. They wear snoods and leg warmers. It is like I am facing a sea of Bananarama and Haircut 100 impersonators! They want to hear nothing but shiny pop. I try to meet them halfway. I have with me the brand new Fall single and I want to hear it *loud*. I'm itching to play it. I can't resist. On it goes. 'Lie Dream Of A Casino Soul' sees people staring open-mouthed as The Fall survey the human wreckage and lost souls lamenting the end of an era and their lifestyle as Wigan Casino closes down. "I got away with that" I think to myself. and flip the record over. It's a scorching thing of pounding drums and cranked up organ – "People tend to let you down, it's a swine" howls Mark Smith. "'Fantastic Life' - indeed it is!", I reflect to myself with quiet satisfaction.

19
GRANDMASTER FLASH & THE FURIOUS FIVE
The Adventures Of Grandmaster Flash On The Wheels Of Steel
The Birthday Party
NO CHART PLACING
Sugar Hill Records

Here was something new for the ears. What we have is Grandmaster Flash scratching, mixing and manipulating records across three turntables in a live mix, a style later dubbed 'turntablism'. Among the most prominent samples incorporated are: Queen's 'Another One Bites The Dust'; Chic's 'Good Times'; Blondie's 'Rapture'; Incredible Bongo Band's 'Apache'; Spoonie Gee's 'Monster Jam'; and The Sugar Hill Gang's 'Rappers Delight'. This was revolutionary stuff, and fascinating, as well as being great dance floor fuel. The likes of Steinski and DJ Shadow would hone this style to the level of high art in the years that followed, but the visceral thrill of first hearing this remains a sweet, sweet memory.

18
PUBLIC IMAGE LTD
Flowers of Romance
Home Is Where The Heart Is
24
Virgin

With Jah Wobble having departed and Keith Levine tired of the limitations of the guitar, 'Flowers Of Romance' was created using hugely experimental and unorthodox methods. Martin Atkins provides a solid back-beat while John Lydon takes a violin bow to the bass and bangs anything he can lay his hands on. Keith Levine meanwhile excels, creating a droning wall of noise that the like of Stockhausen or Lamont Young would have approved. In the midst of the blitzkrieg of dissonance, Lydon produces a beautifully controlled vocal performance as he takes aim at people's reluctance to move on from a romanticised past.

17
DOLL BY DOLL
Main Travelled Roads
Be My Friend
NO CHART PLACING
Magnet

In many ways Doll by Doll could be categorised as the archetypal classic rock band and in many ways they were. Their sound followed the grand tradition - the songs were beautifully crafted and leader and singer Jackie Leven had a rich, smooth as malt whiskey, baritone voice. But Doll by Doll were fuelled by a mixture of psychedelia and aggression, a frightening combination that saw Hawkwind have them thrown off a tour because they were intimidated by their prodigious drug use and sporadic violent behaviour. 'Main Travelled Roads' catches Doll by Doll at the height of their powers. It is a soaring, mystical ballad delivered with steering intensity, concerned with loneliness, pain and honour. It is tragically beautiful and epic in its scope, containing the semi-autobiographical line Jackie Leven is most remembered for: "Eternal is the warrior who finds beauty in his wounds". A remarkable line from a remarkable song.

16
GRACE JONES
Pull Up To The Bumper
53 (1986 REISSUE - 12)
Island Records

Grace Jones was mixing up reggae, funk, disco, punk and chanson styles utilising dub techniques so that ultimately this cocktail of stylings became the distinct Grace Jones sound. Here she accentuates the funkiness and presents an up-tempo slice of irrepressible dance-floor magic. Add to that a purring vocal of blunt sexual metaphors and innuendo that upset the moral watchdogs and caused some controversy. Little wonder the record became absolutely irresistible!

15
IMAGINATION
Body Talk
Body Talk (Instrumental)
4
R & B Records

Imagination made their mark with this, their debut single. 'Body Talk' written by Imagination singers Leee John and Ashley Ingram, along with producers Steve Jolley and Tony Swain, who crafted a sound that while rooted in R&B, contained little American influence. The music is slow, simple and spacious and yet lush and sensuous too. Restraint is the key and the instrumentation is often muted. The three vocalists match the mood, singing the highly suggestive lyrics softly but playfully in the manner of seduction. 'Body Talk' was a brilliant club record, a brilliant radio record, and a brilliant lights down low romantic record.

14
DEXYS MIDNIGHT RUNNERS
Liars A To E
...And Yes We Must Remain The Wildhearted Outsiders
NO CHART PLACING
Mercury

The boldest, most baffling and startling single by Dexys Midnight Runners was without doubt 'Liars A to E' - one part mournful lamentation and one part acid tongued attack on copyists and followers. Snail-paced, with a lone horn and organ providing funereal low end gravitas, whilst the rest of the horn section play stringed classical instruments, Kevin Rowland gives a highly melodramatic performance incorporating a spoken word section. I was mesmerised by this record and utterly besotted. Whilst it proved too difficult to gain radio play and stayed unhappily on record shop shelves, it was nonetheless an artistic triumph.

13
HOLGER CZUKAY
Ode to Perfume (Edited Version) / Persian Love
NO CHART PLACING
EMI

Utterly spellbinding, 'Ode To Perfume' is trippy and slippery. It has a gorgeous, slow motion melody without being remotely 'new age'. Holger's vitality and playful inventiveness make this a riveting listen. B-side 'Persian Love' displays more of Holger Czukay's pioneering spirit. During the 70s, whilst a member of Can, he had used snippets taken from radio during live performance, pre-dating the sampling machine by more than half a decade. And here he mixes Iranian music picked up on shortwave radio, then cut up and spliced into a soundscape along with treated guitar and percussion to create a rich musical tapestry.

12
TOM TOM CLUB
The Genius of Love/Lorelei
65
Island Records

Tom Tom Club was formed by husband-and-wife rhythm team Tina Weymouth and Chris Frantz of Talking Heads fame. The band also included musical heavyweights such as King Crimson/David Bowie/ Frank Zappa guitarist Adrian Belew, Wailers organist Tyrone Downie, and drummer/percussionist Uzziah "Sticky" Thompson of famed Joe Gibbs studio house band The Revolutionaries. 'Genius Of Love' is insanely catchy and is delivered in a childlike sing song style by Tina Weymouth who sings as a woman in jail for drug offences, imagining freedom and being with her boyfriend who is the titular 'Genius Of Love'. Once more having fun together, she name checks the musicians who bring joy to them - James Brown, Hamilton Bohannon, George Clinton and Bootsy, Kurtis Blow, Bob Marley and Smokey Robinson - reminiscing about mystic nights at CBGBs. The whole thing is carried by a quirky, squelchy, extremely funky reggae rhythm. The mélange of these ingredients meant Tom Tom Club cooked up something quite delicious.

11
THE HUMAN LEAGUE
The Sound Of The Crowd
The Sound Of The Crowd (Add Your Voice)
12
Virgin

'Sound of the Crowd' was recorded as a standalone single at producer Martin Rushent's Genetic studio. It was written by Ian Burden and Phil Oakey, was the first to feature the backing vocals of Susan Sulley and

Joanne Catherall, and was deservedly a hit, giving The Human League their commercial breakthrough and the confidence to write and record their classic album *Dare*, 'Sound of The Crowd' being re-recorded for inclusion on that. The track has an arresting synthesiser riff and is up-tempo with absurdist lyrics. As the chorus approaches, the sound swells with the introduction of a droning synth and a slamming electronic drum pattern, while Oakey commandingly ventures the notion that we should "get in line now" and then "get around town" before Susan and Joanne join him in beseeching us to "add your voice to the sound of the crowd". The combination of music and voices creates a disturbing impressionistic vision of our city streets as a dystopian cattle market. We smiled knowingly while we danced at this oh-so-clever subversion of the pop single.

10
RICK JAMES
Super Freak
Super Freak (Instrumental Version)
NO CHART PLACING
Motown

A marriage of convenience between James' inherent funkiness and adopted new wave style keyboard riffs give the already adrenaline-filled song added bounce. The sound is infectious, and Rick James describes in an exaggerated, salacious manner encounters with a sexually liberated and adventurous woman. He commands at one point "Temptations sing!" and incredibly, the Motown legends, including Rick James' uncle Melvin Franklin, are summoned up to provide supporting vocals.

9
WAS NOT WAS
Out Come The Freaks
Hello Operator...I Mean Dad...
I Mean Police...
I Can't Even Remember Who I Am
NO CHART PLACING
ZE Records

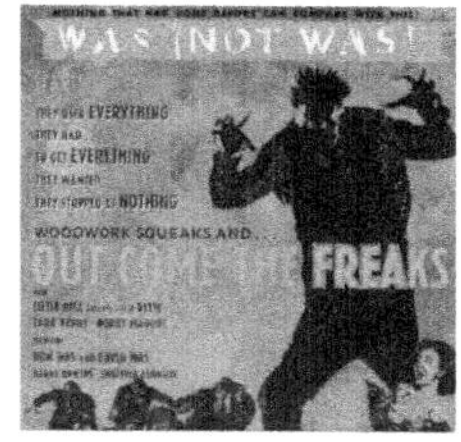

Voices leap out at you as the record begins. "Woodwork squeaks and out come the freaks" they announce before the song kicks in, combining punk attitude with slippery funk. Multiple-voiced and dizzying tales unfold concerning a variety of strange and tragic characters, their hopes and schemes and inevitable mishaps laid bare. Meanwhile, the groove you notice has not let up - it is as unrelenting and punishing as the catalogue of misfortune and heartbreak that has been set before us. I love this song and for all its cartoon quality it makes me cry.

8
YOKO ONO
Walking On Thin Ice
For John/It Happened
35
Geffen Records

John Lennon's final creative act was to record lead guitar for this single on 4th December 1980. On the 8th the recording was complete. Lennon, clutching the master tape from the studio, was murdered that night. On 6th February 1981, the single was released carrying a huge amount of emotional baggage that would understandably engulf mediocre or quite good work. 'Walking On Thin Ice' was strong enough though to emerge as a brilliant piece of work, despite the tragic circumstances that surrounded it. Lennon had heard the B52s and noted the similarities in their approach to Yoko's. He sensed the world was now ready for his wife's avant-garde take on rock and roll. To that end he encouraged, and took on, a supporting role as she fashioned 'Walking on Thin Ice'.

Lyrically, Yoko explores themes of the uncertainties we must live with while remaining true to our spirits. "Walking on thin ice, throwing the dice" is the refrain that acts as a metaphor for the thin line between artistic success or failure and most poignantly the tenuous nature of life and death. Musically, she unleashed a lurching juggernaut of edgy hyper funk that hit hard. John had been extremely proud of what Yoko had achieved and he had every right to be.

7
FẸLÁ ANIKULAPO KUTI
Sorrow, Tears & Blood
(Pidgin English Version
Colonial Mentality (Instrumental)
NO CHART PLACING
Arista

Recorded and released in Nigeria in 1977 as th *Sorrow, Tears & Blood* album, 1981 saw the songs get an international release on the album *Black President* and then as condensed edits on a single. What we received was one of the most powerful records imaginable. Recorded in the wake of brutal police and army raids on Felá Kuti's Kalakuta Republic compound, he addresses these state ordered attacks. "Some people lost some bread, someone nearly die

[...], them leave sorrow, tears and blood, them regular trademark" sings Felá, full of pain but unbroken. The rhythm is measured and mid-tempo, but its chattering percussive groove is unceasing and sinuous, while between the vocals Felá blows snaking saxophone solos. The oppression in Zimbabwe and South Africa is called out amidst the personal reportage. This is truly a record that touches the soul. 'Colonial Mentality' is no less confrontational and well considered, written in the wake of the South African murderous suppression of the Soweto uprising. And once again Felá takes aim at the Nigerian government for their moral weakness, mocking and lampooning their inferiority complex towards western powers.

6

SOFT CELL
Tainted Love –
Where Did Our Love Go
Tainted Love/
Where Did Our Love Go
Tainted Dub

1

Some Bizzare

On a crate digging expedition to America, DJ Richard Searling unearthed a copy of the Ed Cobb written and produced Gloria Jones 1966 single. He popularised the record as he Djed at Va Vas in Bolton and later at Wigan Casino where it became an acknowledged Northern Soul classic, famous for its hand-clapped coda. Gloria Jones released a new version of the song in 1976 produced by her husband Marc Bolan, though frankly it was a mess. Enter Soft Cell.

Marc Almond heard the song in a Leeds club where he worked as the cloakroom attendant and soon it was in the Soft Cell live set. Dave Ball had created a stunning and dramatic arrangement of the song, slower than the original, with a synthesised backing played in a lower key to better match Marc Almond's voice which was incredibly suited to the song. He sounded like a dissolute fallen choir boy as he lisped and gasped a perfect performance which, in combination with the machined bleeps and whirring noises from Ball's instrument, imbued the song with an unmistakable sleaziness. The song was transformed, reinvented and twisted into a shape that suited Soft Cell. It was like a disease, irresistible to anyone exposed to it.

5
KRAFTWERK
Computer Lov
The Model
1
EMI

Released initially with 'Computer Love' as the A-side and 'The Model' as the B-side in July, the record reached number 36 in the charts. A decision was then made to relaunch it as a double A-side and with 'The Model' garnering extensive radio play, Kraftwerk earned a number one single. That is worth repeating – "Kraftwerk earned a number one single!" Just a few years before, that scenario seemed impossible. Sure, 'Autobahn' had been a hit in 1975, but that had been achieved on novelty appeal. It had been the electronic equivalent of Benny Hill's 'Ernie, The Fastest Milkman In The West'. What had changed was that people's ears had finally become attuned to the Kraftwerk sound and they genuinely liked it. Indeed, what wasn't to love? Kraftwerk had never stopped honing and sculpting their sound and had arrived at a point where their melodies were enticingly clean but warm, and their rhythms increasingly crisp. The group's playfulness was as evident as always too. They had mastered the art of addressing important ideas and issues without any condescension. Indeed, their lyrics were delivered through wry smiles. Here on 'Computer Love' they address the coming computer age and predict the loneliness and dissociation that over-reliance may bring. Whilst 'The Model' is simply a song about a model. it is deliberately blank, commenting on superficiality by mirroring it in the lyric.

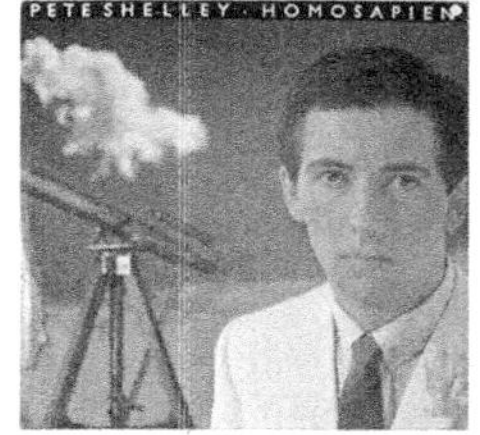

4
PETE SHELLEY
Homosapien
Keats' Song
NO CHART PLACING
Genetic Records

Written in 1974, 'Homosapien' was recorded with producer Martin Rushent as a demo for a possible Buzzcocks' release. After the dissolution of Buzzcocks, Shelley embraced the synthesiser sound of the demo and the track became his first solo single. 'Homosapien' was a stunning dance track with a chugging rhythm accentuated with acoustic guitar. It was designed to move you physically, along with pulsing synths that made the head spin. Aligned to the glorious sound was a provocative lyric delivered in Shelley's defiantly unmasculine voice. The word 'gay' never appeared in the lyric. Nevertheless, the BBC blacklisted the single for its perceived homosexual viewpoint. It is a song with a lot to say about the nature of classification, of branding people and then persecuting them. "I just hope and pray, that the day of our love is at hand [...] and the world is so wrong, that I hope we'll be strong enough" are certainly lyrics where Shelley expresses solidarity with victims of homophobic abuse. This was, and still is, a superb club record. Who could resist pulling shapes to this, played at high volumes amidst triggered laser beams, or on the strobe lit dance-floor?

3
THE SPECIALS
Ghost Town
Why?
Friday Night, Saturday Morning
1
Two-Tone Records

The poorest parts of the country were under attack from Margaret Thatcher's callous and cruel Conservative government. Community, she believed, was a bad thing. She set about destroying it. Shops, clubs and cafés fell to the economic warfare being waged against them; they closed down, and shutters went up. Jerry Dammers had observed all this as The Specials had toured the country earlier in the year and 'Ghost Town' was his comment on the degradation he witnessed. The Specials as a unit were, by this point, extremely dysfunctional and 'Ghost Town' would be their swansong single. It is eerie and menacing. A chill wind blows from speaker to speaker. It is played using minor chords which ramp up the tension. The lyric is sparse but the few words used manage to capture the desperation, despair and rising anger amongst the suffering people. The single caught the nation's mood and as frustrations in the inner city ghettos became riotous and insurrectionary, 'Ghost Town' sound-tracked the scenes of cities burning.

1981

2
LAURIE ANDERSON
O Superman
Walk The Dog
2
Warner Bros. Records

Little known outside the art world, Laurie Anderson released 'O Superman' as a debut single and utilised her artistic skill set in its conception and construction. In doing this she presented us with a new kind of musical language, opening up a doorway to different possibilities. It was thrilling and stimulating as well as being great fun in social situations where, in pubs for instance, one could play it on the jukebox and watch the reactions of people of more traditional tastes. They would express irritation, discomfort and in some cases anger. The record was minimal to the extreme, relying structurally on the exclamation "Ha!" being looped with the aid of a Harmonizer. The lyric revolves around a phone conversation between the narrator and a mysterious voice who first claims to be the narrator's mother before revealing themselves to be "the hand that takes" who informs the narrator that "the American planes are coming". It is puzzling, but never less than intriguing. Laurie Anderson later explained it related to the Iran hostage crisis where a US military rescue helicopter crashed outside Tehran, shaking the government's confidence in its military technology. Be that as it may, this was a without doubt a brilliant utilisation of the pop medium to express highly artistic concepts, and in its unorthodox construction there was vitality and freshness.

1
HEAVEN 17
(We Don't Need This)
Fascist Groove Thang
The Decline Of The West
45
Virgin

Denouncing the rising tide of racism and fascism, and attacking Margaret Thatcher and Ronald Reagan for their discriminatory world-views and policies. Collating this anger and disenchantment into a cohesive lyric. Attaching it to riveting funk track, powered by a swivel hipped bass line and synthesiser riffs. Make it fast and frenzied. Add a momentous shout-along chorus. This had to be viewed as some kind of genius, and indeed it was. Obviously banned by the BBC, fearful that Ronald Reagan was being slandered, the record and its message were still transmitted by club DJs and a clattering cover version recorded by Fire Engines as part of a John Peel session. As Heaven 17's debut release, this record set a high bar for them to match and though they had more successful records of good quality, they never again attained the burning bright, artistic height they had achieved here.

1982

This was the year when the 1970s seemed to end once and for all, the era of beige and brown superseded by a bright, shiny multi-coloured aesthetic. The music press stranglehold of the *NME*, *Sounds* and *Melody Maker* declined as *Smash Hits* appealed to young pop fans who rejected the elitist musical snobbery peddled by snobby elitist critics while the more style conscious opted for *The Face*, *I.D* and *New Sounds and Styles* where how people looked was treated as being more important than what they sounded like. Pop culture theorist and ex-Drones manager Paul Morley championed the slickly produced male-female duo Dollar as torch-bearers of 'new pop'. They were produced by Trevor Horn and record production became a much-discussed topic in the same manner that a guitar player's prowess had once been.

In Manchester New Order, their manager Rob Gretton and Factory Records boss Tony Wilson financed the opening of a nightclub the like of which was previously unseen in the UK and named it The Hacienda and it was fabulous, every time I entered the place (and that was frequently) I knew I was in a special environment and that we Mancunians were privileged indeed to have this adult playpen to enjoy ourselves in. How I loved roaming it's different levels sampling a cocktail or two in The Gay Traitor or dining on a plate of the exotic and previously unheard of hash browns in the cafeteria.

On a personal level I declined the generous offer to audition for a role in the Alan Clarke directed *Made in Britain* which ultimately went to Tim Roth and launched his career towards international stardom. Regrets? Indeed I've had a few... The Do Dos fell apart after a disastrous outdoor gig at Hulme Carnival when the stage monitors were removed before our set in front of a huge crowd with the evening breeze blowing the sound around. Our performance became increasingly shambolic because we couldn't hear each other. My musical tastes had become dominated by a belated embrace of the northern soul scene and though its peak years were passed some of the all-nighters I attended, notably at The Carousel on Plymouth

Grove, were rammed and there was a feeling of euphoria about sliding atop the sprung dance floor to obscure but brilliant records from Memphis, Chicago, Philadelphia and practically every other American city.

One particular outing of note was at the Ritz just a block or two further along the road from the Hacienda. this was a celebration of the Ric-Tic label that rivalled Motown in mid 60s Detroit and featured live performances from Al Kent, Lou Ragland, Pat Lewis and JJ Barnes. I was accepted enough to be asked to DJ at a couple of events and though they were low key it was intimidating and nerve-racking. I formed a new band named The Bears From Belle Vue Zoo and tried to incorporate Northern Soul beats into self-composed material. We were based at a new studio our friend Adam had opened in Ancoats called Out Of The Blue and for a while it went well before enthusiasm simply ebbed away and it died.

This year I was also the subject of a documentary film called *The Other Side of Ian Moss* shot by the head of art at Manchester University, a splendid enthusiastic German named Ulrich Finke. He filmed me in various locations reciting lyrics I'd written. There were a few screenings and it was flattering to be deemed worthy of attention but I wasn't convinced that it was truly representative of the person I was and, hindered by my lack of enthusiasm, that too simply faded away .

NOTABLE EVENTS

Unemployment in the U.K. rises above the 3 million mark, a post-war high

Freddie Laker's Laker Airlines collapses leaving 6,000 customers stranded. It had accumulated a debt of over $270 million.

Syrian president Hafez al-Assad orders his troops to put down a Muslim uprising in the town of Hama. Up to 40,000 civilians are murdered and 1000 troops lose their lives in the conflict

Argentinian forces invade the Falkland Islands in March and Britain declares war sending troops to the islands. A brief, bloody war ensues and Argentina surrenders in June. Argentine military dictator Leopoldo Galtiieri resigns and the previously despised British Prime Minister Margaret Thatcher sees her popularity and standing given an enormous boost as a result of the victory.

Head of the KGB Yuri Andropov is appointed to the secretariat of

Suited, booted, behatted - 1982

The Comunist party of the Soviet Union and later succeeds Leonard Brezhnev as general secretary.

Israel invades Southern Lebanon and war begins.

In Belfast there are a series of killings carried out by the army and police of unarmed Catholics and allegations of a covert 'Shoot To Kill' policy are made.

The body of 'God's Banker', Roberto Calvi, chairman of Banco Ambrosiano otherwise known as 'The Vatican Bank' is found hung beneath London's Blackfriars Bridge.

The Provisional IRA detonates two bombs in central London murdering eight people.

The first compact discs are produced in Germany and Sony launches a Compact disc player.

Ciabatta bread is invented in Verona, Italy

30,000 women hold hands and form a human chain around the perimeter fence of RAF Greenham Common in protest against the deployment of nuclear weapons there.

In Belfast, a Loyalist Gang named 'The Shankill Butchers' led by Lenny Murphy stage a series of kidnaps. Victims are tortured with butchers knives before being murdered. The Provisional IRA execute Murphy with collusion from loyalists who believe he is out of control.

The 1981-82 football season sees Manchester United finish third in the First Division behind champions Liverpool. Frank Stapleton is signed and is top scorer. United also sign midfield enforcer Remi Moses and the country's best footballer Bryan Robson for a British record fee of £1.5 million. Tottenham retain the FA Cup beating QPR in the final. Italy win the World Cup beating West Germany 3-1 in the final in Madrid.

NOTABLE BIRTHS

Joanna Newsom; Kaka; James Anderson; Skepta; Billie Piper; Lil Wayne; St Vincent

NOTABLE DEATHS

Lightnin Hopkins; Alex Harvey; Thelonious Monk; Lee Strasberg; Philip K Dick; John Belushi; Harry H Corbett; Carl Orff; Arthur Lowe; Warren Oates; Lester Bangs; Romy Schneider; Rainer Werner Fassbinder; James Honeyman Scott; John Cheever; Henry Fonda; Patrick McGee; Ingrid Bergman; Douglas Badar; Grace Kelly; Jacques Tati; Leonid Brezhnev; Patrick Cowley; Marty Feldman; Marty Robbins;

NOTABLE FILMS

The King of Comedy; Blade Runner; Fitzcarraldo; The Thing; Sophie's Choice; E.T. - The Extra Terrestrial; Eating Raoul; Diner; Tron; An Officer And A Gentleman; Veronica Voss; The Draughtsman's Contract; The Return Of Martin Guerre.

NOTABLE BOOKS

The Color Purple - Alice Walker
Schindler's List - Thomas Keneally
A Pale View Of Hills - Kazuo Ishiguro
Deadeye Dick - Kurt Vonnegut jr
Cat Chaser - Elmore Leonard
Helliconia Spring - Brian W Aldiss
Great Expectations - Kathy Acker
Ham On Rye - Charles Bukowski

100
SHALAMAR
I Can Make You Feel Good
Help Me
7
Solar

As a spin off from the enormously popular *Soul Train* TV show in 1977, a record was released using session musicians and singers. It was called 'Uptown Festival', credited to Shalamar and became a US hit. *Soul Train* creator and presenter Don Cornelius decided to replace the session singers with two popular dancers from the show - Jody Watley and Jeffrey Osborne - teaming them with several lead singers, until in 1979, Howard Hewett came into the band and created their definitive line up. They had a run of British hits and their popularity was increased when Jeffrey Osborne premièred 'The Moonwalk' which Michael Jackson, an enormous fan of Shalamar, adopted. Not content with that, Osborne introduced the world to 'body-popping'.

'I Can Make You Feel Good' came from the album *Friends* which yielded three huge hits. It is a winning combination of soulful singing, sweet strings, pop hooks and disco rhythms and does exactly what it promises to do in the title.

99
DEXYS MIDNIGHT RUNNERS & THE EMERALD EXPRESS
Come On Eileen/Dubious
1
Mercury

The new Dexys sound had been revealed on the previous single. Fabulous though that was it failed to stir up much in the way of chart action. 'Come on Eileen' addressed that problem. Starting slowly, as the scene is set, the song ignites as the pace is picked up and while no less dramatic, the violins that have replaced riffing horns, are lighter and less ominous. Kevin Rowland delivers a lyric about a romantic/sexual coupling with the titular Eileen, who must constantly be cajoled and persuaded to act against her repressive Catholic upbringing. The song judders to a halt before building up steam once more through a chorus sung in unison, before the blue touch paper is lit once more and the song races to its close.

98
WHAM!
Young Guns (Go For It)
Going For It!
3
Inner Vision

Jittery funk with a Dragnet-style horn embellishment provides the soundscape for Wham! to make their commercial breakthrough, following the failure of debut single 'Wham Rap!'. 'Young Guns' was written by George Michael and lyrically tells the story of a young man advising his best friend that he shouldn't get too serious about the girl he's seeing and should instead enjoy the single life. The girl's part, sung by American Lynda Hayes, is a response as she tells her boyfriend he shouldn't hang around "with that creepy guy". Its brashness is offset by its tongue in cheek nature and the infectious energy of the performance.

97
GODS GIFT
Discipline / Then Calm Again
NO CHART PLACING
New Hormones

Gods Gift were never fashionable or much loved. As a band they were difficult, obdurate, intense, and deliberately confrontational. The only laughter heard at a Gods Gift gig was nervous. These people were deadly serious about their songs. In terms of content and the presentation of these songs, which was in the most non-showbiz manner imaginable, I adored them! I'd seen them play at The Can Club and was entranced. Richard Boon recognised their worth too, giving them a place on his New Hormones record label. 'Discipline' was their second single on that label and third overall. It was also their last. It is stunning, featuring a churning, unchanging riff played hard and a vicious vocal about hopelessness and pointlessness. "He hates his life, he thinks of suicide" sings Steve Edwards, while the voice of orthodox reason preaches the need for discipline.

96
FAD GADGET
Saturday Night Special
Swallow It Live
NO CHART PLACING
Mute

Fad Gadget had toured America and, ruminating on his observations, wrote amongst other songs 'Saturday Night Special' named after a handgun. The song is superficially pretty, featuring a piano and flamenco-style hand clapping. Fad Gadget deliciously croons a lyric that parodies the macho attitudes of the idealised American male and the ludicrous notion that it's okay to carry and use deadly firearms.

95
SCRITTI POLITTI
Asylums in Jerusalem/
Jacques Derrida
43
Rough Trade

Here was a double A-side of delightful intelligent arch pop. I couldn't fully fathom its code, it being far too cryptic lyrically for me to fully grasp what is being conveyed. But 'Asylums in Jerusalem' may be addressed towards the original hardcore Scritti Politti audience with Green Gartside asking them to understand his need to lighten up and have fun. Whilst 'Jacques Derrida' may well be about the deconstruction of a pop song, whatever the rights and wrongs of these suppositions, both are glorious combinations of rhythm and melody, and toe tappers too.

94
ABC
The Look Of Love
The Look Of Love (Part 2)
4
Neutron Records

Art imitates life and then life imitates art, as Martin Fry wrote the lyric to 'The Look of Love' about a hurtful breakup and then recruited the girl who had jilted him to come into the studio and deliver a cold emotionless "goodbye" as part of the track! The song is sweeping and majestic, and Fry plays the lovelorn protagonist in exaggerated theatrical fashion. Strings add to the melodrama, though they are never so cumbersome that they interrupt the rhythmic flow and snappy dance-floor friendliness.

93
THE MEMBRANES
Muscles/
All Roads Lead to Norway/
Entertaining Friends
NO CHART PLACING
Vinyl Drip Records

The youthful Membranes released this as their first single proper, following a flexi-disc which was given away to people by way of an introduction. 'Muscles' was a marvellous record, frothing with energy. Although the band eschewed big guitar chords and displayed nimble subtlety that emphasised the tunefulness of their material. The influence of the band's hometown of Blackpool is evident in the funfair atmosphere created. 'Muscles' pokes fun at overt machismo and aggressive behaviour, with Mark Tilton and John Robb trading distinctly northern-accented vocals. Earning spins in New York's influential Danceteria nightclub, these seaside boys made a big splash with this record.

92
MINUTEMAN
Voodoo Slaves
I Wanna Be Your Minuteman
NO CHART PLACING
Citadel

Minuteman - not to be confused with American band Minute*men* - were an Australian garage band from Sydney who set up their own Citadel record label to release this, their only single, out of necessity as no one else liked their music. 'Voodoo Slaves' is in fact excellent. The band resist the temptation to go overboard with a raft of novelty sound effects. Only on the intro and outro is there a touch of blood curdling howling and chanting. As for the rest of the song, a lean guitar and bass groove suffice, along with a cool disdainful vocal from Dug Lonsdale, who sounds uncannily like Chris Bailey of the Saints. Minuteman disbanded shortly after this release, but Guitarist John Needham continued to run the label and put out records by the likes of Radio Birdman and the Screaming Tribesmen, whilst bassist Clyde Bramley went on to join the Hoodoo Gurus.

91
HUMAN LEAGUE
Mirror Man
You Remind Me Of Gold
2
Virgin

Susan and Joanne coo wordlessly while Phillip is forceful in his delivery, putting plenty of emphasis into each word, with a stomping beat that apes the classic 60s Motown. 'Mirror Man', it has been noted, is comparable to electronic Northern soul. The song is about adopting alter egos, and in doing so, losing something of the soul. Although he kept silent at the time, not wishing to cause offence, Oakey later revealed that the song's subject was Adam Ant, who he perceived as being someone believing his own publicity, and in doing so losing touch with his real self.

90
LAURIE ANDERSON
Big Science/Example #22
NO CHART PLACING
Warner Bros. Records

Anyone fortunate enough to have seen Laurie Anderson perform would attest to the warmth she transmits. She is empathetic and clearly has a love of humanity. That love though is tempered by a healthy distrust of mankind's ability and willingness to do the right thing and act responsibly with care and consideration for others. 'Big Science' is a slow motion stroll through an urban environment that is soulless beneath its stark neon lit streets filled with brand new consumerist constructions. She asks a man she sits next to: "Is it okay if I smoke?" He replies: "It's every man for themselves". A chilling microcosm of the society we are a part of.

89
THE GAP BAND
You Dropped a Bomb On Me Lonely Like Me
NO CHART PLACING
Total Experience Records

Synthesised whistles and a simple, pounding kettle drum pattern open the song before the insistent riff kicks in and the vocals begin to tell a tale of the sexual, utilising a bomb as metaphor. The synths are ramped up higher and higher, whistling and screaming, but never dislocating from the groove. This was funk heaven and in the parlance of the day contained "more bounce to the ounce"!.

88
DINOSAUR L
Go Bang! #5/
Clean On Your Bean #1
NO CHART PLACING
Sleeping Bag Records

Arthur Russell had accompanied poet Allen Ginsberg on cello in the early 70s. He moved on to become musical director of The Kitchen, an avant-garde performance space in Manhattan with a manifesto to promote obscure minimalists. Not one for orthodoxy or restrictions, Russell booked the proto-punk Modern Lovers and Talking Heads into the venue - to the dismay of the purists - as he sought to demonstrate that minimalism existed in music beyond the modern classical sphere.

By 1977, Russell was releasing records himself with a loose group of musicians christened Dinosaur L. Not to be tied down, further releases came out under the Loose Joints name. In 1982, a Dinosaur L album, *24→24 Music*, was released and included a version of 'Go Bang', recorded in 1979. Francois Kevorkian was asked to remix the track for single release. Larry Levan made it a dance-floor smash at the Paradise Garage where its slippery jazz funkiness and outright weirdness, powered by swells of organ and chanted vocals, made this a classic well worth remembering.

87
LONE RANGER
M16 / M16 (Version)
NO CHART PLACING
Channel One

Lone Ranger at this point was recognised as Jamaica's pre-eminent DJ. Where his predecessors had often given short shrift to the dictates of rhythm as they chatted over a track, Lone Ranger was all about rhythm. He stayed on the beat and his flow was unhurried and smooth. M16 utilises the Hugh Roy 'Scandal' rhythm from 1971 and is mixed by Scientist. The 70s had seen a craze for toasters praising their motorbikes but here the subject matter is an automatic weapon, a sign of the times.

86
THE THREE JOHNS
English White Boy Engineer / Secret Agent
NO CHART PLACING
CNT Productions

Three men – Jon Langford, John Hyatt and John Brennan (real name Phillip) - along with a drum machine called Hugo, came together in Leeds in 1981 to play a 'Funk The Wedding' event as a royal coupling was being rammed down the nation's collective throat. They weren't allowed to play as they were too drunk, but undeterred carried on and began issuing singles. 'English White Boy Engineer' was the first and captured them in full flight. It was in fact a song Jon Langford had written for The Mekons, and had been recorded by that ensemble as part of a John Peel show session. Here it is stripped to the bone and baring sharp teeth. The Three Johns make a blood-curdling, guitar-filled racket, though not devoid of melody. Topped by singer John Hyatt's clean and powerful lyrical assault on the hypocritical attitudes toward earning money in apartheid-era South Africa, this is a single that makes a point that needed making, as well as a glorious noise.

85
VIRGIN PRUNES
Pagan Love Song
Dave-Id Is Dead
NO CHART PLACING
Rough Trade

One Part Oscar Wilde, one part T-Rex and one part Salvador Dali, here the Virgin Prunes perform an examination of emotions crippled by repression. They act out the perversions caused by guilt that is drip fed into the soul from childhood - a guilt that is constantly reinforced - creating a negativity to feelings of love, resulting in the hardening of the heart in order to protect against emotion that is contrary to controlling moral dogma.

Drums and whips crack while the idiosyncratic music sways and carries a sense of mystery and bucolic strangeness as we are allowed a look into the dark hearts and minds of the creative force of Dublin's finest musical export.

84
RICHARD AND LINDA THOMPSON
Don't Renege On Our Love
Living In Luxury
NO CHART PLACING
Hannibal Records

Musically sparse, with just Richard Thompson's expressive guitar playing on top of a quick-tempoed skipping beat provided by Dave Mattocks, above which Richard Thompson sings about betrayal in a relationship from the viewpoint of a wronged man. Recorded quickly and cheaply, this bare bones approach lent the song an edge of sincerity and smouldering anger.

83
SOFT CELL
Torch/Insecure Me
2
Some Bizzare

A muted trumpet leads into this song of loneliness and the search for comfort inside the words of sad songs, delivered by a torch singer. Marc Almond sings beautifully in a voice full of hurt. For the last verse and chorus, New York rapper Cindy Ecstasy joins him which is a nice touch. Dave Ball displays much restraint, the keyboard parts allowing the melody and melancholy feel of the song space enough to creep up on the listener.

82
THE FALL
Look, Know/I'm Into C.B.
NO CHART PLACING
Kamera Records

Two relatively straight forward topical songs by Fall standards, with subject matter nobody else was addressing. Delivered in a Brutalist uncompromising style, 'Look Know' finds Marc Riley asking the question, "Do you know what you look like, before you go out?" It is addressed initially to posing nightclub fashionistas who are ridiculed, before the question is turned around and Mark Smith begins addressing himself in somebody else's voice as he often did. Voicing various characters in one voice, the music here is a deliberate ugly dirge, totally at odds with the subject matter.

'I'm Into CB' addresses the craze for Citizens' Band radio sets that were imported from the USA, where it was used constructively by truckers to warn others where police patrols lurked, where traffic was heavy, to score drugs, or simply for company. In the UK there was a four-mile limit on transmissions, rendering it little more than a useless toy, though enthusiasts adopted the colourful terminology of their American counterparts. Mark invents a pair of hapless characters - 'Happy Harry' and 'Cedar Plank' - who fail to grasp the lingo before the Harry character comes to grief as his enthusiasm leads him to a transgression for which he is jailed. This is a perkier number, featuring a recurring xylophone pattern and superb hard-hitting drum performance from Karl Burns and Paul Hanley.

81
DARYL HALL & JOHN OATES
I Can't Go For That (No Can Do
Unguarded Minute
8
RCA

Riding in on a simple drum beat and a bass line that Michael Jackson filched for his song 'Billie Jean', a tinkling keyboard motif signals the start of the song proper. The smooth voiced Daryl Hall adds a cool as can be almost conversational vocal about standing up for yourself and not being pushed around. His ire is aimed at record company executives, though it is a coded message disguised as a personal relationship song. The chorus is sharp and at least semi iconic. A pair of classy saxophone breaks add colour to this restrained gem.

80
FREE ENTERPRISE
Make It On My Own
Foxy Lady
NO CHART PLACING
BMC Records

This electro-disco track written and produced by Bobby Orlando has a lyric about having the determination to carry on against the odds. Stylistically, the track is a precursor of the Hi-NRG sound that Bobby Orlando would pioneer. It also inspired the 'hard times' fashion movement that was briefly chic and saw dressing down become regarded as the ultimate height of hipness.

79
PEECH BOYS
Don't Make Me Wait/
(Alternative Mix)
49
TMT Records

The Peech Boys formed at New York's Paradise Garage and were fronted by a remarkable singer in Bernard Fowler. 'Don't Make Me Wait' was their first single and was produced by legendary Paradise Garage DJ, Larry Levan, who gave it an electronic rhythm topped by gospel style piano and a dub sensibility. At over 7 minutes in length and repetitive to the point that it became mesmerising, this record was a brilliantly innovative dance floor favourite in New York. It was also transported to Chicago when Larry Levan's closest friend Frankie Knuckles opened a club there called The Warehouse. Here house music was born and 'Don't Make Me Wait' was the template for much of that.

78
HÜSKER DÜ
In A Free Land
What Do I Want/M.I.C.
NO CHART PLACING
New Alliance Records

Hüsker Dü changed their approach dramatically for this second single. Gone was post-punk experimentation and in came a double speed hardcore sound that didn't sacrifice the melodic quality the band possessed within the maelstrom. 'In A Free Land' was written by vocalist Bob Mould and amid the wall of noise instrumentation is a lamentation upon flag waving patriotism and the assertion that "the only freedom worth fighting for is for what you think".

77
ORANGE JUICE
Felicity /In A Nutshell
You Old Eccentric
63
Polydor

The initial promise shown on the Postcard Records singles saw Orange Juice sign to Polydor where bigger budgets and better promotion should have seen them achieve pop success. Sadly the magic was waning and the world was moving away from them. They did however show flashes of their brilliance, and this James Kirk penned single was one of those occasions. The twang of guitars is augmented by a sparkling piano and whistle. The lyric seems to address yearning and wistfulness. Edwyn Collins provides a deliciously sardonic vocal - there is a James Brown copped shout of "take me to the bridge" before the frothy concoction closes with a galloping riff over which Edwyn archly trills "happiness… this is the sound of happiness".

76
GEORGE CLINTON
Loopzilla/Pot Sharing Tots
NO CHART PLACING
Capitol Records

Here George Clinton lampoons the lack of imagination displayed by radio stations in terms of programming. He takes a swipe at the rotational plays of the same old songs as if they're on a loop, hence 'Loopzilla'. Using a warped electro backing, voices put through vodocoders, and interpolations from hit songs from the past including The Four Tops' 'I Can't Help Myself' and Martha and the Vandellas' 'Dancing In The Street,' as well as several Parliament/Funkadelic tracks. The track is frenzied and hints at madness induced by prolonged exposure to the radio, leaving George to advise us "don't touch that radio. don't touch that knob!".

75
DURAN DURAN
Save a Prayer
Hold Back the Rain (Remix)
2
EMI

Duran Duran's singles up to this point had grated on me. They seemed to try so hard to sparkle but simply irritated. 'Save a Prayer' was a change of tack - it tells the tale of a meeting between two people leading to a night of sex in unromantic terms. It was slow paced and conveyed a feeling of disappointment in its lilting verses, while the choruses were beautiful but desolate and full of aching pain.

74
ADAM ANT
Goody Two Shoes
Red Scab
1
CBS

The Ants were made to walk the proverbial plank and jettisoned into history, and here was Adam Ant's first solo single. It was, it has to be said, a quite spectacular opening salvo. Wisely retaining Marco Pirroni and Chris Hughes from the band as creative foils, the drum track is as pounding and upfront as the Ants had ever been. But in comes a horn section providing trumpet fanfares and growling saxophone, whilst Adam - perhaps displaying signs of a persecution complex - portrays himself as being hounded by an intrusive media who constantly ask "don't drink, don't smoke, what do you do?". The unspoken answer is, of course, "I have lots of sex!".

73
THE STRANGLERS
Golden Brown/Love 30
2
Liberty

Having watched the majority of their punk peers bite the proverbial dust, The Stranglers were not content to merely survive. They hit a new creative peak and were rewarded with their biggest hit as 'Golden Brown', a waltz in 6/8 time played on a harpsichord, over which Hugh Cornwell candidly details his love for the comfort blanket of heroin, granted them acceptance and respect from a mainstream audience who doubtlessly hadn't got a clue what these elderly reprobates were on about.

72
ABBA
The Day Before You Came
Cassandra
32
Epic

The penultimate single and their last recorded song for 35 years, 'The Day Before You came' was something of a masterpiece. With no trace of frothy pop, it signifies a maturity in approach with nuanced performances. The track is close to six minutes long and has no choruses, relying heavily on a mesmerising clockwork beat. Beneath that is a mostly grey wash of synths and ghostly backing vocals. Agnetha handles the main vocal contrary to her usual style, taking the lyric and acting it out, sing-speaking the words which describe the mundanity of the day, leaving what is unsaid as a powerful and disturbing counterpoint. She imbues the track with a sense of faltering confidence, of certainties becoming doubts. She sounds as though she and her world are in the process of unravelling. The sense of sadness and the tension here are deeply affecting. It is said that Agnetha spent time making sure the lighting in the studio suited the mood of the song before she delivered her performance and then simply walked out of the door and out of Abba.

71
THE TEARDROP EXPLODES
Tiny Children
Rachael Built A Steamboat
44
Mercury

The Teardrop Explodes were fracturing as a band and that fact may well have influenced this song about bewilderment and insecurity. It is fragile in the extreme using only a sombre and simple organ accompaniment. Julian Cope sings in a voice left naked and vulnerable, of being unsure how to proceed. A drum playing a mournful figure is introduced as the song nears its end without reaching any conclusion - it is a beautiful, atmospheric piece of music.

70
THE THE
Uncertain Smile/
Three Orange Kisses from Kazan/
Waitin' For The Upturn
68
Some Bizzare

Travelling to New York specifically to record this single indicates the faith in the talent of the relatively unknown Matt Johnson, aka The The. That faith was rewarded by the quality of the track and the inroads it made building up a word -of-mouth excitement that began an upward career trajectory for him. 'Uncertain Smile' was brooding and atmospheric; cerebral and melodic too. It features a distinctive percussion part played on a wooden device called a xylimba and a mix of flute, saxophone, guitar and subtle electronics.

69
THE GO-BETWEENS
Hammer The Hammer
By Chance
NO CHART PLACING
Rough Trade

Perhaps the first true classic from this band of literate Australians, 'Hammer the Hammer' was written by Grant McLennan and he described it as an "incomplete meditation on loneliness and violence". Others speculated that it was about his growing taste for heavy narcotics by his proximity to The Birthday Party. Whatever the truth of that, it is a twisting slice of pop delivered with urgency and containing a brutal chorus line of the song title repeated with rising emphasis each time.

In contrast, Robert Forster's 'By Chance' is an intelligent piece of jangling guitar pop with a strident vocal, the style of which up-and-coming Mancunians, The Smiths, would soon be replicating.

68
STEREO
Somewhere In The Night
Stereomania
NO CHART PLACING
Carrere

Stereo were a French synth pop duo and 'Somewhere In The Night' is their classic single. They combine a dark ominous synth texture with lighter runs and riffs to add a musical tension. Saxophone is used to provide another flavour and the vocals are matter of fact and mechanical in their delivery. This was cutting edge stuff delivered with great panache - perfect club music.

67
THE GUN CLUB
Fire of Love
Walking With The Beast
NO CHART PLACING
Animal Records

The debut album by the Gun Club is called *Fire Of Love*. This single - also called 'Fire Of Love'- is not on that album but on the follow up called *Miami*. Here The Gun Club, led of course by Jeffrey Lee Pierce - heroin addict and president of the Blondie fan club - sign up to Blondie guitarist Chris Stein's Animal Records label. Stein handles the production and the band serve up a slow-burning tale of love that rests on an immortal throbbing guitar riff which is played with dead-eyed malice, while Jeffrey sings in a characterful voice that carries a ghostly echo of Hank Williams.

66
THEATRE OF HATE
Do You Believe In The Westworld
Propaganda
40
Burning Rome Records

Led by Kirk Brandon, Theatre of Hate serve up an existential cowboy song with a sociopolitical subtext, produced by Clash guitarist Mick Jones. Spaghetti western guitars and galloping drums provide the soundscape for Brandon to unleash his near operatic voice in dramatic, stunning style.

65
DIVINE
Shoot Your Shot (Remix)
Shoot Your Shot
NO CHART PLACING
"O" Records

Divine was a larger than life drag queen, famous for roles in the anarchic films of John Waters who placed faith in her and was rewarded by truly epic performances. Turning to music Divine hooked up with Bobby O, another maverick who intuitively understood the Divine character. This empathy saw him tailor this song and sound into a perfect fit. It is a Hi-NRG classic with a pinballing synthesiser pulse at its core. And given a lyric loaded with sexual innuendo, despite having a highly unconventional voice, Divine delivers a brilliant reading of it full of character, individuality and a sense of lovable mischievousness.

64
MAN PARRISH
Hip-hop, Be Bop (Don't Stop)
Hip-hop, Be Bop (Part Two)
41
Polydor

Although electro as a style was in its infancy, this a sensational crucial cut that has proved to be of timeless quality. Given the nickname 'Man' by Andy Warhol it was the young Manuel Parrish's first release, mostly instrumental with just a snippet of vocal and the sound of a barking dog used decoratively. This was all about the beats and the feel, a record guaranteed to get the party started.

63
XTC
Senses Working Overtime / Blame The Weather / Tissue Tigers (The Arguers)
10
Virgin

'Senses Working Overtime' is a highly intelligent song of bewilderment and distaste, disguised as a happy sing-along by dint of its jaunty, easy-on-the-ear melody. The idea to take the chorus of the Manfred Mann hit '5-4-3-2-1' and reverse it until the sound of Andy Partridge counting off "1-2-3-4-5 senses working overtime", indelibly stamps it into the collective consciousness of any discerning pop music lover.

62
KID CREOLE
AND THE COCONUTS
Stool Pigeon
In The Jungle (Remix)
8
ZE Records

Cool and funky bass, chattering percussion, hand-claps, a divine ringing guitar line and a mighty horn riff, combined with August Darnell's gangster homage lyric about a police informer who betrays his friends and is well rewarded for his treachery. He ends up with a protected identity, relocated and lonely. Delivered with huge style and panache, Kid Creole and the Coconuts had created a genre all of their own as tongue-in-cheek dance-floor masters of consummate skill and flamboyance.

61
ELVIS COSTELLO AND THE ATTRACTIONS
Man Out Of Time
Town Cryer (Alternate Version)
58
F-Beat

Despite his later hypocritical servitude to the institution of monarchy in accepting a tacky gong, and with it membership into a tarnished institution, it shouldn't be forgotten that Elvis Costello was once a formidable songwriter and performer. 'Man Out Of Time' is amongst the very finest of his career. A decision was made to take the aggression and high tempo out of the Attractions' playing and so for

'Man Out Of Time', aside from an opening salvo and a closing flourish, the song is allowed lots of space. It has a lushness and prettiness that are a perfect counterpoint to what, at surface value, is a tale of a government minister hiding away from a sex scandal and seeing his promising career going down the plughole with each revelation. Shades of the Profumo affair of the sixties are evident but as Costello himself attested, often accusatory songs are observations of the writer himself.

60
KATE BUSH
The Dreaming
Dreamtime (Instrumental Version)
48
EMI

Kate's fertile imagination and fearless creativity produced this powerful and unsettling single about traditional and sacred Aboriginal lands being destroyed by white people seeking nuclear weapons grade uranium. The now disgraced ex-TV star, Rolf Harris, plays didgeridoo and famed birdsong impersonator Percy Thrower makes sheep noises. 'The Dreaming' refers to a concept in Aboriginal lore where all living things are as one and Kate paints a word picture of giant mechanical diggers ripping people apart, imagining them to be trees. The sound is, as she described it, is "earthy" and the rhythm and deep sound of the piano create a feeling of doom-laden apprehension.

59
THE CLASH
Know Your Rights / First Night Back In London
43
CBS

Here we go… the most contradictory act of all times were the Clash. On one level, 'Know Your Rights' is simply glib hippy sloganeering about how bad 'the man' is, played in a punk-by-numbers style - pure populist posturing. On the other hand, Joe Strummer invests the song with all the deranged energy and passion of a true believer, so that it is imbued with spirit and is unquestionably exciting due to the adrenalized performance, to the point you find yourself dragged along, convinced of the sincerity being displayed.

58
KOOL & THE GANG
Get Down On It/No Show
3
De-Lite Records

Kool & The Gang were formed in 1969 and their greasy, loose-limbed brand of funk chimed with the times in the early to mid-70s. The arrival of the more sophisticated disco sound saw them become unfashionable, out of step and in need of fresh impetus. To that end they fetched in Deodato as their producer. The move paid dividends as he made them more pop-friendly by concentrating on hooks in their songs and shaving off some rough edges. During this period, they became a hit-making machine releasing singles that people could dance to with memorable tunes. The best, and the band's biggest British hit, was 'Get Down On It' which has an impossibly brilliant groove over which the band exhort the listener to dance, using such memorable phrases as "you gotta get on the groove" and "get your back up off the wall"... the invitation was acceptable to most people.

57
SHRIEKBACK
My Spine Is The Bass-line
Tiny Birds/Feelers
NO CHART PLACING
Y Records

Ex-XTC keyboardist, Barry Andrews and ex-Gang Of Four bassist, Dave Allen were amongst the founding members of Shriekback. 'My Spine Is The Bass-line' was their second single and is driven, as one might surmise, by a splendidly funky bass part. The sound is raw and spare. There is a chanted coda of "no blood, no guts... no brains at all", between thought-provoking lyrics sung with a subtle hint of menace. Aiming at both heart and head, Shriekback scored direct hits with this single.

56
YELLO
Pinball Cha Cha
Smile On You
NO CHART PLACING
Do It Records

Wonderful inspired lunacy from Yello, 'Pinball Cha Cha' conforms to no rules but their own. Voiced in a ludicrously deep baritone, telling a tale of a man who devotes his life to playing pinball to fill the emptiness he feels. The percussion break that fills the middle of the song is simply astonishing and they move out of it with joyous uplifting panache, making this most singularly unusual single a pleasure from beginning to end.

55
GANG OF FOUR
I Love A Man In Uniform
The World At Fault
65
EMI

Sly subversion from Gang Of Four. Banned by the BBC during the Falklands war, presumably because they felt it might demoralise the troops, the song paints a picture of a recruit joining up after falling for the advertising campaigns that sold a notion of machismo to the gullible using slogans such as "they'll make a man of you". He imagines himself transformed into a desirable sex machine and his girlfriend is equally seduced by the image. "The girls they love to see you shoot", he declares, only to be answered by a female voice, "you must be joking, oh man you must be joking", as it seems he can only perform when under orders! The song is played in a smooth, disco style, replete with hand-claps and prominent funk bass as a way of insidiously infiltrating the mainstream, and in a small way begins the demolition of the baseless backward notions we were still being sold.

54
THE CLEAN
Getting Older/Scrap Music
Whatever I do Is Right-Wrong
NO CHART PLACING
Flying Nun Records

The Clean were the leading lights of the New Zealand sound that so brightened the music world and made every *Flying Nun* record release worthy of investigation. This is a belter. It bounces along atop a relentless, fuzzy guitar riff. Abstract trumpet sounds are added and the nagging vocal concerns itself with people unable to adapt to the ageing process.

53
QUADRANT SIX
Body Mechanic
Body Mechanic (Instrumental)
NO CHART PLACING
Atlantic

'Body Mechanic' is an absolutely rocking record with a sleazy edge to it. Composed and recorded by electro pioneer and Arthur Baker associate, John Robie, with assistance from Jellybean Benitez, this was a record that acted like a time bomb going off in city after city as clubbers clamoured for its hard-edged electro beats.

52
THE POINTER SISTERS
I'm So Excited/
Nothin' But A Heartache
NO CHART PLACING
(1984 -11)
RCA Victor

The Pointer Sisters were from Oakland, California and came from a gospel background. They began recording in 1973 and enjoyed intermittent success in a variety of styles, ranging from country to rock. Teaming up with producer Richard Perry, he helped create for them a defined, energetic style based on R&B vocalising aligned to post-disco production. 'I'm So Excited' captured the essence of the Pointer Sisters. Their gospel inflected vocals have a genuine urgent power, and given a high-tempo track that sizzles, to perform over the result is so spectacular that it sounds like the eruption of a giant soda fountain.

51
ODYSSEY
Inside Out
Love's Alright
3
RCA Victor

Written by kilted and helmeted Scottish disco oddball Jesse Rae, 'Inside Out' is a phenomenal record. It features a vocal delivery by Lillian Lopez that expresses emptiness and weariness, while the band's performance is simply magnificent on what is a challenging piece of music full of fragmented pieces of melody atop a funky groove of slap bass and squiggly synthesiser. Add a restrained wash of disco strings and staccato backing vocals – "In… side…out!, In…side…out!" - and you have a genius record that is quite simply unique.

50
BESIDE/FAB FREDDY
Change the Beat (French And English Rap)
Change The Beat (French Rap)
NO CHART PLACING
Celluloid

Fab 5 Freddie came from the graffiti art culture in New York to become a highly-respected artist lauded by the Manhattan hipster elite. He bridged the gap between hip-hop and the punk rock scenes and with Material producing and Bill Laswell playing bass, recorded this single that leapt out of the speakers, such was its freshness and vitality. Rapping in English and French over a sparse but atmospheric backing, 'Change The Beat' opened ears that had been resistant to hip-hop and garnered respect for the movement. The B-side was a French language version of the track by female rapper 'Beside'.

49
TEARS FOR FEARS
Mad World
Ideas As Opiates
3
Mercury

Roland Orzabal, who wrote 'Mad World' and Curt Smith who sang it had become highly interested in Arthur Janov's theories expressed in his book *The Primal Scream*, and these theories influence both songs on this release. 'Mad World' was written as Orzabal looked out onto the street from his flat above a pizza shop in Bath, although he himself noted it wasn't particularly mad and should have been called 'Bourgeoisie World'! Played as a piece of effervescent synth-pop, its cheerfulness cushioned the effect of the lyric which is concerned with depression and anxiety without obscuring it.

48
EVELYN KING
Love Come Down / Love Come Down (Instrumental)
7
RCA

Written and produced by Kashif, who was developing a sparse R&B sound and heavily reliant on synthesisers, 'Love Come Down' was given to Evelyn "Champagne" King, who was one of the most underrated singers in the R&B genre but a real stylist nonetheless. This was an effortless dance classic.

47
YAZOO
Only You/Situation
2
Mute

Vince Clarke had quit Depeche Mode in 1981, fatigued and turned off by pop stardom. He then faced the prospect of being dropped by his record label and so wrote 'Only You' to demonstrate to *Mute* boss Daniel Miller his capabilities. The song was offered to Depeche Mode who declined it, and so Vince Clarke searched for somebody who could sing with emotion. He had come across Alison Moyet singing in blues bands and thought she was a perfect fit. And although she took a good deal of persuading, eventually they formed Yazoo. 'Only You' was released as a first single - it was synth-pop of course but mid-tempo synth-pop, juxtaposed with the warmth and feel of a classic Motown single. The mournful lyric about coming to terms with a failing relationship was given bones by Alison Moyet's soulful voice. It was a deserved hit and a wonderful correlation between two musical traditions meeting and creating something new.

46
EURYTHMICS
Love Is A Stranger/
Monkey, Monkey
54 (1983 - 6; 1991 - 46)
RCA

Synths with a psychedelic tinge play a delightful melody. The percussion sounds like a swarm of marching ants. Annie Lennox has her voice placed high in the mix and sounds flawless. The song is dark – shimmering and swirling. It is akin to Marlene Dietrich meeting J.G. Ballard at a Halloween ball.

45
MALCOLM MCLAREN AND THE WORLD'S FAMOUS SUPREME TEAM
Buffalo Gals (Scratch)/
Buffalo Gals (Trad. Square)
9
Charisma

The middle-aged McLaren cut an unlikely figure as a pop star, particularly one in the hip-hop field. But whatever he lacked in youth, authenticity and talent, he made up for in irrepressible self-belief and a knack for choosing talented people to work with. He had been to a block party where he encountered hip-hop and scratching techniques for the first time as he watched Africa Bambaataa and Universal Zulu Nation. Recruiting Anne Dudley and Trevor Horn as co-writers, the song took shape. DJ scratchers, The World Famous Supreme Team, were brought in for the recording produced by Horn. They combined hip-hop beats with South African Zulu tribal singing and then added calls from square dancing into the mix to create a curious but hugely entertaining Frankenstein's monster of a track.

44
JUNIOR
Mama Used To Say
Mama Used To Say (Instrumental)
7
Mercury

Junior Giscombe, who toured as a backing vocalist for Linx, teamed up with that band's producer, Bob

Carter, to write and record this debut single. I am not being disparaging when I describe its sound as lightweight funk combined with pop soul, because the result was fresh and sweet. Lyrically, the song dealt with advice the young Giscombe received from his mother, telling him to be in no rush to grow old, but to be patient and live life each day. Giscombe sang with a voice that was expressive and full of character. Critics at the time compared him to Stevie Wonder, and it is a compliment to this song that for a brief time, the comparison didn't seem too fanciful.

43
LOU REED
The Blue Mask
Walk On The Wild Side
NO CHART PLACING
RCA

Lou had been hit and miss over the previous few years, with the misses more numerous than the hits and the hits not matching previous triumphs. Now he put together a superb band, featuring guitar stylist Robert Quine, Fernando Saunders on bass and future Jethro Tull drummer, Doane Perry. Together they unleashed this song full of grotesque violent imagery, matched by a nerve-shredding sonic onslaught – "Let me luxuriate in pain" sings Reed with grim fortitude as he trawls through ugly memories, concluding that they have to be faced and shouldn't be hidden behind the blue mask.

42
GRACE JONES
Nipple To The Bottle
Ja Guys (Dub Version Of My Jamaican Guy)
NO CHART PLACING
Island Records

Whilst the groove here is magnificent and Sly Dunbar's bass part is so funky it is stratospheric, this song ultimately rests on Grace Jones' performance which is nothing short of incredible. 'Nipple To The Bottle' is a break up song that is absolutely scathing towards the object of her ire. She is withering in her assessment of his faults, laying out his attempts to manipulate and control her and concluding with the line "you're still a baby", giving it heavy emphasis in a song where practically every line is spat out with venom. Grace Jones was breaking the chain of what a woman - a black woman at that - was perceived to be. She challenged notions of servility, displaying huge self-confidence, and her honesty was brutal. It wasn't a popular stance in conservative times and this single received little in the way of the media coverage it deserved.

41
WAH!
The Story Of The Blues Part One
The Story Of The Blues (Talkin' Blues)
3
Eternal

Motormouth Pete Wylie had been the third part of The Crucial Three, along with Ian McCulloch and Julian Cope. He hadn't shirked from self-promotion, to the point of it becoming tedious hyperbole as he carved out his niche as Wah Heat! A change of approach, signified by a name shortened to simply 'Wah!', saw him deliver a record that was every bit as good as he said it was. Given an expansive arrangement, featuring female backing vocals and a string section, Wylie sings of being battered by hard times but refusing to be defeated by them. Huge stirring choruses are a feature and propel the song into the realms of the anthemic.

40
YELLOWMAN
Zungguzungguguzungguzeng
Who Can Make The Dance Ram?
NO CHART PLACING
Greensleeves Records

Life had been tough for Winston Foster, aka 'Yellowman'. Abandoned by his parents and brought up at Alpha Boys School - famed for the amount of reggae artists nurtured there – he was shunned by others because he was albino, hence the name 'Yellowman'. Despite the seemingly insurmountable problems he faced, Yellowman built a reputation as a top toaster and DJ using self-effacing humour to defuse hostility. Working with producer Henry "Junjo" Lawes, he became an early star of the dancehall style that swept Jamaica. On 'Zungguzungguguzungguzeng' - the record that elevated him to the summit - he toasts over the rhythm from the 1967 Alton Ellis track 'Mad Mad Mad', boasting of his sexual prowess, using colourful expressions and the nonsense phrase of the title in an easy flowing joyful manner.

39
ROWLAND S. HOWARD /LYDIA LUNCH
Some Velvet Morning
I Fell In Love With A Ghost
NO CHART PLACING
4AD

The original version of 'Some Velvet Morning' by Nancy Sinatra and Lee Hazelwood is mysterious and magnificent but New York no wave queen, Lydia Lunch, and Birthday Party guitar-slinger, Rowland S. Howard, match it with a reading that seems to come from the gutter. So soiled and desultory is their treatment of the song that it might well have carried a health warning.

38
A CERTAIN RATIO
Knife Slits Water/Kether Hot Knives (Mix In Special)
NO CHART PLACING
Factory

A.C.R. lived in the shadow of Joy Division/New Order through their Factory Records association, which meant they were never accorded the respect they deserved. By this point in their career they had moved from being a band with ideas beyond their level of musicianship to become highly accomplished players. 'Knife Slits Water' is long and languid. It snakes through its 9:44 minutes eerily, never surrendering its grip on the attention that is seized from its blaring car horn intro through the patterns created using the deep funk bass of Jez Kerr and Donald Johnson's exemplary percussive skills.

37
SHARON REDD
Beat The Street
Beat The Street (Instrumental)
NO CHART PLACING
Prelude Records

Sharon had been part of Bette Midler's backing vocal troupe, 'The Harlettes', before stepping out on her own. 'Beat the Street' is one of the clutch of singles she released before succumbing to AIDs-related pneumonia in 1992. 'Beat The Street', mixed by Francois Kervokian, is disco being re-imagined for a new era. Its machined rhythm is complimented by a wicked guitar lick, while Sharon Redd's R&B style vocal adds warmth and emotion. This evolution of form would eventually result in the birth of house music .

36
WHODINI
Magic's Wand/
It's All In Mr. Magic's Wand/
Magic's Wand (Special Extended Mix)
47
Jive

John "Mr Magic" Rivas was the presenter of the *Rap Attack* on New York's WBLS radio station. An intern named Jalil Hutchins, who helped out answering phones, wrote a rap about Mr. Magic, but wanting a second voice for it recruited a rapper named 'Ecstasy'. Together they recorded the track and Mr. Magic made it his theme tune. Two years later 'Magic's Wand' stirred up interest from London-based label Jive who had the duo rerecord the track with production from Brit synth pop pioneer Thomas Dolby. Only when the record was recorded were the group christened. To tie in with the song title, 'Whodini' was the chosen name. And at that point, a DJ by the name of 'Grandmaster Dee' was added to the group. As for the record, it was great fun as the two rappers exchanged lines in conversational style whilst Thomas Dolby gave the track a fabulous spacey musicality.

35
THE JAM
Beat Surrender/Shopping/
Move On Up/
Stoned Out Of My Mind / War
1
Polydor

Both 'Town Called Malice' and 'The Bitterest Pill (I Ever Had To Swallow)', which preceded 'Beat Surrender' as singles in 1982, had been excellent pieces of work. But having announced his decision to end The Jam, Paul Weller saved the best until last. Taking the title by twisting Anita Ward's 'Sweet Surrender' and the military term 'beating a retreat', he wrote a song that was a final hurrah and a reminder of the qualities he had always tried to instil into The Jam, such as pride and passion. He signalled his future intent by the prominent use of horns rather than the band's traditional guitar attack which he had come to find restrictive. 'Beat Surrender' was a fond wave goodbye to his teenage group The Jam and an introduction of sorts to the more expansive and adult Style Council who would emerge from the ashes.

34
THE CHILLS
Rolling Moon/Bite
Flamethrower
NO CHART PLACING
Flying Nun Records

The Chills were early proponents of the Dunedin sound found on *Flying Nun* releases. Essentially the band is the work of one man - Martin Phillipps and whoever he chooses to play with. As such, the band has a constantly revolving membership, and continues to this day. 'Rolling Moon' was the first single release and captures the essence of The Chills to perfection. It is a feast of melodic chiming guitars underpinned by organ and tambourine, with a genial vocal from Phillipps describing a haunting experience, which concludes with melodic whistling. It is wonderful and bewitching.

33
CRISTINA
Things Fall Apart / Disco Clone
NO CHART PLACING
ZE Records

Written with, and produced by, Was Not Was, 'Things Fall Apart' was included on the *ZE Christmas Album*. Cristina was surely the template upon which Lana Del Ray has built her career. Her delivery is dry and darkly sardonic as, over power chord riffing, she describes a horrendous Christmas Eve that sees her break up with a boyfriend and, bereft of any seasonal goodwill, ultimately concludes: "I caught a cab back to my flat, and wept a bit, and fed the cat".

B-side 'Disco Clone' was the A-side of her 1978 recording debut, a song described by Cristina as "the worst song I've ever heard". Because of this, she takes huge liberties with the track and performs it as musical theatre akin to Brecht and Weil visit Studio 54.

32
THE ASSOCIATES
Club Country
A.G. It's You Again
13
Associates/Beggars Banquet

Rhythmic guitars and violins amidst a lush electronic landscape, combined with an up-tempo beat that Billy Mackenzie uses as a launchpad for the sonic splendour of his incredible voice! My instinct is that the lyrical content behind MacKenzie's explosive crooning is comparing the stifling social constrictions and perceived need for one-upmanship taking place at a country club's exclusive domain, with the behaviour of inmates of a psychiatric hospital.

31
'LECTRIC WORKERS
Robot Is Systematic
Robot Is Systematic (Instrumental Version)
NO CHART PLACING
Discomagic Records

Years and years ahead of its time, this is inventive, expressive, electronic music that transcends its Italo-disco genre.

30
CAPTAIN BEEFHEART & THE MAGIC BAND
Ice Cream For Crow
Light Reflected Off The Oceands Of The Moon
NO CHART PLACING
Virgin

The band seem to be playing the same song at different speeds, but are corralled by Cliff Martinez, whose drums provide shape and a rock solid base. Beefheart himself is on fine form, throwing out line after extraordinary line to create a collage of vivid imagery. His voice is worn, but humorous and warm as he acts as ringmaster for the shape-shifting instrumentation. His harmonica solo that ends the record is hilariously ragged. Miraculously, all this sounds perfect, as intended, which is why Beefheart was that rare thing - a musical genius.

A video was made to promote the single that was rejected by MTV as being "too weird".

29
THE CLASH
Rock The Casbah
Long Time Jerk
30
CBS

With music written in its entirety by Topper Headon, all that was needed was a lyric to match the tune's quality. Topper's original idea was dismissed out of hand as soppy and sentimental, which left Joe Strummer to disappear into the studio toilets to pen 'Rock the Casbah', inspired by the banning of western music in Iran following the Islamic revolution. Topper's original track was piano-led and grooving. Guitars and bass were overlaid along with sound effects and Strummer sang in a playfully exaggerated fashion, the combination of which created perhaps the most pop radio-friendly single of the Clash's career.

28
FRANTIC ELEVATORS
Holding Back The Years / Pistols In My Brain
NO CHART PLACING
No Waiting

Self-released by the band but selling a mere 200 copies, 'Holding Back The Years' was a final nail in the coffin for the Frantic Elevators. Moving way past the groups art-punk origins, the song was an atmospheric ballad with a stream-of-consciousness lyric from singer Mick Hucknall, about the emotional wrench of first leaving home and going out into the world alone. He conjures up a series of family related images that give him resolve - nothing is clichéd or sentimental. It is a tremendous piece of writing matched by a yearning, soulful vocal.

27
EINSTÜRZENDE NEUBAUTEN
Thirsty Animal
Durstiges Tier
NO CHART PLACING
Self-released

Einstürzende Neubauten translates from German as 'collapsing new buildings', which, as names go, is rather uncompromising. However, the name does not match their utterly harrowing and no-compromise approach to making music, as the band bash with jackhammers and other tools to create their sound. On 'Thirsty Animal' they are joined by the banshee-voiced Lydia Lunch as well as Rowland S. Howard of The Birthday Party. Opening with what sounds like a chainsaw or axle grinder amalgamated with shards of guitar noise, courtesy of Howard, an ungodly howl is summoned up by Lydia Lunch that matches the ferocity of the sound that surrounds her. The song runs beyond the nine-minute mark and the intensity level never dips.

26
IMAGINATION
Just An Illusion
Just An Illusion (Instrumental)
2
R & B Records

As sultry and sensuous as ever, Imagination returned and seduced all before them with languid grooves and a lethal combination of angelic voices. They were irresistible.

25
JAPAN
Ghosts
The Art Of Parties (Version)
5
Virgin

'Ghosts' is a minimalist composition written by David Sylvain, drummerless and without bass guitar. The backing track is fragmented, experimental and highly atmospheric. Atop that, Sylvain purrs the autobiographical lyric concerned with disappointment and disillusionment as he contemplates his band's success, which despite being everything he had once dreamed of, has ultimately brought him no happiness or satisfaction.

24
GREGORY ISAACS
Night Nurse/Material Man
NO CHART PLACING
Island Records

It was unedifying, but with Bob Marley's death, record companies sought a replacement, a new reggae superstar who would shift product for them. The most likely was the charismatic and supple-voiced Gregory Isaacs. And so, after a career stretching back over a decade, 'The Cool Ruler' (as he was dubbed) was extensively promoted and deserved success, but success only on his own terms, success in recognition of his own talent. A pale Bob Marley clone he was not, nor would he ever be.

Earlier in the year he had released

the superb 'Cool Down the Pace' single. He topped that though with 'Night Nurse' - a song of heartfelt longing. And over a rhythmic but sympathetic backing, courtesy of 'The Roots Radics' band, Gregory sang it exquisitely with understated good taste and undeniable cool.

23
VIRGIN PRUNES
The Faculties Of A Broken Heart (What Should We Do If Baby Turns Blue)
Chance Of A Lifetime / Yeo
NO CHART PLACING
Rough Trade

Gothic in the manner of Edgar Allan Poe, with a similar confrontationally disturbing style, desperation is captured in every word and note of this song. It leads towards madness and tragedy. 'Baby Turns Blue' (the title of the original 7" single), was produced by Colin Newman of Wire, who streamlines the wild noise to create a track that although harrowing, is presented in as user-friendly a manner as Virgin Prunes could ever be. They achieve this without sacrificing the group's innate primal energy and the hissing and screeching expressionism that was an integral part of their musical art.

22
THE VALENTINE BROTHERS
Money's Too Tight (To Mention)
Money's Too Tight (To Mention) (Instrumental)
NO CHART PLACING
Energy Records

John and Billy Valentine, who had spent three years in the touring company for the musical *The Wiz,* wrote and recorded 'Money's too Tight (To Mention)', which was the ultimate 'hard times' anthem. Over a rolling funk groove, the brothers trade verses detailing the hardships that mount up, blighting their lives as a result of 'Reaganomics', the name given to US president Ronald Reagan's spending cuts which caused terrible hardship to the already poorest people in American society.

21
PATRICK COWLEY
Megatron Man/Teen Planet
NO CHART PLACING
Metronome

Although originally issued in 1981 in the USA, 'Megatron Man' was released a year later in several European and Latin countries. It is nine minutes of relentless synthesised dance floor mastery. Cowley exploits the studio as a creative tool and aligns it with his ear for melody to make 'Megatron Man' a constantly fascinating track, full of changing tones and containing a head spinning series of energised rushes and peaks.

20
NEW ORDER
Temptation/Hurt
29
Factory

'Temptation' holds a special place in New Order's history: it was their first self-produced release; it was re-recorded twice in the years that followed; it was remixed several times; and it has the distinction of being the most played song in the group's live performances. The track was cut from a take that became the 12-inch single, which is a little bit untethered and where the rhythm and beats are the source of most enjoyment. A 7-inch single was released simultaneously. An edit from the full track and in its more concise form, its synth-pop geniality is more pronounced.

19
THE WEATHER GIRLS
It's Raining Men
It's Raining Men (Instrumental)
2
CBS

The Two Tons O' Fun were Martha Wash and Izora Armstead. They had been backing singers and visual foils for disco superstar Sylvester. The couple were giant-sized ladies with giant-sized gospel/soul voices and were extremely charismatic. Paul Jabara (who had written hits for Donna Summer) and Paul Shaffer wrote 'It's Raining Men' and offered it to Donna Summer. She hated it, offended by what she considered its "blasphemy". Cher, Diana Ross and Barbara Streisand also gave it an emphatic rejection. And so it was offered to Two Tons O' Fun. Martha Wash was initially resistant but consented to record the song. Two Tons O' Fun then changed their name to The Weather Girls to tie in with the song's title. The record was embraced by the gay community before infiltrating the mainstream. Its uplifting Hi-NRG post-disco sound, combined with raunchy R&B vocals and the lyrical objectification of men, was a refreshing subversion of the norm. While the song and performance of it were so upfront and celebratory, only the most prudish could possibly take offence.

18
MADNESS
House Of Fun/Don't Look Back
1
Stiff Records

One of four glorious Madness singles released in 1982 - 'Our House', 'Driving in My Car' and 'Cardiac Arrest' are worthy of honourable mentions here. Madness had proved to be a consummate singles act and this was their purple patch. 'House of Fun' is a coming-of-age farce set in a chemist shop, as the 16-year-old narrator - who is of legal age but lacks maturity - attempts to buy a packet of condoms using euphemisms rather than plain language. That leads the nonplussed and irritated female shop assistant to believe he wants balloons from a joke shop. Recorded initially without a chorus, *Stiff Records*' head honcho Dave Robinson asked the band to include one. Keyboard player Mike Barson wrote the catchy classic chorus there and then. The band recorded this separately and it was then inserted into the main song through hours of painful editing.

17
DEXYS MIDNIGHT RUNNERS & THE EMERALD EXPRESS
The Celtic Soul Brothers
Love Part Two
45 (Re-Release 1983, No.20)
Mercury

With Dexys at one point down to a core two-piece of Irish descended Kevin Rowland and Scottish Jimmy Patterson, the lyric to 'Celtic Soul Brothers' was formulated by Rowland as a statement of intent and in tribute to their unity and shared vision. It was the first song to be recorded and released by the revised line-up and a radical departure from the style which they were associated. Incorporating fiddles and mandolins, the new outfit moved as quickly as lightweight boxers - they bobbed and weaved but attacked with deceptive power. Using a melody that leans on The Whispers' 1967 single 'Needle in a Haystack', 'Celtic Soul Brothers' was taken at an up-tempo pace and received one of Kevin Rowland's finest singing performances, making sure every word is clear and understood as he delivered what amounted to a manifesto.

16
INDEEP
Last Night a D.J. Saved My Life (Vocal & Acapella)
Telephone Ringing-Screeching Tires-Flushing Toilet (Sound Effects)
13
Sound of New York

Rumbling deep bass, shrill Chic-style guitar, and soulful conversational vocals telling the tale of a bored and lonely woman who tries to phone her man but gets no reply. She listens to the radio and the DJ plays records that give her a feeling of empowerment. She gets in her car and drives and, as the music touches her soul, she finds empathy in the songs. We have all been touched by certain records, all been moved emotionally, and this record is a tribute to the power of music to heal and to the DJs who keep the discs spinning.

15
PHILIP GLASS
Facades/A Gentleman's Honour
NO CHART PLACING
Epic

Written for a scene in the film *Koyaanisqatsi* but ultimately not used, the title refers to the deserted out-of-hours facades of Wall Street buildings. Glass uses repetitive structures throughout his work and 'Facades' is no exception. It is absolutely beautiful, and the melodies that drift through the coldness of the track are melancholic. They humanise the otherwise impersonal, modernistic edifice that the nagging sawing of violins help us visualise.

14
DAVID BOWIE/
GIORGIO MORODER
Cat People (Putting Out Fire)
Paul's Theme (Jogging chase)
26
MCA Records

Recorded as the theme song for a 1982 film of the same name, starring Natassja Kinski and Malcolm McDowell, the film itself was absolutely dreadful, but this title track was magnificent. Bowie wrote the lyric to music that Moroder had already recorded, very much with the mood of the film in mind, hence the Gothic imagery. For his performance, Bowie sang in a deep baritone and was backed by a female chorus. His tone is measured but as he hits the song's chorus - and on the word 'gasoline'- employs an octave change that jolts the listener - it is staggering and thrilling. Combined with Moroder's trademark mechanised patterns and rock band instrumentation, this makes 'Cat People' full of dramatic moments which are spectacularly good. It is a slightly hidden classic in both artiste's illustrious careers. Bowie returned to the song 18 months later and recorded a version for his *Let's Dance* album that was good, but lacked the energy and magic of this single.

13
SOFT CELL
Say Hello, Wave Goodbye / Say Hello, Wave Goodbye (Instrumental)
3
Some Bizzare

Set in the seedy but seductive streets of Soho where Marc Almond was living, this is a song about furtive, shame-tinged romance. The protagonist is a man who has grown tired of an affair and its attendant baggage. He has realised he can no longer navigate its awkward terrain and with a degree of vengeful cruelty, he is writing its final chapter whilst laying down ground rules for any future chance encounter. "We're strangers meeting for the first time okay?", he decrees. In future we keep things brief, hence, "say hello, wave goodbye". This was a wonderful song - sad and gritty, showing great insight into human behaviour. Soft Cell touched a chord and in doing so marked themselves as exceptional talents.

12
RIP RIG + PANIC
Storm the Reality Asylum (Extended Version)/ Leave Your Spittle In The Pot/ It's Always Tit For Tac You Foolish Brats
NO CHART PLACING
Virgin

Rip Rig + Panic were named after a Roland Kirk album title, contained two ex-members of The Pop Group, had Neneh Cherry as lead vocalist and her father, Don Cherry, as a guest musician. They were a formidable free-wheeling outfit at their best, but too often their wilfully-indisciplined approach made them unpalatable for general consumption. However, here they excelled. They hit a loose piano-based groove which is added to by nimble bass, horns and percussion, while Neneh Cherry and Andrea Oliver sing abstract lyrics containing multiple hooks with cool aplomb, leading to the mighty insurrectionary chorus.

11
THE CLASH
Straight To Hell/
Should I Stay Or Should I Go?
17
CBS

This double A-side single has a claim as the Clash's best ever 45. It is best remembered for 'Should I Stay Or Should I Go' with its classic riff and Mick Jones' perfect whining vocal that carries a stinging petulant rebuke in its delivery and of course the Spanish language backing gleefully hollered by the two Joes – Strummer and Ely. However, it is 'Straight To Hell' that is this single's heavyweight sound. Totally un-rock 'n' roll, the group create a highly experimental and eerie backing track with a bossa nova rhythm for Joe Strummer, who sounds at once both indignant and saddened to sing his song about injustice and exploitation. In the first verse, Strummer sings about the closures of steel mills in northern Britain and the generations of unemployment and poverty that ensue. He then turns to American soldiers, abandoning the children they had fathered to Vietnamese women during the Vietnam War, before his ire is aimed at profiteering developers burning down the houses of poor immigrant communities in New York's Alphabet City, forcing them out of the area so gentrification could commence. It is fiercely impassioned - both the music and vocal contain a haunting quality that touches deeply and stirs up feelings of compassion.

10
ROCKERS REVENGE
featuring DONNIE CALVIN
Walking On Sunshine/Acappella Sunshine
Rockin' On Sunshine/Walking On Sunshine
4
London Records

Rockers Revenge was a studio-based band combining Arthur Baker's prowess behind the mixing desk with reggae singer Donnie Calvin. The first fruits of their labour was 'Walking On Sunshine', a remake of Eddy Grant's 1979 single. They took apart Grant's song, which had a sunshine vibe about it, instilled by a sweet lightness of touch and transformed it into a brooding rumbling epic that felt menacing due to its abrasive edge and Calvin's gritty singing. It sounded big... and the synthesiser hook they used felt like a call to arms. Inside a club, this record was titanic to the point of becoming overpowering, as its blocks of chattering synths and the voices of the female backing singers swirled around your head and seemed to bounce from surface to surface, until you were surrounded by the sound and enslaved by the rhythm.

9
PRINCE
1999
How Come U Don't Call Me Anymore
25 (re-release 1985 – 2 / 1999 – 10/2016 – 49)
Warner Bros. Records

'1999' was one of Prince's signature songs; the fact it charted four times across three decades testimony to its enduring appeal. The opening lines of the song are handed to members of his backing group, The Revolution, sung firstly by Lisa Coleman and secondly by Dez Dickerson before Prince uses his voice. This was a subtle homage to Stevie Wonder who employed the same process on 'You Are The Sunshine Of My Life'. The song's main riff is remarkably similar to the backing vocals of The Mamas and Papas' hit 'Monday Monday' but is delivered in a bold, strutting style while Prince - with Jill Jones now given a line to sing - talks of the cold war insanity of stockpiling nuclear armaments and aiming them at each other. He concludes, however, that it makes no sense worrying and it's better to party - like it's 1999 - which will mean if we get that far, we shall have lived through the nightmare of Reagan and Brezhnev as we enter a new millennium.

8
RHODA WITH THE SPECIAL A.K.A.
The Boiler
Theme From The Boiler
35
Two-Tone Records

'The Boiler' was the first self-written song by The Bodysnatchers, an all-female group who recorded using a ska style for *Two-Tone Records*. Written and performed by Rhoda Dakar, the lyric is a first-person perspective of a woman suffering low esteem issues who is violently raped. Her reference point was a friend who had been raped and Dakar attempted to capture the horror and fear her friend had described in the song. The Bodysnatchers split up with the bulk of the group formed the pop act The Belle Stars whilst Dakar went on tour in America with the Specials where 'The Boiler' became part of their set. Back in the UK, Jerry Dammers began recording the song, slowing it down considerably and replacing its ska inflections with haunting keyboard Muzak stylings. Dakar recorded her vocal but then other projects removed Dammers from the process until 12 months later The Fun Boy Three's defection from the ranks of The Specials saw Dammers re-engage. The song completed, it was released into the world where its subject matter and Rhoda's incredibly harrowing portrayal of the victim meant it received scant media exposure. Nonetheless it charted and the important issues it raised were heard. It remains a record that everyone should hear at least once .

7
MARK STEWART AND THE MAFIA
Jerusalem
High Ideals And Crazy Dreams
Welcome To Liberty City
NO CHART PLACING
On-U Sound

There is of course nothing remotely patriotic about William Blake's 'Jerusalem'. His poem turned into a hymn is in fact a condemnation of the suppression of free thought and expression, imposed by the nationalists of the Napoleonic era in which it was written, which remains valid to this day. Somewhere in time, the meaning of the words were perversely twisted into a glorification of 'Britishness' and more particularly 'Englishness'. They were seen as representing a view that a new Jerusalem could be built here. Mark Stewart and Adrian Sherwood reclaim the song from the flag wavers and deliver it as a fragmented contemporary piece that reflects the multi-ethnic and multicultural makeup of this island nation. Traditional church choirs are represented, as are northern brass bands alongside bold electronics, football crowds and dub reggae effects. Mark Stewart is placed deliberately low in the mix but still refrains from raising his voice and becoming hectoring in manner. His tone is without bombast; he imparts the words in a considered, deadly serious tone. This reading of Jerusalem is no art prank, a trap it could easily have fallen into. Rather, it is a bold and brilliant political statement inside an equally bold and astonishing piece of music making.

6
SUN RA
Nuclear War
Sometimes I'm Happy
NO CHART PLACING
Y Records

'Nuclear War' was the most accessible record the space jazz pioneer Sun Ra recorded in his entire half-century long career, which indicates that this record contained a message that no matter how flippantly it was delivered, was one that needed to be heard. And so, over a laid back funky piano groove, Sun Ra and his Arkestra engage in a call and response dialogue, laying out in street jargon the consequences to humankind of a nuclear war that in 1982 seemed highly probable. "It's a motherfucker!" Ra exclaims. He talks about the effects of radiation poisoning and warns: "If they push that button your ass gotta go". The song's languid pace never detracts from the message and Ra concludes with the declaration: "They're gonna blast you so high in the sky, you can kiss your ass goodbye". And pointed rhetorical question: "Oh what you gonna do without your ass!?"

1982

5
SYLVESTER AND PATRICK COWLEY
Do Ya Wanna Funk
Do Ya Wanna Funk (Instrumental)
32
London Records

Patrick Cowley died in November 1982, an early victim of the AIDS epidemic which would later claim Sylvester as well. Somehow they found time for this final collaboration and it was pure Hi-NRG dynamite - a dance floor monster - with Cowley's pumping synths and machined flourishes a perfect match for Sylvester's magnificent opera-meets-R&B voice, delivering unabashed the innuendo filled lyric with huge aplomb.

4
AFRICA BAMBAATAA
AND THE SOUL SONIC FORCE
Planet Rock
Planet Rock (Instrumental)
53
Tommy Boy

Planet Rock was one of the most influential records released in the 80s. It was a bomb going off, an explosion with a huge wide-ranging aftershock. Tom Silverman needed a hit for his fledgling record label and had put Africa Bambaataa together with producer Arthur Baker. They had made a record called 'Jazzy Sensation' which sold a very respectable 30,000 copies. For the next single they fetched in musician John Robie and set about creating a track that reflected their shared love of electronic music, in particular that of Kraftwerk. A backing track was created, with Robie replicating elements of Kraftwerk's songs 'Numbers' and 'Trans-Europe Express' on synthesiser. A funky beat was added before a three-man rap crew were asked to add vocals. Baker later commented that they "despised" the track but nonetheless MC G.L.O.B.E wrote a rap that celebrates the power of music and a positive outlook. He then developed a rapping style that was half speed and off the beat, christening it 'MC Popping'. The painstaking task of splicing parts with a razor blade and sellotape and mixing the track fell to Baker. And shortly after he completed the job, the record hit the streets and clubs where its mix of electronics, funk and hip-hop made it a sensation. The uncredited writers from Kraftwerk were rightly irked and sought redress, which came in the form of a $1 per sale commission.

3
MARVIN GAYE
(Sexual) Healing
(Sexual) Healing (Instrumental)
4
CBS

The late 70s and the turn of the decade had seen Marvin Gaye at his lowest ebb. He owed a fortune in taxes, was divorced, remarried and divorced again, was in dispute with Motown where his records had stopped selling, and had a titanic cocaine addiction. He tried to tour but was too erratic and unreliable. More lawsuits followed and he attempted suicide by ingesting an ounce of cocaine. It was a failure. This was the backdrop to his move to Europe - first to London where his problems were only magnified. And so as fate would have it, he ended up living in the Belgian port city of Ostend. Here, with a new recording contract secured, he began to cut down his drug use, exercise and regain his health. He rethought his recent approach to making music and returned to the style of his early 70s' 'Let's Get It On' peak. An album was recorded which would prove to be his greatest success, but sadly his last before he was tragically killed. Preceding the album was the single '(Sexual) Healing', basically a paean to spiritual release achieved through joyous physical coupling. Marvin sounds completely rejuvenated artistically. His voice is velvet... seductive but playful. He glides over a backing that contains a strong reggae element aligned to a drum and percussion groove that is highly original and dance floor slinky.

2
GRANDMASTER FLASH
& THE FURIOUS FIVE
The Message
The Message (Instrumental)
8
Sugar Hill Records

Up to this point in time, DJs had been the stars of hip-hop crews, with the MCs seen as interchangeable, their role simply to encourage a party atmosphere in as skilled and entertaining fashion as possible.

How 'The Message' changed that perception - in fact turned the whole theory on its head - was because this particular message was one of social conscience. It spoke of real issues and hardships, and of a system that didn't care enough to try and halt the correlation between poverty and criminality. The listener could not help but hang onto every vitally important word. It contained a killer hook too in "it's like a jungle sometime, it makes me wonder how I keep from going under" followed by nervous laughter. Additionally, the music created broke new ground - it was sinuous and funky but left lots of space for the voices to operate within. It contained a modernist noirish feel as electronic sound effects helped create an aural landscape that felt edgy and dangerous. 'The Message' was a great awakening in the hip-hop community that led to issues of real substance and importance coming to the fore in lyrical content with increased regularity.

1
ROBERT WYATT
Shipbuilding
Memories of You
NO CHART PLACING (1983 - 35)
Rough Trade

Clive Langer - once of Deaf School and at this point a notable record producer - had a tune but not a suitable lyric. At a party he played the tune to Elvis Costello who wrote what he himself described as "the best lyric I've ever written". It concerned the then current Falklands War and it expressed the painful irony of traditional shipbuilding yards that had been in decline which were now thriving once more as new ships needed to be built to replace vessels sunk in the conflict. These new ships then sailed away carrying local recruits to war and possible death. Bitter-sweet was an understatement. Robert Wyatt was approached to sing a version of it for a planned EP containing the song performed by four different artists. Once Robert Wyatt had recorded his vocal, the original EP plan was scrapped. Wyatt's version would clearly be definitive. It was, and still is, enormously moving, pained and poignant. His performance was magnificent. It felt intimate and wise, carrying a weight of emotion that was almost unbearable. The music matched the voice perfectly - delicate and doleful, jazz-tinged and sympathetic to the lyrical content. If there has ever been another song about war as subtle and considered as this masterpiece, I've yet to hear it.

On a personal note, my late Mother used to love this song. She would listen to it attentively with tears welling in her eyes. When she was in her 80s, she would ask me to sing it for her and I would happily oblige. Around this time, I found myself in Clive Langer's company after a Deaf School gig in Liverpool. I told him of the feelings his song induced in my mother, how its sad beauty cancelled out any generational divide, and how it evoked memories of her three uncles who, barely out of their teens, had died in the mud of the Somme during the 1914-18 war. His eyes welled up – "Give her a hug from me" he said.

'Shipbuilding' is a song containing great humanity, and one of its co-authors was displaying his humanity. If Galtieri and Thatcher had shared a shred of that noble feeling in 1982 the lives of the 904 who died in a pointless war would have been spared.

The Fall went to Australia and fetched me back this t-shirt, 1982

1983

The previously highly-unpopular Margaret Thatcher had waged a war and won, the Iron Lady myth was created and she took on regal airs and was compared to Boadicea. In her metaphorical chariot she was swept back into power on a landslide at the general election as the UK's population celebrated victory in disgusting jingoistic style and elected a warmonger as prime minister rather than the principled pacifist leader of the vanquished opposition Michael Foot. She was now free now to wage a new war, this time against trade unions and working class communities that she despised. How musicians reacted to this, if they reacted at all, was either through a party-harder approach that embraced escapism, or at the other end of the scale there was an increase in overt political content from dissenting voices across the board through pop chart acts to the hard-edged though peace advocating anarcho-punks. Attitudes were fragmented, the Tories set out to divide and conquer they were succeeding, the musical mix reflected a nation divided there were a schizoid variety of styles competing for attention when one considers that the USA under Reagan increasingly began to act as the world's bully, funding insurrection against regimes they disapproved of and illegally invading Grenada. Tensions between the USA and the Soviet Union were constantly on a knife edge with the threat of nuclear war a genuine concern, meanwhile on home turf 'Reaganomics' were bringing rising unemployment to those in the poorest inner city neighbourhoods and, as ever with poverty, there comes drugs, violence and crime as a way of life. One way or another this would be reflected in music as hip-hop became angrier and the dance scene increasingly hedonistic.

My own musical life was in a state of flux, I was not in a band for the first time in 4 years and endeavoured to find a vehicle in which I could express myself. I somehow found myself booked as the entertainment for The Youth Communist Leagues' summer gathering in the grounds of the Hollings building (the toast rack) in Fallowfield. I played in partnership with my brother and we were well-received, beyond that I caroused the city's nightspots, went to lots of gigs and bought lots of records, business as per usual .

NOTABLE EVENTS 1983

Nazi war criminal Klaus Barbie is arrested in Bolivia

The wearing of a seatbelt becomes mandatory for drivers and front seat passengers in the UK

The 3D printer is invented by Chuck Hull

Ronald Reagan proposes the Strategic Defence Initiative - a new weapons technology to intercept enemy missiles, the media dub the plan 'Star Wars'.

At Motown's televised 25th anniversary show Michael Jackson performs Billie Jean and debuts the Moonwalk

At the Kursk Nuclear Power Plant in Russia a reactor is shut down due to fuel rod failure.

A total loss of coolant occurs at the Embalse Nuclear Power Station in Argentina it is classified as an accident with local consequences.

Technical failure at the Phillipsburg Nuclear Power Plant in Germany sees the release of Iodine-131 causing contamination.

Soviet Military officer Stanislav Petrov prevents the start of a worldwide nuclear war when he identifies the warning of attack by the US as a false alarm.

Multi Tool Word, soon to become Microsoft Word, is released in the US.

American Cruise missiles arrive at RAF Greenham Common to mass protests

The Brinks-Mat robbery takes place at Heathrow airport - 6,800 gold bars worth £26 million are stolen

Manchester United sign Dutch wizard Arnold Muhren at the start of the 1982-83 season, Frank Stapleton is top goal scorer with 19 goals, the team finish 3rd in the League, lose the League Cup final to Liverpool but win the FA cup beating Brighton and Hove Albion 4-0 in a replay after the original contest was drawn 2-2. 17 year-old Norman Whiteside scores goals in both finals becoming the youngest person to do so. Manchester City are relegated when they lose 2-1 at home to David Pleat's Luton.

NOTABLE BIRTHS

Rafe Spall; Mo Farah; Robin Van Persie; Amy Whitehouse

NOTABLE DEATHS

Dick Emery; Garrincha; Billy Fury; Karen Carpenter; Tennessee Williams; Donald McClean; Herge; Gloria Swanson; Muddy Waters; Chris Wood; Luis Buniel; David Niven; James Jamerson; Jobriath; Klaus Nomi; Ira Gershwin; George Liberace; Ralph Richardson; Barney Bubbles; John Le Mesurier; Slim Pickens; Robert Aldrich; Violet Carson; Dennis Wilson.

NOTABLE BOOKS

The Secret Diary Of Adrian Mole Aged 13 ¾ - Sue Townsend

Shame - Salmon Rushdie

Helliconia Summer - Brian W Aldiss

La Brava - Elmore Leonard

Bluebeard's Egg- Margaret Atwood

Adventures in the Screen Trade - William Goldman

NOTABLE FILMS

Scarface; Monty Python's The Meaning Of Life; Rumblefish; Christine; Videodrome; local Hero; Zelig; L'Argent; The Osterman Weekend; The Dresser.

100
JACKIE LEVEN
Love Is Shining Down On Me
Great Spirit Calls
NO CHART PLACING
Virgin

The great Doll By Doll had been broken; poor sales of now deleted albums and singles meant their wild beauty would be heard no more - they were gone. For the group's leader though, things were looking good. He had signed a deal with Virgin/Charisma and promised them some less bloodthirsty, brighter fare. An album's worth of songs were apparently recorded and this single released. It was breathtaking, bright and summery. Joy cascaded from the grooves. Jackie was in great voice as he duetted with a female partner - probably Carol Wolf – with whom he was pictured on the single's sleeve. He was as poetic as ever. However, the line "silent motorcycles kick themselves to death on a desert highway that goes nowhere", sadly prophesied the fate of this record which, despite its built-in optimism and supremely catchy and uplifting chorus, fared worse than Doll By Doll releases. It received no publicity and no airplay. It simply came and went unnoticed. Another single followed into silent oblivion and this phase of Jackie Leven's career quietly closed.

99
MADNESS
Tomorrow's (Just Another Day)/
Madness (Is All In The Mind)
8
Stiff Records

A genuine double A-side single featuring two songs of high quality. 'Tomorrow's (Just Another Day)', was written by Mike Barson and Chas Smash, and 'Madness (Is All In The Mind)', a Chris Foreman composition. The former sees the group continue to delve into darker, thought-provoking themes whilst disguising the melancholy behind a cheerily played tune and the lugubrious vocals of Graham MacPherson AKA Suggs. The latter features a rare lead vocal from Chas Smash and is played as a slow piano-led blues, leading into a jauntier chorus that nonetheless displays an inherent sense of sadness and a struggle to maintain emotional and mental stability.

98
JOHN HOLT
Police In Helicopter
Police In Helicopter (Version)
NO CHART PLACING
Volcano

The USA were applying pressure on Jamaican authorities to locate and burn down the herb fields in an effort to reduce the amount of marijuana reaching the USA. This was John Holt's musical response. Holt had built his reputation as a performer of love songs with mainstream appeal but had spent a period in quiet reflection and experienced a spiritual epiphany, converting to the Rastafarian faith. As the smoking of "herb" was a central tenet of the religion, Holt proposed striking back and burning down the (sugar) cane fields that the economy relied upon. He performs the song over an easy-grooving rhythm in an almost meditative style. Calm and coherent, his smooth vocals are effortless and his reasoning impeccable.

97
CULTURE CLUB
Victims / Colour By Numbers
3
Virgin

Professionally, Culture Club were on the crest of the wave. They were the most successful British band of the era, an achievement that was replicated worldwide. Singer Boy George had rapidly become a cultural icon and all seemed sweet. However, beneath the surface George was involved in a toxic relationship with drummer Jon Moss. 'Victims' was a song addressing that relationship, about being hurt but finding the strength to overcome the pain. It was performed as an epic, with lavish orchestration adding to the winning melody provided by Roy Hay that Boy George matches with a magisterial vocal performance. There was no denying the Boy had plenty of talent and was a superb singer.

96
THE JONZUN CREW
Space Is The Place
Space Is The Place (Instrumental)
NO CHART PLACING
21 Records

The Jonzun Crew came from Florida and featured three brothers. Heavily influenced by Parliament/ Funkadelic, they took themes and concepts for their own music but did not look backwards when it came to recording them. In 'Space Is The Place', under the supervision of John "Jellybean" Benitez, they give us a thrilling, bleeping, Vocoder-voiced, electro funk jam that was highly futuristic.

95
ELTON JOHN
I'm Still Standing
Earn While You Learn
4
The Rocket Record Company

Although Elton John was still an enormous star, he had been a complete musical irrelevance since 1975. It was then that he released 'Someone Saved My Life Tonight', his last single of any note. Suddenly, somehow he moved through the gears to perform 'I'm Still Standing' as though he meant it. Although Bernie Taupin had penned the lyric as a put down to an old girlfriend as their relationship failed, Elton performed it as if it was a statement of resilience, of bouncing back from the setbacks and heartache that made him (privately) a deeply unhappy and troubled individual. He attacks the song with gusto; it is up-tempo and piano keys are pounded hard while vocally he strains at the top of his register, instilling a feeling of urgency as he proclaims himself a survivor. On this evidence he most certainly was just that.

94
YELLO
I Love You
Rubber West
41
Stiff Records

Another slice of art as dance music from the ever-imaginative and highly entertaining Yello. With a sound pitched somewhere between The Residents and acid house, and a lyric that combines sensual romance with road safety advice, this was a must hear record.

93
QUANDO QUANGO
Love Tempo/(Mix)
NO CHART PLACING
Factory

Mike Pickering would go on to enjoy success with T-Coy and M People but his earliest group was Quando Quango, formed in Rotterdam with Dutch siblings Gonnie and Reiner Rietveld. They moved to Manchester where Pickering DJed at The Haçienda and began releasing music, with 'Love Tempo' the pick of their singles. It is strongly dance-orientated, featuring alongside obligatory electronics, horns and steel drums. They successfully incorporated elements of Latin, reggae and disco, aligned to a distinctive post-punk sensibility to create a potent hybrid that, though rooted in Manchester, looked outward and embraced other musical forms.

92
NEIL YOUNG
Computer Age / Sample and Hold
NO CHART PLACING
Geffen Records

Neil Young's son Ben was born with cerebral palsy and unable to communicate. In hospital they sought ways to get the infant to respond. They were most successful when they used a mechanised robotic voice rather than a natural human voice. This led to Neil Young to record the album *Trans*, as both an artistic reinvention and more pertinently as an attempt to communicate with his child. 'Computer Age' was the outstanding track and selected for single release. It features heavy use of the Vocoder to distort the vocals, as well as a synclavier and electric piano to create a synthetic sound. Within this frame - within the machine so to speak - Young places his soul. And with his words and the pleasing melody, he reaches out and attempts to touch his child as he touches the listener.

91
KING SUNNY ADÉ
& HIS AFRICAN BEATS
Synchro System / Ire
NO CHART PLACING
Island Records

What *Island Records* had done a decade before in sweetening the reggae sounds of The Wailers by adding western style instrumentation and studio polish recognisable to a rock audiences ears, they attempted to replicate with their great African hope, the king of Nigerian juju music, King Sunny Adé. 'Synchro System' had been a Nigerian hit in 1974 as an 18-minute cut, awash with pedal steel guitar over intricate drum patterns. This new reading of the song was excellent in its own right but now came enhanced with a modernist sheen of synthesiser sounds and chattering rhythm machines.

90
PREFAB SPROUT
Lions In My Own Garden (Exit Someone)
NO CHART PLACING
Kitchenware Records

Missing a girlfriend who had gone to study at the university of Limoges in France, Paddy McAloon wrote 'Lions In My Own Garden' to express his feelings of abandonment and insecurity. He took the letters used to spell out the city's name to create the song's title. The image of being watched by lions in his own garden also summed up how abnormal his situation felt. Utilising simple instrumentation, acoustic guitar, bass, drums coloured with vibraphone and harmonica, the song's melody was subtle and crept into the ear before taking residence in the subconscious. Sung with a world-weary sincerity, the track was deemed good enough by the band for them to shell out £800 to self-release it on their own Candle Records imprint before it gained a wider release via Kitchenware Records.

89
MTUME
Juicy Fruit
Juicy Fruit Part II (Reprise)
34
Epic

As a staple of hip-hop sampling, even people who have no idea of the original song have been exposed to its sinuous, rolling groove. Written by James Mtume, he felt he had something special and so phoned singer Tawatha Agee, who was in London between dates on a Roxy Music tour. Duly summoned, she flew back to the USA to work on the song overnight. With no lyric written at that point, Mtume penned the innuendo-laden words one verse at a time, whilst Tawatha Agee sang each part as lyrics were passed to her. The song completed, she flew back to London in the morning. They had created a slow-burning, dance floor delight which oozes sensuality and, despite being only a modest hit, it set the standard for smooching, dim lit, sexual disco-soul.

88

PHILIP GLASS
Cloudscape/Cloudscape
NO CHART PLACING
Island Records

Recorded for the film *Koyaanisqatsi*, 'Cloudscape' is a brooding atmospheric piece of dark and ominous-sounding electronics that perfectly suited the mood of the times. It hinted at uncertainty. It suggested danger. It evoked barely remembered nightmares whose latent horror remains embedded within consciousness.

87
ZED
Plastic Love
Plastic Love (Instrumental Version)
NO CHART PLACING
Fuzz Dance

A true precursor of the house style that came out of Chicago later in the decade, this slice of timeless Italo-disco with futuristic lyrics, features lush synths, a robotic machine beat and a strong female vocal. It was totally out there in 1983 and doesn't feel old today.

86
G.A.N.G.
Incantations
Incantations (Instrumental)
NO CHART PLACING
Discomagic Records

G.A.N.G. were an Italian, studio-based combination of Giorgio Giodarno, Giorgio Dolce and Robert Zanetti - prog rock lovers one and all. They took themes from Mike Oldfield's tracks 'Incantations' and 'Foreign Affair', played them as a medley, and gave it a solid base of drums. They added funk-style licks on guitar and a soaring choral effect, before the pure-voiced Stefania Dal Pino contributes an even more ethereal vocal to the heady mix. The phrase 'blissed out' was surely coined by clubbers who fell under this epic's nine-minute spell - perfect for the Balearic scene that flourished, where it was regarded as a cosmic classic.

85
DEPECHE MODE
Get The Balance Right!/
The Great Outdoors!
13
Mute

Though they still looked like well-scrubbed schoolboys playing at being pop stars, this was where Depeche Mode began to grow up, grow out of, and grow away from their gauche and twee beginnings, 'Get The Balance Right!' was the first single new member Alan Wilder featured on, and it was surely no coincidence that depth was added to the band's usual, highly melodic sound, while Martin Gore's lyric is oblique and of more interest than the 'boy meets girl' pap they had previously peddled.

84
THE SPLASH BAND
Remix From The John Carpenter Film *The End* Pt 1: Disco-Version
Remix From The John Carpenter Film *The End* Pt 2: Sound-Version
NO CHART PLACING
Zanza Records

John Carpenter's theme music from his film *Assault On Precinct 13* is taken and given an electronic Italo-disco makeover. It is played several octaves higher than the original. A 4/4 beat and prowling bass add rhythm and it is supplemented by the imagining of an angelic choir of deep-toned machines. Soaked in reverb to chilling effect, this record had a dance-floor lifespan that spread well into the nineties as it was played by notables such as Laurent Garnier, Juan Atkins and Carl Craig.

83
ROLLING STONES
Undercover Of The Night
All The Way Down
11
Rolling Stones Records

For anyone but absolute die-hard obsessives, 'Undercover Of The Night ' is the final time The Rolling Stones released a single worthy of their reputation. Written by Mick Jagger, under heavy influence from William Burroughs novel *Cities Of The Red Night*, the song uses violent imagery to portray the lives of the poor under politically corrupt regimes in Latin America, with young men given guns and made to fight, and young women forced into prostitution. The song is played as a highly rhythmic and fractured piece, with hard rock guitar and thumping bass courtesy of Robbie Shakespeare, who was chosen over Bill Wyman for the session.

82
HIPNOSIS
Pulstar
End Title (Blade Runner)
NO CHART PLACING
Memory Records

Italian act Hipnosis (sometimes credited as Hypnosis) were another group who looked at recognisable themes from other artists that they could cover in a spacey, futuristic-sounding disco style. 'Pulstar' is originally from the pen of Vangelis, as is 'Blade Runner'. Hipnosis strip the tracks of the grandeur - out go soaring strings and bold synthesiser lines. In their place comes a leaner, cleaner, almost minimal approach. Programmed drums are added - crisp and untreated, but still anchoring these intriguing pieces to the dance-floor. There were not many takers in the UK at the time, but Hipnosis reached the German Top 10 with this.

81
STEWART COPELAND AND STANARD RIDGWAY
Don't Box Me In / Drama At Home
91
A&M Records

'Don't Box Me In' was written as a collaboration between Wall Of Voodoo front man, Stan Ridgway and

Police drummer Stewart Copeland. It was part of the score for Francis Ford Coppola's film *Rumblefish.* The song followed the film's theme about a longing for personal freedom whilst feeling caged. This was expressed in abstract terms, capturing vividly the mindset of the film's ultimately doomed central character, the Motorcycle Boy. With Copeland handling all instrumentation save for the haunting harmonica part performed by Ridgway, the song flows easily through several musical passages while Ridgway's stylised vocal is in-simpatico with this engaging piece of mood music.

80
JULIAN COPE
Sunshine Playroom/
Hey High Class Butcher
64
Mercury

Julian Cope's debut solo single after the demise of A Teardrop Explodes found him in rude health and fine form. It begins with a whimsical, pastoral instrumental passage before abruptly changing style and pace becoming a neo-psychedelic rocker, replete with violins and trumpets. It twists and turns several times yet remains a cohesive and never-less-than-audacious piece. Lyrically, an excited sounding Julian laments the loss of childhood and its innocence, going as far as throwing in a couplet from the children's song 'The Runaway Train'.

79
KC AND THE SUNSHINE BAND
Give It Up
It's Hard To Say Goodbye
1
Epic

KC and The Sunshine Band had experienced a fallow patch stretching back to the 70s in the charts. 'Give it Up' remedied that, but not without a degree of difficulty, as their record label didn't consider it worthy of release. In stepped independent label Meca Records, who issued it in the USA where it became a hit. Shamelessly, Epic then launched the single internationally and reaped the rewards as the single's good natured mix of disco and pop, along with its near addictive chorus, made it unstoppable.

78
DUET EMMO
Or So It Seems
Heart Of Hearts (Or So It Seems)
NO CHART PLACING
Mute

Duet Emmo was a combination of Bruce Gilbert and Graham Lewis who, during Wire's hiatus, were recording together as Dome. They combined with *Mute* head Daniel Miller, who had issued his own music under the nom-de-plumes of The Normal and Silicone Teens. The name Duet Emmo was an anagram of Dome and *Mute*. 'Or So It Seems' was built on a simple but effective synthesiser motif, surrounded by atmospherics and occasional hand-claps as punctuation, whilst Graham Lewis abandoned his harsh vocal style for something unusually soft and emotive. The overall effect is utterly beguiling,

77
MR. FLAGIO
Take A Chance/Take A Chance (Instrumental Version)
NO CHART PLACING
Squish

Mr. Flagio were an Italian, studio-based electronic disco outfit who only worked together for a single year, but in that time they released this jewel of the Italo-disco movement. They take the song from Material, the seminal New York no-wave act. Stripping the funk from its bones, it is transformed into a sleek electro master-class of dynamic synth lines. With heavy use of the Vocoder on the voice, it is almost impossible not to dance to, they captured a sound that genius French duo Daft Punk would lean on heavily as a source of inspiration.

76
YES
Owner Of A Lonely Heart
Our Song
28
ATCO Records

Yes were a band out of time - a musty antiquity from the early 70s prog rock boom. Their style had zero relevance in the new bright shiny 80s. And yet with the aid of new blood in the shape of South African guitarist and principal songwriter Trevor Rabin, new ideas courtesy of ex-singer and a new producer, Trevor Horn, along with contributions from the old guard of bass player Chris Squire, and singer Jon Anderson, they reinvented themselves, delivering this single that they could justifiably feel proud of and that stood toe to toe with contemporary sounds. It took seven months and lots of rewrites and changes of approach to rid it of its original bland Americanisms, but the result showcased Yes as purveyors of bold, modernist pop, possessed of soaring dynamics, a crunching riff and a chorus that was jaw droppingly brilliant.

75
CHRIS & COSEY
October (Love Song)
Little Houses
NO CHART PLACING
Rough Trade

Following the dissolution of Throbbing Gristle, Chris and Cosey began releasing music that incorporated synth-pop elements aligned to the rhythmic base they had provided for TG. 'October (Love Song)' was their first single for Rough Trade and was a tender expression of the love and emotions Cosey felt for Chris. It was also possessed with an almost translucent beauty and had a delicious melody, although the public weren't ready to embrace this in 1983. It was featured in DJ Andrew Weatherall's early acid house sets a few years later as minds were opened and people became more accepting in their tastes.

74
PORTION CONTROL
Raise The Pulse
Collapse/Bite My Head
NO CHART PLACING
Illuminated Records

Portion Control were from South London and described themselves as an electro-punk band. They did not regard themselves as musicians, more as machine technicians, using no conventional instrumentation. The sound here is one of squiggly rhythms. They were the first people to use the Roland 303 on record, a good five years before its squelching bass lines became a staple of acid house records. Over the choruses, the intensity is ratcheted up several notches and they introduce sections of brutal stomping. The sound is completed by a thoughtful, though thoroughly pessimistic, lyric that is aggressively shouted out with feeling.

73
PETE SHELLEY
(Millions Of People) No One Like You/If You Ask Me (I Won't Say No)/(Millions Of People) No One Like You/If You Ask Me (I Won't Say No) (Dub Mix)
94
Genetic Records

Pete Shelley was still making superb melodic pop songs that had choruses as big as the heart he put into his songs. Unfortunately, without the Buzzcocks' brand name to grab attention, they were fairly widely ignored. 'No One Like You' was a glorious combination of pulsing electronics and a guitar that added edge, while Shelley's melodic gifts and plaintive singing voice remained as uniquely impressive as ever.

72
HASHIM
Al-Naafiysh (The Soul)
Bonus
NO CHART PLACING
Cutting Records

Jerry Calliste Jr. taught himself how to play keyboards by ear using a hand held Casio player. He had been DJing since he was 12 and promoting parties soon afterwards. At this young age he abandoned his Catholic upbringing and converted to Islam, taking the name Hashim, which translates from Arabic as 'decisive'. He was undoubtedly decisive too! His next move was to found Cutting Records and create the label's first release, 'Al Naafiysh (The Soul)', which is deservedly recognised as one of the best electro tracks of all time. He was 17 by now, and his record was the hottest sound in the hottest clubs in New York. It was also being blasted from boom boxes by any self-respecting b-boys on the streets, happily spinning on their heads and break-dancing to the most impossibly nasty and gloriously filthy, synthesised hip-hop groove imaginable.

71
THE WATERBOYS
A Girl Called Johnny
The Late Train To Heaven
80
Chicken Jazz

The Waterboys were a Scottish-Irish band led by Mike Scott and named after a line used by Lou Reed in his song 'The Kids'. However Patti Smith was Scott's main inspiration. He published a fanzine about his heroine and this debut single was an homage and comment on her seemingly indomitable spirit. Stylistically it was out of step with any of the current musical trends, being led by a near vaudeville sounding piano and featuring a wailing saxophone. Mike Scott's voicing of his poetic lyric was strong and assured too. All in all it was a bold opening statement for a young band. Being prepared to stand apart meant that this is a track that has weathered the ravages of time very well indeed.

70
JAMES BROWN
Bring It On…Bring It On
The Night Time Is The Right Time
45
Sonet

The great James Brown was at this stage adrift and rudderless. Now recording for a small independent label, the parent album of this single was inconsequential and dispensable but on these A- and B-side cuts, he and his band returned to the hard funk style that he had practically invented and hit the sweet spot one more time.

69
HEAVEN 17
Temptation/We Live So Fast
2
Virgin

Often cleverness that manifested itself in overly high ambition and heavy conceptual theories weighed down the music of Heaven 17 and made it stodgy and difficult to stomach. Here though, they pulled off the marriage between conceptual thought and highly enjoyable pop. The concept came from Martin Ware to write a song about rising sexual tension where the music keeps rising alongside the emotions, and based on 'The Lord's Prayer'! It sounds preposterous, but they pulled it off. They added the voice of Carol Kenyon to go alongside that of Glenn Gregory, it lit the blue touch paper and the track had lift-off. It climbed and climbed, higher and higher until the tension was finally released in a finale where Carol Kenyon hits a series of high notes until she sounds absolutely spent and unable to continue any longer.

68
RUN-D.M.C.
It's Like That
Sucker M.C.'s (Krush Groove 1)
NO CHART PLACING
Profile Records

This was the debut single of Run-D.M.C. and it changed the direction of hip-hop. It ushered in a new generation of artists of a more abrasive nature who would talk about their lives on the streets and point the finger at those in authority who both neglected their welfare and persecuted them. The sound was tough and strikingly stark. While the two rappers spat out lines about high prices, unemployment, war, and a sense of accepting these as inevitabilities, they conclude on an optimistic note, encouraging people to put aside prejudices and find strength in unity.

67
U2
Sunday Bloody Sunday
Endless Deep
NO CHART PLACING
Island Records

Never issued as a British single, this most iconic U2 song was nonetheless widely available as an import from the Netherlands. The song looks at the events of the Bloody Sunday massacre of 1972 through the eyes of a horrified onlooker. Explicit lines that make plain its rejection of all paramilitary groups on both sides of the conflict contained in the original lyric were removed when the song came to be recorded - a necessary omission to protect the group from real danger of retaliation by gunmen. Musically, the song is a scorching powerhouse of a performance and is sung with true passion as befits a song that preaches humanitarian love over the cycle of perpetual violence that seemed to be consuming Ireland.

66
TOM WAITS
In The Neighborhood/Singapore
Tango Till They're Sore/16 Shells
NO CHART PLACING
Island Records

While Tom Waits' earlier music had been more than respectable, here he took a quantum leap, stylistically and qualitatively. 'In The Neighborhood' is one of his finest songs – he uses the waltzing style and sound of a New Orleans funeral procession whilst vividly describing the day-to-day lives of a collection of down-at-heel characters in an entertaining and sympathetic portrait of a neglected community.

65
DAVID SYLVIAN AND RYUICHI SAKAMOTO
Forbidden Colours
The Seed And The Sower
16
Virgin

Sakamoto had starred alongside David Bowie in the flawed cinematic portrayal of life in a Japanese prisoner of war camp that was *Merry Christmas, Mr Lawrence*. What was beyond criticism in the film was the score written by the ex-Yellow Magic Orchestra leader. It was outstanding and featured this version of the main theme with a lyric and vocal courtesy of ex-Japan singer David Sylvian. With a title taken from a novel by Yukio Mishima that, like the film, deals with repressed homosexuality, Sakamoto's piece is stark, oriental-flavoured and haunting. Sylvian's performance is equally haunting - his approach to the song is measured to perfection as he gives voice to the internal strife of a man torn between his longing and his faith.

64
JUNIOR DELAHAYE
Working Hard For The Rent Man
Mystic Revelation
NO CHART PLACING
Wackie's Disco 709

Junior Delahaye was a prodigious talent - writing, singing, producing and playing all the instruments on his releases. This gem decries the injustice of life working for little pay and the struggle that ensues. He is sweet-voiced and the groove is gentle, featuring a distinctive guitar accompaniment, dub stylings, melodica and scat singing.

63
D.J. AFRIKA BAMBAATAA
Death Mix/Death Mix
NO CHART PLACING
Paul Winley Records

This was recorded at a live jam at James Monroe High School in the Bronx in 1979 on a hand-held tape deck. Copies were passed around, and in 1983 these 19 minutes were committed to wax and released, much to Bambaataa's displeasure. It's murky and there is tape hiss to contend with, but beneath that is the sound of Bambaataa spinning and cutting tracks, such as Yellow Magic Orchestra's 'Computer Games' and The Jackson Five's 'Great To Be Here'. Meanwhile rappers 'The Cosmic Force' are on hand to throw down some jive and high-spirited chanting. This is an iconic record, capturing a taste of the atmosphere of a thrilling moment in time. Even the cover art proved to be iconic, as it was later recycled in tribute by no less a figure than DJ Shadow.

62
THE FALL
The Man Whose Head Expanded
Ludd Gang
NO CHART PLACING
Rough Trade

Opening with the sound of a saloon bar space invader machine, the song moves through several stages - from a steady drum and bass riff to almost nothingness, before speeding up and featuring a keyboard part from Craig Scanlon who, at the finale, picks up his guitar to play out on. Lyrically Mark Smith describes in humorous style a man who becomes paranoid by swallowing misinformation, who believes people on television steal his words. Another example of the utterly compelling and peerless genius of The Fall.

61
THE VERLAINES
Death And The Maiden
CD, Jimmy Jazz And Me
NO CHART PLACING
Flying Nun Records

References within the lyric to the shooting of Arthur Rimbaud by fellow poet and lover Paul Verlaine (from whom the band took their name), as well using the titular phrase "death of the maiden", referring to a painting by Egon Shiele which depicts a woman embracing a skeleton, indicates what a cultured bunch this New Zealand outfit were. Aided by a quickly strummed guitar, they create a jangling sound that breaks into razor sharp staccato bursts through the choruses and adds a free-form electric organ section into its middle. The song unfolds as an intoxicating mix of arresting imagery and ramshackle tuneage.

60
CASCO
Cybernetic Love / Cybernetic Love (Instrumental)
NO CHART PLACING
CGD

Salvatore Cusato is perhaps *the* major figure in Italo-disco music. He had been a DJ playing a mixture of soul and glam rock when a series of chance encounters with Giorgio Moroder introduced him to the synthesiser and gave him a passion for electronic music. His DJ career flourished but alongside it he began to make his own recordings as Casco (Italian for 'helmet') the most iconic and enduring being 'Cybernetic Love'. The track was strikingly elegant, pushed along by a bass that sounds like liquid. Melodic synth lines are woven together into a luscious texture whilst robotic vocals sit atop the creation like the cherry on a cake waxing lyrical about love between man and machine.

59
THE GO-BETWEENS
Cattle And Cane / Heaven Says
NO CHART PLACING
Rough Trade

Sat in Nick Cave's London apartment with Cave in a heroin-induced comatose state, Grant McLennan picked up Cave's acoustic guitar and composed this song consisting of snapshots of life at home in Queensland, reflecting the homesickness he felt. With help from Robert Forster, its stumbling and jerky time signature came together. Lindy Morrison played an exceptional drum part, McLennan sang as though in a dream, and the complete song captured a feeling of lost innocence. It was yet another subtle, minor masterpiece from The Go-Betweens that was destined to be ignored by media and general public alike. It must have been, at best, bitter-sweet when their unacknowledged influence enabled the likes of Arcade Fire to become global stars, utilising a coarse approximation of The Go-Betweens' sound.

58
BAUHAUS
She's In Parties / Departure
26
Beggars Banquet

Northampton's Bauhaus were too derivative a mix of The Birthday Party darkness and Bowiesque flash to ever be considered a great band. They did, though, have fabulous cheekbones, giving them teen appeal, and intermittently released some fabulous singles. This was a prime example, and the band's swansong. They borrowed the cavernous atmospherics that Martin Hannett had gifted to Joy Division and incorporate added hooks, both musical and lyrically, and then let singer Peter Murphy perform a vocal which is stylistically somewhere betwixt 'Ziggy Stardust' and 'The Laughing Gnome'. It is high camp. It is boys dressing up posing and preening. And it is great pop!

57
THE S.O.S. BAND
Just Be Good To Me
Just Be Good To Me (Long Version)
13
Tabu Records

The S.O.S. Band's name was an abbreviation of 'Sound of Success', and from their 1977 beginnings they did enjoy success. But it was the introduction of Jimmy Jam and Terry Lewis as producer/writers that took them to a higher plateau of artistic and commercial achievement. 'Just Be Good To Me' was an electro-funk epic of *Ben Hur* proportions. At the base of the song is an extraordinary rhythm created using a Roland drum machine, and over that are layers and layers of musical colourings. It is grandstanding for sure, but with impeccable taste displayed. Lead vocalist Mary Davis excels by using the muscular rhythms as a springboard to deliver a performance that is supple and nuanced.

56
PUBLIC IMAGE LTD
This Is Not A Love Song
Public Image
5
Virgin

John Lydon's response to the accepted wisdom that "love songs yield hits" was to release the mischievous 'This Is Not A Love Song' which gave PiL their highest chart placing. Also tackled in the lyric is the accusation that Lydon had sold out. He sticks his tongue firmly into his cheek whilst claiming he was "going over to the other side". With guitar and drums as accompaniments, a vocal of dripping sarcasm is unleashed between the high voltage rocker riffs - conceptualism in the guise of pop music.

55
WALL OF VOODOO
Mexican Radio
Call Of The West
64
Illegal Records

Originating in Los Angeles, Wall of Voodoo combined synthesiser and drum-machined new wave style with spaghetti western and country and western leanings. This mix was perfectly captured in 'Mexican Radio', a skewed tribute to the cross-border broadcasts they would pick up. With singer Stan Ridgway's already highly distinctive delivery enhanced with echo placed on his vocal, and mariachi-style harmonica break featuring prominently in the song, it transported this listener from his damp Mancunian surroundings to the sunbaked, dusty, desert towns of southern California.

54
PRINCE CHARLES AND THE CITY BEAT BAND
Cash (Cash Money)
Jungle Stomp
78
Virgin

Timing is vitally important, and Prince Charles and the City Beat Band were unfortunate in getting their timing badly wrong. They appeared peddling a brand of electro funk in a post-Funkadelic style, dressed like a gang in street tough threads. They'd worked hard on their sound and their image, but to no avail as the music world was consumed with hip-hop, and to a lesser extent, go-go music. There wasn't room for another form of black music in the white-dominated media, so they went unnoticed. The shame was they were damned good, as illustrated on this single - a riot of squelching synth bass, cool call and response vocals, and a flute solo that is sublime in its funkiness.

53
N.O.I.A.
The Rule To Survive / Night Is Made For Love
NO CHART PLACING
Italian Records

Another innovative Italo-disco record. Instrumentally sleek and stylish, its synthesiser lines are crystalline, and the male vocal has an otherworldly quality, almost as if it was performed by an android.

52
FELT
Penelope Tree / A Preacher In New England / Now Summer's Spread Its Wings Again
NO CHART PLACING
Cherry Red

Penelope Tree was a top swinging 60s fashion model associated with photographer to the stars, David Bailey. Here, atop a backing that combines Tom Verlaine-style elegance with Hank Marvin-like twang, the lyric reveals singer Lawrence examining the dislocation from normality and sense of loneliness that Ms. Tree must have experienced within her bubble of fame. Troublingly, he reveals these feelings are easy for him to imagine.

51
THE THE
This Is The Day
Mental Healing Process
71
Some Bizzare

A very young Matt Johnson wrote this song addressed to himself, as his life was on the cusp of change - there are myriad possibilities, so many that life can feel overwhelming. "This is the day when things fall into place" he sings, seemingly unconvinced. The song is universal in its sentiments but personal in its execution. And it is carried on a lilting melody by a haunting harmonica that drifts through the sensitively-paced backing track.

50
THE SMITHS
This Charming Ma
Jeane
25 (1992 - 8)
Rough Trade

The Smiths were big news, and this, their second single, was good enough to live up to the sky high expectations that were placed on their slender shoulders. It was recorded at Stockport's Strawberry Studios and its punchy production was a cut above the sound quality of a typical independent release. Tunesmith Johnny Marr was an excellent guitar player who was tenacious in his quest to achieve the sound he heard in his head. To that end he worked hard in the studio to create a multi-textured tapestry of guitar takes. He was aided by a rhythm section who operated wonderfully well together and were perfectly suited to the Smiths' sound. Andy Rourke grooved on bass like Motown's James Jameson, whilst the drumming of Mike Joyce was crisp and propulsive.

The singer was quick-witted and theatrical, his use of arcane language highly imaginative. His lyrics portrayed himself as a sensitive soul, somewhat out of step with the harsh modern environment. He would create his own world, based on studied good manners, a portrayal of kindness and seemingly high principles. This record captured all of this, and The Smiths became a beacon of light to a swathe of devoted fans who bought into this image of outsider sensitivity. They invested their love and belief into the group, placing them atop a pedestal, only to be left bereft when in later years, the band's former singer and chief beneficiary of their affections, revealed himself as a sinister, deeply cynical, racially motivated bigot. In doing so, he betrayed the faith of a generation.

49
BOB MARLEY
AND THE WAILERS
Buffalo Soldiers
Buffalo (Dub)
4
Tuff Gong

Two years on from Bob Marley's death came this single, recorded in 1978, that would prove to be one of the most popular tracks ever released bearing his name. 'Buffalo Soldiers' were an American army cavalry regiment formed in 1866 comprising black ex-slaves who were sent to assist white settlers to forcefully take native American lands in the so-called 'Indian Wars'. Marley delves into this history to make points about the mistreatment and oppression of black people in modern America, despite the role they played in helping to create it. The song was co-written by Noel "King Sporty" Williams, who supplied a lively, dance-infused rhythm, while Marley, with such weighty subject matter, delivers in a serene and stately manner.

48
BANANARAMA
Cruel Summer/Summer Dub
(Special C.B. Mix)/Cairo
8
London Records

Bananarama were three young women housed, courtesy of Paul Cook, above the Sex Pistols' old rehearsal space. They named their band as a tongue-twisted version of Roxy Music single 'Pyjamarama' and came to the public's attention through collaborating with The Fun Boy Three. They were fun!

Writer/producers Swain and Jolley worked in conjunction with them and hit followed hit. 'Cruel Summer' was a subtle downbeat song in its lyric, bemoaning an oppressive heat that seems endless, accentuating the longing, the waiting, and wanting somebody to stop the loneliness. It is lifted by a gorgeous melody, and the relatable 'girls next door' style natural vocals blended together so well, that they melt cynicism and lift spirits.

47
WHAM!
Club Tropicana
Blue
4
Inner Vision

When taken at face value, what sounds like an ode to an escapist, hedonistic lifestyle, reveals itself on closer inspection to be a tongue-in-cheek critique of the then booming, '18-30' package holidays. The lyrics parody holiday brochure promises of smiling faces, brushing shoulders with stars, romance and a free bar. To match the lyric, the groove - which is heavily indebted to The Gap Band hit 'Burn Rubber On Me' - is given a makeover of Latin-flavoured horns and piano.

46
STOPP
I'm Hungry
Caramba Mix
NO CHART PLACING
Discomagic Records

Here was a record truly ahead of its time. It pre-dated acid house by half a decade. It is squelchy. It bounces. It is Italian, but found a home in Chicago.

45
HOWARD DEVOTO
Rainy Season
Rain Forest (Variation N16)
97
Virgin

Taken from Howard Devoto's only solo album, *Jerky Versions Of The Dream*, this was the obvious choice as a single. Where much of the album was dense to the point of being opaque, 'Rainy Season', whilst lyrically weighty, was handled with a lightness of touch and had a shimmering brightness. Dave Formula remains present from Devoto's former band, Magazine. His piano is at the heart of the song and is incandescent, whilst Devoto sings without the affectations that could be off-putting, delivering an outstanding performance.

44
GRACE JONES
Living My Life (Long Version)
Living My Life (Dub Version)
NO CHART PLACING
Island Records

This is a song with a curious history, as well as being an absolutely fantastic creation. 'Living my life' was recorded as the title track of Grace Jones' album of the same name, but omitted from the release. It has been suggested that its sparkling style clashed with the more restrained reggae feel of the album. Or alternatively, litigation was threatened by *Virgin Records* for the taking, without consent, of the Deutsch Amerikanische Freundschaft (DAF) track, 'Als Wär's Das Letzte Mal', as played here by the Compass Point Allstars. Eventually it was released as a blink-or-you'll-miss-it 12-inch single in the UK where those who heard it experienced Grace in titanic form, proudly singing an anthem of strength through defiance and self-determination - a rallying call for the persecuted outcasts at the margins of society, be they people of colour or those whose sexualities offended the puritanical.

43
THE GO-BETWEENS
Man O'Sand To Girl O'Sea
This Girl, Black Girl
NO CHART PLACING
Rough Trade

The Australian trio here became a quintet for the first time on record, with the addition of Robert Vickers on bass guitar. Whether it was his presence or mere coincidence, this single revealed another facet to The Go-Between's sound. Previously, the group had been restrained and introspective. On 'Man O'Sand to Girl O'Sea', they are as literate as always but express wretched desperation in a forceful manner, over a neo-garage rock stomp that leads to a thudding monosyllabic chorus. It is a song full of great lines and wonderful moments. No other Go-Betweens record would ever match the fervour of this magnificent single.

42
SOFT CELL
Soul Inside
You Only Live Twice
16
Some Bizzare

Their commercial peak was waning, as Soft Cell pushed themselves into explorations of sounds and feelings and resisted music industry pressure to present a cleaner cut, twee, synth-pop sound and image. On 'Soul Inside' the synths are more heavily textured than before, at points sounding frighteningly industrial. A whirling cacophony ensues that winds ever upwards, seemingly intent on becoming untethered from its moorings. Within this cyclone of sound Marc Almond, revealing his best Scott Walker-like croon, waxes existential, and cries that his damaged soul is being torn. The end was looking nigh for Soft Cell but they were exiting under their own terms.

41
VIRGINIA ASTLEY
Love's A Lonely Place To Be Soaring
NO CHART PLACING
Why Fi

Virginia Astley - a classically trained pianist, flautist, soprano, and ex-Ravishing Beauty - was not a prolific artist, but all her releases were worthy of investigation. Here she creates a sunny pastoral sound, evocative of a summer's day, and attaches to it a bitter-sweet lyric of longing for love, in a voice of church choir innocence.

40
THE STYLE COUNCIL
A Solid Bond In Your Heart
It Just Came To Pieces In My Hand
A Solid Bond In Your Heart (Instrumental)
11
Polydor

Paul Weller's decision to end the highly popular group, The Jam, was immediately vindicated. 1983 saw a run of superb singles that displayed the confident musical progression of their main creator. 'Speak Like A Child', 'Long Hot Summer' and 'Money-Go-Round' all took Weller's song-craft in different directions and all were deserved hits. This fourth single of the year was a song that had been recorded by The Jam and earmarked as their farewell single before 'Beat Surrender' was ultimately selected. In The Style Council's hands, the song is transformed and infinitely superior. It grooves with a classic soul feel, where previously it simply thumped. Weller sings without the strained machismo that had been evident and constricting in The Jam days. Every instrument seems to have space that makes the track flow effortlessly, and the seemingly free-form saxophone that is liberally sprayed across its surface, is masterful. Weller's lyric too, about striving for spiritual fulfilment, sounds sincere and uncontrived, and was an indication of his artistic growth.

39
ZZ TOP
Gimme All Your Lovin
If I Could Flag Her Down
10
Warner Bros. Records

In 1983 the world went crazy for ZZ Top. MTV picked up their video for 'Gimme All Your Lovin' and the sight of this trio of dusty dudes from the desert, in cowboy hats, shades and ridiculously long beards (except for the clean-shaven Frank Beard), having fun with the coolest looking car imaginable, was irresistible. The secret was out, and the best bar room boogie band on planet earth became hit-making superstars.

'Gimme All Your Lovin' was indeed a prime slice of ultra-sharp ZZ Top boogie; catchy, funny, rocking, were all applicable adjectives. Add one of Billy Gibbons' extraordinary guitar solos to the mix and it was no surprise that this record went stratospheric.

38
WESTWOOD/CASH
Psycho For Your Love
Work Those Joints
NO CHART PLACING
Southern Sun Records

Danan Potts spent time at the Detroit Recording Institute where he took an interest in what future Detroit techno wizard and producer Juan Atkins – then a student on the production course - was creating. Influenced to do something himself, some of Atkins' style was appropriated and Potts released an early techno single titled 'Go Bananas', under the name Superlife. Following that, he did some work with PFunk head George Clinton, before teaming up with Orlando Cash and releasing 'Psycho For Your Love' - a lethal combination of techno and funk. It is dance floor manna from heaven that still tickles.

37
THIS MORTAL COIL
Song To The Siren
Sixteen Days Reprise
66
4AD

Tim Buckley had included 'Song To The Siren' on his album *Starsailor*, a wild, thrilling journey into the soul of the singer with shining moments throughout. And yet 'Song To The Siren' is the song that shines brightest - a devastatingly beautiful epic with a lyric by Larry Becket that uses imagery from Greek mythology of sirens luring sailors to their doom.

Here, as part of the project instigated by Ivo Watts of 4AD to record versions of obscure songs using his label's artists under the name This Mortal Coil, Elizabeth Fraser and Robin Guthrie of the Cocteau Twins were tasked with serving up an interpretation of Buckley's masterpiece. They treated it with great reverence, as a hymn, and delivered an extraordinary performance of incandescent wonder. Over a minimal backing, Fraser uses her magnificent voice superbly, exercising great restraint. It is a marvel, and stands as equal to Tim Buckley's original take on the song.

36
FUN BOY THREE
Our Lips Are Sealed
Our Lips Are Sealed (Urdu Version)
We're Having All The Fun
Going Home
7
Chrysalis

The GoGo's were the support act to The Specials on a British seaside tour, and Jane Wiedlin and Terry Hall briefly became a couple. When Wiedlin returned to Los Angeles, she received some lyrics in a letter from Hall and wrote music to them. The resulting song was 'Our Lips Are Sealed'. It was recorded by the Go-Go's as the opening track on their debut album *Beauty and the Beat.* Upbeat and infectious, it subsequently became a hit single. Two years later Hall was no longer a member of The Specials but part of the Fun Boy Three. With David Byrne of Talking Heads producing, they recorded their version of the song in a much gloomier style, ridding it of its bounce and revealing the song's lyrical dark heart. It was hypnotic and compelling, and also the last Fun Boy Three single to chart before they split.

35
TOOLS YOU CAN TRUST
Working And Shopping / The Work Ahead Of Us
NO CHART PLACING
Red Energy Dynamo

Tools You Can Trust consisted of core duo Ben Stedman and Rob Ward, with additional members coming and going. They were based in Hulme and I knew them well, played gigs with them and liked them a lot. Their sound was heavily percussion-based, combining drums and metallic objects with added tape effects and minimal guitar. They sang heavily-politicised songs of truth. On 'Working And Shopping', over a frenetic beat, Rob barks out, along with yelps and grunts, the tale of a hard-working man unable to afford his daughter's wedding dress.

34
VIOLENT FEMMES
Gone Daddy Gone / Add It Up
NO CHART PLACING
Slash

Violent Femmes hailed from Milwaukee, and were to folk rock what The Cramps were to rockabilly - strange, dark cousins. 'Gone Daddy Gone' was written by singer Gordon Gano, although he drops in a full verse from Willie Dixon's 'I Just Wanna Make Love To You'. It is played at full tilt and powered by xylophone with two highly eccentric xylophone solos. It is a song to twitch and tap toes to, a song that makes people feel happy. It was featured on Gnarls Barkley's 2006 album *St Elsewhere,* and released as a single to make another generation feel happy.

33
EDDY GRANT
Electric Avenue
Walking On Sunshine
2
ICE

'Electric Avenue' - so named because it was the first British market street to get electric lighting - is in Brixton, which, with its vibrant Caribbean population, became synonymous with racist policing in the 70s and 80s . Harassment and brutality were everyday occurrences that provoked the riots in the area in 1981. Eddy Grant was moved to write 'Electric Avenue' as a musical response. He uses a reggae rhythm played electronically, with guitar chords as punctuation. It is positively explosive-sounding, and a suitable base for a lyric describing the violence. It is militant, and Grant sings in an angry, harsh manner. Yet his knack for melody and his pop music nous, meant that the song's sing-along chorus resonated with people. The record became a huge international hit, despite its subject matter.

32
LOOSE JOINTS
Tell You (Today)
Tell You (Today) Part I & Part II
NO CHART PLACING
4th & Broadway

Loose Joints duo, Arthur Russell and Steve D'Aquisto, together with occasional collaborator Jocelyn Bowden who supplied a silky vocal, unleashed this brass-laden stomper onto the dance-floor. It's a jazz heavy thing of style and substance, that slips easily from the blazing horns into a piano frenzy, via a whistled solo. They were pushing the boundaries of what disco music was allowed to be - opening minds - and in doing so blazing a trail and providing inspiration for a generation who would follow in their wake.

31
ORANGE JUICE
Rip It Up / Snake Charmer
8
Polydor

Steven Daly and James Kirk had quit Orange Juice to form a new band called Memphis. They were replaced by Malcolm Ross from Josef K and Zeke Manyike, a drummer of repute who worked with The Style Council and The The. Undoubtedly, some ramshackle charm was lost in the change, but the compensation was a higher degree of musicality, whereby ideas that previously had been clutched at could now be grasped. 'Rip it Up' demonstrated the new band's strengths admirably. It's an excellent song about stubborn pride impinging on happiness. Full of fabulous lyrical allusion, it is blessed with a completely unforgettable chorus. It also charmingly alludes to Buzzcocks' song 'Boredom', both lyrically and musically, acknowledging an influence. The song is played with unhurried assurance and precision utilising Nile Rogers' style funk guitar and a synthesiser - previously unheard on an Orange Juice record - to add texture and enhance the groove.

30
AFRIKA BAMBAATAA
& SOUL SONIC FORCE
Renegades Of Funk
Renegades Chant
Renegades of Funk (Instrumental)
30
Tommy Boy

Heavy percussion, wild electro-funk and rapped lyrics, drawing parallels between the present day crop of street artists and the revolutionaries of the past. Ideas, words and sounds in a collision, aimed at waking up people to the vitality of what was current. "No matter how hard you try, you can't stop this now" was the opening statement - this record went boom!

29
MADONNA
Holiday/Think Of Me
6
(Re-release 1985, No.2, 1991, No.5)
Sire

Madonna's previous singles, 'Everybody' and 'Burning Up', had marked her as being "interesting", in a very niche, post-disco way. But with 'Holiday' her true potential was unleashed, and her unstoppable rise began. Written by members of disco act Pure Energy, the song was sourced by producer John "Jellybean" Benitez who saw in it a potential hit. Madonna concurred, and the two of them worked on an arrangement. The song is slender but has a universal appeal in its celebration of taking a vacation. It was performed with a deft lightness of touch, and without sacrificing any dance-floor potency, its overt poppiness was brought to the fore.

28
BARBARA MASON
Another Man
Another Man (Rap)
45
West End Records

Barbara Mason had been a hit making soul singer in the mid-60s who was now reinventing herself as a kind of post-disco diva. Her singing voice retained all its expressiveness, and over a delicious crawling electro groove, with a filthy bass sound, she recounts the tale of stealing a man from a love rival, only to discover he is bisexual, and with huge regret she realises she is losing him to another man.

27
CABARET VOLTAIRE
Yashar/Yashar
NO CHART PLACING
Factory

Taken from their album *2X45*, and put into the hands of John Robie, this single offers up two of his mixes of the track. Although funk elements had been embedded in Cabaret Voltaire's music from their beginnings, it had never been overt. Robie was tasked with locating that element and steering this music towards the dance-floor. He retains the song's *The Outer Limits* sampled vocal intro, but from there reconstructs much of the track, introducing an Italo-disco style piano part, whilst retaining the original machine groove. The treatment is a huge success, transforming the sound of the group, while retaining their essence.

26
ECHO AND THE BUNNYMEN
The Cutter
Way Out And Up We Go
8
Korova

'The Cutter' is a fine combination of eastern influences echoing The Beatles' mid-60s experiments in psychedelia, along with scything guitar and a relentless rhythmic base that propels the song towards a series of crescendos. Ian McCullough, meanwhile, conveys a sense of unease as he sings a lyric that seems to look inwards, and strives to address an issue of obsessive self-criticism and constant editing of ideas in pursuit of perfection.

25
WAS NOT WAS
Knocked Down, Made Small (Treated Like A Rubber Ball)/
Man Vs. The Empire
Brain Building
NO CHART PLACING
Geffen Records

Was Not Was released the album *Born to Laugh at Tornadoes* to huge critical acclaim but sales-wise it tanked. The obvious single was 'Knocked Down, Made Small' which effervescently told a tale of defiance, and despite adversity, finding the resilience to triumph. The song's chorus was unforgettable and lead vocalist Sweet Pea Atkinson sang it with complete conviction. It should have been a hit.

24
THE POLICE
Every Breath You Take
Murder By Numbers
1
A&M Records

Despite their popularity and run of hits that were absolutely impossible to avoid, I was sniffily indifferent to the dubious charms of The Police. Their cod-reggae stylings seemed cold and calculated. Furthermore, the affected voicings of the singer were stomach-churning and made me want to puke. And then they released 'Every Breath You Take' which silenced my critical voice. It is a song about possessiveness to the point of obsessiveness - creepy and nasty. It's genius lies in hiding its true meaning by being disguised as a love song. It is performed with huge economy, which adds a hint of menace to the song that is adorned by a guitar part played by Andy Summers, influenced by the classical composer Bartok.

23
THE CURE
The Lovecats
Speak My Language
7
Fiction Records

Apparently influenced by Patrick White's novel *The Vivisector*, and performed in a playful faux-jazz style 'The Lovecats' seems to be a metaphorical exploration of the cruel treatment of society's most vulnerable - here being thrown into a sack and hurled into the sea to drown. Then again, it might not be! Either way it's a cracking tune, and Robert Smith's vocal purrs are highly entertaining and worthy of Eartha Kitt.

22
CYBOTRON
Clear / Industrial Lies
NO CHART PLACING
Fantasy

Kraftwerk samples and ground-breaking electro-looping with hard hitting beats and treated robot voices - all the elements of a future techno style were in place on this thrill-a-minute sonic adventure, created by Juan Atkins, Richard Davis and John "Jon 5" Housely. The early 80s often felt as though the future had arrived - 'Clear' soundtracks that feeling.

21
DAVID BOWIE
Modern Love
2
EMI America

Bowie reflects cynically upon the complexities of the world, upon faith and love. He stands apart yet cannot disguise his longing for involvement and human interaction. He channels his love for the music of Little Richard's old time rock 'n' roll in the pounding piano and drum base of this song. He incorporates a call and response style into the chorus, that is a 50s throwback. On board he has Stevie Ray Vaughan, a guitar player who can unleash powerful intensity, and leaves him sidelined as a crisp horn section play the riffs and solos that speaks the musical language of a bygone age. And yet these elements do not seem nostalgic, existing as ghostly traces within something utterly contemporary - mere echoes. This was a masterful, intriguing, shape-shifting David Bowie single. None of his sure-footed artistic instincts were misplaced just yet.

20
EURYTHMICS
Sweet Dreams (Are Made Of This)
2
RCA

Here was a song that came from an unhappy place in the soul of Annie Lennox. It had been written in the aftermath of the split of her previous band, The Tourists. She described herself as being in a dream state, feeling depressed and nihilistic. It came together when Dave Stewart began playing a bass riff on a synthesiser and Annie Lennox added a second synth part. The record company were reluctant to release the song as a single - it had no chorus, and despite Dave Stewart adding a few uplifting lyrics, it was still for the most part dark and gloomy. Common sense finally prevailed and Eurythmics had the breakthrough hit they had sought.

19
JOHN CALE
I Keep A Close Watch
Close Watch
NO CHART PLACING
Island Records/ZE Records

The mercurial Welshman, John Cale, originally included 'I Keep a Close Watch' on his 1975 album *Helen of Troy*. He returned to this outstanding track whilst recording the experimental *Music For A New Society*, adding bagpipes to an otherwise stark reading of the song. Here the two versions were placed on one single. It is a beautiful, brilliant song, slight in construction, but filled with expressive power. Cale flips from magisterial to anguished over the course of these twinned takes of one of his most memorable songs, that was allegedly at one point considered by Frank Sinatra as suitable for him to record.

18
THE SPECIAL AKA
Racist Friend/Bright Lights
60
Two-Tone Records

In the aftermath of The Specials' bitter split, Jerry Dammers steered a newly-configurated line up into the bleakest places pop music had ever ventured. The Special AKA's first single - 'The Boiler'- had been a harrowing account of rape, the second - 'War Crimes' - about Israel's bombing of Lebanese civilians in Beirut. Now came this polemic about racists within our midst. Many condemned it as being too preachy, too extreme, too dogmatic. I thought it was a brilliant simplification of a troubling issue - as Jerry put it, "if you have a racist friend, now is the time for your friendship to end".

17
FREEEZ
I.O.U.
I Dub U
2 (re-release 1987, No.23)
Beggars Banquet

Written by and produced by Arthur Baker, remixed by John "Jellybean" Benitez, this is electro that is utterly captivating. Its chorus is inane, but that was the whole point. It utilised repetition superbly - even today it continues to conjure up images of beat-boxes, body popping and BMX's. Arthur Baker would use this song's DNA to create New Order hits 'Confusion' and 'Shellshock'.

16
GRANDMASTER
& MELLE MEL
White Lines (Don't Do It)
White Lines (Don't Do It)
7
Sugar Hill Records

'White Lines' is no doubt a superb record, but its background is cloaked in duplicity. Firstly, it is a famous anti-drug song that concerns itself with the negative aspects of drug dealing as a career, and drug use as a lifestyle choice. But it was originally conceived as a celebration of a cocaine-fuelled party lifestyle, until commercial considerations saw the theme changed and the "don't do it" message introduced. It was then credited to Grandmaster & Melle Mel to give the impression that this was a Grandmaster Flash record. Flash had in fact severed ties with Sugar Hill Records by this point. Add to these points the fact that the track was a direct uncredited lift of 'Cavern', a single issued by Liquid Liquid on 99 Records, and the whole process looks alarmingly slipshod and compromised. And yet, the performance of the track by the Sugar Hill house band, particularly that of bassist Doug Wimbish, is razor sharp. And Melle Mel rides the rhythm with huge aplomb, so that ultimately we must conclude that this record truly shines.

15
RUFUS AND CHAKA KHAN
Ain't Nobody/Sweet Thing (Live)
8
Warner Bros. Records

'Ain't Nobody' was the biggest singles success enjoyed by Rufus in their decade long career. It perhaps felt bitter-sweet. Chaka Khan, by this point, had a flourishing solo career and had been tied to Rufus only due to contractual obligations. As a final goodbye for the band, she was persuaded to join them in a live farewell and album called *Stompin' at the Savoy* which included 'Ain't Nobody' as one of four studio tracks. Warner Bros. were not keen on issuing it as a single. Rufus keyboardist and song composer, David Wolinski, threatened to give the song to Michael Jackson for his *Thriller* album unless they relented. They did, and whether her heart was in it or not, Chaka Khan produced a scorching vocal performance as she proclaimed how good her man made her feel. Enhancing the voice was a track built around a looped keyboard part that was pure intoxication, and live drums imitating the programmed variant of Wolinski's demo recording.

14
MALCOLM MCLAREN
Double Dutch
She's Looking Like A Hobo
3
Charisma

Cultural magpie Malcolm McLaren, in cahoots with Trevor Horn, pilfers a tune called 'Puleng' by South African Mbaqanga group, The Boyoyo Boys, who instigated legal action to gain payment. He uses that to bring attention to the world of competition skipping and specifically the 'Double Dutch' - a skipping game name checking several troupes of practitioners from New York. In doing so, a great piece of eccentric pop was created. It was joyous and energetic and opened ears to a musical style that deserved a wider audience.

13
HERBIE HANCOCK
Rockit/Rough
8
CBS

Herbie Hancock was looking for a change of musical direction. He'd been an integral part of Miles Davis' 60s band that recorded the seminal albums *On the Corner, Jack Johnson* and *In a Silent Way*. His skills on keyboards were utilised on sessions with players such as Eric Dolphy and Grant Green. He formed his own genre-mashing group The Headhunters. Now his challenge was to remain contemporary in a new era. To that end, he hooked up with Michael Beinhorn and Bill Laswell of New York band Material and built a track incorporating programmed beats mixed with live Cuban bata drums. A guitar stab was sampled from a Led Zeppelin record. Deejay duo, The Infinity Rappers, provided a scratched section, and Hancock contributed the melody. It was dynamite, but they didn't know it until they played a tape loud through large speakers at a hi-fi shop. It attracted a group of amazed neighborhood youths, their reaction being the first indication that 'Rockit' would be a hit.

12
TALKING HEADS
Burning Down The House/
I Get Wild/Gravity
NO CHART PLACING
Sire

Talking Heads had 14 charting records in the UK but bizarrely 'Burning Down The House' didn't register at all, despite being the group's highest charting single in the USA. The song was inspired by Tina Weymouth and Chris Frantz attending a Parliament/Funkadelic show at Madison Square Gardens where the crowd chant of "burn down the house" lodged in Chris Frantz's memory. During a band jam that was locked into a funk groove, he kept shouting out the phrase. David Byrne amended it into 'Burning Down The House' and wrote a colourful, though meaningless, lyric where the words were chosen to fit the groove. It was an approach that served Talking Heads well - the song was a seamless and spinning ball of uplifting energy that had natural rhythm and dance-ability.

11
MICHAEL JACKSON
Beat It
Burn This Disco Out
3
Epic

Producer Quincy Jones encouraged Michael Jackson to write a rock song similar to 'My Sharona' by The Knack. Although he had never attempted to do anything similar, Michael Jackson set to work. He wrote a lyric about a gang fight, something that was alien to him as his upbringing had sheltered him from the street. He took inspiration from *West Side Story* and his imagination. For the music, he built a track heavy on synclavier, and a hybrid of real bass and a machined version. Drums and guitars were added - all that was needed was a guitar solo that needed to be dramatic and powerful. Eddie Van Halen obliged, adding scorching intensity. The creation was masterful, a combination of pop, dance and rock. It was a crucial record for Michael Jackson that hugely expanded his audience.

10
THE FALL
Kicker Conspiracy
Wings/Container Drivers/New Puritan
NO CHART PLACING
Rough Trade

This came as a two-single pack of four great songs, including two from their classic 1980 John Peel session ('Container Drivers' and New Puritan'). Lead track 'Kicker Conspiracy' had considerable impact - in 1983 football and football supporters were sneered at by liberal elitists. I suspect that Mark Smith partially wrote the song to antagonise Rough Trade who Mark perceived as middle class, liberal hippies. It is prescient nonetheless, predicting the be-suited money men stealing the game away from the working classes off the field, while on the field the rise of muscular athletic drones replaced the less dedicated but infinitely more skilled and entertaining likes of George Best. Given a drum-heavy, tribal sound and a chanted call and response vocal hook, this was The Fall standing totally at odds with the rest of the music business.

9
THE IMPOSTER
Pills and Soap/
(Extended Version)
16
Imp Records

Disturbed by the political climate in Thatcher's Britain and inspired by Grandmaster Flash single 'The Message' in that it spoke of the ugliest aspects of life, Elvis Costello (for he was the thinly-disguised Imposter), put pen to paper and headed for the studio. Over a stark arrangement of little more than drum machine and piano, he poured out his bile in a lyrical stream that compared the treatment of this country's ever-increasing economic underclass with the barbarous mistreatment of animals in the manufacture of cosmetics. Hard-hitting, accusatory and defiant, it was a brilliant piece of music that acted as a rallying cry against the uncaring and immoral high and mighty. It came at a time when opposition to Tory rule was largely unheard. They basked in a post-Falklands sea of grubby, jingoistic triumphalism, and the cult of personality built around their glorious, but evil, 'Iron Lady' filled them with the confidence to make ever more punitive attacks on the lower echelons of threadbare society.

8
DAVID BOWE
Let's Dance
Cat People (Putting Out Fire)
1
EMI America

For the next stage of his career David Bowie decided to become a superstar and have gigantic hits. To that end he recruited Chic rhythm guitarist extraordinaire Nile Rogers as producer and creative foil. Rogers, at Bowie's behest, eliminated the strange alien element that had long been a feature of Bowie's work, and replaced it with something solid and tight. Something with guaranteed dance-ability as the winning ingredient. Meanwhile Bowie simplified his approach - his lyric was slight and empty of meaning, but he sang it with power and precision hammering home the choruses. Blues guitarist Stevie Ray Vaughan plays a fiery solo towards the song's conclusion. Bowie had changed tack again - this unexpected swerve into the mainstream was brilliantly executed and delivered with huge panache. 'Let's Dance' was a huge triumph, though later attempts at replicating its success would see Bowie losing his musical soul along with a huge chunk of his original audience.

7
MICHAEL JACKSON/THE JACKSONS
Wanna Be Startin' Somethin'
Rock With You (Live)
8 (re-release 2009, No.57)
Epic

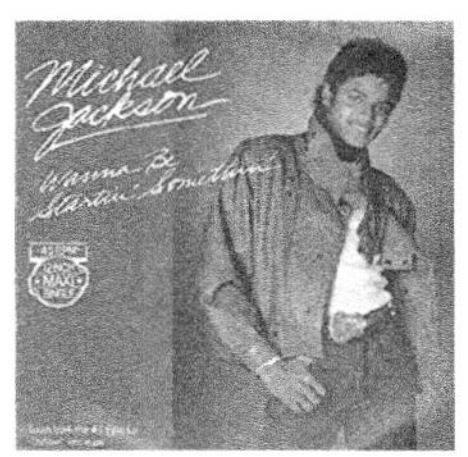

Michael Jackson supposedly wrote 'Wanna Be Startin' Somethin'' for his sister La Toya. It was a comment on her troubled relationship with her sisters-in-law, a riposte to the hurtful gossip she was subjected to. Ultimately, it was Michael who recorded the song, though it also featured in La Toya's live performances. A version was cut in 1978 for inclusion on his *Off The Wall* album, but ultimately omitted. This new take was made in 1982, and became the opening track and fourth single from his *Thriller* album. It is a sparkling, bright, upbeat song, combining disco with precision funk. A complex rhythm pattern propels it, while it also features sharp horn riffs and prominent female backing vocals. Jackson's singing performance is stupendous. He is at the edge of hyperactivity, absolutely frenzied though always just about in control. Michael's vocal range was wide, and he utilised it to thrilling effect. When he hits the top notes, the listening experience is one of head-spinning astonishment.

6
CYNDI LAUPER
Girls Just Want To Have Fun
Right Track Wrong Train
2
Portrait

Cyndi Lauper would prove over the years to be a formidable songwriter. But for her debut solo single, she chose to cover a song written by Robert Hazard who had recorded a demo version himself. 'Girls Just Want To Have Fun' had been conceived as being sung from the male perspective, but Cyndi Lauper changed the emphasis and in doing so created a feminist anthem, celebrating female camaraderie. Her point made, Cyndi Lauper goes to town with it and has an absolute ball with the song. She romps through it mischievously, fills it with her playful character whilst not neglecting to sing it superbly. It is a wild, weird, wonderful, and quite glorious jamboree of a record that might well have proved an impossible to follow 'albatross' to a lesser talent than Cyndi Lauper.

5
FRANKIE GOES TO HOLLYWOOD
Relax (Sex Mix)
Ferry 'Cross The Mersey/Relax
1
ZTT

Liverpudlian band Frankie Goes to Hollywood, featuring Holly Johnson (ex-Big In Japan) as lead vocalist, received a huge boost from appearing on Friday teatime TV staple, *The Tube.* They were an unsigned act and performed 'Relax', replete with a verse filched from David Lynch's *Eraserhead* soundtrack. Seen by Trevor Horn, they were signed to his label and work commenced on recording the song.

For the ensuing sessions the Frankies, with the exception of Holly Johnson, were jettisoned as Trevor Horn took control of what went on within the studio. A version with Ian Dury's Blockheads performing the track, was completed, and then scrapped as old-fashioned, before a more electronic version was attempted. With programmed rhythms, samples, heavy keyboard use, and stabs of guitar, it was built piece by piece. Holly Johnson gave his all vocally, and the record was released. ZTT minister of communication, Paul Morley, launched a bold advertising campaign, confidently highlighting the record's overt gay sex theme. It crept stealthily up the chart, taking nearly three months to hit the top position. The BBC, of course, banned it for its salacious, immoral content, but the record was unstoppable, clocking up a total of 59 weeks in the Top 75.

4
KRAFTWERK
Tour de France
Tour de France (Instrumental)
22 (remix 1999, No. 24)
EMI

The members of Kraftwerk were keen cyclists, celebrate the joy of riding and the most famous and iconic cycle race, the Tour de France. It was a stylistic departure for Kraftwerk following their explorations of hi-tech computers and their influence on human life. They now sound-tracked the altogether more primitive, but life-enhancing, bicycle, the ultimate 'man machine', where human engineering and physicality combine to provide an exhilarating eco-friendly mode of transportation. A simple percussive pattern forms the base of the song. It is aligned to a sweeping melody, and samples of voices and mechanical sounds associated with cycling - such as gears changing and wheels spinning - whilst the hard breathing and the human heart of the cyclist are also represented. Recorded in German, French and English it was released in multiple mixes so there is no definitive version of the song, but however it is heard, it is a true delight.

3
NEW ORDER
Blue Monday
The Beach
9 (re-released 1988 - 3; 1995 - 17;
2004 - 76; 2006 - 73)
Factory

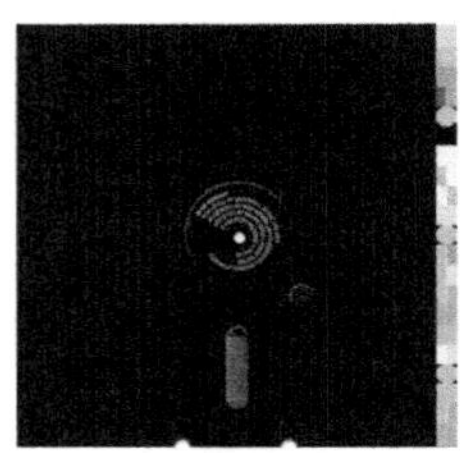

'Blue Monday' is a mishmash of ideas and influences that were coalesced by New Order to create a single that bridged 70s disco, punk attitude, Italo-disco and the electro grooves emanating from New York, creating something unique. The record established the group as a major force and would be a huge influence on the acid house scene towards the decade's end. It certainly bears a striking resemblance to the Gerry and The Holograms' single by C.P. Lee and John Scott from 1979. Equally, it is true that Bernard Sumner had visited exiled Mancunian Mark Reeder in Berlin and had returned with a pile of 12-inch dance singles he had heard in that city's clubs. These certainly bled into the recording, as did Peter Hook's spaghetti western influenced bass line. Ultimately, none of this matters because 'Blue Monday' transcends these influences and stands proudly as a monumental achievement for a group who had come together following tragedy, and not enjoyed an easy ride since their inception.

2
PRINCE
Little Red Corvette
Horny Toad/D.M.S.R.
54 (re-release 1985 - 2; 2016 - 70)
Warner Bros. Records

Where previous songs such as 'Head' and 'Dirty Mind' had been so blatant in their sexual content and had frightened away many sensitive types, 'Little Red Corvette' disguised its content in metaphor that helped make it more accessible. It is a song about a one night stand with a woman with a promiscuous history, who Prince advises to slow down and in essence find something more meaningful and spiritually rewarding than just the sexual act. Played completely by Prince, with the exception of a glittering guitar solo by Revolution band member Dez Dickerson who also sings backing vocal alongside Lisa Coleman and Jill Jones (Prince has them perform in a manner borrowed from Sly and the Family Stone). This is a sparse and percussive piece of funk, with choruses that explode gloriously. It tells its story eloquently - there is no excess instrumentation and no flim-flam, making it a classic single in classic single style.

1
MICHAEL JACKSON
Billie Jean
It's The Falling In Love
1
Epic

Every sound, every phrase, every element of this song was scrutinised to see if it could be improved. Perfection was being chased and between them Michael Jackson and Quincy Jones got close to touching that holy grail. Billie Jean is a futuristic feast of funk, chiselled to a razor sharp edge. It is also a psychological chiller, as Jackson refutes absolutely the allegations from the titular Billie Jean that he is the father of her son. There is, despite its prowling dance groove, a deep sadness at the heart of the song. We are left questioning, who is the father of the child? Why is the claim of paternity being made by the mother, and then in turn denied out of hand by the perceived father ? What will become of the child at the centre of the claim? Jackson handles the darkness of the material with a perfectly nuanced singing performance, taking much of it at the lower end of his vocal range using his falsetto to emphasise certain lines, before finally unleashing all his vocal ticks and squeals as the song builds towards its finale. Michael Jackson was already a huge star, possessed with an indisputable talent. Billie Jean took the perception of him to the next level, marking him as a musical genius.

1984

With the Conservative party emboldened by a landslide election victory in the aftermath of the Falklands war, the prime minister turned her attention towards a full frontal assault on the working classes and the trade unions whose members' actions had in a large part brought down the previous Conservative government under Ted Heath. Pit closures were announced in the nation's coal fields and a strike inevitably ensued as Thatcher picked a fight with the equally intransigent N.U.M president Arthur Scargill. The resulting war of rhetoric and ego-driven one-upmanship spoke more of doggerel than deep-seated convictions, meanwhile outside in the real world striking miners and their families were experiencing real hardships and deprivation as the authorities attempted to starve them back to work, the Police Force were co-opted as the government's army to wage war against pickets. With uniform numbers hidden and truncheons drawn they brutalised those carrying out legal union-approved action which brought the country close to civil war.

Battle lines were drawn, support for the miners was strong and collections of food and money to help them were organised on a regular basis from members of the dockers and railway workers unions who supported the miners. Violence soon escalated and in June what came to be known as 'The Battle of Orgreave' took place when a mass picket was met by police units in riot gear deploying dogs and riding horses into the crowds beating anyone to a pulp who's head could be smashed with a baton. The simultaneous threat of Nuclear war had not gone away either and nor had the Women's peace camps at Greenham Common although they were forcibly evicted for a second time in a dawn raid one April morning, many had returned by evening facing further vilification from the media and oppression from the authorities, they were highly-principled, noble women who were demonised. This was not a happy country ,

More trivial than these events, though still significant to me, was my social life. In Manchester any alternative scene was based around The Hacienda, there were few other places offering live music and a space to meet like-minded people for more hedonistic nights. A club night in Bernard's Bar (later South nightclub) called 'Stuffed Olives' offered electronic dance music and illicit thrills in one the city's first gay nights. Meanwhile I improved my mind by reading a good deal and killed brain cells by overindulgence in recreational drinking and potion abuse. Somehow my group, The Hamsters, reformed and played gigs at Manhattan's, The Hacienda (twice) and Manchester Polytechnic before falling out again and splitting, it was frustrating and disappointing. Still, life rolled on as I watched live gigs, bought more records and bowled about the country watching football.

NOTABLE EVENTS 1984

The space shuttle *Challenger* is launched, Astronauts Bruce McCandless and Robert L Stewart make the first untethered space walk.

Constantine Chernenko succeeds Yuri Andropov as General secretary of the Communist Party of the Soviet Union.

The Miners Strike begins in March and lasts throughout the year.

Sinn Fein's Gerry Adams and three others are shot and wounded in an attack by the UVF.

WPC Yvonne Fletcher is shot dead by a gunmen leading to a police siege on the Libyan Embassy in London.

Researchers in the USA announce their discovery of the AIDS virus.

Barefoot South African runner Zola Budd, controversially granted British citizenship, collides with USA athlete and 'face of the games' Mary Decker at the Olympic Games in LA, neither win medals.

Unaware he is on air during a radio broadcast President Ronald Reagan announces 'we begin bombing (Russia) in five minutes'.

The UK and the Republic of China sign an agreement to return Hong Kong to Chinese rule in 1997.

The first episode of *Thomas The Tank Engine* is broadcast, narrated by Ringo Starr.

The provisional IRA plot to assassinate Margaret Thatcher fails - a bomb is detonated in the Grand Hotel, Brighton during the Conservative Party conference on the eve of her speech - five innocent victims die.

A BBC television news report by Michael Buerk reveals the enormity of the humanitarian disaster brought on by famine in Ethiopia and prompts Boomtown Rats frontman Bob Geldof to form Band Aid - the resulting single reaches number one at Christmas.

Indian prime minister Indira Gandhi is assassinated by her two Sikh bodyguards. Anti-Sikh riots break out and many thousands of people are murdered in Hindu majority areas.

The Sandinista Front wins the Nicaraguan general election.

The Bhopal disaster in India sees more than 23,000 die and more than half a million injured following a chemical leak at an American-owned pesticide plant - it is the worst industrial accident in history.

Crack cocaine appears in Los Angeles and soon spreads across the USA creating what is termed the crack epidemic.

The unconquerable West Indies cricket team, led by Lancashire captain Clive Lloyd and starring Viv Richards and Malcolm Marshall, steamroller England 5-0 in the summer test series in what their supporters proclaim a 'Blackwash'.

During the 1983/84 football season Manchester United are knocked out of the FA Cup by Third Division Bournemouth and eliminated from the League Cup by Oxford United but, typical of United at this time, they somehow turn around a two-goal deficit against mighty Barcelona (including Maradona) in the Cup Winners' Cup before narrowly losing narrowly to Juventus. They briefly threaten to join the title race but yet another injury to Bryan Robson means they trail in fourth behind 'you know who'.

NOTABLE BIRTHS

Darren Fletcher; Andres Iniesta; Mark Zuckerberg; Duffy; Bastian Schweinsteiger; Dizzee Rascal

NOTABLE DEATHS

Alexis Korner; Johnny Weissmuller; Jackie Wilson; Yuri Andropov; Marvin Gaye; Tommy Cooper; Count Basie; Diana Dors; Andy Kaufman; John Betjeman ; Eric Morecombe; Big Mama Thornton; Ed Gein; James Mason; Richard Burton; Truman Capote ; JB Priestley; Leonard Rossiter; François Truffaut; Indira Gandhi; Sam Peckinpah.

NOTABLE FILMS

Once Upon a Time In America
The Terminator
Paris, Texas
Ghostbusters
Blood Simple
The Killing Fields
Gremlins
The Karate Kid
A Nightmare on Elm Street
Indiana Jones and the Temple of Doom
Amadeus

NOTABLE BOOKS

The Unbearable Lightness of Being - Milan Kundera
The Wasp Factory - Iain Banks
Empire of the Sun - JG Ballard
The Witches of Eastwick - John Updike
Money - Martin Amis
Finding the Centre - VS Naipaul
The Man Whose Teeth Were All Exactly Alike - Philip K Dick
Ma Rainey's Black Bottom - August Wilson
The Night of the Ripper - Robert Bloch
Unsung Heroes of Rock'N'Roll - Nick Tosches

100
THE FUZZTONES
Bad News Travels Fast/Brand New Man (and a Brand New Car)
NO CHART PLACING
Midnight Records

Taking their name from the guitar effect used by The Rolling Stones on their single '(I Can't Get No) Satisfaction', these New Yorkers were doing nothing new or particularly original. But what they did was achieved with spirit and panache. This has a riff nicked from Jethro Tull's 'Locomotive Breath' – it's revved up, offering a snotty lyric that leads to a catchy chorus. A psych-style guitar break is thrown into the mix and that's it! A glorious slice of rock 'n' roll.

99
DAVID BOWIE
Blue Jean
Dancing with the Big boys
6
EMI Records

Second-rate Bowie still wasn't bad, and this was second-rate Bowie, easily his worst single since 'The Laughing Gnome'! It was, nevertheless, a stand-out track compared to much of the dross served up on his *Tonight* album. Based around an Eddie Cochran-style riff, it's an up-tempo rocker performed immaculately well and given a beautiful studio polish, also containing a lovely saxophone part. Those plus points must be balanced against the fact that 'Blue Jean' is little more than a collection of clichés in its construction with a tawdry, mildly-offensive lyric designed to appeal to his new undiscerning mass audience.

98
THE SMITHS
William, It Was Really Nothing/How Soon Is Now?/Please, Please, Please, Let Me Get What I Want
17
Rough Trade

Mancunian rockers The Smiths enjoyed a successful 1984 with three Top 20 singles, turning them into bona fide pop stars. This one is widely perceived as a bitchy, coded message aimed at Billy McKenzie of The Associates who Smith's singer Stephen Morrissey had briefly been close to.

97
SECESSION
Touch (Part 3)/Touch (Part 4)
NO CHART PLACING
Beggars Banquet

Secession came from Edinburgh and went through numerous line-up changes before arriving at this point where they found a musical style with which they were comfortable. 'Touch' is electro-pop of the highest order. The band conjure up a highly atmospheric piece. Synthesisers add colour and texture over chattering rhythms on a track that lends itself to the sombre melancholic vocals.

96
PLUSTWO
Mad Radio/New Sensation
NO CHART PLACING
MIO Records

An elegant Italo-disco track on one hand, it also has a zany light-heartedness about its vocals that lend the track a naïve charm. This is utterly beguiling and sounds like listening to separate songs played on the radio at the same time.

95
NEWCLEUS
Automan (Special Edit)
Where's the Beat (Special Edit)
Automan (Dub Version)
NO CHART PLACING
Sunnyview

Newcleus were an electro group from Brooklyn NYC. Their single, 'Jam on Revenge', was a highly-prized and highly-rated track amongst the hip-hop fraternity. 'Automan' is a glorious slice of electronic funk with a pulsing riff that seemed like it was beamed down from a spaceship orbiting earth. It reappeared in sampled form to send the track 'Rhythm is a Dancer' by Snap to the top of the charts in the early '90s.

94
SCOTT WALKER
Track Three/Blanket Roll Blues
NO CHART PLACING
Virgin Records Ltd.

Informally titled 'Delayed', 'Track Three' was Scott Walker's comeback single. It was his first since the brief Walker Brothers resurrection ended with the release of 'The Electrician' in 1978. It turned out to also be the last UK single he would ever release. Walker melds his voice with that of backing vocalist Billy Ocean. They harmonize fabulously well together, their voices soaring. The musical backdrop is atmospheric and other worldly and there are no musical hooks or choruses. 'Track Three' is uncompromised and uncompromising.

The flip side, 'Blanket Roll Blues', is notable for containing the only song lyric written by playwright Tennessee Williams, originally sung by Marlon Brando in the film *The Fugitive Kind.*

93
RUN DMC
Rock Box
Rock Box (Vocal Dub Version) Rock Box (Dub Version)
NO CHART PLACING
Profile Records

Run DMC had not wanted to do it – "it" meaning using guitar on a hip-hop track. They had sorted out the beat using a DMX drum machine. Rhymes were written which compared other rap crews unfavourably with themselves. Ready to go, they laid down the track in a traditional hip-hop manner and went home. At this point Larry Smith, who co-produced alongside Russell Simmons, took matters into his own hands, adding bass, tambourine and keyboards. He then fetched in his friend Eddie Martinez to play wigged out hair metal guitar to the track. Run DMC did not like it and the record label were unsupportive. DJs, however, were massively enthusiastic. It was fresh and new. 'Rock Box' reached the ears of white rock kids and altered the trajectory of Run DMC's career. Hearing it inspired The Beastie Boys to adopt the rock-rap formula that launched their commercial breakthrough.

92
BANANARAMA
Robert De Niro's Waiting/Push!
3
London Records

Brilliant summer pop that's as bright as a button and full of hooks in all the right places. Intriguingly, beneath the surface lurks a darkness. The song is ostensibly concerned with a girl's hero worship of Robert De Niro, in which she has a fantasy relationship with the film star, and is idealised into something sweet and safe. It is, however, implied that the reason she takes refuge inside illusionist thought is that she has been the victim of a date rape and no longer has enough trust or confidence to engage in the real world with real people.

91
SONIC YOUTH FEATURING LYDIA LUNCH
Death Valley '69
NO CHART PLACING
Iridescence Records

Referencing the Manson Family and The Beatles' track 'Helter Skelter', which had been misunderstood so dramatically that it was interpreted as a message to commit the Tate-Labianca murders, Sonic Youth, with the help of a chillingly deranged little girl lost vocal from Lydia Lunch, create a swirling vortex of raging, guitar-led, thrillingly intense noise that evokes the madness of the song's subject matter.

90
FLYING LIZARDS
Sex Machine (Extended Version)/
Machine Sex/
Flesh and Steel (Extended Version)
NO CHART PLACING
Statik Records

Stripped of its soul, this cold, emotionless reading of James Brown's classic, retains its funky flavour. It is delivered in a robotic style, performed by David Cunningham with beautifully enunciated vocals from Sally Pearson. These Flying Lizards were now very much a marginal act, commercially speaking. However, they remained just as amusing and thought-provoking as they had been in their chart heyday.

89
SMILEY CULTURE
Cockney Translation
Roots Reality
NO CHART PLACING
(1985 - 71)
Fashion Records

David Emmanuel – AKA Smiley Culture - was a British reggae artist using dancehall style. In 'Cockney Translation' - his first single - he was fast-talking, cheeky and cheerful and without really knowing it, musically radical. He had the idea to mash up the two prominent, though conflicting, cultures in his life and delivered this quick-witted lyric comparing the respective similarities and differences between the black and white communities sharing the same London Street in a combination of street slang. To illustrate his lyric he switches rapidly between the Cockney popularised by Chas and Dave and the Jamaican Patois used by disenfranchised black youths. It was brilliantly conceived, and as well as being funny, highlighted the fact that Englishness was now a multi-ethnic and multi-cultural mix. Smiley Culture was the forerunner of British rap, his style informing the next generation. His death during a police raid on his Surrey home in 2011 is said to have been a contributory factor in anti-police riots in August that year.

88
BOB DYLAN
Jokerman
Isis (From the Film *Renaldo & Clara*)
NO CHART PLACING
CBS Inc.

Be it a series of biblical allusions or political allegory, the simple fact is that this six-minute epic of stunning imagery is a brilliant song, one of Bob Dylan's finest. That it retains a sense of mystery, rather than blatantly revealing its meaning, adds rather than detracts from its quality. It received an impassioned live reading on the *David Letterman* show with Dylan backed by a punk rock group called The Plugz. For this recording though, an all-star cast including Sly and Robbie, Mick Taylor and Mark Knoffler provide a more measured accompaniment that Dylan responds to with a stellar performance.

87
MALCOLM MCLAREN
Madame Butterfly
(Un Bel Di Vedremo)
First Couple Out (Extended Mix)
13
Charisma

McLaren's interest in cultures that he pillaged for inspiration may well have been ephemeral, but he had a mind full of ideas, and they needed to be explored. Here he sets out to integrate the high art of Puccini's opera with the low art of 80s pop by way of hip-hop beats introduced into the score. Against all odds he succeeds in creating a seamless piece, brilliantly executed, and quite revolutionary. Deborah Cole gifts him a singing performance of magnificence that elevated the track way beyond mere novelty status and ensured even opera buffs couldn't get too snooty about the outcome.

86
BROKEN GLASS
Style of the Street (Dance Mix)/
Streetstyle/Street Repeat/
Style of the Street (Original Mix)/
Streetbeat
NO CHART PLACING
Streetwave Ltd.

Mancunian mainstays galore combined here. Among those involved former Magazine drummer Martin Jackson, future Swing Out Sister keyboardist Andy Connell, Hacienda DJ Greg Edwards, and future Ruthless Rap Assassin and Black Grape man Kermit. They provided the music for Broken Glass, who were one of the original British B Boy crews, local Mancunian superstars who could be seen break-dancing around Piccadilly Gardens before becoming a Hacienda Saturday night staple and touring the country's clubs. What was recorded was fabulous electro-funk that was worthy of comparison with what was coming out of New York. If not revolutionary in content it was perfectly functional, fresh-voiced and crisp.

85
HÜSKER DÜ
Celebrated Summer / New Day Rising
NO CHART PLACING
SST Records

Renowned noise makers Husker Du were less one-dimensional than often imagined and here on 'Celebrated Summer' a 12-string acoustic guitar is the featured instrument for Bob Mould's song that displays wistful imagery in a nostalgic remembrance of youthfulness, before questioning the validity of those memories. The band's melodic gifts were displayed on this single, but without any compromise to the passion that fuelled them and without rendering them toothless. They still bit, and bit hard.

84
RED GUITARS
Good Technology
Heart Beat Go (Love Dub)
NO CHART PLACING
Self Drive Records

Red Guitars, from Hull, built up a following around the country by playing benefit gigs for various left-leaning causes. Their music was an intriguing blend of African rhythms, folk-blues and punk attitude. The self-released 'Good Technology' sold 60,000 copies - an incredible amount for a record without a promotional budget. The band showed great awareness of the power gained by the simple expedient of leaving space. Within and around it guitar and bass weave and the drums remain steady as an anchor. Meanwhile intelligent, pointed and prescient lyrics about the constructive and destructive effects of technology pour forth: "We've got plastics that are indestructible, We've got deodorants that make us smell of flowers, We've got detergents to clean up the sea, We've got sounds that can tear us inside out".

83
ARTHUR BAKER

Breaker's Revenge
Breaker's Revenge (Dub Mix Vocal)
Jazzy Break Down (Instrumental)
NO CHART PLACING
Atlantic

The film *Beat Street* was a drama-dance film set in New York and featuring hip-hop culture. From the soundtrack came 'Breaker's Revenge', a huge slab of electro-funk with a fabulous piano break amidst the scratching and slamming beats. It has echoes of Blaxploitation-era James Brown in its DNA that is reinforced by a vocal uncannily similar to JB himself.

82
PSYCHIC TV
Roman P/Neurology
NO CHART PLACING
(1986 - 48)
Sordide Sentimental

Disturbing lyrics about Roman Polanski's corruption of young girls and the murder of his wife Sharon Tate by the Manson clan are sung gleefully to a rip-snorting riff from guitarist Alex Fergusson that leads into a glorious and pointed sing-along chorus of "Are you really free? Are you really free?". Transgression never sounded quite so cheerful as in the hands of this Psychic TV line-up.

81
DAVY DMX
One for the Treble (Fresh)
One for the Treble (Fresh)
Instrumental/Bonus Beats
NO CHART PLACING
Tuff City

David Franklin Reeves Jr became Davy D and began touring as the DJ for rapper Kurtis Blow. He also found time to form and play in a band named Orange Krush who released a single in 1982 called 'Action' which, when re-purposed as 'Krush Groove' was appropriated and sampled by a legion of hip-hop acts such as Run DMC, Jay Z, Kanye West and De La Soul. For his first solo record he billed himself as DMX in recognition of the drum machine that he favoured to provide his beats. 'One for the Treble' is basically a hip-hop instrumental except for sampled voices. It is scratch heavy and has a joyous momentum that hasn't aged.

80
THE STRANGLERS
No Mercy/In One Door
37
Epic

The oldest punks in town were still rocking but here they offer light relief by introducing backing singers for the first time. The song is a long, miserabilist litany of complaints about life's tendency to grind one down. It is heavily repetitive, but The Stranglers had a melodic gift that turned unlikely songs like this into gems. The song leans upon a quirky, memorable and insanely catchy guitar phrase. At points it is cut by a brooding psychedelic keyboard part that works terrifically well whilst singer Hugh Cornwell performs admirably and displays an almost cheerful lightness of touch that is somehow perfectly-suited to the song.

The record sold a modest amount but took on a renewed life as samplers moved in to pillage it for their own work. Fatboy Slim, The Chemical Brothers, De La Soul and Prince Paul are amongst the many who visited this track to assist in the creative process.

79
ROCKMASTER SCOTT AND THE DYNAMIC THREE
The Roof Is On Fire
The Roof Is On Fire (Scratchin')
The Roof Is On Fire (Jivin')
NO CHART PLACING
Reality Records

In these early days of hip-hop culture, the DJ was regarded as being higher up the totem pole than the rappers. The billing here reflected this perception. The balance of power was changing though, and the only participant on this record not to receive a song-writing credit was Rock Master Scott. 'The Roof Is On Fire' had first appeared on the previous single as the B-side to the excellent 'Request Line'. They had incorporated into it the P. Funk chant of "the roof, the roof is on fire, we don't need no water, let the motherfucker burn". Radio play was not forthcoming, so this cleaned up version was released as the group hoped it would get them an appearance on *Soul Train*. They failed in that aim, but the song's stripped--to-the-bone beat and scratched sounds were a perfect springboard for the Dynamic Three to exult the skills of the DJ in fine style.

78
TOOLS YOU CAN TRUST
Show Your Teeth
Messy Body Thrust
NO CHART PLACING
Red Energy Dynamo

Down to the core duo of Ben Stedman and Rob Ward, Tools You Can Trust tread a musical path somewhere between Suicide and Einsturzende Neubauten, but with a more frenzied and brutal energy. They are at their purest and most breathtaking on this single's two sides.

77
VAN HALEN
Jump/House Of Pain
7
Warner Bros. Records

Van Halen abandoned their hard rock constituency and leapt into the charts with this anthemic piece of glam metal that substitutes the guitar as lead instrument with synthesiser. It may well have offended the most puritanical head-bangers in their audience but for the rest of us it offered much welcome light relief. Catchy as measles and as jumpy as a March hare, 'Jump' was hard not to love. And just to remind us that this was a Van Halen record, they squeezed a guitar solo onto the track as well.

76
THE MEMBRANES
Spike Milligan's Tape Recorder
All Skin And Bone
NO CHART PLACING
Criminal Damage Records

A tribal drum stomp, guitar as noise, bass pumping and Mark Tilton shouting out the lyrics. It was loud and ramshackle but it seemed to me like the sound of people celebrating life itself and having a huge amount of fun.

75
FRANKIE PAUL
Pass The Tu-Sheng-Peng
War Is In The Dance
NO CHART PLACING
Greensleeves Records

Frankie Paul was born almost blind. On a visit to his school, Stevie Wonder heard him sing and offered praise, spurring the young Frankie to pursue a career in music. He had an exuberant style and a rasp in his voice that belied his youthfulness. 'Pass The Tu-Sheng-Peng' is in the great tradition of reggae songs written in praise of marijuana. It was recorded with The Roots Radics band who provide a tight as a nut rhythm for Frankie Paul to extemporise over in a gleefully upbeat manner.

74
BRUCE SPRINGSTEEN
Dancing In The Dark
Pink Cadillac
28 (1985 - 4)
CBS

Although he was a global star, Bruce Springsteen was not immune to record company interference and having recorded his *Born In The USA* album it was suggested he write a commercial song to be issued as a single. He was angry and frustrated but acquiesced and that night wrote 'Dancing In The Dark', in which he expresses his unhappiness with his life, seeking consolation and comfort in the sexual act. That isn't happening for him either – "you can't start a fire without a spark", he sings imploringly. The song was delivered at a brisk pace, synthesiser pulses adding a dance feel. It was a song that people who generally weren't keen on Springsteen could enjoy, and it gave the record company the hit they wanted from him.

73
X-POSED
Point Of No Return
Dub Of No Return
NO CHART PLACING
Pantera Records

X-Posed - or Expose as they were also known - were a group consisting of three women from Miami. They updated the '60s sounds of groups like The Supremes and Marvelettes, placing that vocal style into a dance synth-pop zone. 'Point of No Return' was their finest moment - smart and cool and extremely sleek and luxurious sounding. It generated little interest at the time but was rerecorded in 1987 and sailed into the American Top 5.

72
FELT
Mexican Bandits
The World Is As Soft As Lace
NO CHART PLACING
Cherry Red

Felt at this point were making largely instrumental music, and 'Mexican Bandits' is a highpoint of this era for the band. Lawrence and Maurice Deebank play guitars that intertwine as the tune gallops along over a rock solid drumbeat. The music they created was a long way from being rock-orientated but where they had once sounded fey and uncertain, they now projected a knowing confidence in their own abilities.

71
A. AVENUE
Golden Queen (Vocal)
Golden Queen (Instrumental)
NO CHART PLACING
Discover Records

Italo-disco heaven was achieved with 'Golden Queen'. It contains stuttering drum rhythms, multiple synths (some that sooth and some that sound threatening), voices that sound ethereal and spoken passages with alien-like voices that mesh together. Imagine a combination of Vangelis, Sparks and Sylvester making a record with Arthur Baker programming the drums, then you'll have a pretty good idea of the scope displayed here.

70
WHODINI
Freaks Come Out At Night
Grandmaster Dee's Haunted Scratch
Freaks Come Out At Night (Instrumental)
97
Jive

Having previously worked with German producer Conny Plank, Larry Smith was brought in this time around following his work on Run DMC's records. Jive hoped Smith would replicate the Rap-Rock hybrid that worked for Run DMC, but neither he nor Whodini wished to be copyists. Here then the R&B quotient is ramped up from previous releases but the sound is all electronic - it is in fact closer to the sound George Clinton was mining than generic hip-hop.

69
SHINEHEAD
Billie Jean/Mama Used to Say
NO CHART PLACING
Hawkeye

Shinehead - English born, Bronx raised - created a seamless fusion between dancehall reggae and hip-hop. There was daring wit, sparkle and positivity in his work. Here he takes recent mega hits for Michael Jackson and Junior Giscombe and makes them over in a fresh style that displays perfectly his personality and talent.

68
THE STAPLE SINGERS
Slippery People (Club Version) Slippery People (Instrumental)
On My Own Again
78
Epic

Gospel-soul legends The Staple Singers got a new lease of life after being persuaded to record this Talking Heads song. Writer David Byrne had evoked the spiritualist preacher in the Talking Heads original but here in The Staple Singers' hands, with Byrne playing guitar, the church theme is made explicit. The vocals are in a call-and-response gospel style where Pops Staples takes on the preacher role and daughter Mavis the answering congregation. Her performance is mind bogglingly brilliant. At points she appears lost in an emotional frenzy and to be speaking in tongues. Here was a record that went deeper and transcended the excellence of the original. It was truly stunning and gloriously funky.

67
R.E.M.
Don't Go Back To Rockville
Wolves, Lower
NO CHART PLACING
I.R.S. Records

Originally a punk rock style number played in a fast Ramones-like tempo, here it was jokingly played in a country style in the studio and its charm was revealed in that recast form. 'Don't Go Back To Rockville' was a straightforward and appealing song penned by bass player Mike Mills as a plea to a female friend not to return to Rockville for the summer. Taking liberties with the facts, he penned a list of reasons why it would make each of them unhappy. It had a sweet, wistful essence - a great tune with a memorable chorus. It wasn't a hit anywhere but it opened a few more ears to the fact that R.E.M. were doing very interesting things with their music.

66
JULIAN COPE
The Greatness And Perfection Of Love/24a Velocity Crescent
52
Mercury

Julian Cope was at this point a classicist in his approach to music making. This nugget is a beautifully created facsimile of 1960s psychedelia, conjured up in Julian's mind as the kind of pop that coloured his childhood imagination. Upbeat and sun-dappled, it starts with a glorious fanfare and never flags. Julian sings majestically with purpose and clarity. His reputation as shambolic acid casualty got in the way of his music, he was filed away as a wasted talent. But the truth was that his gifts remained intact and he allied those to a craftsmanship which served his artistic efforts very well indeed.

65
DEPECHE MODE
People Are People
In Your Memory
4
Mute

Lyrically gauche but with compassion at its heart, 'People Are People' saw Depeche Mode embracing serious universal themes of racial hatred and aggression and standing firmly against them. This message was aligned to a highly imaginative electronic track full of intriguing sounds that nonetheless served, rather than overpowered, the song in no small part due to the simple though effective vocal melodies. 'People Are People' was arguably over-earnest but that also lends the song appeal. It is so free of cynicism that one can't help feel uplifted when hearing its unmistakable opening electronic salvo.

64
SEVERED HEADS
Dead Eyes Opened/Bullett/Mount
NO CHART PLACING
Ink Records

This was Australian band Severed Heads' first single. They operated with one foot on the dance-floor and the other in the field of experimental noise. On 'Dead Eyes Open' they sample a 1950s BBC radio broadcast of actor Edgar Lustgarten narrating a grizzly chilling extract from a show based on the 1924 murder of Emily Kaye. His voice fits perfectly into the track, luring the listener with its quiet measured tone and only then reveals….the Horror!

63
FRANKIE GOES
TO HOLLYWOOD
The Power Of Love/The World Is My Oyster/Holier Than Thou
1
ZTT

The Frankies were everywhere! They were a sensation, their music soundtracking nights out and their range of 'Frankie Says' t-shirts the most highly-visible fashion item on the high street. 'The Power Of Love' was their grand gesture, a symbol of their hold on the nation. It was a romantic epic of biblical proportions, heady and luxurious, totally disregarding the concept of restraint. No excess was too excessive, and yet its charms more than compensated for its vulgar bombast. For at its heart was a spirituality in Holly Johnson's belief that love held a redemptive power.

62
SHOCK HEADED PETERS
I, Blood Brother Be (£4,000 Love Letter)/Truth Has Come/
Katabolism/Hate On Sight
NO CHART PLACING
El Records

Karl Blake formed Shock Headed Peters following the demise of The Lemon Kittens. This was their first release, delightfully contrary and in opposition to whatever musical fashion was currently hip. 'I, Blood Brother Be' is played mostly as a walking jazz with a huge and cinematic finale. The lyrics portray homosexuality in a positive way and is sung in an assured baritone. DJ John Peel refused to play the song as he considered it distasteful and indecent which was a ludicrous and hypocritical position for him to adopt considering the amount of hetero-themed sexist nonsense that he played without censure.

61
ART OF NOISE
Beat Box (Diversion Six)
Beat Box (Diversion Seven)
92
ZTT

Art Of Noise were formed from the emergence of sampling technology. Utilising this new creative tool, they set about examining new ways of composing and performing music and this first release set the template. It was experimental in its incorporation of the sounds of household appliances in alignment with percussive samples which were cut up and reassembled. An electronic instrumental that possessed humour and wit, found an appreciative audience in the hip-hop crowd.

60
KILLING JOKE
Eighties (The Coming Mix
Eighties
60
EG

Killing Joke were an enormously popular and respected band, though I never quite got it. After their first dub-influenced single, it all seemed to get very safe and predictable to me. However, I couldn't help but enjoy 'Eighties', which had a great riff that Nirvana would snaffle for their own 'Come As You Are' single and played over an almost tribal drum beat, they sounded like an angrier Adam and the Ants.

59
BARRINGTON LEVY
Murderer/Murderer [Version]
[Credited to I Life Players]
NO CHART PLACING
Jah Life International

Reggae music in the digital age held much less appeal to me than the roots rockers sound of the 70s. The dancehall style usually left me cold, but of course there are always exceptions to the rule. In this case I kept my ears open for Barrington Levy's tracks which seemed possessed of greater substance than many others. 'Murderer' is a case in point - a brilliant record over a mid-tempo groove, Levy sings in an assured tenor voice that seemed to convey much more pain and wisdom than a 19-year-old should really have experienced.

58
VIOLENT FEMMES
It's Gonna Rain
Jesus Walking On The Water
NO CHART PLACING
Slash (Rough Trade)

Wisconsin band Violent Femmes returned with a swinging countrified sound and lyrics with plentiful allusions to biblical matters. This one is about building the Ark in preparation for the prophesied great flood. Critics thought they were being ironic. They weren't. Whether you are a believer or not didn't matter ultimately because this sounded so good.

57
HARD CORPS
Dirty/Respirer (To Breathe)
NO CHART PLACING
Survival Records

Three male sound engineers made a chilly dance infused piece of electronica that came with a brutal edge and then adding as a counterpoint the highly emotional vocals of Regine Fetet. The human element combined with the hardness and precision of the instrumentation. 'Dirty' spoke eloquently of where we were as a society in terms of having to learn how to strike a balance between technology and humanity.

56
WHAM
Freedom/Freedom (Instrumental)
1
Epic

Written while George Michael was still a teenager, he felt that this song was a great leap forward and was the point he began to take himself seriously as a writer. It is about committing to a monogamous relationship rather than 'playing around'. Musically it is performed as an up-tempo Motown-esque stomper with pounded piano to the fore. It wasn't innovative. It wasn't edgy. But it was near perfect pop and absolutely delightful.

55
SOFT CELL
Down In The Subway/Disease And Desire/Born To Lose
24
Some Bizzare

Soft Cell's final single in their original incarnation saw them covering a song written by Jack Hammer who most famously co-composed 'Great Balls of Fire'. Surprisingly, they approach it in a more traditional style than previous offerings. Live drums are played with aplomb and apparent gusto by Dave Ball. Saxophonist Gary Barnacle plays a honking riff that adds an authentic R&B element to proceedings. And backing vocalists ramp up the song's tension providing a counterpoint to Marc Almond, who mines the lyric with theatrical flair, locating the song's heart of loneliness and desperation which he delivers with relish.

54
CAMEO
She's Strange/Groove With You
37
Club

Cameo had been around since 1974 and had released 10 albums when 'She's Strange' opened the door a little and gave them and their brand of deep funk a taste of mainstream success. That they achieved this with a positive portrayal of a trans-gender person was something worth celebrating. That the track was also so sinuously funky, riding an insanely contagious groove was further evidence that this band were a substantial force.

53
POGUE MAHONE
Dark Streets Of London
The Band Played Waltzing Matilda
NO CHART PLACING
PM

Pogue Mahone would soon sign to Stiff records who would re-release this single under the band's new and less offensive (to some), The Pogues. For now though, this single came in a pressing of 2,000 copies on their own label. 'Dark Streets Of London' - written and sung by the inimitable and hugely-talented Shane McGowan - is a vivid evocation of the drinking classes in the Irish hostelries of North London, played gleefully by a merry band of co-conspirators on banjos, fiddles, whistles and other traditional instruments.

52
THE FALL
C.R.E.E.P/Pat-Trip Dispenser
NO CHART PLACING
Beggars Banquet

The Archie's 60s hit 'Sugar Sugar' provides the tune that is served up in a mangled re-imagining. Keyboards and bass are to the fore and new band member Brix Smith is prominent on backing vocals while husband Mark is acid-tongued in his portrayal of a person who has drawn his formidable ire, describing him at various points as "a horrid trendy wretch" an "ugly gawk", and of course, a "c.r.e.e.p".

51
THE GO-BETWEENS
Part Company
Just A King In Mirrors
NO CHART PLACING
Sire

'Part Company' is a beautiful, heart-wrenching song, penned and sung by Robert Forster over a swell of acoustic guitar and wandering bass, given structure by Lindy Morrison's fine drumming. Forster sings the eloquent words of sadness and regret, imbuing them with resolve, despite uncertainty. It is projected as a break up song, signifying the end of a relationship, though Forster claimed it was written about leaving their Australian home to attempt to further their career in the UK .

50
QUEEN
Radio Ga Ga/I Go Crazy
2
EMI

Since 1981's 'Under Pressure' – co-written and performed with David Bowie - there had been no major hit singles for Queen. 'Radio Ga Ga' would remedy that situation and etch itself into the collective consciousness of music lovers around the globe. Written by Roger Taylor, it related the waning influence of radio, as the visual medium of MTV gained ascendency. Much work in terms of arranging, polishing lyrics and supplying harmonies came from Freddie Mercury who's vocal on the track was titanic. It should also be noted that for a band who had once proudly and somewhat pompously proclaimed the fact that they did not use synthesisers, here was a record built on drum machines, synth-bass, vocoder and all manner of electronica.

49
EVERYTHING BUT THE GIRL
Each And Every One
Laugh You Out The House
28
Blanco Y Negro

Tracey Thorn and Ben Watt were already well known to watchers of the music scene through their solo endeavours and Thorne's stint in The Marine Girls. Now, combining their talents to great effect, Everything But The Girl stood apart from the wave of synth-pop bands by adopting a jazzy bossa nova style. This single captured their essence to perfection. Clipped rhythm guitar is at the heart of the song but muted trumpet, congas and Thorn's throaty but subtle vocal combine to great effect and add an air of sophistication to the already highly melodic song.

48
THE CARS
Drive/Stranger Eyes
5 (1985 - 4)
Elektra

'Drive' is a gorgeous ballad performed over an electronic soundscape with a melody suffused with a sad, aching quality. Sung by Cars' bassist Benjamin Orr, rather than regular lead vocalist Ric Ocasek, he delivers a touching heartfelt performance. The song was a deserved No. 5 UK chart hit on release. A year later, the song was used as background music to a montage of film clips depicting the Ethiopian famine at the Live Aid concert at Wembley stadium and the record charted again as a result. The Cars donated the money earned from this success to the Band Aid Trust, Ric Ocasek presenting a cheque for £160,000 to trustee Midge Ure.

47
THE IMPOSTER
Peace In Our Time
Withered And Died
48
Imposter Records

Although recorded under his own name and included on his lacklustre album, *Goodbye Cruel World*, for some reason Elvis Costello chose to release this single under his Imposter alias. It was stylistically a world away from the cluttered synthesised sound he was burying his songs beneath in this period and benefited enormously from that fact. At heart 'Peace In Our Time' is a folk song, deeply cynical of the intentions of world leaders' rhetoric and hidden agendas. The lyric moves from Neville Chamberlain's attempt at appeasement of the Nazi war machine, through to Ronald Reagan's nuclear lunacy in pursuing his 'Star Wars' missile program. The song is funeral-paced and features a pump organ and mournfully played trombone.

46
COLOURBOX
Say You/Fast Dump
NO CHART PLACING
4AD

Colourbox existed on the outskirts of the arty synthesiser band's scene. Their influences included hip-hop, soul and reggae, which set them apart from their contemporaries. Here they take on U-Roy's wonderful 70s classic 'Say You', giving it a cool, mellow and highly melodic treatment with a superb, soulful vocal from Lorita Grahame.

45
FRANKIE GOES
TO HOLLYWOOD
Two Tribes/War (Hide Yourself)
One February Friday
1
ZTT

The Frankie's second monster single 'Two Tribes' was an anti-war, hard rock/disco/Russian classical hybrid that ridiculed the so called 'superpowers' and poured scorn on their vain, posturing old men leaders - cowboy Ronald Reagan and Cossack Konstantin Chernenko. Musically, its two competing elements are American style funk and a dramatic string-laden approximation of Russian folk. Trevor Horn's production is perfect for the material, creating a dynamic, multi-layered aural blitzkrieg with Holly Johnson's fabulous vocal sitting like a cherry on top.

Actor Patrick Allen provides snippets of dialogue from the *Protect and Survive* public information films. And from *Spitting Image,* voiceover actor Chris Barrie imitates Ronald Reagan, quoting from speeches by Adolph Hitler and Fidel Castro. This was a record that encapsulated the fears and abhorrence many felt about the power possessed by idiots like Reagan, Chernenko and Thatcher. Once heard, never forgotten, this was a truly inspired and important record.

44
ECHO AND THE BUNNYMEN
The Killing Moon/Do It Clean
9
Korova

One of three singles released by Echo and the Bunnymen in 1984 (the others being 'Silver' and 'Seven Seas') that were all high quality. 'The Killing Moon' was clearly the most outstanding and quite possibly the finest song the group ever produced. It was not simply the subject matter, being concerned with the inevitability and acceptance of death. But it also came with a sense of importance, perhaps due to the refinement and dignity attached to the song's arrangement. It certainly transcended any labelling of generic jangly pop.

43
WAS (NOT WAS)
(Return To The Valley Of) Out Come The Freaks
(Predominantly Funk Version) Out Come The Freaks
50
Geffen Records/ZE Records

The Was brothers and trusty entourage returned to 'Out Come The Freaks', one of their signature songs from 1981. This re-imagining of the song is significantly different in mood and tempo, a sympathetic and more positive reading, slowed down and containing real gravitas. A brand new lyric introduces a separate cast of characters from society's margins. The chorus, while lyrically unchanged, is sung as an endlessly sad refrain by Harry Bowers rather than chanted in loud and proud defiance of the freak label. Was (Not Was) were a marvellous act and this was a marvellous record. But just like the 'Freaks' they profiled, they were at this point struggling for the recognition they deserved.

42
TALK TALK
It's My Life
Does Caroline Know?
46 (1985 - 93/1990 - 13)
EMI

Talk Talk mastered the art of mixing traditional song-craft and instrumentation with the modernity of synthesisers to great effect. They created a seamless, sophisticated easy-on-the-ear sound and had the intelligent, lyric writing and emotional vocal style of Mark Hollis to call upon. All this made for a potent brand of musical expression which came with glorious melodicism and hooks aplenty.

'It's My Life' is written from the point of view of a man in a troubled and painful situation. Although he knows the solution to his problem is to leave, he asserts "it's my life" and chooses to stay. Quite an insightful look at his existential dilemma and thought patterns for a catchy pop single.

41
THE STYLE COUNCIL
My Ever Changing Moods
Mick's Company
5
Polydor

This is a smoothly grooving treat with a touch of Latin flavouring featuring brilliant drumming and fabulous trumpets. Paul Weller's squeals, emulating the great Curtis Mayfield, make me smile, while the lyric has depth and great substance, capturing as it does the bewildering and terrifying mood of the times.

40
LIZZY MERCIER DESCLOUX
Mais Où Sont Passées Les Gazelles
Les Dents De L'amour
NO CHART PLACING
CBS

Sparkling pop, using Somalian rhythms and instrumentation, over which Lizzy good-humouredly enquires "but where have the G] gazelles gone?". As I don't speak French that is the only phrase I understand! But it doesn't spoil my delight or dampen my enthusiasm for this record which is possessed by a magical quality.

39
DEPECHE MODE
Master And Servant
(Set Me Free) Remotivate Me
9
Mute Records

Depeche Mode were stretching their wings and learning to fly, pushing themselves into darker areas. Here they sing about S&M role-playing and examine the correlation between these sexual games and everyday life. The track utilises whip and chain sound effects that seem to come from a dungeon. Despite the explicit subject matter, they escaped censorship, in all likelihood because this was still essentially brilliant catchy pop.

38
THE FLIRTS/DIVINE
Helpless (You Took My Love)
Native Love '84
NO CHART PLACING
Black Sun

As well as producing a host of other artists such as Divine and The Pet Shop Boys, Bobby Orlando had formed The Flirts where, along with a revolving cast of female vocalists, he recorded his own work. 'Helpless' was aimed squarely at the dance floor. It had pristine light-footed rhythms as its base and a clarity of sound that was enhanced by a dramatic vocal. It was a superb club record that gave off a cool but sensual vibe. It was impossible to be affected by its charms as its rhythms seemingly controlled the way I walked and carried myself.

37
FAD GADGET
One Man's Meat
Sleep (Electro-Induced Original)
NO CHART PLACING
Mute Records

With a fuller sound than ever before due to the incorporation of a band into recordings, 'One Man's Meat' was a glorious, though still strange, pop record with a sound not a million miles away from that of hit-making label mates Depeche Mode. Hopes for a taste of commercial success were not completely unrealistic though, perhaps undermined by Fad's vocal grunts and growls, which would have seemed incongruous and somewhat disturbing residing in the pop charts. This turned out to be the last Fad Gadget release as that nom-de-plume was removed and future recordings bore the moniker of 'Frank Tovey'.

36
FELIX
Tiger Stripes
You Can't Hold Me Down
NO CHART PLACING
Sleeping Bag Records

Arthur Russell and Gallery/Studio 54 DJ Nicky Siano teamed up for this project, but tensions became frayed during the recording as Russell became annoyed at his collaborator's hyperactive personality. Meanwhile, Siano was irked by Russell's perfectionism and the changes he introduced. Things came to a head when Russell scrapped the original vocal by Evelyn Thomas, at which point Siano recorded a lead vocal which appalled Russell so much he walked out. When the record was released it featured a vocal by Maxine Bell and Russell used the alias 'Killer Whale' for his credit. As for the record, despite its turbulent history, it was quite superb. It was sparse, percussive and slinky, with a spirit of playful eccentricity married to a hip shaking groove and cool jazz vibe.

35
PUBLIC IMAGE LIMITED
Bad Life/Question Mark
71
Virgin Records Ltd.

P.I.L. further fragmented during the recording of the abandoned album *Commercial Zone*. Keith Levine departed, leaving John Lydon as the band's only original member. Several *Commercial Zone* songs were rerecorded for the album, *This Is What You Want... This Is What You Get*, including 'Bad Life', which in its original form had been called 'Mad Max'. It was a smart rant over rattling rhythms and a furiously riffing saxophone. Lydon's vocal was deliciously sarcastic, and his chanted phrases used as choruses lodged within the brain. Another P.I.L. single with the power to make us smile, dance, and think was no bad thing at all.

34
QUEEN
I Want To Break Free
Machines (Or 'Back To Humans')
3
EMI

The hard rock and pomposity of Queen's 1970s were receding into memory as they hit their artistic stride and revealed themselves as a superb pop act. Written by John Deacon, there is no pretentiousness at all, just simple, joyous tunesmithery aligned to a magnificently uplifting chorus. The song was embraced as an anthem in Europe and South America where its message was perceived as being pro-democratic and anti-authoritarian. But in the USA it was largely disliked because the video that accompanied the track showed the group in drag paying homage to *Coronation Street* and English humour, which the uptight American media perceived as promoting transexuality and sexual perversion.

33
WORKING WEEK
Venceremos (We Will Win)
Bottom End
64
Paladin/Virgin

Featuring vocals by Claudia Figueroa, Tracy Thorn and Robert Wyatt, this was the debut and most successful single by British jazz band Working Week. It is both a tribute to the Chilean protest singer Victor Jaro and a condemnation of the brutal regime headed by Margaret Thatcher's close friend General

Pinochet who murdered him. Played in a Latin jazz style that lends itself to exuberant dancing, whilst simultaneously being a perfect vehicle for political messages, the melding of voices and instrumentation made this a must-have record.

32
GIORGIO MORODER WITH PHILIP OAKEY
Together In Electric Dreams
Instrumental
3
Virgin Records Ltd.

Steve Barron, who had directed the video to The Human League single 'Don't You Want Me', was directing his first feature film. He enlisted Giorgio Moroder to provide a musical score and, wishing for an emotional song to play as the end credits rolled, he suggested to Moroder that Human League front man Philip Oakey might be a suitable candidate to sing. Moroder had the track completed and recorded Oakey's vocal in 10 minutes! The single was a huge success that eclipsed the film. Moroder and Oakey released a collaborative album, but lightning did not strike twice.

'Together in Electric Dreams' was their magical moment when the stars aligned. It is simultaneously futuristic yet retro sci-fi, with Oakey adding flesh and blood to the piece that captures a euphoric optimism and has a built in universal bonding mechanism, such is the song's heart-warming message of fraternity.

31
THE CHILLS
Doledrums/Hidden Bay
NO CHART PLACING
Flying Nun Records

Martin Phillipps was a superb songwriter who proved himself time and time again. His band, The Chills, had some of the organ-led trebly sound of Syd's Pink Floyd, and Phillips shared with Mr. Barrett the gift of being able to turn everyday feelings and events into extraordinarily rich and perceptive songs. Here, he looks at his life of unemployment and the 'doledrums' that he finds himself in when money is tight, only for these feelings to subside into joy when mail arrives through the letterbox. "The benefits arrive and life goes on", he cheerfully trills, to bring to a close this succinct pop gem.

30
DEAD OR ALIVE
You Spin Me Round
(Like A Record)/Misty Circles
1 (2003 - 23/2006 - 5)
Epic

Dead or Alive had been notable only for the flamboyant style of singer Pete Burns, and his friendship with ex-Cramp Bryan Gregory. Their music had been up to this point a kind of murky, tuneless Gothic-infused mess. They had recently breached the lower reaches of the chart with a cover version of KC & the Sunshine Band classic 'That's The Way I Like It' and teamed up with production team Stock, Aitken and Waterman, who's hit-making form was unrivalled. By all accounts, the band's record label was unenthusiastic about 'You Spin Me Round' and the band funded the recording themselves. It only goes to show that record companies often know nothing about music because this was a surging Hi-NRG rush of irrepressible disco magic, containing elements of Wagner's 'Ride Of The Valkyries'. It pumped and pulsed relentlessly, delivered with considerable aplomb by all concerned, particularly Pete Burns who's moment had well and truly arrived.

29
WOMACK & WOMACK
Love Wars/Good Times
14
Elektra

The musical pedigree of husband-and-wife outfit Womack and Womack was of the highest order. Linda was the daughter of Sam Cooke, while her husband Cecil had been a member of The Valentines, alongside his brother, soul legend Bobby Womack. This pair were wonderfully expressive singers and fine writers. They made a virtue of the tradition that shaped their music and, in an era dominated by drum machines and programmed sounds, their old style R&B style was highly refreshing.

'Love Wars' tells of a painful relationship, where admissions of wrongdoing are made amidst the realisation that the fighting has to stop to save them from parting. The musical backing consists of a mid-tempo, funk groove, lit up by a superb imaginative arrangement. Music of this quality doesn't pander to fashion and can never go out of style.

28
MALCOLM X
No Sell Out
No Sell Out (Instrumental)
60
Tommy Boy

Inspired by hearing Grandmaster Flash using the "do you feel lucky punk?" line from the film *Dirty Harry* over a record, drummer Keith LeBlanc began experimenting with spoken word pieces in conjunction with drumbeats. After being granted permission to use extracts from speeches by Malcolm X by his widow Betty Shabazz, LeBlanc built the track with key passages from speeches by the inspirational black activist, whose fiery oratory and message of peace and empowerment through the struggle for equality was as relevant in 1984 as it had been in the sixties. The combination of Malcolm X's voice with the brilliantly programmed beats was spine chilling. LeBlanc had made a masterpiece that was brazenly political and highly provocative and challenging towards those in power who maintained the status quo. He had also jump-started a new era in hip-hop where conciseness would increasingly be at the fore.

27
THE SPECIAL AKA
What I Like Most About You Is Your Girlfriend
51
Two-Tone Records

The world-view expressed in the songs of Jerry Dammers was extremely bleak, all the more so as you would find yourself nodding in agreement at the reality contained within his sentiments. 'What I Like Most About You Is Your Girlfriend' offered, on the face of it, some light relief from the rapes, racism, and bombings of recent singles. However, it comes with a cynical black heart and its humour is laced with darkness. The song is played in a slinking jazz style, featuring tremendous horn parts from Dick Cuthall and Rico Rodriguez. Dammers himself takes the lead vocal in exaggerated slime-coated, high-pitched style. He adopts the role of a duplicitous nightclub predator, befriending a man at the bar and hiding behind his charming exterior the fact that his intention is to steal away the girlfriend from this new found friend. It's an unforgettable performance, and this was another top notch Specials single and the final release by the iconic Two-Tone record label.

26
TIME ZONE
World Destruction
World Destruction
44
Celluloid Records

This collaborative single brought together Afrika Bambaataa and John Lydon along with producer Bill Laswell. It was the collision point between hip-hop and punk; a dense, howling claustrophobic beast of a record. The contrasting vocal styles of Bambaataa and Lydon - the former declamatory, the latter delivered with an edge of suspicion and paranoia - create a ping-pong effect, given further emphasis by Martin Atkins' pounding drum beat and the synthesiser fanfare.

25
PRINCE AND THE REVOLUTION
I Would Die 4 U
Another Lonely Christmas
58
Warner Bros. Records

Up-tempo and funky, for this outing Prince audaciously casts himself as the Messiah rather than mere mortal. He evokes the messages Jesus gives to his followers in the Bible forgiving their evil, stating that all he needs is belief. And of course, that he "would die 4 U". Only someone of supreme talent could pull off a song like this without sounding entirely ridiculous. Prince did just that, with considerable ease.

24
PREFAB SPROUT
When Love Breaks Down/Diana
NO CHART PLACING (1985 - 25)
Kitchenware Records

The 'sophistipop' category that this record fell into could often be an excuse for bland tunelessness masquerading as being subtle and important. 'When Love Breaks Down' was assuredly *not* that. It was rather a quiet and measured pop gem, albeit with a glorious big(ish) chorus. From its opening keyboard notes, the sound is rich and seductive, played with restraint but not without a sparkle. Songwriter Paddy McAloon sings wistfully of his regret and pain of a valuable relationship slipping away beyond his grasp. He is a superb lyricist and his words of heartbreak, given their soulful delivery, ring true and sincere.

23
CHAKA KHAN
I Feel For You/Chinatown
1
Warner Bros. Records

'I Feel For You' was written by Prince, used on his eponymous album (1979). It was subsequently offered to Patrice Rushen who declined to record it however Chaka Khan took the song to an entirely different level. Rather than replicate Prince's falsetto vocal, she turned on the power and emotion of her own formidable voice and unleashed something that felt primal and cathartic. That is not to say this is an unsophisticated recording - legendary producer Arif Mardin used the most up-to-date tools at his disposal, Melle Mel of The Furious Five provided raps, and Stevie Wonder played chromatic harmonica and provided vocals via samples taken from his 1962 hit 'Fingertips'. Everything gelled, and the immediacy of Chaka Khan's singing was thrilling.

22
STYLE COUNCIL
You're The Best Thing
The Big Boss Groove
5
Polydor

Laid back and jazz-infused, 'You're the Best Thing' was shimmering and so light it seemed to float. Against that, Paul Weller sang the song in immaculate style, sounding soulful and emotional. His lyric is personal and free of major statements, displaying the tender side of his personality.

21
PROPAGANDA
Dr. Mabuse (A Paranoid Fantasy
Dr. Mabuse (An International Incident)
27
ZTT

'Dr Mabuse' was a creation of author Norbert Jacques, who was made famous as the lead character in three films directed by Fritz Lang and portrayed as a demonic, cunning, criminal mastermind. German act Propaganda used the character as inspiration for this debut single, wrapping the song inside a truly epic production by Trevor

Horn who creates a fearful Gothic soundtrack of swirling synths and driving beats. The crystalline voiced Claudia Brucken produces a vocal of otherworldly uniqueness that is the equal of the instrumentation. The single taken as a whole seemed huge, cinematic and extraordinary.

20
MADONNA
Like A Virgin/Stay
3
Sire

'Like a Virgin' was the first iconic statement song of Madonna's career, cementing her superstar status in the public imagination. Written by Billy Steinberg and Tom Kelly, it related the feeling of starting afresh and renewed at the outset of a relationship, of writing off the past and rediscovering a purity of thought and emotion. Nonetheless the word 'virgin' in every chorus gives the song a racy edge, and Madonna singing at the top of her register revels in the ambiguity and irony of the lyric. In her hands, the song has added depth and becomes multi-faceted.

Produced by Nile Rogers, and with a bass line very similar to that used by Michael Jackson for 'Billie Jean', Toby Thompson and Bernard Edwards – Rogers' Chic band-mates - provide the dynamic rhythmic swing for the track. This was a guaranteed floor filler and a sure fire hit. It made Madonna world-famous.

19
THE DREAM SYNDICATE
John Coltrane's Stereo Blues (Special Edit)
John Coltrane's Stereo Blues
NO CHART PLACING
A&M Records

'John Coltrane's Stereo Blues' was the centrepiece of The Dream Syndicate's second album and was thankfully released as a single. The Dream' Syndicate were seen as the leading lights in a scene dubbed 'the Paisley Underground'. While the band's first album displayed 'cool' influences, such as The Velvet Underground, this album was widely-disparaged by critics. It was more wide-screen and loose – Faulkner rather than Burroughs. There was a grandeur in its scope, and it served up a taste of American Gothic mixed with the churning guitar epics played wildly by the out of fashion Neil Young and Crazy Horse. The song attempts to conjure a feeling of free-thinking adventure - at certain points the guitars could peel paint. It is passionate and ambitious and these are qualities I admire.

18
DIVINE
You Think You're A Man
Give It Up
16
Proto

Previous singles 'Love Reaction' and 'Shake it Up' had both charted in the lower reaches of the Top 100, but here was the wonderful trans superstar

Divine, produced by the up-and-coming team of Stock, Aitken and Waterman, achieving a genuine fully fledged hit. Written by ex-Leyton Buzzards singer Geoff Dean, along with Keith Millar and it fitted Divine like an exquisitely tailored glove. Cut in Hi-NRG style, here was a song that was anthemic from the moment the first vocal is heard. It was cheekily provocative and loveable to anybody with an open mind. Of course, not everybody has that faculty, so predictably when Divine appeared on *Top of the Pops*, the BBC received a barrage of complaints from irate, prudish, intolerant, heterosexuals.

17
SADE
Smooth Operator / Spirit
19
Epic

Sade were a band named after their singer, Sade Adu, formed from the ashes of previous band Pride. They played a highly-refined mixture of soul and jazz in a measured, sophisticated style. This was topped by vocals that were cold and aloof. It was a formula that set them apart from their peers and their best work, such as 'Smooth Operator', had a spine-chilling tension contained within their pristine production.

'Smooth Operator' dated back to 1982 when Pride were still together and was written by Sade Adu and Ray St. John. On the face of it, the song condemns a con man who uses women to obtain his income with no care for their injured feelings. Another reading of the song is as an allegory concerning the perniciousness of global capitalism. It rode on chattering Latin influenced percussion, a sensuous bass line and a velvety saxophone that snakes through the track.

16
PRINCE AND
THE REVOLUTION
Let's Go Crazy (Edit)
Take Me With U
7
Warner Bros. Records

Opening with a funereal organ piece, over which Prince delivers a eulogy for the "dearly beloved", the song kicks into gear, introducing a chugging riff with the organ now swinging and sweetening the sound. Prince peels off one blistering guitar solo before later adding a second of fiery intensity. He excitedly sings his exhortations to live a life of high ethics, but also with fun with the drums high in the mix. 'Let's Go Crazy' is an ultra-energetic showcase of supreme talent that crams multiple ideas and brilliant musical performances into the record's grooves.

15
BRONSKI BEAT
Smalltown Boy/Memories
3 (1992 - 32)
Forbidden Fruit

To be openly gay in this era was courageous. The three members of Bronski Beat combined their stories of being oppressed in the provincial towns where they were raised before fleeing to London to find a sense of community. They wrote the semi-autobiographical 'Smalltown Boy' together, combining their words to the electronic Hi-NRG sound they danced to in London's gay clubs. This was a bold statement of intent, unleashing upon the world Jimmy Summerville's astonishing falsetto. Combined with the emotional force he brought to the lyric, it made for an unforgettable record that, as well as being a piece of brilliant pop, was also a jab in the eye for the repressive and intolerant Conservative government who's rampant homophobia was barbaric and abhorrent.

14
GIL SCOTT-HERON
Re-Ron/'B' Movie (Intro)
NO CHART PLACING
Arista

Uniting with Bill Laswell meant a change of style for Gil Scott-Heron. Out went the congas and flutes and in came Laswell's electro-fused hip-hop beats. However the message remained unaltered, and as always highly potent. It was a calling out and a ridiculing of the buffoonish president of the US, Ronald Wilson Reagan, the frighteningly inept ex-Hollywood B-Movie actor who was standing for re-election. This voice of opposition points out the corrupt nature of the president and the foreign policies that included the illegal invasion of Grenada and the funding of terrorists in Nicaragua. His voice unwavering, this was a measured but withering rebuke, from the ever articulate Scott-Heron, of the barely coherent bigot in the White House and of those who chose to re-elect him.

13
EURYTHMICS
Here Comes The Rain Again
Paint A Rumour
8
RCA

Eurythmics were now a self-contained hit-making machine, with Annie Lennox and Dave Stewart co-writing the songs. Annie sang them magnificently and Dave produced them with a masterly touch. This, for me, was their creative zenith. Though remaining hugely successful, from this point they began a slow, lingering slide towards mediocrity. However, this was an absolute triumph. A song cloaked in melancholy, it conveys the feeling of the final moment of beauty before inevitable decay begins its process of breaking down and making that decimation a sad, painful memory. Members of the Philharmonic Orchestra play the string part that is blended with the synthesised backing track, to create a sense of high emotion and grandiosity that Annie Lennox amplifies with her brooding and mournful vocal.

12
JOCELYN BROWN
Somebody Else's Guy
Somebody Else's Guy (Dub)
13
4th & Broadway

Jocelyn Brown had appeared on scores of hits for other artists as an uncredited singer: Chic, Cerrone, Inner Life, and Disco Tex & The Sex-O-Lettes had all borrowed her gospel-formed voice to enhance their own recordings. 1984 saw her debut album which yielded 'Somebody Else's Guy' which she co-wrote and produced. She opens the track with solo piano and in an anguished howl explains the predicament she finds herself in as the third party in a relationship meant for two. The song takes off, embellished with funk guitar, piano, horns and a hand-clap rhythm. It is superbly constructed, but Jocelyn Brown's lead vocal performance, along with the imaginative use of male backing singers, are what make this a remarkable record.

11
MADONNA
Borderline (U.S. Remix)
Borderline (Dub Remix)
Physical Attraction
56 (1986 - 2)
Sire

'Borderline' was the fifth single from Madonna's eponymous debut album, written by producer Reggie Lucas. Madonna had not been entirely happy with the version they recorded and this resulted in an association-ending disagreement with Lucas. Subsequently John 'Jellybean' Benitez was tasked with remixing the track to better suit Madonna's vision.

'Borderline' follows the R&B/soul template of classic Motown or Philadelphia International singles but is given a modernist synthesised backing. Madonna's vocals are pitched up, a device that made her sound younger than her 24 years. But they do not make her sound like 'girl next door' material. She sounds knowing and strong, even as she performs these lyrics about needing more emotional commitment from a relationship. This was not the catchiest or most hook laden of Madonna's portfolio of hit songs but it had real depth and substance beyond its exceptional groove.

10
GEORGE MICHAEL
Careless Whisper
Careless Whisper (Instrumental)
1
Epic

Written by George Michael when just aged 16, with assistance from Wham! band-mate Andrew Ridgeley, 'Careless Whisper' had a long gestation period before its release. A version was cut at the famed Muscle Shoals Sound Studio with legendary producer Jerry Wexler. To George Michael's ear it was unsatisfactory, and he fought not to have it released. Eventually a new version was cut in London with less-celebrated musicians which became the official release as a track on the Wham! album *Make it Big*. It was subsequently released as a Wham! single in most countries, though in the UK it became George Michael's first credited solo single. The song is aching and wistful in its melody with its main riff performed on saxophone. The vocal is handled extremely well and with a certain gravitas as the semi-autobiographical tale of cheating within a relationship is examined.

9
CYBOTRON
Techno City
Techno City (Instrumental)
NO CHART PLACING
Fantasy

Their home town and base – Detroit - was at this point collapsing. People were leaving in search of improved prospects and the neglected city fell into disrepair and ruin. To counter the bleak reality of their present, Cybotron looked towards the future for inspiration, a high-tech, machine-enhanced future. Their music reflected this, and 'Techno City' was perhaps their most fully realised piece. They take inspiration from the funk of Parliament/Funkadelic, and equally from European synth pioneers Kraftwerk and Gary Numan, using synthesiser melodies as sweet as sugar in conjunction with brutal machined hand-clap rhythms. Distorted voices and snippets of wailing rock guitar combine to create this early techno masterpiece.

8
ROCKWELL
Somebody's Watching Me
Somebody's Watching Me (Instrumental)
6
Motown

Rockwell is Kennedy Gordy, the son of Motown head Berry Gordy. His father was unconvinced by his son's musical prowess and took some convincing before releasing 'Somebody's Watching Me'. One avenue of persuasion was that Kennedy had managed to get Michael and Jermaine Jackson to sing backing vocals for him. Another was the undeniable quality and commercial potential of the song he presented to his father. Kennedy was given the name 'Rockwell' because single name artists Madonna and Prince were enjoying huge success.

When it appeared the single was infectious and fun, a tale of exaggerated paranoia played in a punk/funk/pop style with synthesiser the most prominent instrument. Rockwell sings his lines in a highly exaggerated fake British accent straight from *Hammer Horror* films. An uncredited Michael Jackson is heavily-featured as a vocal foil, his unmistakable voice ensuring his participation was the worst kept musical secret of the time.

7
PRINCE AND THE REVOLUTION
Purple Rain
God
8 (2016 - 6)
Warner Bros. Records

'Purple Rain' was conceived as a collaborative Nicks of Fleetwood Mac, in a country music style. When that plan failed to reach fruition, he took it to rehearsal with his band The Revolution. As they jammed around the basic structure, Wendy Melvoin began adding guitar chords which inspired Prince to see the song differently. Rather than being a mellow, country-flavoured track, it was transformed into an anthemic power ballad of huge potency. A lyric of great imagery and imagination was written, describing the sky's discoloration as it bleeds and cries - it is the beginning of the apocalypse. Faced with the person he loves and his faith in God guiding him, the song begins with a lone guitar but rises as instruments are added and the emotional intensity grows more feverish. Elements of rock, gospel and orchestral flourishes combine to make this one of the towering monuments to Prince's talent.

6
THE GO-BETWEENS
Bachelor Kisses
Rare Breed
NO CHART PLACING
Sire

The Go-Betweens

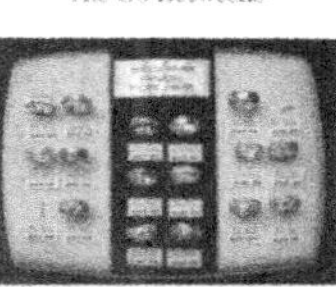

Bachelor Kisses

Grant McLennan was in love, and that love inspired this beautiful, open-hearted song. It is rich and melodic with a lyric full of evocative phrases that carry sincerity and a depth of feeling, as faithfulness is promised amid a landscape where unfaithfulness is commonplace. The rhythms are light and nimble, the guitars sparkle and chime, and McLennan - assisted by Ana De Silva of The Raincoats on the chorus - sings unaffectedly but with true soul.

5
23 SKIDOO
Coup
Version (In The Palace)
NO CHART PLACING
Illuminated Records

Formed in London in 1979, 23 Skidoo's were produced on early releases by like-minded artists such as Cabaret Voltaire along with Genesis P-Orridge and Peter Christopherson from Throbbing Gristle. They were difficult to categorise as they drew influences from a variety of esoteric sources. But in 1984, following the breakup of Linx, they recruited bass player extraordinaire Peter 'Sketch' Martin, who played on the album *Urban Gamelan*, featuring the track 'F.U.G.I' which was re-tooled to create this 12" single. 'Coup' is an extraordinary record, where the funk element of the band's sound is fully unleashed. Two separate bass lines coil around each other and very likely influenced Chemical Brothers' 'Block Rockin' Beats' 13 years later. The horn section - on loan from Aswad - play an incendiary riff. Percussion chatters, gunshot sounds and snatches of dialogue from the film *Apocalypse Now* add to the already dread atmospherics. It is easy to get lost within its layers of sound - on one hand an ear-worm of great potency it is simultaneously brooding, unsettling and somewhat claustrophobic.

4
CYNDI LAUPER
Time After Time
I'll Kiss You
3
Portrait

'Time after Time' was written towards the end of sessions for Cyndi Lauper's debut album, for the simple reason that one more song was needed. She was paired for the writing process with Rob Hyman from U.S. band The Hooters. It was a fortuitous partnership. Sparks flew, and the product of their union was this beautiful bitter-sweet ballad. Built over simple keyboard chords and embellished by bright jangling guitar and tic-toc percussion, it effortlessly touches the heart, dealing as it does with a love between people that is not perfect, but that remains strong and true. "If you're lost, you can look and you will find me, time after time" runs the chorus. It is a statement of commitment: straightforward, uncomplicated and rings true. Delivered as it is by a singer capable of investing genuine emotion into the words, 'Time after Time' is simply irresistible.

3
THE JESUS AND MARY CHAIN
Upside Down
Vegetable Man
NO CHART PLACING
Creation Records

Hailing from East Kilbride, siblings Jim and William Reid formed The Jesus and Mary Chain, recruiting teenage drummer Murray Dalglish whose kit consisted of two drums, and bassist Douglas Hart who had three strings on his instrument (though he later decided one of them was superfluous). They combined the energy and noise of *White Light White Heat*-era Velvet Underground with the pop classicism and harmonies of The Shangri-Las - bottled it, shook it up, and finally drenched it in feedback so that they sounded unlike anyone else. 'Upside Down' - their debut single - was a statement of intent, an assault on orthodox thinking and the mundanity that surrounded them. It was loud, brash and brilliant. They had the exquisite good taste to cover the officially unreleased Syd Barrett gem 'Vegetable Man' and put it on the flip side of the single. I loved them! How could I not?

2
PET SHOP BOYS
West End Girls
Pet Shop Boys
NO CHART PLACING
Epic

I came across this record by the intriguingly named Pet Shop Boys, who I had no knowledge of, in a remainders bin in a record shop in Ashton-under-Lyne. I forked out 25p for it on the strength that Bobby Orlando had produced it. What I listened to when I got home was a record unlike anything I'd ever heard before. The component parts seemed to be a rhythm track similar to Grandmaster Flash and the Furious Five's 'The Message' with a man who sounded like Noel Coward rapping in a posh English accent, taking lines from highbrow literature (T.S. Eliot's *The Wasteland*, and Edmund Wilson's *To The Finland Station*) mixing them with lyrics concerning paranoia and sex and adding a brilliantly memorable pop chorus that was immediately stuck in the head. It worked as a pop record and as a dance record. It defied genre classification as it broke new ground, but seemed to be one of those oddities whose charms had limited appeal. Sadly only a few were privy to the genius of 'West End Girls' seemed at the time. And then in early 1986 a new, more sumptuous, re-recorded version of the song hit the nation's airwaves like a bomb. It was unstoppable. It was everywhere. It hit the charts. Pet Shop Boys were like a quiet, understated, very British version of Sparks. The record went to Number One in the hit parade and Pet Shop Boys were on their way to becoming one of the finest pop bands of all time, with their combination of killer tunes and intelligent witty lyrics delivered in supreme style year after year.

1984

1
PRINCE
When Doves Cry
17 Days
4 (2016 - 26)
Warner Bros. Records

Doves, the symbol of peace, are here evoked as a metaphor. These doves though are crying, and the reason for their tears is that rather than bearing witness to peace, they see in the troubled relationship that the song depicts, war, hurt, jealousy, suspicion, and blame. There in a nutshell is the subject matter for what was one of Prince's signature songs. Further embellishments add depth to the lyric - the mother and father of the narrator are examined for clues in their behaviour that may have led to their child repeating their mistakes and facing the same sad consequences. Animals too are used as a symbolic device to emphasise the unhappiness felt. Prince composed the line "animals strike curious poses" to display that these innocent creatures sense something is wrong, and adopt stances to shield themselves from harm. Prince combines the lyric and his wonderfully assured vocal with a deliberately stripped back funk accompaniment. A drum machine and guitar are the only instruments used for the bulk of the song although a synthesiser solo, recorded at half speed and then sped up, is incorporated into the piece. An intended bass part was recorded, but ultimately discarded, leaving empty spaces that displayed in Prince a bravery to defy musical orthodoxy, along with the faith in his own innate fine taste and self-belief that this gossamer thin production - one that defined the expression "lightness of touch" - would function as a dance-floor filler and a pop radio staple. It did of course, even as it stunned, and nobody in their right mind at this time could have any doubt that the centre of the pop music world was based in Paisley Park Studios, Minneapolis, and the man at the controls was the audacious purple-clad supreme talent that was Prince.

1985

This year saw me unemployed and living in the town of Glossop at the bottom of the snake pass that leads to Sheffield. I was cut adrift to a large extent from what was happening culturally in Manchester and didn't particularly feel I was missing out. I lived quietly and cheaply. I'd rented a house from a friend who had moved to Scotland, I was a little isolated but that suited me fine, the 'greed is good' mantra of Thatcherite Britain repulsed me, I had no TV but read plenty of books, took long walks , attended karate classes and of course I had music. The Smiths and New Order dominated the Manchester scene and indeed were the most credible acts nationally too. The Fall were a rung or two beneath them in terms of popularity though as ever streets ahead musically. Swing Out Sister enjoyed success with their brand of jazzy, sophisticated pop and releasing their first singles and building up expectations were The Stone Roses and Happy Mondays. Other than The Fall I could take or leave most of what was on offer, I still went to gigs when I could and The Hacienda was an occasional treat too, it was football though that was my major diversion , it was at this point cheap enough for even someone as hard up as I truly was to go to games. One excursion saw me at Hillsborough towards the end of the season as an away supporter. I stood in the Leppings Lane section of the ground and experienced an emotion I had never experienced at a football match before: fear. The terrace was so packed that in the crush of the crowd my feet were not touching the floor as I was swept up and down. I had no control at all, it was very frightening. Football and the authorities that governed needed to get their house in order, sadly they only reacted when just a few weeks later the twin tragedies of the Bradford fire claimed 56 lives and the killing of 38 Juventus supporters before the European cup final in Brussels were followed in 1989 by the huge loss of life that occurred at Hillsborough on that same terrace. So much unnecessary death finally forced their hand into making stadia safer for spectators.

In the wider world the famine in Ethiopia needed to be dealt with and to the great shame of governments the help needed came not from our democratically elected leaders but pop stars who staged the globally watched Live Aid events in London and Philadelphia in July that raised millions.

NOTABLE EVENTS

The Sinclair C5 Velomobile is commercially launched.

Vodaphone launches the first UK mobile phone network

The border between Gibraltar and Spain which had been closed by General Franco in 1969, is reopened.

Mikhail Gorbachev becomes General secretary of the Soviet Communist Party and de facto leader of the Soviet Union.

Australian television soap opera *Neighbours* debuts on BBC1.

Mohamed Al-Fayed buys the London department store and British institution Harrods.

The FBI brings charges against the suspected heads of the five mafia families in New York City.

Approximately 10,000 people are killed in Bangladesh as a result of 'Tropical Storm One'.

A fire at Bradford City's Valley Parade ground, caused by a discarded cigarette, kills 56 people. Eighteen days later rioting Liverpool fans cause the deaths of 39 Juventus supporters whom they attacked at the crumbling Heysel stadium in Brussels before the European Cup final. UEFA bans all English clubs from Europe within weeks.

Scientists at the Antarctic discover a hole in the ozone layer caused CFC gas common in aerosols and fridges.

The Discovery Channel is launched

The iconic American highway ' Route 66' is officially decommissioned.

Greenpeace vessel *Rainbow Warrior* is sunk in Auckland harbour by French DGSE agents.

Live Aid concerts in London and Philadelphia raise over £50 million towards famine relief in Ethiopia

A state of emergency is called in South Africa as expressions of unrest grow in Black townships.

The worst single air disaster in history occurs when Japan Airlines Flight 123 crashes killing 520 people, Only ten days earlier Delta Airlines Flight 191 had crashed in Dallas Texas killing 137 people.

Richard Ramirez, the serial killer known as The Night Stalker, is captured in Los Angeles

Riots break out in Brixton following the shooting of Dorothy Groce by Metropolitan Police.

The Nintendo home video game console is released in the USA.

22 year-old Gary Kasparov becomes the youngest ever world chess champion after defeating Anatoly Karpov.

DNA is first used as evidence in a criminal case

Manchester United defeat League champions Everton 1-0 in the FA Cup final despite Kevin Moran being sent off late in the game. The ten men defended admirably in extra time and 20 year-old midfield colossus Norman Whiteside scores an exquisite goal of immense skill to seal victory. Buoyed by this success United start the following season winning a club record ten games in a row from the start of the season and 14 out of 16 establishing a 13-point lead over Liverpool. A league title in 1986 looks a mere formality...

NOTABLE BIRTHS

Lewis Hamilton; Cristiano Ronaldo; Lily Allen; Chris Froome; Lana Del Ray; Luka Modric; Wayne Rooney.

NOTABLE DEATHS

Konstantin Chernenko; Michael Redgrave; Zoot Simms; Marc Chagall; Enver Hoxha; George Brown; Louise Brooks; Jock Stein; Laura Ashley; Rock Hudson; Nelson Riddle; Yul Brynner; Orson Welles; Ricky Wilson; Phil Silvers; Big Joe Turner; Philip Larkin; Robert Graves; Ian Stewart; D Boon; Ricky Nelson.

NOTABLE FILMS

Back to the Future

The Breakfast Club

Pee Wee's Big Adventure

The Color Purple

Brazil

Ran

Kiss of the Spider Woman
My Beautiful Launderette; Subway
My Life as a Dog.

NOTABLE BOOKS

The Handmaid's Tale - Margaret Atwood
Perfume - Patrick Suskind
Love in the Time of Cholera - Gabriel Garcia Marquez
The Cider House Rules - John Irving
White Noise - Don DeLillo
Lake Wobegon Days - Garrison Keillor
Galapagos - Kurt Vonnegut jr
Less Than Zero - Brett Easton Ellis
Oranges Are Not the Only Fruit - Jeanette Winterson
Mermaids on the Golf Course- Patricia Highsmith

100
MEAT PUPPETS
Swimming Ground
Up On The Sun
NO CHART PLACING
SST Records

Kirkwood brothers, Curt and Kris, along with drummer Derrick Bostrom, hailed from rural Arizona. Their band, the Meat Puppets, had started out playing hardcore punk that had been sweetened by country flavours. Now, in the wake of their recreational drug use, a lysergic feel and psychedelic tinge was added to the mix. That said, 'Swimming Ground' is, at its core, a nostalgic look back to idyllic days when as youths, the local swimming pool provided solace from the endless hot summer days, while the overhead clouds pass without bringing rain. The guitars are clean and summery, the sound is a trifle ramshackle and the vocals are on the sloppy side. All of which goes to make 'Swimming Ground' an absolutely charming single.

99
JESSE JOHNSON'S REVUE
Be Your Man/Special Love
NO CHART PLACING
A&M Records

Jesse Johnson had been the guitar playing singer in The Time who had been affiliated to Prince and had recorded the original version of 'Nothing Compares to You'. Following the group's demise he struck out on his own although Prince's influence was an obvious and indelible feature of his music. His look mirrored that of his mentor, from the pencil moustache to the paisley frock coat. It is to his credit that he showed enough pizazz to be perceived briefly as a rival to Prince and 'Be Your Man' displayed why. It is a piece of snaky, loose-limbed funk, dominated by guitar and keyboard and Jesse Johnson's voice that sounds like… you know who, sighing and squealing through a list of reasons why the object of his affection should select him as her paramour. Derivative? Yes, but it grooves in fine style.

98
PREFAB SPROUT
Appetite/Heaven Can Wait
92
Kitchenware Records

'Appetite' was the third single taken from the phenomenally excellent Prefab Sprout album *Steve McQueen*. It was at least the equal of preceding singles ('When Love Breaks Down' and 'Faron Young'). Composed over a hip-hop style beat and fleshed out further by a genius bass line and keyboard and production flourishes courtesy of Thomas Dolby, Paddy McAloon's lyrics are fascinating, concerning the naming of a newborn child and choices which reflect the parents' emotions. 'Heartache' is suggested at one point but discarded as not being a boy's name. They finally concludes that 'Appetite' is the most suitable choice as it reflects the parents attitude towards life.

97
BRYAN FERRY
Slave To Love
Valentine (Instrumental)
10
E.G. Records Limited

Bryan Ferry's first solo release for seven years displayed the journey from artful experimentation to luxurious romanticism that the Roxy Music main man had undertaken. 'Slave to Love' was akin to being wrapped in velvet while inhaling the finest and most exclusive fragrance known to man. It was dreamy and intoxicating and Ferry sounded the epitome of a louche, sophisticated lothario.

96
SIOUXSIE AND
THE BANSHEES
Cities In Dust/An Execution
Quarterdrawing Of The Dog
21
Wonderland (Polydor)

Having never become enmeshed in the punk orthodoxy that rendered many of their peers to become hamstrung, The Banshees sought to constantly refresh themselves and expand their musical vocabulary. 'Cities in Dust' saw a move into dance rock territory without sacrificing their individualistic stamp. It was also their first release to feature new guitarist John Valentine Carruthers. The song depicts the destruction of Pompeii following a huge volcanic eruption. It opens to the sound of a synthesised chiming that evokes alarm bells ringing. From there, the horror and fear of the city's population is imagined. Drums are rhythmic and rock solid while the guitar and bass play a choppy near funk riff. It is a glorious sound but the centre of the performance is yet another tremendous raw and passionate vocal from Siouxsie.

95
ANTHONY RED ROSE
Tempo/Tempo (Version) (Credited to King Tubbys All Stars/
Tempa (Credited to King Asher)
NO CHART PLACING
Firehouse

Recorded at the newly opened King Tubby studios, this digital rhythm was a dancehall smash. Its minimalism relies upon Anthony Red Rose providing melody with his buoyant vocal. Swathes of intermittent echo provide a change in sound with no diminishing of the haunting quality on offer here.

94
FELT
Primitive Painters/Cathedral
NO CHART PLACING
Cherry Red

Having approached his hero Tom Verlaine to produce Felt (named after the way Verlaine intoned the word 'felt' on the Television song 'Venus De Milo') band-leader Lawrence turned to Robin Guthrie of Cocteau Twins fame to helm recording sessions. 'Primitive Painters' was intended to be as much a statement as a record. It was to be cloaked in myth and splendour, an expression of bold artistic ambition. Its spiralling guitar part was composed by Maurice Deebank, the classically trained guitar foil to Lawrence, who would leave the band following these recording sessions. Adding to the sound was teenage keyboardist Martin Duffy. It was already a fine piece when, in an inspired moment, Guthrie had his band-mate, Elizabeth Fraser, sing alongside Lawrence. Her distinctive soaring voice in combination with his sing-speak style worked perfectly, and though 'Primitive Painters' did not trouble the chart compilers, it was the highest selling single Felt would enjoy, and a triumph in every other sense.

93
R.E.M.
Wendell Gee/Crazy
NO CHART PLACING
I.R.S. Records

Wendell Gee' was a businessman known and liked by members of R.E.M. The song alludes to him being respectful but seemingly lost in illusions. It is a typically mystical and obscure lyric penned by Michael Stipe to fit the music written by Mike Mills as an homage to Fleetwood Mac. Mills performs much of the track solo while a grumpy Peter Buck, who hated the song with a passion, provides a skittish banjo solo that enlivens the song's pretty overtones but Gothically funereal crawl.

92
THE WINANS
Let My People Go
Let My People Go (Instrumental)
71
Qwest Records

The Winans were a four-brother gospel outfit from Detroit. Their recording career began in 1981, forging a link between their church roots and the sound of secular contemporary funk and R&B. At this point they were newly signed to Quincy Jones' *Qwest* label, and the release of 'Let My People Go' consequently reached a wider audience than previous records. Over a churning, rumbling groove, The Winans lent their voices to this plea for justice and freedom. What voices they possessed! Their sound was utterly beguiling and the passion they conveyed genuinely moving. Added to that, the skill of their harmonies was stunning.

91
MEAT WHIPLASH
Don't Slip Up/Here It Comes
NO CHART PLACING
Creation Records

Hailing from East Kilbride, Meat Whiplash named themselves after a song by The Fire Engines, who in turn were named after a song by the 13th Floor Elevators. Later, Meat Whiplash would morph into a group called Motorcycle Boy, named after a character played by Mickey Rourke in the film *Rumblefish*. Enough!

'Don't Slip Up' is a cool, noisy pop record that matches together the styles of The Television Personalities with that of fellow East Kilbridians, The Jesus and Mary Chain. Essentially it is a twee, very sweet concoction, with an extremely fey vocal, given a tougher sonic outer-coating of feeding back guitar noise.

90
JOHNNY OSBORNE
Budy Buy
Budy Buy (Version)
NO CHART PLACING
Jammy's Records

Johnny Osborne had succeeded in riding each evolutionary change within reggae music since his recording debut in 1969. His voice was flexible and warm. He could adapt it convincingly to multiple styles and was perfectly at home in each at the peak of his popularity in the 80s dancehall era. Here, recording with Prince Jammy, the ubiquitous 'sleng teng' riddim is used. It had reputedly been the first time in reggae that the live band was replaced with a programmed sound and therefore the start of the Jamaican digital musical revolution. Massively infectious and an undoubted floor filler, this was joyfully constructed party music.

89
DANIELLE DAX
Fizzing Human Bomb/ Yummer Yummer Man/Bad Miss 'M'
NO CHART PLACING
Awesome Records

Brilliant guitar pop from the stupendously talented Danielle Dax. Rockabilly drums are at the base of this cracking pop record with a psychedelic edge. The vocal performance is of the usual sublime, high quality we expected from Dax.

88
STEVIE WONDER
Part-Time Lover
Part-Time Lover (Instrumental)
3
Motown

The 70s had been illuminated by the genius music released by Stevie Wonder. But following his 1980 album *Hotter than July*, which was stuffed full of hits, Stevie seemingly lost his mojo and his music barely sparkled. Fortunately 'Part Time Lover' displayed vigour and zest. Although it didn't dazzle in the manner 'Superstition' or 'Sir Duke' had done in the past, it certainly twinkled appealingly. The song borrows the tempo and feel of The Supremes' 60s hit 'You Can't Hurry Love' atop of that adrenalised rush of sound, Stevie - along with Luther Vandross - provides a stellar vocal performance, describing a man cheating on his wife with his mistress who discovers she in turn is cheating on him. Syreta Wright and Philip Bailey of Earth, Wind and Fire lend support on the choruses making this a truly star-studded affair where the song is strong enough to carry the weight of expectations.

87
JAMES
Hymn From A Village
If Things Were Perfect
NO CHART PLACING
Factory

The ingredients that would make James hugely successful were on display at this early stage of their career. Fewer people were listening, that is all. 'Hymn From A Village' was as equally witty and literate as the hits that would follow - it was tuneful enough to whistle, all jangling guitars at the fore but with a solid base of thumping drums and elastic bass supporting the structure. It was self-deprecating lyrically, concerning a band's striving for success, sung with nonchalant panache by Tim Booth. It was clear this was a group whose trajectory was skyward.

86
ISLEY JASPER ISLEY
Caravan Of Love
I Can't Get Over Losin' you
52
Epic

Seeking a fresh sound, the original trio of Isley Brothers had introduced youngsters Ernie and Marvin Isley along with cousin Chris Jasper into the line-up and enjoyed renewed success during the 70s. As the hits dried up again, creative differences caused a gulf between the old and new factions and so Ernie, Marvin and Chris set up independently as Isley Jasper Isley. This single was nearly a hit for them that displayed their pedigree to the full. Written largely by Chris Jasper, who takes the lead vocal, it is an aching evocation of Christian values and a call for love and cooperation between people as a way towards creating a better society. It has a meditative, head-nodding groove and these thoroughbred performers blend their honey sweet voices in hymn like unity. The following year British jangle pop act, The Housemartins, released an acapella version of the song that topped the hit parade.

85
STYLE COUNCIL
Walls Come Tumbling Down
The Whole Point II/Blood Sports
6
Polydor

Swinging and up-tempo, 'Walls come Tumbling Down' was a turbo-charged criticism of Thatcher's evil authoritarian leadership and the class system in the UK. The downtrodden working class are not excused their responsibilities, being urged to turn off their TVs and open their eyes to life's realities, to the blackmail of promised jobs, to the slavery to HP payments. 'Unity is strength' is the message, and this is a heartfelt, thought-provoking cry for the masses to recognise the enemy and rise up against them.

1985

84
EINSTÜRZENDE NEUBAUTEN
Yü-Gung/Seele Brennt/Sand
NO CHART PLACING
Some Bizzare

The sonic terrorism that Einstürzende Neubauten had become renowned for was scaled back on this Adrian Sherwood remixed single. That is not to say that 'Yü-Gung' represented an easy listening experience for the uninitiated. It was wildly experimental, and its palette of sounds was far from tame. Whilst Blixa Bargeld's vocal alternated between whispers and visceral screams, it did have a recognizable structure and an incessant beat that in certain adventurous clubs one could actually dance to.

83
PATTI PALLADIN
AND JOHNNY THUNDERS
Crawfish/Tie Me Up
NO CHART PLACING
Jungle Records

'Crawfish' was the opening number from the 1958 musical film *G.I. Blues*, sung by the film's star Elvis Presley in a duet with Kitty White. The song was reprised here by ex-New York Doll and Heartbreaker Johnny Thunders, in cahoots with ex-Snatch vocalist Patti Palladin. They take it in that loose and louche style that the Rolling Stones mined in their *Exile on Main Street* heyday. Thunders is reunited with the Heartbreakers' mighty rhythm section of Jerry Nolan and Billy Rath along with Only Ones guitar ace John Perry. The vibe is swampy - saxophone, wailing harmonica and congas supplement the core band and add to the atmosphere, while Johnny and Patti sing with gusto. Anyone who loves rock 'n' roll is guaranteed to adore this record.

82
JOHN WAYNE
Call Di Police
Version: "Sleng Teng"
NO CHART PLACING
Jammy's Records

The Rubbery 'sleng teng' riddim is ridden again. Thankfully, it was absolutely titanic and bore repeated listens because a large number of Jamaican releases used it. Here, the unlikely named John Wayne tells a tale from the point of view of a ghetto-dwelling victim of robbery.

81
KID FROST
Terminator
Terminator (Instrumental)
NO CHART PLACING
Electrobeat Records

This is written, played and produced by Dave Storrs, although rapper Kid Frost gets the main billing. Originating in Los Angeles, 'Terminator' was a near perfect slice of electro - futuristic but with a street edge provided by Frost's snapping delivery and its stuttering machine rhythm.

80
THE POGUES
Sally Maclennane
The Wild Rover
The Leaving Of Liverpool
54
Stiff Records

'Sally Maclennane' is one of the brilliant drinking songs written by Sean McGowan and performed with skill and much gusto by The Pogues. The titular Sally Maclennane is in fact a name given to stout which, along with the fun and camaraderie of the pub dwelling fraternity, is celebrated in the song which also carries an understanding of life's brevity. The combination of raucous high spirits with a serving of pathos was at the heart of what The Pogues were all about, and the reason their songs have become woven into the fabric of our society .

79
MADONNA
Crazy For You
I'll Fall In Love Again
(SAMMY HAGAR)
2 (1991 - 2)
Geffen Records

Madonna signed up to provide a track for the film *Vision Quest* in 1983. By the time it was released in 1985, Madonna was arguably the biggest musical star in the world. It was written to reflect the film's script and was the first ballad released by Madonna whose lyrics expressed sexual desire between lovers, couched in innuendo laden couplets. Madonna's label, *Sire*, were not keen to see 'Crazy for You' released, fearing over-saturation of the market. They needn't have feared - her audience lapped it up, and this demonstration of her versatility, if anything, broadened her appeal.

78
LAIBACH
Die Liebe/Grosste Kraft
NO CHART PLACING
Cherry Red

'Love is the greatest power which creates everything' is the message of this song, and an arsenal of sonic power is deployed to convey it. It lurches upon a hammered, militaristic beat that sounds like metal being hammered against metal. Hunting horns blare and the Sten gun rhythm vocals are shouted with great intensity. Here was music that roared. They came bedecked in neo-military uniform and utilised the iconography of harsh oppression to their own ends. We learned they were from Yugoslavia, where the group's parodies of nationalism and totalitarianism earned them the status of subversive dissidents.

77
THE CURE
In Between Days
The Exploding Boy
15
Fiction Records

The Cure had at this point developed the knack of constructing pretty, upbeat pop confections which were musically bright and breezy. These housed downbeat introspective lyrics, which pulled at the heartstrings even as one whistled the tune, this single being a prime example. 'In Between Days' presents a warm, friendly sound, perfect for radio. Acoustic guitar is used in combination with a melodic synthesiser line and the bass is a doppelgänger for something Peter Hook would perform with New Order. Robert Smith meanwhile wistfully sings a lyric full of regret at the breaking down of a relationship he is unable to fix or leave cleanly.

76
PENGUIN CAFE ORCHESTRA
Music For A Found Harmonium
Air A Danser
NO CHART PLACING
Editions EG

Simon Jeffes was a classical musician who grew tired of the constraints of the form. He had dabbled in rock music but found that equally constricting. He turned to folk music as a way of releasing his creativity but his folk music did not rely on tradition - it was a vehicle for his dream-like abstractions. He formed The Penguin Cafe Orchestra in the early 70s, an enigmatic loose aggregation of talents creating subtle musical delights that were eagerly devoured by a faithful following. 'Music For A Found Harmonium' was a piece written by Jeffes on a discarded harmonium he found and retrieved from a backstreet in Kyoto, Japan. It is a beautifully eccentric piece that acts as a comforting sticking plaster to cover a battered and bruised soul. It lifts the spirit in even the darkest of days and has become recognised by a wider audience due to its appearance on several Hollywood film soundtracks.

75
MR FINGERS
Mystery Of Love
Mystery Of Love (Dub Version)
NO CHART PLACING
Alleviated Records

Larry Heard had been a drummer in a rock band. However his enthusiasm for new technology and the sounds that could be manipulated from it was not shared by his more conservative fellow band-mates. Heard nonetheless purchased a synthesiser and drum machine and set to work building tracks. His first two efforts produced 'Washing Machine' and 'Mystery of Love'. Pleased with them, he made acetates and gave copies to DJs Frankie Knuckles and Ron Hardy who both made claims of being the track's originator. Flattered, rather than disillusioned by this back handed compliment, Heard credited himself as Mr Fingers and released 'Mystery of Love' on his own Alleviated Records label.

The house music explosion had not really begun at this point and compared with the brash high energy of hip-hop and go-go, this record seemed slow and repetitive. The UK audience did not yet embrace nor accept its sensuous charms - the sleekness of the synth lines and the complexities of the machined rhythms seemed alien. Twelve months later, following the chart success of Farley Jackmaster Funk's 'Love Can't Turn Around' *The House Sound of Chicago* album was released, containing 'Mystery of Love' and at that point the audience was ready. This track was then recognised as the true innovative classic it truly is.

74
WISEBLOOD
Motorslug/Death Rape 2000
NO CHART PLACING
K.422

Wiseblood were a duo formed by drummer/producer Roli Mosimann, who had made his name in the band Swans, and Jim Thirwell of Foetus notoriety. Together, they created monolithic slabs of industrial noise with in-your-face sexual imagery as lyrical grist to the mill. 'Motorslug' is somewhat sweeter than that. Drums pound relentlessly as usual but not unpleasant sound effects are deployed to provide respite. Thirwell, in his inimitable hiccupping style, provides a vocal that conjures an image of a demented Elvis impersonator stuck in a hell consisting entirely of lounge bars. At one point there is a detour into Doors territory and Thirwell evokes the Lizard King while Mosimann steps into the musical shoes of Ray Manzarek. The track lasts beyond the nine-minute mark but remains fabulously entertaining and always interesting.

73
LLOYD COLE AND
THE COMMOTIONS
Lost Weekend/Big World
17
Polydor

Lloyd Cole and the Commotions rode a wave of critical acclaim for a couple of years that reached a peak with the release of their debut album, *Rattlesnakes,* in 1984. Its patchier follow up, *Hard Times,* was slammed by the press, although the pair of singles it yielded were fine literary guitar pop jewels. First came 'Brand New Friend' followed by 'Lost Weekend' which describes a desultory stay in Amsterdam involving overindulgence and its consequences. The tune is played in a quick tempo with twanging guitar to the fore while Cole pours out colourful couplets in the manner of a young Bob Dylan.

72
BEASTIE BOYS
Slow And Low/Slow And Low
NO CHART PLACING
Def Jam Recordings

In 1984, Run DMC cut 'Slow and Low' as a demo but in the end never completed the track for release. It was instead passed onto the Beastie Boys' producer, Rick Rubin' who reworked the beat and the Beastie's added the line "white castle fries only come in one size". It was performed with all the cheerful zest and vigour the three Beastie Boys possessed, aligned to a blast of AC/DC sampled guitar. This was undoubtedly crude, and unsophisticated, but it was exciting and fun.

71
JOHN CALE
Dying On The Vine
Everytime The Dog's Bark
NO CHART PLACING
Beggars Banquet

I didn't like this single's parent album very much at all. *Artificial Intelligence* came with that horrible eighties production sheen that made me want to puke. It also came with Larry Sloman writing the lyrics to Cale's melodies, several of them nonsensical rubbish. Cale also chose to record using Nico's backing band, The Faction, who frankly sounded run of the mill at best. 'Dying on the Vine' was the exception to the rule. It is such a strong and beautiful song that it survives the vile sonics employed. It has a haunting quality, suggesting that the narrator's reminiscences are laced with bitter pain. Cale sings the song perfectly. He is as strident as ever, but each word seems lacerating and regretful. His performance dominates every other component part of the recording, making this an important song in his illustrious canon of work

70
THE KINKS
Living On A Thin Line
Sold Me Out
NO CHART PLACING
Arista

Here was an oddity - a Kinks single written and sung, not by Ray Davies, but by his younger sibling Dave. He reprises the themes explored by his big brother on the 1968 *The Village Green Preservation Society* album, lamenting the loss of the characteristics that had once defined Britain: decency, a sense of fair play, good manners, humour and tradition. Dave's tone is harsher than Ray's had been. He rebukes the nation's politicians while simultaneously commenting on the precarious path that The Kinks had navigated during their long tenure of high peaks and low troughs. Guitar chords are played with barely concealed aggression as the song broods and crackles with latent energy, making this the best Kinks single since the early 1970s 'Celluloid Heroes'.

69
THE COMMODORES
Night-shift/I Keep Running
3
Motown

'Night-shift' was written by drummer Walter Orange along with producer Dennis Lambert and Franne Golde, as a tribute to Marvin Gaye and Jackie Wilson who had recently died. It depicts them as working the night-shift in heaven where they are playing some sweet sounds. Marvin's song 'What's Going On' is mentioned, along with Jackie's 'Higher and Higher' and 'Baby Workout'. Walter Orange sings lead, but it is the harmonies with JD Nichols where the song truly soars and takes on the feel of a spiritual requiem for the two lost soul music giants.

68
RON HARDY
Sensation (Long)
Sensation (Short)/Sensation (Dub)
NO CHART PLACING
Trax Records

Ron Hardy was a seminal figure in the early Chicago house scene alongside Frankie Knuckles. Hardy DJed at the Music Box in a manner that was the opposite of the smoothness Knuckles employed at The Warehouse. His sets were characterized by their energy and volume, mixing up Philadelphia disco, Italo-disco and new wave, often shifting the pitch upwards to maximise the drama and emotion. His recorded legacy is slim as he was hamstrung by a heroin addiction that would kill him aged 33 in 1982. 'Sensation' however was a ground-breaking release that went a long way towards establishing the house sound and the iconic Trax Records label it was released on. Produced by label boss Larry Sherman and with a brilliant vocal from Adrienne Jett, who would record one more track with Jamie Principal before disappearing, this remains an absolutely sublime record.

67
BIG BLACK
Rema Rema
NO CHART PLACING
Forced Exposure [White Label]

'Rema Rema' is a one-sided single version of a song by the band Rema Rema. Its 300 copies pressing was given away to subscribers of *Forced Exposure* magazine. It is at the more accessible end of Big Black leader, Steve Albini's, oeuvre. It pounds in a ceaseless fashion while guitars buzz. Meanwhile a sinister laughing vocal sits in the midst of the noise. It is disconcerting but recognizable as pop music too. In 1991 the recording received a proper release.

66
MARC ALMOND
The House Is Haunted (By The Echo Of Your Last Goodbye)/
Broken Bracelets/Cara A Cara/
Medley (Unchain My Heart/
Black Heart/Take My Heart/
Burning Boats
55
Virgin/Some Bizzare

Marc Almond was highly prolific - a laudable trait as long as one's quality control remains of a high standard. Thankfully he excelled in that area. His ear for a tune was remarkable, and while he had proved himself no slouch in penning very fine songs for himself, his impeccable taste in choosing other people's material to record was an undoubted asset also. 'The House is Haunted' was a little-known ballad of lost love dating back to 1934. Almond invests into it his heavily-dramatised, wildly emotional style. playing the role of a lonely heartbroken ex-lover to a pained tee.

65
CYBOTRON
R-9 / R-9 (Instrumental)
NO CHART PLACING
Fantasy

Whilst Chicago was spawning house music, the equally powerful musical force of techno was being birthed in Detroit. Cybotron were absolutely at the forefront of that creative explosion. Their music was growing ever more potent and fully realised, though soon after this release Juan Atkins would leave the band due to irreconcilable differences about musical direction with partner Richard Davis. Here however they return to formative influences and combine their passion for Kraftwerk and George Clinton to forge a futuristic, funk master-class, based on the biblical texts relating to Revelation 9. It grooves and rocks fabulously, whilst its bass line is positively evil.

64
MICRODISNEY
Birthday Girl /Harmony Time/
Money For The Trams
NO CHART PLACING
Rough Trade

Microdisney hailed from Cork, and were led by co-writers Sean O'Hagan and Cathal Coughlan. Intelligence and integrity were key components in their sound, aided by excellent tunesmithery. On 'Birthday Girl', they play a jolly easy-on-the-ear piece led by a keyboard that seems to signify good times. It disguises a pessimistic and angry lyric, detailing the miserable and squalid lives acted out between birth and death. It is sung with an enthusiasm close to perverse relish by Coughlan.

63
SCHOOLLY-D
P.S.K.-What Does It Mean?
Gucci Time
NO CHART PLACING
Schoolly-D Records

From the streets of Philadelphia came Schoolly D and his self-released, reverb drenched, social commentary 'P.S.K.' single, P.S.K. being the abbreviation for 'Park Side Killers', a gang to whom Schoolly D was affiliated. He talked graphically of drugs, sex and guns, and in doing so sowed a seed that spread through the hip-hop community like wildfire. He changed perceptions of what could be done with the form. His record was not radio friendly - it was anti-establishment, energetic, raw and real. It was where the spirit of the wildest free jazz and punk rock were taken up by rap crews. It was gangsta rap, two years in advance of NWA. It was revolutionary art. Listen closely to the Radiohead track 'Idioteque' from their *Kid A* album (2000), and the beat is basically a sped-up version of 'P.S.K'.

62
WHAM!
I'm Your Man
Do It Right (Instrumental)
1
Epic

Energy and joy are combined here on a song George Michael knocked out to kill time on an aeroplane flight. It is up-tempo, given a breathless, soulful performance that is totally uplifting. Six months later, Wham!

were over as George Michael began a solo career aimed at a more adult audience, confirming his astonishing talent. However, the most magical pop thrills that were his legacy were the singles he released with Andrew Ridgeley as Wham!.

61
LL COOL J
I Can't Live Without My Radio
I Can Give You More
NO CHART PLACING
Def Jam Recordings

Rock guitar riffs and turntable scratches combine over a crunching beat. While LL Cool J salutes the sounds coming out of his ghetto blaster in hyperactive raps, it is dated - unmistakably the sound of 1985, but that sound was big, bold and mighty.

60
DAVID BOWIE
Loving The Alien
Don't Look Down
19
EMI America

David Bowie's album *Tonight* was atrocious - mostly terrible songs swamped in horribly excessive production. However a few were good songs swamped in horribly excessive production. This fell into the latter category. Edited and remixed it was a good, if not great, Bowie single. The artist had put his heart into the song and 'Loving the Alien' was Bowie laying bare his dislike of organised religion. So, although the fussiness of its studio polish diminished the song of several degrees of its power, the beauty at its heart was still glimpsed. It retained its haunting melodic pull, and there was, without any doubt, serious intent locked into Bowie's ominous sounding vocal.

59
THE CHILLS
This Is The Way/Never Never Go/
Don't Even Know Her Name/ Bee
Bah Bee Bah Bee Boe/
Whole Weird World/Dream By
Dream, Dream By Dream [Parts
One to Four]
NO CHART PLACING
Flying Nun Records

Under the umbrella title of *The Lost EP* came this 12-inch package of unhinged genius from everybody's favourite New Zealand band on our favourite New Zealand record label. The death of drummer Martyn Bull in 1983 brought about a period of mourning that caused huge instability in the line-up. Martin Phillipps went through over 20 different band members inside two years. "Fill your head with alcohol, comic books and drugs" runs a line in 'This Is The Way', which offers an indication of Phillipps' state of mind. The music remained as beautiful and psychedelically tinged as ever, although it is certainly dark-hued on the monotone voiced 'Whole Weird World' and the shape-shifting five parts of 'Dream by Dream'.

58
DEXYS MIDNIGHT RUNNERS
This Is What She's Like
(Full Length Version)
Marguerita Time
78
Mercury

Don't Stand Me Down was the Dexys album released in September. It came with a new look for the band - preppy Brook Brothers style suits were now the chosen apparel. The music press ridiculed them, saying they looked like double glazing salesmen. The undoubtedly challenging material was, by and large, scorned too. Although there was a notable minority who heralded it as tremendous work, songs did not behave in the conventional manner. The use of conversational dialogue between and within songs was not to the liking of the critics. Kevin Rowland initially refused to countenance a single release to support the album, but terrible sales forced his hand and a three-minute edit of the album centrepiece, the 12-minute 'This Is What She's Like' was released. It was too late to stimulate sales - negative attitudes were already entrenched and the failure of the album, the failure of the single, and a disastrous tour in half-empty theatres signalled the beginning of the end for the band and the spiralling out of control of Kevin Rowland's mental health. The shame was that, particularly in its unedited form, 'This Is What She's Like' was a thing of rare beauty - a three-part suite of interconnecting musical themes and a lyric that was about love and desire, but also incorporated themes of class division into its musings.

57
WALLY BADAROU
Chief Inspector (Vine Street)
Chief Inspector (Hill Street)
46
4th & Broadway

Wally Badarou was a close associate of Level 42 and contributed his keyboard, production and writing skills to their material. He became a sought after session musician and producer. A part of The Compass Point Allstars, he worked with many acts including Felá Kuti, Marianne Faithful, Grace Jones, Talking Heads and Mick Jagger. He did not neglect his solo work and his 1984 album *Echoes* yielded this daring piece of instrumental dance-floor exotica. It was an absolute compulsory DJ selection in British soul clubs - its dirty groove, spy film horn riffs and tropical percussion combining to make 'Chief Inspector' a one-of-a-kind, impossible-to-replicate bomb of a record.

56
RUEFREX
The Wild Colonial Boy
Even In The Dark Hours
NO CHART PLACING
Kasper Records

This Irish band fearlessly addressed an emotive political issue with 'Wild Colonial Boy' and their unambiguous condemnation of people in far off places (USA) who have romantic notions of noble struggle, funding terror in the land of their forefathers (Ireland) is delivered with all the forensic skill of a surgeon cutting out a harmful cancer. Guitars blaze, the vocal is contemptuously angry and every word is scalpel-sharp. "It always gives quite a thrill, to kill from far away" is just one example of the power of language on display.

55
BOBBY WOMACK
I Wish He Didn't Trust Me So Much
Got To Be With You Tonight
NO CHART PLACING
MCA Records

The speed with which he had married the widow of his great friend Sam Cooke meant whispered rumours of wrongdoing were forever associated with their union. Those persistent rumours gave this song the feeling of being a confessional, even though it was not written by Womack. It is a song about romantic duplicity and the guilt felt about the betrayal of a friend whose wife the narrator is involved with. The song is given a stripped-back, feather light touch instrumentally, with Bobby Womack singing the life out of it at the fore. His gritty voice expresses pain and regret in what is a brilliant performance.

54
COIL
Aqua Regis/Panic/Tainted Love
NO CHART PLACING
Force & Form

Coil were formed by Peter 'Sleazy' Christopherson and John Balance, refugees from Psychic TV. They were joined in the studio for this release by Jim Thirwell, acting as producer. 'Aqua Regis' is an instrumental, connected to 'Panic', which explores the concept of using fear as key to unlocking creative potential. Guitar feedback and machine rhythms accompany John Balance's self-styled feral vocals that culminate in a chant of "the only thing to fear is fear itself". The other side of the single features an atmospheric funeral-paced version of Ed Cobbs' 'Tainted Love', popularised by Soft Cell. A reflection of the emerging HIV/AIDS epidemic that was decimating the gay community, it is a stunning and harrowing recording. The extraordinary vocal offered up by Balance is assisted by Christopherson, wrenching the singer's arm up his back to add real pain to the performance, helping to make this a record that is deeply moving and quite unforgettable.

53
TENOR SAW
Ring The Alarm / Ring The Alarm (Version)
NO CHART PLACING
Techniques

Clive Bright (AKA Tenor Saw) was a 19-year-old upstart competing at the first Jamaican dancehall sound clash. He was pitted against Black Scorpio, King Jammy's Hi Fi and Arrows International. Tenor Saw stole the show and claimed the crown as he freestyled his way into the crowd's hearts with his lethal put downs of his rivals. 'Ring the Alarm' was the title of his triumphant piece and it was recorded for Winston Riley's *Techniques* label. It was a Jamaican smash and Tenor Saw's youthful, clear and unhurried vocal style was massively appealing. Sadly, aged just 21, Clive Bright lost his life in Texas to an alleged hit and run driver.

52
DOUBLE D & STEINSKI
Lessons 1 – 3: - Lesson 3 (History Of Hip-hop Mix)/The Payoff Mix (Mastermix of G.L.O.B.E. And Whiz Kid's: "Play That Beat Mr. D.J.") /Lesson 2 (James Brown Mix)
NO CHART PLACING
Tommy Boy

Double D & Steinski were older than many of their peers in the world of hip-hop aged 27 and 31 respectively, but they were steeped in the culture and had encyclopedic musical knowledge. They teamed up to enter a promotional competition run by the Tommy Boy label to remix the track 'Play That Beat Mr. D.J.' and their sampled collage won first prize. It was a dizzying piece, containing elements of disco and funk records with snippets by The Supremes, Little Richard, Humphrey Bogart and instructional tap dance records. They followed that success up with further lessons. Their treatment of a whole sequence of breaks taken from James Brown records was simply mind-blowing.

51
THE TRIFFIDS
You Don't Miss Your Water (Till Your Well Runs Dry)/Convent Walls/Beautiful Waste
You Don't Miss Your Water (Till Your Well Runs Dry) (Instrumental)
NO CHART PLACING
Hot Records

The Triffids take William Bell's 60s country-tinged soul classic on a trip to the Australian outback, where the country aspect of the song is magnified with the use of fiddles and steel guitar. The song is slowed to a snail's pace and David McComb sings as though he is absolutely parched. The presence of previous single 'Beautiful Waste' as an added track on this 12-inch was further reason to celebrate this record's existence.

50
CAMEO
Single Life/Hangin' Downtown
15
Club

Moving with the times, Larry Blackman had slimmed down Cameo from a Funkadelic-sized and sound-alike large ensemble, replete with horn section, to a sleek three-piece whose effect was no less funky. Now thoroughly modern and powered by synthesiser, they were here celebrating - at least superficially - a hedonistic, free-wheeling, bachelor lifestyle. Although there was a knowing tongue-in-cheek element to Cameo that implied they were not to be taken seriously, their power was not in their message but inside their infectious grooves.

49
ERASURE
Who Needs Love Like That
Push Me Shove Me
55
Mute

This was the debut single for Erasure following the breakup of Vince Clarke's highly successful Yazoo and in many ways it is very much a continuation of that band's style, with new singer Andy Bell almost mimicking Alison Moyet's vocal phrasing. That said, this is an excellent single, with an up-tempo dance groove that goes hand in hand with a gorgeous melody. It is lyrically clear-sighted in its examination of the emotional fallout caused by a destructive relationship. This new partnership would soon find its feet and become more individual and expressive. Huge success would come too and in 1992 a frankly inferior remixed version of 'Who Needs Love Like That' would give the band a Number 10 chart placing.

48
ANDRÉ CYMONE
The Dance Electric/Red Light
NO CHART PLACING
CBS

André Simon Anderson, aka André Cymone, was a teenage friend of Prince who moved into the Anderson household aged 12, following a disagreement with his father. They played together in a band called 94 East, and following the release of Prince's debut album, André became the bassist in his pre-Revolution touring band. Tensions between the two saw a split, but the relationship was patched up well enough for Prince to gift this song to André. It is a truly outstanding slice of electro-funk with lyrical themes expressing positivity and love, advocating loving our enemies at several points. With Prince producing and Andre following the purple one's guide vocal, this is as close to a slice of prime Prince funk as one can get.

47
COCTEAU TWINS
Aikea-Guinea/Kookaburra
Quisquose/Rococo
41
4AD

The three-piece Cocteau Twins had created a musical universe in which they were the sole inhabitants. Their music was a previously unheard language for us to decipher. Aikea-Guinea - titled from a Scottish colloquialism for a seashell - was one of their regular bulletins beamed down to we mere mortals on planet earth. It is a floating, ethereal wonder - at its core simple bass, drum and guitar, but it swirls and moves like a bird in flight, graceful and awe-inspiring. Touches of piano and a synthesised choir are added by Robin Guthrie, whilst Elizabeth Fraser sings beautifully, her voice seemingly carried on gossamer-thin wings.

46
YELLO
Vicious Games / Blue Nabou
NO CHART PLACING
Elektra

Yello lost founder member Carlos Peron between the release of 'Gotta Say Yes To Another Excess' and the recording of 'Stella', which yielded four excellent singles including 'Vicious Games'. The group's focus is sharper than before as they pursue a European pop dance direction. There remained though an unsettling undercurrent to their music. It was theatrical and melodramatic, voiced exquisitely by Rush Winters and painstakingly produced by Boris Blank. This was a record of high ambition that stood out as being individualistic and of rare quality.

45
THE LONG RYDERS
Looking For Lewis And Clark
Child Bride
59
Island Records

The Long Ryders had formed at the beginning of the decade and had been a part of the psychedelically tinged, paisley underground scene. This gave way to a more roots-flavoured combination of country and classic rock. They seemed poised to be huge in the manner of R.E.M. or Tom Petty, signing to Island Records in the UK who released 'Looking For Lewis And Clark' as a single. It kicked like a mule. It rocked. Syd Griffin barked out the lyrics that referenced Tim Buckley and Gram Parsons as though his life depended on it. Harmonica gave it colour, and it rode out on a wigged-out guitar solo - great stuff! A year later they allowed their music to be used in a beer commercial. Credibility was lost, momentum came to a juddering halt and The Long Ryders were yesterday's news.

44
SHAYNE CARTER &
PETER JEFFERIES
Randolph's Going Home
Hooked, Lined and Sunken
NO CHART PLACING
Flying Nun Records

Shayne Carter led bands Bored Games, Straitjacket Fits and the Doublehappys while Peter Jeffries was a key man in This Kind of Punishment and Nocturnal Projections and they teamed up for this single which is Lo-Fi but nonetheless truly epic carried by the emotion of the playing and the desperate edge in the vocal. It is a transportive and truly moving piece of music, perhaps the best record from the whole Dunedin-based musical scene from where came many truly great records.

43
GRACE JONES
Slave To The Rhythm (Blooded)/
Junk Yard/Annihilated Rhythm
12
Island Records

Co-Written by Bruce Woolley, Simon Darlow, Stephen Lipsom and produced by Trevor Horn, the original intention was for the song to be given to Frankie Goes To Hollywood as the follow up to 'Relax'. That plan changed and Grace Jones became the recipient of a song that fit her like a glove.

Production wise Horn pulled out all the stops in sculpting the sound while Grace Jones offered up a sublime vocal delivered with her customary bite as she comments on America's shameful history of slave plantations and exploitation in general terms.

42
THE BANGLES
Manic Monday
In a Different Light
2
CBS

Prince wrote 'Manic Monday' for the group Apollonia 6 in 1984 but ultimately held it back and offered it to Bangles' rhythm guitar player Susanna Hoffs. It was recorded in their guitar pop style with Prince credited as 'Christopher', the name of the character he portrays in his film *Under the Cherry Moon*. The song is clever though slight. It describes a woman waking at 6am on a Monday morning and bemoaning her busy schedule as she would rather return to her dreams of the romance she enjoyed on Sunday. The Bangles bring a refreshing joyousness to the song, it is sunny and vibrant with lots of nice production touches atop its sparkling piano bedrock. Radio-friendly and full of irresistible hooks it gave The Bangles their first and most memorable hit.

41
TOM WAITS
Downtown Train/Tango Till They're Sore
NO CHART PLACING
Island Records

Nobody captured bruised romance quite like Tom Waits. Nobody wrote songs from the point of view of a tattered and torn misfit like Tom Waits. Nobody else stepped into the world of the ragged bohemian as effortlessly as Tom Waits. 'Downtown Train' inhabits the same world Roy Orbison sang of in his lonesome sixties tearjerkers. Now though, the landscape is more ragged and desolate and its inhabitants, like the narrator of this song, are world weary and have a near tragic desperation in their longing for love and shelter.

40
DIANA ROSS
Chain Reaction/More and More
1
Capitol Records

Star-studded records don't always guarantee success. Diana's previous release, 'Eaten Alive', had got no higher than number 71 in the chart, despite being written and produced by The Bee Gees and Michael Jackson, so it must have been with some trepidation that 'Chain Reaction' was issued. It was another song written and produced by the Gibb brothers. They had been unsure about offering it to Ross, fearing she would reject it as being too Motown-like, after her deliberate act of distancing herself from her sixties hits and persona. Nobody need have worried - a good song is a good song and 'Chain Reaction' was very good indeed. It certainly echoed the Motown formula, though the relentless chugging R&B rhythms and gigantic choruses cloaked in eighties production techniques. Inside the grooves, Diana seemed totally comfortable, and her characteristic breathy vocal was the perfect counterpoint to the motorised beat.

39
THE SMITHS
How Soon Is Now?
Well I Wonder/Oscillate Wildly
24 (1992 - 16)
Rough Trade

How peculiar that 'How Soon Is Now?' is widely-acknowledged as being The Smiths' best song whilst being the least representative of their usual sound. Written by Johnny Marr and with a working title of 'Swamp', for indeed it was swampy sounding, it grooves, has an intoxicating atmosphere about it, and rather than incorporating lots of chord changes, as was standard practice in Smiths' songs, 'How Soon Is Now?' is hypnotic and repetitive, based largely around a single chord. A sound is conjured that is one part Bo Diddley shuffle, another part Can space-rock, combined with an unchanging beat holding it together and ratcheting up the tension. Recorded through the night, amidst a haze of marijuana smoke and crimson lights, the track was sent over to Stephen Morrissey, who provided a lyric and vocal the next morning.

38
ART OF NOISE
Moments In Love
Beat Box (Diversion Ten)
87
ZTT

Perhaps this record slipped through the cracks because Art of Noise were a faceless studio-based aggregation of musicians and conceptual theorists playing, on this occasion, a subtle instrumental piece of music worthy of Debussy. Whatever the reason, somehow this gorgeous peon to sensuality, set to the pace of a human heart, received next to no radio play, a fact that meant its sales were disappointingly terrible.

37
JULIAN COPE
Sunspots
I Went On A Chourney
76
Mercury

Julian was, by 1985, largely perceived to have lost his marbles. And he certainly embraced the role of maverick eccentric. While the record company and general public regarded him as a spent force, he was left to please himself. The pressure of serving up hits was removed and he could make music without compromise. 'Sunspots' was fabulous, recycling the kind of riff that The Rolling Stones used for their neo-psychedelic 'Citadel' and adding a plodding bass with an amusing squelching sound. Julian sings in a lovely plummy voice as though reading aloud *Winnie the Pooh* to a group of fascinated children. For further amusement, he constructs and executes a chorus that finds him impersonating the sound of a passing motor car. This was charming, magical stuff indeed.

36
JAMIE PRINCIPLE
Waiting On My Angel
Waiting on My Angel
(Instrumental Dub-Mix)
NO CHART PLACING
ZYX Records

Jamie Principle was a fairly unique proposition on the Chicago house music scene. His tracks drew influence from David Bowie, Prince and Depeche Mode, whereas the majority of acts were working from a blueprint laid out by Parliament/ Funkadelic. As a consequence, Principle's recordings had a lyrical quality not heard elsewhere. He was championed by Frankie Knuckles, although increasingly he would come to feel exploited by the legendary DJ. 'Waiting On My Angel' was a track Principle had recorded at home using synth and playing live drums several years before its release. It is a majestic mid-paced piece, equally effective as a dance-floor filler or simply for listening and luxuriating to in its groove and playful sensuality. Principle sings in a style pitched somewhere betwixt Bowie and Prince and the recording is enhanced by occasional peels of maniacal laughter that help make this truly memorable.

35
THE JESUS AND MARY CHAIN
You Trip Me Up/
Just Out Of Reach
57
Blanco Y Negro

Their gigs amounted to 15 minutes of drunken, incoherent noise that inevitably finished in full scale riots. The band were nobody's idea of what a professional act sounded like but they looked great - like the bastard offspring of the Velvet Underground - and they gave off a genuine, couldn't-give-a-fuck attitude that was refreshing, and more exciting than anything else on offer in UK clubs.

Having sacked their preposterously young drummer and replaced him with Bobbie Gillespie, who had no discernible ability, they stretched minimalism to its limit. He looked great though, and crucially he clearly got it! 'You Trip Me Up' was brilliant – tuneful, sweet-hearted pop, turned upon its head by a hateful lyric. No idealised version of romance for these boys. Its prettiness was almost completely drowned out by rumbling bass, hissing guitars and the sound of rock traditionalists' jaws dropping and smashing on the floor.

34
MADNESS
Yesterday's Men/All I Knew
18
Zarjazz

Even Nutty Boys grow up eventually. Madness were no exception, and their much-loved cheeky chappy personas were discarded for this quiet meditation on life. It is gloomily introspective and melancholy but beautifully conceived and delivered. The transient position they occupied as pop stars in decline left them feeling tired, drained and undervalued. They captured their collective emotional state perfectly. The beginning of the end for Madness had actually begun when Mike Barson had quit the band the year before. 'Yesterday's Men' constituted a glorious top quality last hurrah.

33
TEARS FOR FEARS
Shout/The Big Chair
4
Mercury

This was simple and repetitive. It didn't require sophistication and didn't receive any. Out went introspection and subtlety and, to deliver this song without ambiguity, in came power chords, thumping percussion, and even a guitar solo. For the mantra like lyric, Roland Orzabal chanted his encouragement of people questioning the dictates that are issued from above, examining what they entail, and if in disagreement, not simply accepting this state of affairs passively, but using the power of their voice to protest and protest loudly.

32
GODLEY & CREME
Cry/Love Bombs
19
Polydor

Kevin Godley and Lol Creme had arrived at a point where their fame and earning potential was much higher as video makers than as song-writing musicians. Through their video work they met Trevor Horn, famed producer and head of the ZTT Record label. They asked him to work with them and he acquiesced, only to discover they had little in the way of songs that were complete. 'Cry' was a germ of an idea with just the first verse written. That verse set the scene of a man whose partner is lying and cheating on him. Horn put Godley into the vocal booth and asked him to make up the song as he sang, line-by-line, piece-by-piece. It came together, with an added Featherlight-synthesised backing track that worked brilliantly it gave the duo a record that bore comparison with the immortal 'I'm Not In Love', their 10cc masterpiece from the mid-1970s.

31
NICO
My Funny Valentine
My Heart Is Empty
NO CHART PLACING
Beggars Banquet

'My Funny Valentine' is a bitter-sweet torch song written by Rogers and Hart, popularised by superb performers such as Ella Fitzgerald and Chet Baker. For a non-conventional singer such as Nico, it could have represented a challenge to pull off a performance of the song that wouldn't be derided by critics. She overcame the challenge with grace and displayed a versatility few would have foreseen. She abandoned her favoured style of the period - a stern and authoritative bellow - replacing it with a smooth rendition that displayed fragility. Nico sounded wounded and vulnerable in what was a moving, emotional master-class of understatement, aided by a sparse piano and muted trumpet accompaniment. With John Cale producing her for the first time in more than a decade, the stars were aligned and suggested a brighter future. Tragically, the next year she suffered a minor heart attack whilst cycling and died as a result of her fall.

30
THE POGUES
A Pair Of Brown Eyes
Whiskey You're The Devil
Muirshin Durkin
72
Stiff Records

Accompanied by a tune that is a stumbling distant cousin of 'Wild Mountain Thyme', a story unfolds from the perspective of two men taking solace in a bar. A young man who has lost his love to a rival laments that loss in self-pity, whilst an old man sat beside him speaks of his pain as he recollects the suffering and loss of life of his soldiering days. Shane McGowan penned the lyric in a painterly fashion, setting the scene so that we visualise the men sitting together but each equally alone lost in their reminiscences. On the jukebox, Johnny Cash sings 'A Thing Called Love', his bruised, slightly slurred voice conveying all the poignancy and the nuances of the encounter.

29
ASHFORD AND SIMPSON
Solid/Solid (Dub Version)
3
Capitol Records

Nick Ashford and Valerie Simpson were the husband and wife writer/producers of scores of hits including Chaka Khan's 'I'm Every Woman', Diana Ross's 'Ain't No Mountain High Enough' and Marvin Gaye and Tammi Terrell's 'You're All I Need To Get By'. They had simultaneously maintained their own career as performers since the early sixties and finally had a huge hit under their own names with 'Solid'. It is a song about a long term couple and their enduring love, a recognition of the fact that going through bad times together and retaining faith in the relationship strengthens the bond, until it is as 'Solid' as a rock.

28
DAF
Brothers (Robert Gabi's Mix) Brothers (Mike Hedge's Mix)
NO CHART PLACING
Illuminated Records

The fierce aggression and jagged edges of previous releases were swapped for something altogether more sensuous and smooth for this regrouping of DAF. Here they immerse themselves in the subject of male-on-male love. They project the love they speak of as being innocent and brotherly. The insinuation of a more physical bonding is in the song's undercurrent and gives it a highly sexual frisson.

27
PSYCHIC TV
& THE ANGELS OF LIGHT
Godstar/Godstar (B.J. Mix)
67
Temple Records

With Alex Ferguson hammering out a very Rolling Stones-style riff on guitar, and Chris Thomas - famed for his production work with Roxy Music and Sex Pistols - this was in many ways the most orthodox Psychic TV release. The exception is, of course, Genesis P-Orridge, who had a deep obsession with Brian Jones, and takes the opportunity to tell an extremely prejudicial version of that doomed guitar player's life story. His band-mates are cast in a most unfavourable light, accused of stealing glory. They are described as "laughing friends", unwilling to help as Jones goes to his death "like a lamb going to slaughter". It was, no doubt, uncomfortable listening for those in the Stones camp. It was vicious in its attack on them and its apportioning of blame. But this unpleasant telling of (a version of) the truth did also celebrate Jones' undeniable talent in absolutely rollicking fine style.

26
THE CLASH
This Is England
Do It Now/Sex Mad Roar
24
CBS

This was The Clash in name only. With Mick Jones having joined Nicky Headon in receiving a P45 from Joe Strummer, this was now a band without a soul and barely a tune. Somehow, for some reason, Strummer allowed the band's manager, Bernie Rhodes, to become his equal creative partner. It was a disastrous move. An album called *Cut the Crap* was released, which would have been more appropriate and honest if it had been simply titled *Crap*! Of the 12 songs on the album, 11 were dreadful. Any quality they may have possessed was lost in the cack-handed way the songs were produced, using massed crowd chanting and drum machines that sounded like car crashes. The exception was the magnificent 'This is England', which proved to be the last Clash single, one of the best records bearing the band's name. It is a frenzied, angry, state-of-the-nation address from Strummer, who talks about alienation, violence, racism, the shrinking of the country's industrial base and subsequent joblessness. He condemns Thatcher's triumphant Falklands War and despairs at the subservience and complicit silence of so many British citizens at the obvious wrongs within society. Sound-wise too, 'This Is England' hits the spot. A guitar buzzes through it that resembles a chainsaw. The electronic rhythms are sparse and appropriate, as is the football crowd chorus.

25
DAVID BOWIE/
PAT METHENY GROUP
This Is Not America
This Is Not America (Instrumental)
14
EMI America

Collaborative soundtrack work yielded good results for David Bowie, and this teaming up with noted jazz guitarist Pat Metheny and his band, taken from *The Falcon And The Snowman* film score, proved no exception. The genesis of 'This Is Not America' is in the Pat Metheny instrumental track 'Chris', which was adapted for the newer piece titled from a piece of film dialogue spoken by a Mexican guard in a scene revolving around Sean Penn. The song has a mournful quality, is extremely understated and minimal, whilst Bowie's lyrics follow the film's plot about American political interference in the affairs of other countries. The Pat Metheny Group are quiet and tasteful in their playing. There is no grandstanding, leaving room for a deft vocal performance from Bowie, whose phrasing is immaculate, while his reshaping of the word 'America' is the major conveyor of shifts in dramatic feel.

24
KATE BUSH
Cloudbusting
Burning Bridge
20
EMI

Kate Bush read *A Book Of Dreams* by Peter Reich, the son of Wilhelm Reich, a psychoanalyst who had invented a machine he called a 'cloudbuster' to make rain. He was arrested because of his theories, his books banned and destroyed and he died in prison. Kate sings the song from the perspective of the son. It is not a song about his father or his work but about the love he felt for him, the appreciation of his father's courage in espousing unpopular views that he believed were to mankind's benefit. It is a song about feelings, a song about loss, and a child's wish to help his father. It is a lyrical masterpiece that conveys wonder, joy, fear and forlorn hope. The music created for the song is every bit as powerful - a repetitive piece that feels like a march, powered by dramatic and moving, sawing cello. Another thrilling and audacious single from this young woman who was touched by that rarest of gifts, genius.

23
NEW ORDER
Sub-Culture/Dub-Vulture
63
Factory

The self-written and produced 'Sub-Culture' was a track on New Order's *Low-life* album. For its release as a single it was radically altered and stretched by New York electro giant John Robie whose remix aimed the song firmly towards the dance-floor. Famed sleeve designer Peter Saville found the result not to his taste and so the record was issued in a plain black sleeve as he deemed it unworthy of his talent. I thought it was smashing!

22
FINE YOUNG CANNIBALS
Blue/Wade In The Water
41
London Records

As members of The Beat, bassist David Steele and guitarist Andy Cox had nailed their political colours to the mast, performing the straight to the point 'Stand down Margaret'. Their anger remained unabated and, with the soulful voiced Roland Gift equally in accord, Fine Young Cannibals released this unambiguous statement. They use a seductive melody to get their message across. Acoustic guitar and piano are combined with programmed drums to fine effect while Gift announces he's having a bad day and proceeds to lay the blame for the way he feels firmly at the Conservative government's door. How he feels, he explains, is wronged by their lies and their policies of hateful discrimination that are destroying communities. Angry at the misery they inflict uncaringly, he concludes that even the colour of blue that they sport is cruel, and life would be better without it.

21
THE JESUS AND MARY CHAIN
Just Like Honey/Head
45
Blanco Y Negro

If we presumed that The Jesus and Mary Chain were a one-trick pony, we presumed wrong. Out went the corrosive assault upon the senses, and for this single in came a quite gorgeous melody, that from its drummed Ronettes 'Be My Baby' intro, heads off into a Phil Spector-like wall of sound. The lyrics suggest conflicted emotions of acceptance mixed with resentment. Sexual metaphors abound within the layers of meaning and feeding back guitars that are used exquisitely.

20
LEONARD COHEN
Hallelujah/The Law
NO CHART PLACING (2016 - 36)
CBS

At this point in his career, Leonard Cohen and his music had become extremely unfashionable. His image was that of a depressing folk singer who had been hip in the 60s. This was, of course, nonsense, but an image, no matter how inaccurate, is a hard thing to shake. 'Hallelujah' came from the album *Various Positions*, which was Cohen's first release in five years and his record company hated it. He was reunited with producer John Lissauer, whose sense of theatre had helped make 1974s *New Skin for the Old Ceremony* an artistic triumph, although it sold very poorly. Cohen had changed in the preceding decade, synthesiser replaced acoustic guitar as his song-writing tool of choice, and his voice had deepened considerably. 'Hallelujah' was one of the high points of the album, and an obvious choice to be a single. It was highly poetic and concerned itself with sex, love, betrayal and other such matters, using biblical allusions as metaphors. It was cut down from its 80 written verses to a manageable four-and-a-half minute length and played in 12/8 time, evoking a waltz over which Leonard dead-pans the lyrics. It was magnificent and almost completely ignored until John Cale recorded a version in 1981 and opened the floodgates of recognition for a magnificent song.

19
MARK STEWART
AND THE MAFIA
Hypnotized/As The Veneer Of
Democracy Begins To Fade
NO CHART PLACING
Mute

Once Mark Stewart was teamed with U.S. imported musicians Keith Leblanc, Skip McDonald and Doug Wimbish - who constituted 'The Mafia' - there was not a more ferocious sounding outfit operating anywhere in the music world. The fact that the man sat in the producer's chair and adding keyboards to the sonic blizzard was Adrian Sherwood elevated the whole thing to stratospheric heights. 'Hypnotized' represents one of this collective's great moments. It is dissident, anti-capitalist, anti-authoritarian, cavernous dub, coming from a darkly, funky place where voices drift in and out of the spine-tinglingly electronic mix.

18
THE THREE JOHNS
Death Of The European
Heads Like Convicts
NO CHART PLACING
Abstract Records

The Three Johns kick up a veritable storm here: guitars slash and the drum machine rhythm is hammered as John Hyatt expresses his colourful lyric pertaining to Europe's surrendering its cultural identity to the nation of Mickey Mouse and burgers. A delightful bonus in the shape of live favourite, Marc Bolan's '20th Century Boy', nestled on the flip of this rip snorting cracker.

17
MANTRONIX
Needle To The Groove/Jamming
On The Groove (Dub Version)
NO CHART PLACING
Sleeping Bag Records

This record is aggressively forward thinking - it mixes rap, robotic voices, scratching, beats and slabs of synthesised noise with great finesse. In doing these things, the groove never gives up and remains jumping, fresh and funky.

16
PROPAGANDA
Dual/Jewel
21
ZTT

'Dual', backed by the more aggressive version of the same song named 'Jewel', introduced the sound of Propaganda to daytime radio listeners and even an appearance on *Top of the Pops* for which Stewart Copeland of The Police guested on drums and percussion. The song is a dissection of a relationship that is painfully failing, and each deception and betrayal is compared to a knife cut. It is sung magnificently with real conviction by Suzanne Freytag, despite ZTT main man Trevor Horn's opinion that she could not sing. That opinion had forced the group to recruit second vocalist Claudia Brücken.

15
MODEL 500
Night Drive/No UFO'S (D-Mix)
NO CHART PLACING
Metroplex

Following on from Juan Atkin's Model 500 debut 'No UFOs', which was a jaw-droppingly brilliant record, came 'Nightdrive' which I thought even better. Inspired by the nocturnal missions of Atkins' driving along the interstate across the state of Michigan, he captures a feeling of speeding beneath neon. The garbled vocal is only intermittently audible and adds edginess to the sleazy, squelching electronic funk. This was Kraftwerk's 'Autobahn', transported through space and time to a darker and more dangerous place all together.

14
ROBERT WYATT
& SWAPO SINGERS
The Wind Of Change/Namibia
86
Rough Trade

The 'Wind Of Change' referred to here is one needed to rid Namibia of rule by the brutal apartheid government of South Africa and allow self-determination. It is a protest song taken from an album by The SWAPO Singers – SWAPO standing for South West African People's Organisation. This single was rearranged by Jerry Dammers who turned it into a swinging, ska-tinged, big band workout, featuring Dammers, Lynval Golding and Dick Cuthal from The Specials, with Robert Wyatt's plaintive voice added to that of the SWAPO Singers. The intention is clearly to bring the issues of people seeking freedom and justice to a wider audience and it is an infectious and uplifting piece of music full of optimism and hope.

13
FINE YOUNG CANNIBALS
Johnny Come Home
Good Times And Bad
8
London Records

Fine Young Cannibals had sent their music to practically every record label in the country and been rejected. Somehow, an appearance on the Friday evening TV show *The*

Tube was wangled. It was a brilliant showcase, and was seized upon by the band, whose performance was tuneful, energetic and highly visual. Suddenly, the phone never stopped ringing with offers. 'Johnny Come Home' was the debut single and rocketed them into the chart. It detailed the plight of a teenage runaway learning the harsh lessons of the street - friendless, penniless, homeless and ripe for exploitation. The choruses come from the perspective of his parents who acknowledge their faults now it is too late, as well as their desperation for their son to return home. Played briskly in a hybrid rock/ska style with a head spinning jazz trumpet solo added, it benefited also from a vocal full of passion, adorned with hiccups and a hyper intensity that grabbed listeners by the throat.

12
STEINSKI &
THE MASS MEDIA
The Motorcade Sped On
The Motorcade Sped On
NO CHART PLACING
Tommy Boy

Cutting up sound sources and reassembling them to create something new offended the sensibilities of traditionalists. But when the results are as spectacular as they are on this record, then the issue of legitimacy becomes moot. This was a genius track, using reports of the Kennedy assassination over hip-hop beats, capturing the tragedy and sense of loss. We cannot help but run the unforgettable footage through our minds and feel the very real and human devastation of Jackie Kennedy as we hear her cry of "oh no!" and picture the look of devastation on her face. It is powerful stuff and doesn't end with Kennedy's slaying, but changes scene to the courthouse in Dallas where to the sound of calypso ring out the words "Oswald is shot! Jack Ruby! Jack Ruby!". Lee Harvey Oswald was silenced forever, leaving more questions than have ever been answered.

11
TALK TALK
Life's What You Make It / It's Getting Late In The Evening
16
EMI

'Life's What You Make It' catches Talk Talk in transition from lightweight synth-pop act to creators of thoughtful, meditative head music. They were, at this point, looser and funkier than they'd been, as they adopt an organic approach to their music-making. This starts with a rhythm filched from Kate Bush's, 'Running Up That Hill', but it is the presence of an insistent, pounding piano riff that hooks the listener. Guitar responds to the piano's promptings, and a swampy organ provides texture. It is highly physical music and Mark Hollis matched that approach as he sang with intensity, lyrics that are concise, concerned with seizing what is good from life rather than allowing it to drift.

10
WORLD DOMINATION ENTERPRISES
Asbestos Lead Asbestos
Beats Baby Hi
NO CHART PLACING
Karbon

World Domination Enterprises were a band formed by Keith Dobson, better known as Kif Kif Le Batteur, who had been the drummer for free festival stalwarts Here and Now. This, though was music for a new era. 'Asbestos Lead Asbestos' was a lot less friendly than anything Here and Now had served up. Where that band had revelled in spontaneous free-form jams, World Dom were much more song based. Their mode of sonic attack was short, sharp bursts of hard-hitting noise that fused hip-hop and punk in a fierce uncompromising manner. They were satirists and pranksters at heart, taking aim at big corporations who pollute the planet for profit. 'Asbestos Lead Asbestos' was a spit in the eye of the capitalist system - the sound of the small acorn in opposition to the powerful and filthy rich.

9
THE FALL
Cruiser's Creek
L.A.
92
Beggar's Banquet

In this period The Fall made the effort to release some decidedly catchy pop singles, although there was an awkwardness still at play that prevented true success. 'Cruiser's Creek' epitomises this. It has an up-tempo rhythm aligned to a nagging stop-start riff and a repetitive vocal hook. This contends with Mark Smith's disdainful vocal, along with a lyric that gathers the likes of Paul Weller, Trevor Horn and Paul Morley at an out-of-control hipster party culminating in a lit cigarette and an opened gas tap, causing an explosion to presumably wipe out the guests.

8
TALKING HEADS
Road To Nowhere
Television Man
6
EMI

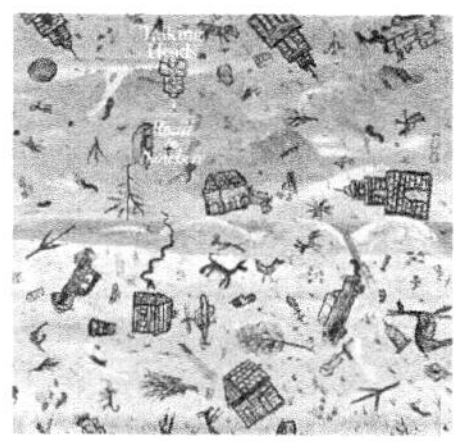

Opening with a gospel choir, before moving into a brisk, cheerful rodeo rhythm, replete with fiddles and squeeze-box, 'Road to Nowhere' is, as David Byrne put it, "a joyful look at Doom", playful, poignant and sardonic. This was commentary on the ultimate uselessness of existence, delivered with a wry smile and wit.

7
JESUS AND MARY CHAIN
Never Understand
Suck
47
Blanco Y Negro

Even before hearing this record the boldness of the stark black script on the blood red sleeve was striking. The music on the disc was equally non-reticent. It screeched and howled like a machine grinding its gears. Painfully distorted guitars thrilled as they were tethered to beautiful pop, just discernible amid the fuzz and fog. This was so crude as to be exhilarating. The band seemed to have been formed purely to give definition to the word 'brat' but that was preferable to the self-important pseudo compassion offered up by pop singers who fancied themselves as messiahs and role models to the lesser beings who bought their records. The Jesus and Mary Chain were an antidote to the excess of the era and a refreshing alternative to the creeping smug blandness of many contemporary guitar bands.

6
PET SHOP BOYS
Opportunities (Let's Make Lots Of Money)/ Was That What It Was?
NO CHART PLACING (1986 - 11)
Parlophone

Written in 1983, when Chris Lowe asked Neil Tennent to write something around the phrase "let's make lots of money", Tennent constructed a parable about greed culture where an aspiring chancer who perceives himself as being intelligent and superior, is engaged in recruiting somebody he sees as of lower intelligence to provide brawn to a joint enterprise to get rich. Inevitably, the claims of intelligence and achievements prove to be without substance and neither person makes any money. Laced with heavy irony and given a dashing dance floor backing, 'Opportunities' revealed the Pet Shop Boys as archly humorous social commentators and brilliant pop auteurs.

5
NICK CAVE AND THE BAD SEEDS
Tupelo
The Six Strings That Drew Blood
NO CHART PLACING
Mute

Heavy on the atmospherics, this startling piece of throbbing swampy neo-blues borrowed from Leadbelly and John Lee Hooker, relating the story of the birth of Elvis Presley, during a violent storm in Tupelo, Mississippi. Biblical imagery is delivered by Nick Cave in fire-and-brimstone preacher style, whilst The Bad Seeds match his fervour with their instrumental attack.

4
PRINCE AND THE REVOLUTION
Raspberry Beret
25
Paisley Park

Prince could not be accused of resting on his laurels. His approach and sound were constantly in a state of flux. And so, in the blink of an eye, he moved on from the startling skeletal funk of 'Kiss', to the lovingly-created psychedelic pop of 'Raspberry Beret', which retains a killer groove whilst entering a sound world similar to that of The Beatles circa 1967. The song itself is as sweetly innocent as anything Prince would write, concerning a lowly shop worker who is disparaged by his boss, seeing a woman enter the store wearing a raspberry beret and the pair striking out together for a romantic adventure. It is sung coquettishly throughout, the dreamy verses that lead into insistent, quite brilliant choruses, enhanced by a string part created by Lisa Coleman.

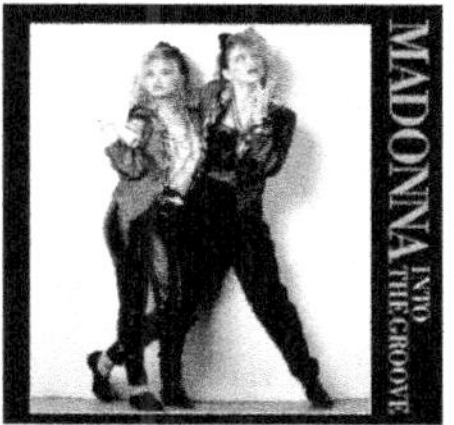

3
MADONNA
Into The Groove/
Everybody/Shoo-Bee-Doo
1
Sire

'Into The Groove' was a mesmerising record. It displayed Madonna's confidence to the hilt, as she performs the lyric that ostensibly is an invitation for someone to dance with her, but is also loaded with sexual innuendo. She handles the material adroitly and controls the narrative so well that it is easy to picture her alone in the night, seeking a partner. Her freedom and liberation from society's moral structure is simply a nailed-on fact. The song is given a synthesised dance groove with a busy programmed beat. Madonna's vocals are double-tracked for the choruses. Its simplicity gives the song its raw energy, and within that simplicity is exquisitely good taste and pure talent.

2
KATE BUSH
Running Up That Hill/
Under The Ivy
3 (2012 - 6/2014 – 51/2022 - 1)
EMI

Always intriguing, here Kate Bush writes about the relationship between a man and woman, about the complexities and the fragile state in which their love exists. She proposes a deal with God, whereby each partner would inhabit the other's body for a short period. Each would experience a greater understanding of the other's thoughts and feelings, allowing them to coexist in a more harmonious state. It is a joyous supposition that is given an uplifting and dramatic musical treatment. Kate Bush enunciates every word with precision, without sacrificing emotion, it is a brilliant singing performance. The programmed drums are suggestive of perpetual motion, while synthesisers bubble as liquid heated in a cauldron, reaching peaks and crescendos - a spellbinding piece of music that gave her greater commercial success than anything else she released in the eighties. That may not have been the case had the song's title not been changed from 'A Deal With God', which may well have been perceived as blasphemous in religious countries and faced blacklisting. Playing a crucial role in the plot of Season 4 of Netflix series *Stranger Things*, cemented its role as a classic, and it shot to Number One in the UK charts, 37 years after its initial release.

1
HÜSKER DÜ
Makes No Sense At All
Love Is All Around
NO CHART PLACING
SST Records

The melding of punk attitude and aggression with pop sensibilities found its perfect synthesis in this short, sharp, shock of a song. 'Makes No Sense At All' is a blast of energy - drums kick viciously, guitars buzz and explode into flurries of fevered noise. Bob Mould wraps his voice around a lyric of sweet, simple profundity. Passion and frustration pour from him in a torrent of questioning emotion. One unforgettable hook follows another in a breathless torrent. With this song, Hüsker Dü achieved immortality. It was unquestionably brilliant, in a year where guitar based music was increasingly derided as being out of date and deeply uncool. 'Makes No Sense At All' was the coolest sound around, its vitality proving the virtue of a great song well performed being beyond the fickle vagaries of fashion. This was a great record and great records stay great - they are timeless.

Whipcrackaway, 1987

1986

I'd enjoyed many aspects of my quiet life in Glossop , the nearby countryside had been a source of wonder and pleasure for a man with time on his hands; walking aimlessly about in no great hurry to be anywhere, I had rested and filled many hours with my nose between the cover of a book, I'd drunk less alcohol than at any point since I'd left school in 1973 and the occasional psychedelic experience fuelled by 'magic' mushrooms had done no harm, I was in a state of undeniably good health both mentally and physically. However I was bored, that was the truth of my situation, bored and somewhat isolated, I knew very few people in this town, the grinding poverty I lived with was depressing me too, the challenge of living on my giro money was wearing me down, managing my budget by subsisting on bland vegetable stews put together from the bruised end of day cast-offs from the local market no longer seemed the triumph of ingenuity it had once been, it now seemed tiresome and even a little humiliating. I needed money and to get money I needed a job.

Unemployment under the Conservative government had reached record levels. The old adage 'it's not what you know but who you know' had never seemed more apt. I knew nobody in Glossop who could help me find employment. I didn't drive, I had little alternative but to reluctantly give up my present dwelling, which I truly loved, and find lodgings in an area where the availability of work would be advantageous to my situation. So I moved into a house in Denton with my old friend and ex-band-mate Bob who had recently suffered a romantic split from a girlfriend and was glad to have me as a lodger. It was a happy arrangement, I was around friends once more, my social life improved considerably, work was sourced and life was easier, I didn't want to fall too readily into unhealthy habits though and so to keep myself fit I joined a full-contact Karate class. Unfortunately I am clumsy and as a result dangerous! Within weeks I'd broken a sparring partner's leg and it seemed a good time to abandon my martial arts career.

Instead I was tempted into fronting a band. My new band-mates were my landlord Bob and British Olympic wrestler Nick Kokotaylo. We rehearsed and it seemed pretty good although our best song was written by three female friends - Karen, Sue and Rhonda, who gifted us a spoof country tearjerker called 'The Horse's Tale'. The band was christened 'Oochikomis' which seemed stupid to me. We played a debut gig and, high on adrenaline, it was a triumph of sorts. A second gig a week later found me pondering what on earth I was doing this for mid-set. I had no faith in the band or our material and so, to the amazement and shock of my fellow performers, I delivered a 'Ziggy Stardust' speech and retired from the stage to a barely-interested audience.

The Hacienda was still the main place I would go to unwind and hear music although a new smaller club called The Boardwalk opened its doors this year and fairly soon it was a rare Saturday night when I could not be found there. The mainstream was dominated by a conveyor belt of well-scrubbed pretty boys and girls making pretty awful, though often superbly produced, records. The old adage that 'you can't polish a turd' frequently came to mind. Outside the mainstream this was a golden age of creativity and much exciting and durable music was on offer to the curious and adventurous listener.

NOTABLE EVENTS

The U.S Space Shuttle *Challenger* disintegrates 73 seconds after take off before a live television audience, the seven crew members, including a female teacher, are killed instantly.

The Soviet Union launched the Mir space station.

The General Secretary of the Soviet Communist party, Mikhail Gorbachev, delivers a speech to US Congress using the keywords 'Glasnost' and ' Perestroika' in his mandate to open up the Soviet Union to western business.

Swedish prime minister Olof Palme is assassinated as he walked home from a cinema in Stockholm.

The UK and Netherlands governments sign a peace treaty formally ending a war that began in 1651.

Swedish scientists detect unusual

In April, there is a meltdown at the Chernobyl nuclear plant near the city of Pripyat in the Soviet Union in what is now Ukraine. The Soviet government cover up the severity of the event but soon the entire population of the area was evacuated never to return. Many historians blame the disaster for the subsequent break up of the Eastern Block and the fall of the Soviet Union.

Mikhail Gorbachev and Ronald Reagan meet in Reykjavik to discuss scaling back nuclear weapons in Europe.

The M25, Greater London's ring road, is opened by a triumphant Maggie Thatcher.

The Sandoz chemical spill occurs in Basel, Switzerland polluting the Rhine.

Somehow Manchester United finish fourth in a two-horse title race with Liverpool as their 13 point lead in October becomes a 12-point deficit by May. Manager Ron Atkinson sells Mark Hughes to Barcelona and replaces him with Peter Davenport from Nottingham Forest and Terry Gibson from Wimbledon, he is sacked in October. Firebrand Aberdeen manager Alex Ferguson is appointed as his replacement but fans are sceptical and attendances will decline over the next few seasons.

Diego Maradona single-handedly wins the World Cup for Argentina in Mexico. In the quarter-final he scores with his 'Hand of God' then displays skills sent from heaven to dribble through half the England team to score the second.

NOTABLE BIRTHS

Alex Turner; Jamie Bell; Lady Gaga; Usain Bolt; Drake; Oscar Pistorius; Amir Khan;Nani

NOTABLE DEATHS

Christopher Isherwood; Phil Lynott; L Ron Hubbard; Frank Herbert; Richard Manuel ; James Cagney; Simone De Beauvoir; Jean Genet; Benny Goodman; Jorge Luis Borges; Pat Phoenix; Cary Grant; Harold Macmillan.

NOTABLE BOOKS

An Artist of the Floating World - Kazuo Ishiguro

Tourist Season - Carl Hiaasen

The Bridge - Iain Banks

The Old Devils - Kingsley Amis
Forrest Gump - Winston Groom
Count Zero - William Gibson
Zodiac - Robert Graysmith

NOTABLE FILMS

Blue Velvet
Ferris Bueller's Day Off
Platoon
The Mission
Top Gun
Down By Law
Crocodile Dundee
Stand By Me
Aliens
The Fly
Sid and Nancy
Labyrinth
Henry portrait of a serial killer
Something Wild
The Hitcher

100
ST. CHE
Be My.... (Temptation: The Sound Of It's Condition)/
The Exquisite Act
NO CHART PLACING
Siren

St. Che was, I am led to believe, Alex Johnson, who had been the singer in Liverpool band Modern Eon. I asked producer Adrian Sherwood about this record some years ago and he confirmed the singer was from Liverpool, so that fits. The record itself is absolutely striking - once heard, it's hard to forget. It floats on a thin electronic groove, with a thumping, simple, drum machine pattern at its base. Vocals are shared between Che, who sings with whining desperation, and Fats Comet, who counters with a measured baritone. There is a third, presumably sampled, voice speaking the word "powerstation" intermittently. I can't make head nor tail of what is being implied, but it all sounds fabulously strange. I liked the cut of its jib then, and like it still.

99
MARC ALMOND
A Woman's Story/The Heel/
A Salty Dog/The Plague/
The Little White Cloud That Cried/For One Moment/
Just Good Friends
41
Some Bizarre

This seven-song single has a running time of 24 minutes and in the order they are presented showcases songs originally performed by Cher, Eartha Kitt, Procol Harum, Scott Walker, Johnny Ray, Lee Hazelwood, and Peter Hammill. It is a fascinating collection - a glimpse into the influences Marc Almond drew upon for his own compositions.

'A Woman's Story' was rightly made the title track. It is a melodramatic piece, perfect for Almond, sung from the perspective of a woman who has been easily seduced into the arms of a succession of men who have taken their pleasure and then discarded her. Now she feels she is truly loved and has a chance of a life spent with one man. She is determined to make the relationship last. We are left wondering if her feelings are reciprocated or if she will once again be left hurt and alone.

98
SAMPSON "BUTCH" MOORE
House Beat Box / House Beat Box (Instrumental)
NO CHART PLACING
Trax Records

Everything released on Chicago's Trax record label was worthy of attention and this disco-infused house cut was no exception. It was the only release credited to Sampson "Butch" Moore. Co-written and produced by Steve "Silk" Hurley, it melded a delicious piano part over tempting dance beats and was topped by a light-as-a-feather vocal.

97
KREEM
Triangle Of Love (Dub Mix)
Triangle Of Love (Vocal)
Triangle Of Love (Instrumental)
NO CHART PLACING
Metroplex

This was the first recording made together by Juan Atkins and Kevin Saunderson who would go on to be recognised, along with their friend and colleague Derek May, as the founders of Detroit techno. The dub mix of the track is startlingly fresh and innovative, its skeletal beats leading into a sonic playground. The vocal cut is less radical, but still a fabulous dance track where the genres of techno and house become entwined.

96
THE CHILLS
I Love My Leather Jacket
The Great Escape
NO CHART PLACING
Flying Nun UK

Drummer Martyn Bull, who had died from leukaemia, bequeathed Martin Phillipps his leather jacket in his will. And this was the spirited, but extremely touching and tuneful, musical response from Phillipps; a salute to the memory of his lost friend and a declaration to love and cherish the aforementioned jacket, which symbolised the time they had shared together.

95
TACKHEAD
Mind At The End Of The Tether
Is There A Way Out
NO CHART PLACING
On-U Sound

Taking a title from the HG Wells short novel *Mind At The End Of Its Tether*, this is a sample-heavy industrial/hip-hop piece that displays a real sense of desperation at the loss of liberty in this high-surveillance age. It is brilliantly played by this group of outstanding musical forces, with particular kudos to drummer Keith Leblanc whose performance is explosive.

94
MICK KARN
Featuring DAVID SYLVIAN
Buoy/Dreams Of Reason/
Language Of Ritual
63
Virgin

The tensions that had caused the split of Japan were to a large degree attributable to the rift between Mick Karn and David Sylvian. But a respect for each other's talent saw the pair reunited. Karn was a gifted multi-instrumentalist, and plays a variety of exotic sounding horns here, while his sinuous fret-less bass playing is melodic and lyrical. Sylvian in turn delivers a sonorous vocal - it is cool and unhurried, suiting the track's gently drifting lilt.

93
JOE LOUIS
The Love Of My Own (Instrumental)
My Own (Dub)
NO CHART PLACING
Target Records

The epitome of deep Chicago house music, its grooves are subdued and moody, while a bright synth pattern adorns the surface and the programmed drums, although relatively unobtrusive, provide a sense of movement. Written and produced by Joe Louis, it was mixed by Larry Heard, whose importance to the burgeoning scene was beyond dispute.

92
A.R. KANE
When You're Sad (Long Version)/
When You're Sad/Haunting
NO CHART PLACING
One Little Indian

Guitars crunch in the intro, the attack ceases and from then they bleed and drone. A drum pattern of great simplicity is at the front of the mix. The bass wriggles around the beat and, faraway, a voice conveys sadness, although the words are lost in the distance. This was a record of few antecedents but would inspire a stylistic movement of what became known as 'shoegaze' bands.

91
TENOR SAW
Golden Hen/Golden Dub
NO CHART PLACING
Up-tempo Records

Tenor Saw captured something special with this mashing up of dancehall rhythms and horns that wouldn't have been out of place in the ska era. His voice is reedy and real as he adopts the persona of a pimp, with the 'golden hen' of the title being the working girl who fetches home the money - the brutal economics of prostitution laid bare.

90
DEPECHE MODE
Stripped/But Not Tonight
15
Mute

Although 'Stripped' was written by Martin Gore, it follows the darkening of the band's sound brought out by newest member Alan Wilder. The track is a jigsaw puzzle of imaginative sampling - a car's ignition and fireworks are used while the beat is the sound of an idling motorcycle engine slowed down to the required tempo. It is an ominous, challenging pop single that features sexually suggestive lyrics sung commandingly by Dave Gahan with evident relish, aligning his voice to the bitter-sweet melody of the tune.

89
THE PASTELS
Truck Train Tractor
Breaking Lines
NO CHART PLACING
Glass Records

The Pastels were raw, without any hint of aggression. Their music sounded amateurish but unthreatening. Macho posturing and power plays were not in their vocabulary. This was a contrary and radical stance to take, in an industry where displays of strength are lauded. The Pastels stood for something kinder and infinitely better. They were heartily refreshing for their lack of pretentiousness, and easy to love. 'Truck Train Tractor' was a great Pastels' record. Sound wise, it nods towards *Loaded*-era Velvet Underground in the use of fuzzy guitars and primitive drums. It is nonetheless a sunny song, as its pop heart is very evident in its cheerful delivery and the choice of vehicle metaphors used to describe the changes of pace and place we experience in our lives.

88
SANTOS
Work The Box / Work The Box (Vocals) / Space The Box / Beat The Knuckles
NO CHART PLACING
Trax Records

Co-written by Ron Hardy with Santos, and a pair of mixes each from Adonis and Frankie Knuckles, meant this was a coming together of some of the biggest Chicago house music names. The Adonis mixed side is well tooled, fairly minimal, repetitive and designed for dance floor action, whereas the Frankie Knuckles mixed tracks are cloaked in darkness and given a dangerous edginess that pre-dates the hardcore sound by several years.

87
THE WOODENTOPS
Good Thing/Travelling Man
NO CHART PLACING
Rough Trade

The Woodentops were a South London group formed by singer and sole songwriter Rolo McGinty who had been a member of The Wild Swans. Later in their career they would become experimental and dance-orientated but at this point they played in a frenetic, jangly guitar pop style. 'Good Thing' was more mid-tempo than many of their offerings, but within its rattling effervescence was a joyous warmth that delivered a spring in the step to listeners wowed by its feel-good factor.

86
SEVERED HEADS
Petrol (Short Mix)
Petrol (Cutup Mix)
Son of (Bigot Mix)
NO CHART PLACING
Normal

Severed Heads projected a bleak world-view. Pessimism and despair were their main subject matter - they saw ugliness and horror at every turn and held a mirror up to the sickness of society. Musically they often presented a harsh and hostile industrial sound, and yet 'Petrol' moved them into territory that might lure in listeners with its incorporation of pleasing hooks. It was pop, albeit a twisted pop with a sharp edge.

85
MARSHALL JEFFERSON
Ride The Rhythm (Ron Hardy Mix)
Ride the Rhythm (Frank Knuckles Mix)
NO CHART PLACING
Trax Records

One side mixed by Ron Hardy, the other by Frankie Knuckles, on this single from Marshall Jefferson who became known as the father of house music. He introduced piano as the featured instrument on his records and was fundamental in shaping the deep house sound, through numerous productions of other artists. 'Ride the Rhythm' incorporates all his techniques designed to guarantee dance floor utopia, with a smooth vocal by Curtis McClain exhorting listeners to give in to the music. This was, of course, irresistible.

84
THE STRANGLERS
Always The Sun
Norman Normal
30 (1990 REMIX - 29)
Epic

The Stranglers knew that this was a high-quality piece of work and confidently expected it to yield them a huge hit. For some baffling reason, that failed to materialise and the failure seemed to hit them hard. 'Always the Sun' was a beautiful, reflective, mature piece of work. Over a gorgeous melody, Hugh Cornwell's lyrics concern the inability to control the chaos all around us. He concludes that we must accept that state of affairs and content ourselves with the certainty that the sun will rise each day. Jean Jacques Burnell provides delicious harmonies, and the playing is subdued and tasteful - not to mention ego free - all lending support to the strength of the song.

83
ULTRA MAGNETIC M.C.'S
Ego Tripping/Ego Bits
Funky Potion/Funky Extension
NO CHART PLACING
Next Plateau Records Inc

Ultra Magnetic M.C.'s came with an entirely fresh approach to rap. They had a wider perspective on what was permissible, rejecting orthodoxy. The stream of consciousness lyric of 'Ego Tripping' was delivered in complex verbal polyrhythms by Kool Keith and Ced Gee. The sound of the record was revolutionary too, utilising blasting synth riffs atop the pounding drum track sampled from 'Synthetic Substitution', a 1973 B-side by Melvin Bliss. Following its use on this track, it would become one of the most sampled tracks in hip-hop history. This was a truly gifted group - they rhymed and flowed effortlessly and were genuinely funky to boot.

82
FELT
Ballad Of The Band/
I Didn't Mean to Hurt You/
Candles In A Church/
Ferdinand Magellan
NO CHART PLACING
Creation Records

Borrowing Bob Dylan's wild mercury sound of whining organ and harsh guitar, Lawrence vents waspishly at the departure from the ranks of founder member and creator of Felt's sound, Maurice Deebank, for a perceived lack of faith and loyalty. In his defence, Deebank was clearly at the end of his tether, with the stifling of ideas by the autocratic Lawrence, who goes for the jugular in similar fashion to Dylan on 'Like a Rolling Stone' He fails, of course, to hit the same artistic heights of that epic song, but nonetheless creates an excellent addition to the run of fine singles issued by Felt.

81
THE THE
Heartland/Flesh & Bones/
Bron in the New S.A.
29
Epic

With an undemonstrative backing featuring piano, strings and harmony vocals, Matt Johnson quietly but effectively sinks his teeth into the sick state of the UK. Thatcher and her cronies are taken to task for the division they have wrought over the country. Working class Tories are admonished for their betrayal of morality and compassion and, to top it, Johnson points out the erosion of our national identity – as the irreversible slide into Americanisation gets under way. "This is the 51st state of the U.S.A." he sings, somewhere between a pained lament and a bitter accusation, while watching any moral fibre or shred of decency we once could claim as a nation, being flushed down the pan.

80
MODEL 500
Testing 1-2/Bang The Beat (Vocal)
Bang The Beat (Instrumental)
NO CHART PLACING
Metroplex

Juan Atkins - once more under his Model 500 alias - displayed an uncanny ability to produce music that sounded like the future, and indeed it was a harbinger of change. 'Testing 1-2' was a quick-paced track with a chattering rhythm and elegant neo-classical synth lines, while 'Bang the Beat' ups the tempo and, over a brutal robotic synth riff, electrically-treated voices spit out instructions. Heard loud in a club through good speakers, this felt like flying through outer space.

79
R.E.M.
Superman/White Tornado
NO CHART PLACING
I.R.S. Records

One thinks of R.E.M. as being a consummate writer's band. Indeed they were, but this was the rarest of things - a cover version of a song by another group released as a single. 'Superman' was originally released by Texas band, The Clique. It caused some disagreement within R.E.M. ranks as Michael Stipe was not keen on the idea of recording the song. Due to his reluctance, Mike Mills debuted as lead vocalist for this track. It was less complex than much of the band's repertoire and sounded like a refreshing vacation from the serious business of creating songs with one eye on career advancement. 'Superman' was bigger and bolder sounding than many REM singles. It had a Byrd's-like feel due to its layered vocals, chiming Rickenbacker guitar sound and thumping 4/4 beat.

78
SPARKS
Music That You Can Dance To
Fingertips
NO CHART PLACING
Consolidated Allied Records

Sparks had dropped off my radar for several years when I came across this single and took a punt on it. I was delighted to find they'd returned to an electronic dance sound similar to the one they had explored with Georgio Moroder at the end of the 70s. This time they augmented the machines with a dynamite live rhythm section which propelled their grooves in a harder dynamic fashion. Russ Mael's voice remained a thing of high camp, near operatic wonder, and the whole was tinged with the band's trademark eccentricity. The B-side of the record was a marvellous playful romp through the Little Stevie Wonder classic, 'Fingertips', which bore similarity to The Residents' treatment of James Brown's, 'It's A Man's Man's World' in its loving irreverence.

77
ALEX CHILTON
No Sex/Underclass/Wild Kingdom
NO CHART PLACING
New Rose Records

Alex Chilton had spent half a decade in self-imposed exile, working as a producer, side-man for the likes of Tav Falco's Panther Burns, as well as taking jobs outside the music industry. He returned with an EP called *Feudalist Tarts* in 1985 and followed it with this more confident offering. 'No Sex' a song about the HIV/AIDS crisis that was gaining attention as it spread.

There had been much speculation as to how the virus was transmitted, but now it was common knowledge that sex was a prime source of transmission. Chilton cut this song at Ardent Studios, his favoured work environment from his days in Big Star. Despite its subject matter, the song was neither depressing nor maudlin, based around a swaggering tight but loose guitar riff, with saxophone colouring the sound. Chilton barked out darkly humorous lyrics about the possibility that a night of sex could be a death sentence – "Come on baby, fuck me and die" being the most brutal and unsentimental couplet on offer.

76
X RAY
Let's Go (A Mix)
Let's Go (Dub Mix)/Untitled
NO CHART PLACING
Transmat

The seemingly endless stream of musical classics emerging from the fertile mind and hard-working fingers of Juan Atkins continued with this collaboration with Derrick May. It finds the pair exploring a hard, dark-hued version of techno, with brutalist beats to the fore and whispered, growled vocals rattling in the midst of the mix. Anybody who equated dance music with mindless euphoria needed to be confronted with this snarling beast of a record - they would doubtless reassess their opinion.

75
HALF MAN HALF BISCUIT
The Trumpton Riots/
All I Want For Christmas
Is A Dukla Prague Away Kit
NO CHART PLACING
Probe Plus

Sounding something like a pub-rock version of The Fall, nobody listens to the Birkenhead-based Biscuits for musical innovation, but rather the genius lyrics of Nigel Blackwell that are gleefully shouted out and have made the band national treasures and a bulwark against Americanisation, musicians who took themselves too seriously and production line pop.

These are two of the finest songs from the group's early days, which are chock full of mordant wit, cultural references, serious points and surrealism. Totally non-conformist in attitudes and approach, the group's very existence is a cause for celebration.

74
LEONARD COHEN
Take This Waltz (Pequeño Vals Vienés)/
Grido A Roma (Grito Hacia Roma/
Asesinato
NO CHART PLACING
CBS

Recorded in Paris for a tribute album to Spanish poet Federico Garcia Lorca, 'Take this Waltz' uses a loose translation of the poem 'Pequeño Vals Vienés' as its lyric. Leonard Cohen imbues the song with his natural grace and gravitas. There is longing and regret expressed in the lyric, voiced with the conflicting emotions of joy and sadness. It is beautifully framed by what else but a sweeping, elegant waltz, and is a true delight that scored Cohen a Number One hit single in Spain. Sadly, that success was not replicated in other regions.

74
THE SAINTS
Just Like Fire Would/East Is East
NO CHART PLACING
Polydor

With just singer Chris Bailey remaining from the immaculate, original version of The Saints, this new version of the band sounded nothing like their predecessors. They were still fine though, and potent. Gone was the adrenaline and raw power of yore. Here they display a more wide-screen melodicism incorporating acoustic guitars, pipes, fiddles and strings! This new sound was closer to Van Morrison than The Stooges, but it was effective, with Bailey still bruised-sounding but singing with soul. Metaphors aplenty and a hint of mysticism peppered his lyrics. It was a highly satisfactory new chapter for The Saints and 'Just Like Fire Would' was later borrowed by Bruce Springsteen for his live shows.

73
VIRGIN PRUNES
Love Lasts Forever/True Life Story
NO CHART PLACING
Baby Records

A cast of so many strong individualistic characters were bound to eventually pull themselves apart, and so it proved with Virgin Prunes. This was their swansong single and was a fitting farewell. Structurally it owes something to the rhythmic, robotic, building blocks of sound employed to great effect by Wire. But there is an added creepiness to 'Love Lasts Forever' that is produced by the scraping of violins and discordant tinkling of piano keys. Gavin Friday is completely over-the-top in his mannered vocal that reeks of malevolent insincerity. Playful and disturbing in equal measures to the very end, Virgin Prunes had illuminated the decade thus far with their sense of theatre and wild imaginings. They departed with integrity and dignity intact.

72
INDIAN OCEAN
Treehouse/School Bell/
School Bell/Treehouse
NO CHART PLACING
Sleeping Bag Records

Penned and produced by Arthur Russell and mixed by Walter Gibbons, this is experimental mutant disco at its finest. Live drums play a tribal beat and a variety of other instruments slip in and out of the mix. Russell sings a hard-to-fathom vocal as if in a dreamy trance. This owed nothing to other records or styles, coming completely out of left field and entrancing adventurous night owls.

71
HÜSKER DÜ
Don't Want To Know If You Are
Lonely/Helter Skelter (Live)/
All Work And No Play
(Extended Mix)
96
Warner Bros. Records

With the muscle of the mighty Warner Brothers empire behind them Hüsker Dü enjoyed their biggest chart success; one week at number 96 on the Hit Parade. It was a kick in the teeth for perhaps the best American guitar band of the era.

'Don't Want To Know If You Are Lonely' was written by Grant Hart and was another demonstration of their signature sound of scorching but melodic guitars, jack-hammer rhythms and impassioned singing. The inter-band musical chemistry was remarkable. In many ways they resembled The Beatles. It was fitting that a furious live version of 'Helter Skelter' featured on the single's flip side.

70
XTC
Grass/Dear God
100
Virgin

XTC had matured into a special band at this point and 'Grass' was a single plucked from the splendid album *Skylarking*, produced by Todd Rundgren. Using the chords from Thunderclap Newman's 'Something in the Air' as a starting point and borrowing the idea of mixed violin and guitar from John Lennon's 'How Do You Sleep?', Colin Moulding's pastoral musings about Coate Water park in Swindon - with Moulding singing in a kind of David Bowie style, if indeed Bowie had been born in rural Swindon rather than metropolitan London - this was an absolutely charming single. Its relative failure saw the Andy Partridge penned B-Side, 'Dear God', issued as a single in its own right. It fared slightly better than 'Grass' reaching the number 99 position.

69
THE STYLE COUNCIL
Have You Ever Had It Blue (Uncut Version)/Have You Ever Had it Blue (Cut Version)/
Mr. Cool's Dream
14
Polydor

'Have You Ever Had It Blue' was a song recorded for the film *Absolute Beginners*. It was produced by jazz legend Gil Evans, famous for his work with Miles Davis. Fittingly, it is the most horn-dominated of The Style Council singles and skips to a cool bossa nova rhythm. Paul Weller sings of unfathomable disappointments and Mick Talbot tinkles the ivories with aplomb on this smoothly satisfying track.

68
STEINSKI & MASS MEDIA
We'll Be Right Back
We'll Be Right Back (Dub)
We'll Be Right Back (Bonus Beats)
NO CHART PLACING
4th & Broadway

Cut up maestro Steinski assembled this beat driven commentary on the perniciousness of the advertising industry and the bombardment we face from it. The happy, barking dog about to get fed samples was surely included to signify the contemptuous opinion big business has of its customers.

67
E.S.P.
It's You + five mixes (Instrumental/ Untitled Mix 1/Untitled Mix 2/ Underground Mix/ Instrumental Reprise)
NO CHART PLACING
Underground

Tom Adams was the DJ at the Onyx Club in Chicago. As more and more DJs began making their own music using drum machines and synthesizers, he decided to follow suit, with his background as a live drummer to support him. He recruited friend and fellow musician Daniel Ellington and they recorded 'It's You' which was released by Underground, an offshoot of DJ International Records. It is a minimalistic piece of deep house that rides on a simple three-note hook. The instrumental version picked up club plays, but the vocal cut is superbly atmospheric.

66
fIREHOSE
Brave Captain/Perfect Pairs
NO CHART PLACING
SST Records

While the house, hip-hop, and techno scenes were all flourishing - albeit away from where a mass audience would look - so too were American guitar bands of the alt-rock variety. Amongst the best of them had been Minutemen, who were brought to an abrupt end by the accidental death of guitarist/vocalist D. Boon. His grieving band-mates, Mike Watt and George Hurley, had little appetite to make music again, but the persistence and enthusiasm of Minutemen fan Ed Crawford, to play with them eventually saw the pair persuaded. Crawford was renamed 'Ed fROMOHIO', and the band fIREHOSE was formed. One of their earliest songs was 'Brave Captain' and it was obvious the three component parts had merged into a powerful individual entity. The song about doubt was fascinating - it had real energy, passion and melodicism. Each instrumental performance shone without being self-indulgent. It was reminiscent of The Who in their late 60s pomp. That comparison is not hyperbolic - it is deserved high praise.

65
P.I.L.
Home/Round
75
Virgin

Bill Laswell produces, jazz drummer supreme Tony Williams plays an outstanding part, matched by guitar virtuoso Steve Vai's metallic soundscape while John Lydon lets rip with an attack on disingenuous politicians whose lust for power meant the probability of war casting a long shadow over everyday living. "Better days will never be" is Lydon's refrain, that perfectly expresses his anger and disappointment with governments and the escalation of threat from the nuclear weapons build up, along with his pessimism for the prospect of a better future.

64
SLEEZY D.
I've Lost Control (Space Side)
I've Lost Control (House Side)
NO CHART PLACING
Trax Records

Experimenting with newly purchased equipment in 1984, Derrick Harris - AKA Sleezy D. - along with his buddy Marshall Jefferson, tried to capture the sound of a nervous breakdown on vinyl. Using a bass synthesiser, they created a modular waveform sound that would inspire a legion of acid house tracks. Released in 1986 and played extensively by

Ron Hardy at The Music Box, one can only imagine the pandemonium and euphoria this track generated as it blasted from the speakers and hit the dance floor. Squelching synths and piston-like beats underpin the maniacal screaming of Sleezy D. on top of the pitched down spoken vocal. This was revolutionary music.

63
BOOGIE DOWN PRODUCTIONS
South Bronx (Vocal)/
South Bronx (Instrumental)/
The "P" Is Free
NO CHART PLACING
Streetwave

The first hip-hop beef started with this track, which was an answer to MC Shan's 'The Bridge', where he claimed hip-hop originated in Queensbridge, Long Island. Here rapper KRS-One and DJ Scott La Rock, with assistance from Ced-Gee of Ultramagnetic MCs, firmly refute that claim, and over samples of James Brown's 'Get Up Offa That Thing', 'Funky Drummer', and 'Get Up, Get Into It, Get Involved' convey raw menace. They pour scorn upon their rivals, and in doing so they created a template that heavily influenced the gangsta rap genre.

62
TELEVISION PERSONALITIES
How I Learned To Love The Bomb
Grocer's Daughter
Girl Called Charity
NO CHART PLACING
Dreamworld

The darkly satirical lyrical genius of Dan Treacy is evidenced on 'How I Learned To Love The Bomb' as he professes to have been converted to the theory that nuclear weapons keep us safe. Of course, nagging voices in his head tell him, "don't you be so stupid" and "if you make bombs, you're longing for war". Set to a cheerful rhythm with a sing-along chorus, this was delicious subversion. On the reverse side, Margaret Thatcher is ridiculed and belittled as being "only the grocer's daughter". Laughter aimed at the pompous and powerful is a highly effective weapon in pricking their aura of supposed invincibility.

61
STAN RIDGWAY
Camouflage
Rio Greyhound
4
I.R.S. Records

Idiosyncratic in his dramatic and distinctive approach to singing and highly imaginative as a songwriter, 'Camouflage' transcended the cult status enjoyed by Stan Ridgway and briefly made him a household name. 'Camouflage' is a supernatural story set to music and tells, in conversational style, the tale of a young marine cut off from his comrades in the jungle who fears his days are numbered. Enter a big marine named Camouflage who guides them through the long night back to safety. They come under attack, and he is shielded by Camouflage who is seemingly unaffected by bullets. Safe at the edge of the camp, Camouflage leaves the young marine. He tells his story and is informed that Camouflage had been on his deathbed until the night before he died, he expressed his last wish as being able to save a young marine.

60
CHANNEL ONE
Technicolor (Radio Mix
Color Dubbing/
Technicolor (Long Mix)
NO CHART PLACING
Metroplex

Another alias under which Juan Atkins released another electronic classic, this one comes with big beats and a robotic rhythm, in combination with fine clean synth lines. Berry Gordy had made Detroit synonymous with the Motown sound. Now, in this new era, Juan Atkins was spearheading his own musical revolution, which once again would make the motor city a place with an original defining sound.

59
SONIC YOUTH
Starpower (Edit)/Bubblegum/
Expressway (Edit)
NO CHART PLACING
Blast First

Written by Thurston Moore and sung by Kim Gordon, this was the single that made Sonic Youth visible to me. Sonically speaking, it alternately throbs and squeals, steadfast in its medium pace, in no hurry at all to speed up simply because it is the expected device employed by guitar bands. There is a confident swagger about 'Starpower'. Its latent power is implicit. It doesn't shout and it doesn't scream. It doesn't have to - it's cool!

58
JOSEY WALES
& ADMIRAL BAILEY
Ballot Box/Ballot Box (Version)
NO CHART PLACING
Jammy's Records

The gruff voiced Rasta-fixated Josey Wales was a star in decline, as the pre-eminent Jamaican DJ sound was that of slackness which he wouldn't countenance. The chatty, effervescent Admiral Bailey was, on the other hand, hot property when Josey Wales fetched him over to King Jammy's. They teamed up to record 'Ballot Box' where they traded quick-fire lines over an infectious rhythm, with their distinctive voices see-sawing to brilliant effect.

57
JULIAN COPE
World Shut Your Mouth
Umpteenth Unnatural Blues
19
Island Records

With a crunching up-tempo variant of the 'Louie Louie' riff being hammered out on guitar and a drum beat that is best described as stomping, Julian set aside subtlety to create this monster record with a giant-sized genius chorus of snotty simplicity - punk as fuck and as bold as brass!

56
THE FALL
Hey! Luciani / Entitled
59
Beggars Banquet

With future head Lightning Seeds person Ian Broudie producing and crisp new drummer Si Woolstencroft making a first appearance, this was a snappy close-to-pop Fall single - a very fine one too. It has Mark Smith using the conspiracy theory surrounding the death of Alberto Luciani on 28 September 1978 - who was Pope John Paul I for just 33 days - as a writing device, without attaching much credence to the theory. The lyric tells of how Luciani became Pope and was subsequently murdered at the behest of the Vatican Bank, fearful of the reforms the new pope intended to introduce. Unusually for a Fall single, the sound is dominated by keyboards and a punishing rhythm with guitar used sparingly. Mark spits out the vocal in his inimitable manner and towards the song's close his then wife Brix adds spirited backing vocals that could have come from a Go-Go's or Bangles record.

55
THE SOURCE
featuring CANDI STATON
You Got The Love (Extended Vocal), (Radio Edit), (Club House), (House Apella)
95 (1991 – 4 / 1997 - 3 / 2004 - 60 / 2006 - 7)
Streetwave

Recorded originally as a direct-to-video piece to accompany a film about the struggle of an obese man attempting to lose weight, it was discovered by British DJ Simon Harris who took it to Morgan Kahn who licensed it and released it on his Streetwave label. It remains one of the great dance singles, and Candi Staton's vocal is extraordinarily powerful and soulful. The track is rooted in the gospel tradition and quite simply touches an emotional chord within people, making them feel good. It has become ubiquitous, following countless re-releases, re-mixes and high-profile cover versions, yet its potency is undiminished.

54
NEW ORDER
Bizarre Love Triangle
Bizarre Dub Triangle
56
Factory

Despite its relative commercial failure, this was the finest pop single New Order released. Their trademark style was simplified so that the gorgeous melody of the song comes to the fore. There is a sunniness that shines through in the sparkly keyboard effects. The lead bass makes its customary appearance and Bernard Sumner's concise lyric is, on this occasion, perfectly adequate in conveying a feeling of being lost.

53
THE GO-BETWEENS
Spring Rain/The Life At Hand
NO CHART PLACING
Beggars Banquet

The Go-Betweens rarely - if ever - disappointed. This was another top-notch release. Penned by Robert Forster, who abandoned his usual painstaking lyricism and embraced a spontaneous 'first thought, best thought' approach as he looked back at his teenage self in Brisbane from the vantage of being resident in London and a decade older. Played in a jangling, wide open country style, with a thrilling lift leading to a glorious chorus, Forster himself compared the song's style to that of Creedence Clearwater Revival. And in a more just world, the remarkable Go-Betweens would occupy a place in the pantheon of great guitar groups, alongside the likes of Creedence and Fleetwood Mac.

52
COLOURBOX
featuring LORITA GRAHAME
Baby I Love You So/
Looks Like We're Shy One Horse/
Shoot Out
NO CHART PLACING
4AD

Colourbox more than do justice to this track. Originally cut by Jacob Miller with Augustus Pablo and King Tubby, they slow it down so it glides on a slinky and sumptuous bass track. Lorita Grahame handles the vocal with confidence and panache. Samples from *Escape from New York* and *Captain Scarlet* are dropped into the mix without distracting from the awesome groove.

51
STEVE 'SILK' HURLEY
Jack Your Body (Club Your Body), (Dub Your Body), (Home Made)
Steve 'Silk' Hurley
1
D.J. International Records

The first house track to hit the top of the UK charts, 'Jack Your Body' paved the way for acid house. It was minimal, stripped-down electronica with a pumping, bass-synth rhythm and machined drumbeat, while the equally minimal vocal is a simple exhortation to "jack your body", which was - in Chicago speak - to dance vigorously to the house sounds in the city's clubs.

50
KRAFTWERK
Musique Non Stop
Musique Non Stop
82
EMI

Kraftwerk had been leaders for a long time. Their music had been ahead of its time and a huge influence on others, many of whom by this point had caught up. 'Musique Non Stop' finds Kraftwerk displaying the influence of acts who had been influenced by them. They adopt hip-hop beats as the basis for their song, adding a female robotic voice speaking the titular phrase in English, followed by the phrase being repeated in French by a robotic male voice. 'Musique Non Stop' is remarkably simple, yet its quirkiness and mastery of rhythm make it highly impressive.

49
THE GO-BETWEENS
Head Full Of Steam (Remix)
Don't Let Him Come Back
NO CHART PLACING
Beggars Banquet

Chasing the elusive hit that might have moved them out of cult status towards a position of recognition and reward, Beggars Banquet had 'Head Full Of Steam' remixed from its original album track form, into what would surely be an irresistible sparkling gem. The ploy failed - the world simply did not respond to these genius Australians who, it could be argued, were the finest guitar band of the 80s. 'Head Full Of Steam' does indeed sparkle. The guitars of Grant McClellan and Robert Forster synchronise in a blissful jangle. The lyrics carry an element of despondency in an unsuccessful pursuit of unrequited love. Its chorus is memorable and euphoric - beautifully sung, with the added bonus of Tracy Thorn's contrasting voice. 'Head Full Of Steam' was another artistic triumph and commercial failure for The Go-Between'.

48
ROBERT OWENS
Bring Down The Walls/(Dub)/(Inst.)
NO CHART PLACING
Trax Records

It tended to be producer-DJs that gained attention in house music circles, but Robert Owens bucked that trend. With his friend and future Fingers Inc. partner Larry Heard producing, he released this slice of minimal electronica that relied heavily on his purring, reverb-soaked tones. It is heavily atmospheric, and Owens sounds positively spooked, on what is a superb, though somewhat eccentric, record.

47
THE TRIFFIDS
Wide Open Road / Time Of Weakness
NO CHART PLACING
Hot Records

'Wide Open Road' is a truly haunting song, given a perfectly judged performance by The Triffids. It is suggestive of a drive through a seemingly endless desert, the wide-open spaces signifying the emotional distance between two people. Lyrically, a picture is painted of a feeling of emptiness that is astute in its observation. The music echoes the feeling - a simple drum machine pattern at its base, melodies sweeping across it and an insistent, wandering bass steering the song through the bleak, uncomfortable terrain.

46
YELLO
Goldrush/She's Got A Gun
(Live At The Palladium N.Y.)
54
Mercury

Parodying the 'greed is good' culture of the decade, Yello's 'Goldrush' made us smile as we digested its insane rhythm and expressive vocal, which made a serious point about the horrible nature of avarice, and made us dance like lunatics. Now that's what I call music!

45
ADONIS
No Way Back (Vocal)
No Way Back
NO CHART PLACING
Trax Records

Aged just 19 when he put this track together (although it was another couple of years before its release), 'No Way Back' is recognised as one of the first acid tracks. It has a bass groove that is relentless and killing. The vocal - over a minimal lyric - is menacing and desperate. It was fresh and exciting in 1986 and still sounds lean and vital to this day.

44
THE LEATHER NUN
Gimme Gimme Gimme (A Man After Midnight)/Lollipop
NO CHART PLACING
Wire Records

These Swedish industrial rockers were one time affiliates of Throbbing Gristle and were accordingly subversive in their approach, having gained a degree of notoriety from their showing of hard core pornography at live shows. Here they take on one of Abba's golden hits and pummel any innocence and light out of it, transforming it into a harsh, dark, unapologetic hymn to pure lust for male flesh.

43
MADONNA
Open Your Heart/Lucky Star
4
Sire

Originally a rock song called 'Follow Your Heart' which was intended for Cyndi Lauper, it was heard by Madonna's management and duly offered to her. Madonna reworked the song, with producer Patrick Leonard in particular adding a bass line which transformed it into a dance track. 'Open Your Heart' was energetic and upbeat, with a lyric that people could relate to. Sung straightforwardly by Madonna who, while not blessed with a conventionally great voice, extracts the maximum from herself and delivers to great effect.

42
TALK TALK
I Don't Believe In You
Does Caroline Know (Live Version)
96
Parlophone

This song about abandoning belief in someone - or perhaps some value system - is excellent. It glides on a bed of drums and organ, with a bass line of taste and economy pushing it along. The vocal is haunting and soulful, and topping it off is that rarest of things, a guitar solo that adds to the song. It cuts into proceedings around two thirds of the way in - hypnotic and passionate, almost heart-stopping. It doesn't outstay its welcome, but ratchets up the already high emotional intensity to near breaking point.

41
COLOURBOX
The Official Colourbox
World Cup Theme
NO CHART PLACING
4AD

Released simultaneously with 'Baby I Love You So', this track was a full-on, celebratory, near euphoric instrumental. Upbeat and uplifting, it was considered for usage on the BBC's *World Cup Grandstand* programme though ultimately not chosen. It is an absolutely huge-sounding record, with energy that scorches. Play it while watching Diego Madonna slalom through the England team to score that most iconic goal, and the drama and poetry in the combination of sight and sound is astounding.

40
VERLAINES
Doomsday/New Kinda Hero
NO CHART PLACING
Flying Nun Records

Although this was a record built on the jerking rhythms and jangly guitar style combined with hummable melodies that characterised many of the Flying Nun stable of acts, it was differentiated by its aggression and angry snarl, not to mention a thumping piano outro. Songwriter Grahame Downes sings of a relationship about to come off the rails and crash. His voice reflects the bleakness of his vision of what the future has in store in a most convincing manner.

39
THE WEATHER PROPHETS
Almost Prayed/Your Heartbeat
Breathes The Life Into Me
NO CHART PLACING
Creation Records

Singer and songwriter Pete Astor, along with drummer Dave Morgan, had been part of The Loft, who in 1985 had released the excellent 'Up The Hill And Down The Slope' single, before messily and publicly splitting up on stage whilst supporting The Colourfield at Hammersmith Palais. From the ashes, The Weather Prophets were formed and 'Almost Prayed' was their first release. Original it was not - it shamelessly wore its debt to The Velvet Underground, from the simple drum beat and the two-chord guitar riff, to the single-note piano part used percussively. Astor sang a quasi-mysterious lyric with studied nonchalance and settled on a brilliant three-word chorus. It seemed to be played on rotation at The Boardwalk - it was part of the atmosphere and sounded fantastic.

38
RUN DMC
Walk This Way
Walk This Way (Instrumental)
8
London Records

This was another record that was hammered at The Boardwalk, displaying a disregard for the barriers of musical genres. It hadn't been unusual for Run DMC to use rock guitars to add power to their raps, but this taking of Aerosmith's already established song, and working with them in the studio to create a new version, meant that the rap-rock collision was now a two-way street that broke down barriers for performers and audiences alike.

This sounded terrifically exciting, though remarkably none of the performers viewed this track as a potential single. It was released reluctantly, resulting in a career revival for Aerosmith, catapulting Run DMC to prominence, and kicking down doors of prejudicial thought for the likes of The Beastie Boys, Faith No More and even Marc Riley and the Creepers to use this formula in their own work.

37
PET SHOP BOYS
Love Comes Quickly
That's My Impression
19
Parlophone

Absolutely hypnotic rhythms signal another fabulous Pet Shop Boys moment. There is a sense of brooding sadness in the song that gives way to the deep romance of the chorus. It is a measured and sophisticated piece of pop craftsmanship where Andy McKay, of the always tasteful Roxy Music, makes an appearance on saxophone, and symbolically pass on the torch of intelligent stylish pop music-making to Messrs. Tennant and Lowe.

36
HALF PINT
Greetings/Greetings (Version)
NO CHART PLACING
Power House

Powered by a rhythm section featuring Sly Dunbar and Robbie Shakespeare, this is a quick-footed celebratory record that acts as a tonic and lifts tired spirits. Half Pint sings and spreads positivity in a light-as-a-feather style, and the world seems to be a warmer, brighter place as he does his thing.

35
JAMIE PRINCIPLE
Your Love (Club Mix)/
(Radio Mix)/ (Dub/Rodapella Mix)
NO CHART PLACING
Persona Records

Jamie Principle wrote 'Your Love' and recorded a home demo. It was given to Frankie Knuckles who, although having never worked on an original piece, agreed to help. He made some adjustments and began playing the record in his sets. It stunned and amazed the ecstatic crowd. After some further work on the song by DJ Mark "Hot Rod" Trollan, it was released a year later on Persona Records, the third release of Jamie Principle's fledgling career. A year after that it was released again unofficially on Trax Records. Jamie Principle had signed no agreement with that label - it amounted to theft with the record now credited to Frankie Knuckles. The track though is an indisputable classic that pushed house music into a more experimental area. Its arpeggiated synth lead and pulsing bass line were ear-worms in themselves and the vocal was a cool master-class in economy. This was a record that went beneath the radar on release but it was taken by The Source, with a vocal by Candi Staton, to become 'You Got The Love', a classic in its own right and a UK hit in 1991.

34
NICK CAVE & THE BAD SEEDS
The Singer (a.k.a. The Folksinger)
NO CHART PLACING
Mute

With the turmoil of The Birthday Party era receding, Nick Cave put together a collection of cover versions for his *Kicking Against the Pricks* album. This allowed he and the Bad Seeds to record material in a variety of styles and expand their musical range. 'The Singer' was one of the highlights of the album and made for a fine single. It is a barely-remembered Johnny Cash song, loaded with pathos and with a hurtful ache close to the surface. It is given a skeletal, musical reading with unobtrusive strings helping ratchet up the tension. Cave sings unconventionally but brilliantly, his voice a deep purr that masterfully expresses the misery of the lyric.

33
ELVIS COSTELLO
& THE ATTRACTIONS
Tokyo Storm Warning (Parts 1 & 2
Black Sails In The Sunset
73
Imp Records

This record howls. This record rampages. This record is brutal and savage. Absolutely compelling and completely bewildering, this is loud, unhinged, violent, fucked up and fascinating. This is one of the great writer's greatest performances, in conjunction with his magnificent band. Swallow a gram of speed and a thesaurus, walk over hot coals whilst singing, and you might, just might, touch the wild extremes of this titanic blast of poetic, diesel-soaked garage rock.

32
SHINEHEAD
Who The Cap Fit
Billy Jean - Mama Used To Say
NO CHART PLACING
Virgin

Shinehead was the moniker adopted by Carl Aitken, a Jamaican who began his career toasting for reggae dancehall sound systems in New York, notably the Bronx-based Tony Screw's Downbeat the Ruler. He also used a live backing band that contained a young Jeff Buckley on guitar and backing vocals. His first record was 'Who The Cap Fit'. Released independently, it was given a UK release by *Virgin*.

I don't know why I bought this - I had never heard of it or the artist. Perhaps I was intrigued to hear versions of much-loved familiar songs. It proved to be a very wise purchase. Shinehead took Bob Marley's brilliant 'Who The Cap Fit' and refreshed and retooled it in his own rap/reggae style. It was a bold stroke to ride roughshod over such a well-loved classic, but the audacious approach paid off. It was a brilliant interpretation. What the A-side did for Bob Marley, the B-side did for Michael Jackson and Junior Giscombe - pure quality!

31
KATE BUSH
The Big Sky (Meteorological Mix)
Not This Time/The Morning Fog
37
EMI

This was a song that captured the times as a child where we lie on our backs staring at the sky, watching clouds as they shift shape. We see pictures in this phenomenon and allow our imagination free reign, and then we find that we feel too old for such frippery and allow ourselves to lose this magical key to a secret world. Struggling to find the right sound for the recording, Martin 'Youth' Glover of Killing Joke was recruited to play bass. It was a master stroke - his playing is hard and rhythmical, and in conjunction with the drums, he lends the song a tribal feel, which acts as a springboard for Kate Bush to emote unencumbered and free.

30
MAN TO MAN
Meets MAN PARRISH
Male Stripper (Part One)
Male Stripper (Part Two)
4
Bolts Records

Miki and Paul Zone were brothers who had been members of The Fast, a New York new wave act who were associated with the scene based around Max's Kansas City night club and had a string of record releases. At the start of the eighties the brothers struck out on their own as Man 2 Man. They changed their style, going completely electronic, and toured with the likes of Sylvester and Divine. For 'Male Stripper', which had originally been recorded with Bobby Orlando in 1982, they teamed up with electro pioneer Man Parrish, and what resulted was dance-floor dynamite with a cheeky homoerotic sexual energy. The record hovered around the chart for 26 weeks but sadly Miki Zone was already dead from an AIDS-related illness by the time of the record's chart peak.

29
THE JESUS AND MARY CHAIN
Some Candy Talking
Psychocandy/Hit
13
Blanco Y Negro

Everything about The Jesus and Mary Chain reflected their immersion in rock 'n' roll iconography, from their big Bob Dylan hair through their Gretch guitars to the coded language of their lyrics. 'Some Candy Talking' suffered a BBC ban due to the insistence of moral watchdog DJ Mike Reid who perceived the song to be about shooting up heroin. It was nothing of the sort - what the coded language almost certainly referred to was the mutual joy in the act of cunnilingus. It is played at a meandering pace, heavy on reverb-soaked guitar atmospherics with stark drums and whispered vocals. It is utterly beguiling.

28
ARTHUR RUSSELL
Let's Go Swimming (Coastal Dub/ (Gulf Stream Dub)/ (Puppy Surf Dub)
NO CHART PLACING
Rough Trade

"Mixed with love by Walter Gibbons" is written loudly across the record label - indeed Gibbons deserved credit for his work here. Arthur Russell's original take of 'Let's Go Swimming' is charming. It is a magical, cello-led, drummer-less piece, almost folky, with Russell's naïve stream of consciousness lyric. Gibbons adds electronics and percussion with intuitive good taste which gives the track greater body and dance-floor appeal without ever cluttering its spaces or undermining its wondrous eccentricity.

27
PRINCE & THE REVOLUTION
Mountains/Alexa De Paris
45
Paisley Park

'Mountains' was written by Prince, along with Revolution members Wendy Melvoin and Lisa Coleman as part of the musical soundtrack to the film *Under the Cherry Moon.* It is simple and yet delicious and passionate. Prince was never constrained by musical genres. He could never be pigeon-holed, and that is evidenced here as influences as disparate as James Brown, The Beatles, Sly Stone and Love can all be detected, although in combination they amount to something that is uniquely the sound of Prince.

26
SIGUE SIGUE SPUTNIK
Love Missile F1-11
Hack Attack
3
Parlophone

Tony James re-emerged half a decade on from the breakup of Generation X with sci-fi punk outfit Sigue Sigue Sputnik. This was their debut single, produced by Giorgio Moroder, one part Suicide, one part Donna Summer, with T. Rex swagger. Dressed up like extras from a trash glam version of Mad Max, they were a wild, over-the-top flash of vibrant colour, and this was a dizzying, rampaging aural equivalent of the look, with thumping beats and hiccupping vocals.

25
MADONNA
True Blue / Ain't No Big Deal
1
Sire

Motown-inspired dance pop was the order of the day for Madonna. She was head over heels in love with Sean Penn and the title 'True Blue' is taken from one of his favourite expressions, an avowal of the love she felt. Its retro leanings incorporate a chorus in similar style to the Dixie Cups' 1964 hit 'Chapel Of Love'. It is up-tempo and saccharin sweet, with a bounce that is irreplaceable - to put it quite simply, this was great pop.

24
BEASTIE BOYS
(You Gotta) Fight For Your Right (To Party)
Time to Get Ill/Paul Revere
11
Def Jam Recordings

Playing up their snottiness and acting like brats to satirise the mindless hedonism of party animals backfired on the Beasties. The irony of 'Fight For Your Right' was lost on an audience who took them at face value, as did a rabid tabloid press who were looking for new corruptors of morals to vilify. But even though the song's message was lost in translation, this remained a thrilling record full of hard rock guitar hammering out a hypnotically dumb riff of simple genius, drums that sound like they are taking a severe beating, and shouted vocals that come together like a deranged, quite absurd, football crowd chant.

23
MR FINGERS
Washing Machine
Can You Feel It/
Beyond The Clouds
NO CHART PLACING
Trax Records

Mr Fingers was, as we have previously ascertained, the alias used by DJ Larry Heard to release his own music. 'Washing Machine' was one of his finest pieces, and indeed a true house music classic. It bleeps and squelches, and as surmised from the title, follows the rhythm of a washing machine's cycle. Conceptually sound and great fun, its companion tracks were of similar high quality, 'Can You Feel It' being a masterful piece of techno infused head music in combination with a dance sensibility. 'Beyond The Clouds' meanwhile was a sprawling, moody piece of techno house, similar to the pieces Juan Atkins was recording in Detroit.

22
JANET JACKSON
What Have You Done For Me Lately
3
A&M Records

Janet Jackson had lived in a gilded cage. She had been controlled by her father who acted as her manager, performed on a TV show she disliked and recorded a pair of albums that she had no input into. She left the Jackson's family home, married James Debarge against the family's wishes, only to separate and begin divorce proceedings shortly afterwards. In the midst of this, she signed to A&M records where she was teamed up with Jimmy Jam and Terry Lewis, a writer/production team who had been affiliates of Prince and members of The Time. Together they composed 'What Have You Done For Me Lately', which reflected Jackson's feelings about the neglect she felt during her marriage. Jackson succeeded in displaying her maturity, strength and independence. She delivered it fearlessly and fiercely over a stripped back, deeply funky groove.

21
CICCONE YOUTH
Tuff Titty Rap
Into The Groovey/Burnin'Up
NO CHART PLACING
Blast First

Following the death of best friend and Minutemen band-mate D. Boon, bassist Mike Watt spent time with Kim Gordon and Thurston Moore of Sonic Youth, who were at the time recording their *Evol* album. They wished to encourage Watt to begin playing again and he recorded two tracks with them. The Ciccone Youth project was born from this alliance. 'Into The Groovey' was a sincere tribute to Madonna's talent and an acknowledgement of her roots in New York's No Wave scene. Samplers and drum machines were incorporated into the rebooting of the iconic Madonna single without sacrificing Sonic Youth's trademark guitar-bleeding dissonance. It clattered and buzzed and featured a deadpan vocal from Moore. Blasts of noise and a genius musical hook further added to its allure. The other Madonna cover song on the release - 'Burnin' Up'- was cut by Mike Watt with no Sonic Youth involvement and lent the single and Ciccone Youth experience a conceptual edge.

20
THE FALL
Living Too Late/
Hot Aftershave Bop/
Living Too Long
97
Beggars Banquet

The lyrical content of 'Living Too Late' is a verbalising of the disgruntled thought process of a middle-aged suburban male. Musically it plods along on one chord, except as verses end it breaks down - only the keyboard and vocal remain. It is the sound of madness, of a mind at the end of its tether, and Mark Smith disturbingly yodels through these parts. Mark's performance is wonderful - the sound of a man at the peak of his powers. He is confident and utterly convincing in his depiction of the draining tedium and waning power the narrator experiences. Equally prominent is Steve Hanley whose bass playing is extraordinary, he uses the instrument to act simultaneously as the song's anchor and melodic lead. He grooves and makes the whole band groove along with him.

19
THE MEKONS
Hello Cruel World
Alone & Forsaken
NO CHART PLACING
Sin Record Company

The instrumentation sees The Mekons move away from the guitar-led post punk sound that had launched them. It moves them towards a different sonic landscape of countrified violin, though this is no jig or reel 'Hello Cruel World' is a desperate sounding, grinding howl sung plaintively by Tom Greenhalgh that is moving and emotional. The Mekons were a voice of sanity and reason - their collective conscience compelled them to speak unpleasant truths wrapped up in music that was slightly ramshackle and bruised but nonetheless quite beautiful.

18
NITRO DELUXE
Let's Get Brutal/(Dub)/
The Brutal House
24 (1987)
Cutting Records

Nitro Deluxe was the chosen alias for Philadelphia born Young Manny Scretching Jnr. He had played with a variety of funk and jazz ensembles including Sun Ra's Arkestra, before recording solo.

'Let's Get Brutal' was a huge tune in popularising house in the UK. It was guaranteed to put feet on dance-floors in euphoric communion with the DJ. Its strength is actually its subtlety, working its way into the head and filling the heart with joy. Every note is downplayed and yet the synth riff at the heart of the tune is mesmeric - a truly timeless classic.

17
CAMPER VAN BEETHOVEN
Take The Skinheads Bowling/
Colonel Enrique Adolfo Bermudez
NO CHART PLACING
Rough Trade

Camper Van Beethoven were a Californian band who mixed up all manner of musical styles ranging from ska to country rock. They combined these musical elements with offbeat, deliberately quirky lyrics that in truth grew to irritate me to an extreme degree. Their most absurdist song was their first single, 'Take The Skinheads Bowling' - completely meaningless, relating the size of bowling alley lanes and finding gangs of skinheads on the lawn. Its brilliance lay in its joyous exuberance and the refreshing sense that here was a band not taking themselves even slightly seriously. They were having fun and we listeners were in on the joke. Any song with a lyric as great as "had a dream last night I was licking your knees" gets my vote as one of the best of 1986.

16
FARLEY "JACKMASTER" FUNK & JESSE SAUNDERS
Love Can't Turn Around (Club Mix)/(Radio Edit)
Dub Can't Turn Around
10 (1996 - 40)
House Records

The cold facts of the matter are as follows. Isaac Hayes released a disco-flavoured single in 1975 called 'I Can't Turn Around' which remained a club favourite for many years and was often heard in the influential Chicago club The Warehouse. In 1986 Steve "Silk" Hurley cut a house version of the track which inspired his house-mate Farley "Jackmaster" Funk to team up with producer Jesse Saunders to record his own version which incorporated new elements alongside elements from both Hayes' and Hurley's versions. The vocal hook of 'I Can't Turn Around' was transposed into 'Love Can't Turn Around. And then, the true genius moment arrived when Darryl Pandy was recruited to sing. Pandy had a background in Broadway operatics and gospel. He brought power and sweet silkiness to his outstanding flamboyant performance, which made hearing this record an unforgettable delight.

15
THE LEN BRIGHT COMBO
Someone Must Have Nailed Us Together/Mona
NO CHART PLACING
Empire Records

The Len Bright Combo paired the ramshackle rhythm section from The Milkshakes in the form of Bruce Brand and Russ Wilkins, with singer-songwriter extraordinaire, and equally ramshackle guitar player, Wreckless Eric. They were my favourite live act of the day and I attended as many of their gigs as possible. I was always delighted to receive the newsletters they sent out. Who cared that they were technically sloppy musicians who valued feel over virtuosity? Who cared that they weren't dressed to the nines and didn't have incredible hairstyles? What they had was energy to burn and songs that were utterly sublime. 'Someone Must Have Nailed Us Together' was one of the best - a brilliant observation on love that has faded between a couple who stay together simply because they can't fathom a way to part. It is bathed in pathos and yet is also a rowdy sing along, comparable to the classic 60s hits penned by Ray Davies for The Kinks. There is no higher praise I can offer than that!

14
KATE BUSH
Hounds of Love
The Handsome Cabin Boy
18
EMI

'Hounds of Love' is direct, stripped back and completely compelling. Only a rigid drum pattern and Fairlight provide a backing. The voice does the rest, supplying the melody and drama, as Kate sings about running away from the clutches of unwanted love, comparing herself to a fox being pursued and hunted by a pack of dogs. Kate Bush was at a creative peak and her music defied classification - this woman gave us the wonderful treasure of her music.

13
PET SHOP BOYS
Suburbia/Paninaro
8
Parlophone

Inspired by the cinematic depiction of the suburban nightmare in Penelope Spheeris' film *Suburbia*, but also the Brixton riots of 1981 and 1985, The Pet Shop Boys portray the boredom and drudgery of suburban life that leads to a ratcheting up of tension and the threat of violence erupting out of the slightest provocation. The song understandably has a dark edge of menace. The imagery of packs of dogs running through the dark streets is disturbing and vivid. Thankfully that is tempered by a pretty and elegant keyboard part and the cultured pronunciation in Neil Tennant's singing voice, turning ugly subject matter into glorious pop nirvana.

12
MADONNA
Papa Don't Preach/
Ain't No Big Deal
8
Sire

The 28-year-old Madonna singing a song from the perspective of a pregnant teenage girl confiding in her father should have sounded ridiculous. The reason it isn't is down to how Madonna handles the lyrics with empathy and conviction. She pulls it off magnificently, and in doing so created one of her signature songs. Controversy followed as pro-abortion groups in the US saw in the song an anti-abortion sentiment. This was codswallop, as the young female protagonist in the song examines both options open to her before concluding she will keep the baby. To my mind, the lyrics are pro-individual choice. Musically the track is excellent, utilising classical elements to soundtrack the emotion of the song. It morphs into a quick-paced dance track without ever sounding contrived and the subtle use of acoustic guitar and strings is highly effective.

11
CAMEO
Word Up/Urban Warrior
3
Club

'Word Up' was the most deliciously funky slice of R&B heard in years. From its opening nod to Ennio Morricone's theme to *The Good, the Bad and the Ugly*, the listener is grabbed by the throat and propelled to the dance floor where abstract shapes are pulled to this abstract reassembling of old forms. 'Word Up' was a hip colloquialism of the conversational phrase "you bet". It acts as a fabulous vocal hook incorporated into the easy-to-sing-lyric that accompanies a riff of exquisite simplicity and monstrous proportions. Synths whistle and whirr amidst the track's percussive chatter. And for the duration it is difficult not to wear a grin from ear to ear.

Northern Soul DJing in a gold lamme suit

10
MARSHALL JEFFERSON
Move Your Body /Dub Your Body
Drum Your Body/House Your Body
NO CHART PLACING
Trax Records

Marshall Jefferson recorded 'Move your Body' using friendly co-workers from his job at the post office where he worked on the night-shift. He used piano to give it an uplifting feel and wrote a lyric sung by his workmate Curtis McClain that celebrated the euphoria and social communion felt in clubs such as The Warehouse and Music Box. Trax Records head Larry Sherman was very dismissive of the track and highly reluctant to release it. He claimed it didn't sound like house music at all. He was persuaded to finally issue the single when a group of British journalists reporting on the Chicago scene were escorted around five or six clubs where DJs were playing 'Move Your Body' on cassette to an ecstatic reaction. Marshall Jefferson pointedly had "The House Music Anthem" emblazoned across the record label and finally 'Move your Body' hit the streets. Its impact was profound - a powerful celebration of a scene built by outsiders and social outcasts. The piano chord progression was a sensational musical device that would be copied and used as a template on records for decades to come.

9
ROBERT PALMER
Addicted To Love
Remember To Remember
5
Island Records

Robert Palmer had been a perennial figure, seemingly always on the brink of success. I'd first encountered him as a member of rock soul band Vinegar Joe and had been an eager purchaser of his fantastic 1974 album *Sneakin' Sally Through the Alley*. In 1986, the stars were aligned, and his overdue major success arrived courtesy of 'Addicted to Love'. The song was originally conceived as a duet between Palmer and Chaka Khan but she was not allowed dispensation from her record company to appear on another label, so Palmer recorded the track as a solo. He had a stellar cast of musicians on board including

Wally Badarou, Andy Taylor of Duran Duran, Tony Thompson of Chic and his band-mate Bernard Fowler producing. They served up a swaggering riff that jerked and lurched in a fashion that was riveting while Palmer was at once sophisticated and soulful and the combination of these elements made for a near perfect pop record.

8
CYNDI LAUPER
True Colors/
Heading For The Moon
12
Portrait

'True Colors' was written by Billy Steinberg and Tom Kelly, the pair responsible for The Bangles' 'Eternal Flame' and Madonna's 'Like a Virgin' among others. Steinberg had written the lyrics as an ode to his mother, and it was presented to Cyndi Lauper as a traditional piano ballad. She dismantled it and created an arrangement that breathed life into the composition. The song is uplifting and a testament to the strength and goodness in a person's nature. Cyndi Lauper tapped into the spirit shown by a recently deceased friend, Gregory Natal, who had succumbed to the HIV/AIDS virus. It gave her singing performance a heartfelt emotional edge that resonated with the listener. It is a truly outstanding and beautiful record that became a standard for the gay community. Some years later Cyndi founded the True Colors Fund, dedicated to eradicating homelessness amongst LGBT teens.

7
P.I.L.
Rise
Rise Instrumental
11
Virgin

With a supergroup gathered around him, John Lydon recorded his most memorable single since debut P.I.L. single 'Public Image' back in 1978. With Shankar's electrified and electrifying violin very much to the fore, Lydon unleashes a series of images related to the cruel and morally corrupt system operating in apartheid-era South Africa. He points out that change will come because of indomitable human spirit – "Anger is an energy" he chants, making the point that channelling a negative energy can lead to a positive outcome. The music is a spectacular mix of global styles and Lydon's Irish roots are displayed in the chorus, "may the road rise with you", which originated in the first line of a Gaelic blessing, literally translated as "may the road rise up to meet you".

6
PAUL SIMON
You Can Call Me Al
Gumboots
4
Warner Bros. Records

'You Can Call Me Al' was the lead single from Paul Simon's politically sensitive, though brilliant album *Graceland*. It utilises an army of musicians, some Western and some African. They create a dizzying kaleidoscopic musical backing for Simon's tale of middle-aged disappointment, which is delivered in quick-fire conversational style akin to David Byrne's method of performance with Talking Heads. A synthesised horn part created by Adrian Belew acts as punctuation, as well as being a brilliant musical hook. The song has a chorus referencing a meeting at a party with French composer Pierre Boulez who mistakenly called Paul Simon 'Al', and his then wife Peggy as 'Betty', an incident that instigated the writing of the song.

5
GWEN GUTHRIE
Ain't Nothin' Goin' On
But The Rent (Club Mix)/
(Dub Mix)/ Passion Eyes
5 (2005 REMIX VERSION - 42)
Boiling Point

Gwen Guthrie got her first professional break by singing backup to Aretha Franklin in 1974. From there her career snowballed, writing songs for the likes of Roberta Flack and Ben E King, and singing on records by Stevie Wonder, Madonna, Peter Tosh and a host of others. Her solo career ran concurrent to her session work, being dubbed "first lady of the Paradise Garage", as several of her tracks found favour at that venue. She teamed up with DJ Larry Levan and had a huge club hit with 'Padlock' which featured The Compass Point Allstars. Her big moment came with 'Ain't Nothin' Goin On But The Rent', in which she cheekily referenced songs by James Brown,

Billy Preston and First Choice in lyrics that proclaimed solvency as a prerequisite for romance. She was accused of being materialistic, presumably by people who had never been poor enough to appreciate how poverty damages relationships. The song was funky and fresh and its title became a catchphrase for those struggling financially.

4
DAVID BOWIE
Absolute Beginners/
Absolute Beginners (Dub)
2
Virgin

'Absolute Beginners' was far and away Bowie's greatest musical achievement of the 80s, one that proved his talent wasn't spent, even though it had been misplaced for some considerable time. The song was the title track for a film directed by Julian Temple, for which Bowie agreed to provide the theme song in exchange for a small acting role. Returning for the first time since 1971's *Hunky Dory* sessions was pianist Rick Wakeman, who excels on a track which is a breathtaking thing of great beauty. It features an incredible saxophone solo from Don Waller that erupts violently and passionately whilst Bowie delivers a classy, crooned vocal. The whole is an extremely satisfying romantic declaration of deep love.

3
THE FALL
Mr. Pharmacist /
Lucifer Over Lancashire/
Auto Tech Pilot
75
Beggars Banquet

'Mr. Pharmacist' can stake a claim as being one of the most iconic Fall singles. It contains all the ingredients and essence of what made these Salfordians/Mancunians the most interesting band of the decade. It is hard hitting and punchy - no flab, just a great pounding riff. A shouted vocal, a mad speedy interlude and it's over. It is lyrically brilliant, and its pro-drug message fits like a glove. Oddly, it is not self-composed but a cover of a forgotten 1966 garage rock classic by The Other Half, which discerning record collector Mark Smith decided was perfect for The Fall, whose playing on this single is thrillingly brutal.

2
PRINCE AND THE REVOLUTION
Kiss/
Love Or Money
6 (1988 - 76, 2016 - 38)
Paisley Park

PRINCE AND THE REVOLUTION/KISS

Originally a song given to funk band Mazarati, who began developing the track in a recording studio room next door to where Prince was working, Prince decided the song was too good to be given away and reclaimed it. He retained the funky rhythm that producer David Z had introduced, along with Mazarati's backing vocals, stripped the song of bass, added a wiggly guitar line and topped it off with distinctive "ah-wah-ah" backing vocals cribbed from Brenda Lee's 'Sweet Nothin's'. The result was minimalistic to the point of being skeletal, but with a superb arch vocal from Prince, the finished article was delicious and unique. His record label was unimpressed and didn't want the song to be released. Prince stood his ground and won the day. 'Kiss' was a much-loved and admired single and garnered much praise, with successful cover versions by Age of Chance and Art of Noise.

1
ELVIS COSTELLO
AND THE ATTRACTIONS
I Want You/
I Hope You're Happy Now
79
Imp Records

Not only is this one of the most bloodlettingly naked songs ever written - laying bear jealous, ugly emotions - it is equally one of the most painful and intense performances committed to wax. Lyrically, vocally, and musically, this song is akin to a framed photograph of a once-loving couple being hurled violently against a wall. Glass smashed, it drops to the floor where it is angrily ground beneath a boot heel until it is completely obliterated. 'I Want You' is riveting from first note to last, from the opening creepy vocal salvo, through the self-lacerating bulk of the song to the final exhausted self-pitying gasp. Its sound is stark, stripped of romance. A loveless, brutalist dirge, 'I Want You' is unforgettable. It relates the painful, bitter and twisted feelings of the narrator at the loss of his lover to another. It cripples and destroys any concept of dignity or self-respect. 'I Want You' speaks eloquently of a darkness inside the soul. It is extreme, but full of truth about the flawed nature of the human condition - a genius record.

Poised for stardom - Whipcrackaway, 1987

The Thin Men 1987 featuring Marc Riley (guitar), my brother Neil (bass), Mike Joyce of The Smiths (drums) and myself with a bottle of Irish whiskey.

1987

This was my 30th year of life, I took a look around; my peers seemingly lived happy stable lives replete with wives, children, cars, houses and careers while I had nothing - what had I been doing? I'd had good times along the way but I was rootless and pretty disappointed with myself. I vowed to change, I got a steady job with a steady income and I moved into a house and got a mortgage, of course ultimately these things made me unhappy but I was trying desperately hard to see if conformity might bring contentment, I had money for things and so I bought a thing manufactured by Amstrad, it played records and tapes and also functioned as a crude though very complicated recording device. I stood no chance of figuring out how to use it but my brother came to the rescue and we found time each week to write and record a song together, it was very stimulating.

Buoyed by this activity I was persuaded by former Oochikomis band-mate Gene to help him and my friends Sue, Karen and Rhonda to record a demo of their song 'The Horse's Tale'. I played it to Fall bassist Marc Riley and he released it on his In Tape record label. We named the group Whipcrackaway and the single was savaged by the *NME*! In his *Manchester Evening News* column Mick Middles claimed that we sounded like drunkards, Capital Radio ran a spoof feature on it. Gene was mortified initially, though soon regained his composure. The girls didn't give two hoots and I was highly amused, still I did argue with Roger Eagle about it. I held Roger in the highest regard but his claim that we were insulting the country music genre he held dear I found pious and overly puritanical. I gathered myself, Gene and friends, including Marc Riley, to record some more songs. One night in the Hacienda I bumped into Smiths drummer Mike Joyce and asked if he would care to come and play on a version of Marc Bolan's 'Baby Strange', he was delighted to accept and once permission was granted by Messrs Morrissey and Marr we committed the song to tape. At a gig by Nico at Manchester Central Library I encountered Peter Hook of New Order, popped a similar question to him and a fortnight later we convened at Suite 16 in Rochdale and cut 5 tracks

- it was great fun. The press got wind of what was happening and briefly rumours of a supergroup circulated. I was having fun, I was out and about a lot in various clubs and venues and heard, felt and witnessed a musical and societal change as acid house swept across the city on a wave of ecstasy and genuine enthusiasm. Local bands picked up on the sound, they became looser and funkier and 'baggy' was born. I found myself in the role of fascinated spectator; this was somebody else's party - I loved lots of the music and the attitude but accepted my place on the fringes of this changing landscape.

NOTABLE EVENTS

In New York Mafia boss 'Fat' Tony Salerno is sentenced to 100 years imprisonment for racketeering

The special envoy to the Archbishop of Canterbury, Terry Waite, is kidnapped in Lebanon, he is held until 1991.

The cross channel ferry 'Herald of Free Enterprise' capsizes killing 193 people in Zeebrugge, The Netherlands.

The Simpsons is first shown as part of *The Tracey Ullman Show.*

Former SS guard Klause Barbie, known as 'The Butcher of Lyon', is put on trial for war crimes. Found guilty he is sentenced to life imprisonment.

The Conservative Party wins another general election by a landslide, Margaret Thatcher remains as Prime Minister.

Former Deputy Fuhrer Rudolph Hess is found dead in his cell at Spandau Prison aged 93. Hess had been arrested in 1941 having flown to Scotland in an attempt to negotiate Britain's exit from the war.

Michael Ryan murders 16 people in Hungerford, Berkshire. It is mainland Britain's first mass shooting.

Legendary jockey Lester Piggott is jailed for three years for tax evasion.

12 people are murdered by the provisional IRA at a remembrance service at Enniskillen, Northern Ireland.

31 people die and 100 more are injured following a fire at Kings Cross tube station.

Ronald Reagan and Mikhail Gorbachev sign the INF Treaty eliminating shorter range nuclear missiles.

Alex Ferguson's first year as Manchester United boss is mixed at best. United finish 11th in his first season and are knocked out of the FA Cup by eventual winners Coventry City. The only highlight of the season is doing the double over Liverpool, the win at Anfield is United's only away win all season, helping Everton win the league. Fergie signs Viv Anderson and Brian 'Choccy' McClair but the 1987-88 season begins with Liverpool, with new signings John Barnes and Peter Beardsley, back at the top of the league.

NOTABLE BIRTHS

Edison Cavani; Joss Stone; Andy Murray; Novak Djokovic; Kendrick Lamar; Lionel Messi; Sebastian Vettel; Frank Ocean.

NOTABLE DEATHS

Alistair MacLean; Liberace; Andy Warhol; Dean Martin; Primo Levi; Carlton Barrett; Rita Hayworth; Fred Astaire; John Huston; Lee Marvin; Peter Tosh; Jaco Pastorius; Henry Ford; James Baldwin.

NOTABLE BOOKS

The Bonfire of the Vanities - Tom Wolfe
Misery - Stephen King
Le Ballade De I'mpossibble - Haruki Murakimi
The Black Dahlia - James Ellroy
The Neon Rain - James Lee Burke
The Rules of Attraction - Bret Easton Ellis
The Passion - Jeanette Winterson
The Child in Time - Ian McEwan
Psychotic Reactions and Carburettor Dung - Lester Bangs
I'm With the Band , Confessions of a Groupie - Pamela Des Barres

NOTABLE FILMS

Wings of Desire; Matewan; RoboCop; The Untouchables; Full Metal Jacket; Fatal Attraction; Empire of the Sun ; Good morning Vietnam; Predator; Dirty Dancing; Wall Street; The Last Emperor; The Belly of an Architect; Prick Up Your Ears; Barfly; Withnail & I; Radio Days; Au Revoir Les Enfants; Bagdad Cafe.

100
WAS (NOT WAS)
Spy In The House Of Love
Dad I'm In Jail
21
Fontana

Overdue chart success arrived for Was (Not Was) with this old style, funky soul number. The band's inherent strangeness and quirky songs were put on the back burner as they proved themselves capable of playing it straight to gain the recognition they deserved. The song swings, the horns roar and Sweet Pea Atkinson takes the lead vocal with aplomb - it is gritty and passionate.

99
PULP
They Suffocate At Night/Tunnel
NO CHART PLACING
Fire Records

The original line-up of Pulp had departed and with them had gone the light, almost folky sound of their earliest work. Only Jarvis Cocker remained, and he was joined on this record for the first time by Russell Senior. They are noticeably darker in mood and sound than before and have begun to home in on the approach that will transform them into pop stars in the mid-90s. 'They Suffocate At Night' finds Cocker singing atop an insistent, almost pretty keyboard motif. It is a little wonky, but that suits a song about sad misfits - a loveless couple having bad sex and feeling bad about it. It is a picture of bleak despair, a fragment of a kitchen sink melodrama, and a glimpse of what was to come from Pulp.

98
PUBLIC ENEMY
[E Side] You're Gonna Get Yours (Vocal Mix)/ (Dub/Terminator X Getaway Version)/[F Side] Miuzi Weighs A Ton (Vocal Mix)/Rebel Without A Pause (Vocal Mix)
88
Def Jam Recordings

Although the subject matter concerning Chuck D's choice of car (an Oldsmobile 98) is light-hearted fare for Public Enemy, this record still hits hard. It is urgent, energetic, and highly insistent. Chuck D raps with speed and wit, while the beats and effects give the impression of an action film soundtrack. Always exciting and often thought provoking, when one considers the quality of 'Rebel Without A Pause' and 'Miuzi Weighs A Ton' that were part of the package, this was a superlative single.

97
JUNGLE WONZ
Time Marches On (Vocal)/(Club)
NO CHART PLACING
Trax Records

Jungle Wonz was an alias used by Marshall Jefferson, and this was the second release under that name. It is a sublime piece of deep, deep house, very understated musically while being sinuous and grooving. Harry Dennis's delicious vocal relates the changes we must accept and learn to embrace.

96
SISTERS OF MERCY
This Corrosion/Torch
7
Merciful Release

Goth rock was a sub-genre of punk, attracting an audience devoted to the look and the lifestyle of black clothing, eye shadow …. and miserableness! It was big business. The top goths were The Cult, The Mission and Sisters of Mercy, the latter led by Andrew Eldritch. Subtlety was not his forte, being one for grand sweeping gestures. For 'This Corrosion' he employed Jim Steinman as producer, fresh from his huge success with Meatloaf. A deliberately huge and over the top 40-piece choir was employed and Eldritch uses the song to put down deserters from his band's ranks, particularly Wayne Hussey, who had gone on to form The Mission. It was spiteful and a bit silly but somehow it made for great pop.

95
SINÉAD O'CONNOR
Troy/Still Listening
48
Ensign/Chrysalis

The debut single from Sinéad O'Connor pulled no punches. It is stunning and heart-wrenching. She uses the song as catharsis, unburdening herself of the anger she felt towards her mother who she claimed subjected her to emotional mistreatment and physical abuse. The ancient city of Troy is used as a metaphor for the destruction of love between mother and child - as Troy burned so their relationship turns to ashes. Sinéad's voice is incredible. At certain points, it is feminine and tender, at others it is a lion's roar. Full of passion and power, strings accompany her through what is a true epic and a marker of what was to follow, from this unique supreme talent.

94
CRIMINAL ELEMENT ORCHESTRA
Put The Needle To The Record/(Dub)/(Bonus Beats)
63
Cooltempo

Arthur Baker was the man behind this jumping electro track, benefiting from scratching by the "magic disco machine" over pure rockin' beats and Prince samples, one that raised pulses and the temperature on dance-floors.

93
HOLGER HILLER featuring BILLY MACKENZIE
Whippets/Waltz
NO CHART PLACING
Mute

Holger Hiller had been the singer in German synth band Palais Schaumburg, and had begun a parallel solo career in 1980, becoming one of the first Europeans to use a sampler as his main instrument. The vocals on 'Whippets' comes courtesy of the extraordinary Billy MacKenzie, who gives a madcap performance without restraint over slabs of orchestrated noise and oriental-flavoured percussion. It is avant-garde pop at its most extreme. Two decades later, Scott Walker would release 'Tilt', which sounds a lot like 'Whippets', and fans and critics would be equally bemused by it.

92
SCREAMING TREES
Asylum/Take It To The Tree
NO CHART PLACING
Native Records

Most music lovers will see the name Screaming Trees and presume this is the American pre-grunge outfit who were fronted by Mark Lanaghan. But this is an English act of the same name hailing from Doncaster, playing an edgy, urgent style of electronica, incorporating a fabulous bass line and a vocal that is anxious and urgent.

91
THE SEA URCHINS
Pristine Christine
NO CHART PLACING
Sarah Records

Hailing from West Bromwich, this single was the first release by seminal Bristol label Sarah Records who would become synonymous with the fey jangle pop that found favour amongst fey floppy-fringed boys and girls sporting flowered dresses and Dr Martens boots - the C86 generation. 'Pristine Christine' was, in truth, a fine example of swoon-worthy guitar pop; the sound harks back to that of The Byrds of the mid 60s and is topped by a yearning vocal that suggests sensitivity and bookishness, too much of this kind of thing would turn anyone's brains to mush, but taken in isolation this is an extremely charming and adorable sound.

90
RISSE
House Train (L.A. Radio Mix/
(Chicago Mix)
77
Jack Trax

Written and produced by Steve "Silk" Hurley, this leant heavily on the pre-house Salsoul Records label formula of marrying disco beats (and what amazing beats there are on this record) with strong, expressive vocals supplied here by Charisse Cobb, in what is essentially an update of the formula of name checking cities used on 'Martha and the Vandellas' 60s classic, 'Dancing in the Street'.

89
GEORGE HARRISON
Got My Mind Set On You
Lay His Head
2
Dark Horse Records

Visiting his sister in Illinois in 1963, George Harrison spent time in record shops buying albums not available in the UK. One was by James Ray, which contained the Rudy Clark song 'Got My Mind Set On You'. It registered strongly enough for Harrison to record a version himself 24 years later, with Jeff Lynne producing and playing bass, Jim Keltner drumming and Jim Horn and Ray Cooper adding saxophone and percussion - a high quality grouping of musicians. The magic flowed, making this Harrison's best single since the early 70s. It was snappy and infectious fun. Very, very repetitive, but that didn't matter. Everybody seemed to be having a great time singing and playing and this was transmitted to listeners who found themselves singing along, almost as a reflex action.

88
EPMD
It's My Thing (Club)
You're A Customer (Club)
97
Cooltempo

'It's My Thing' was the lead single from the seminal hip-hop album, *Strictly Business*. EPMD were a duo comprising Erick Sermon and Parrish Smith, EPMD standing for "**E**rick and **P**arrish **M**aking **D**ollars", which revealed their serious intent. 'It's My Thing' was a great introduction to their sound, which was sample heavy, dexterously rapped party music. Here they sample James Brown band co-singer Lyn Collins, to add a touch of her soulful delivery to the seriously funky rhythm being served up.

87
NITZER EBB
Let Your Body Learn/
(Instrumental)/(Seven Inch Edit)
NO CHART PLACING
Mute

Classified as an EBM (Electric Body Music) act, Nitzer Ebb described their music as being "international funk aggression", which fits perfectly. 'Let Your Body Learn' is utterly relentless. It has a fast, powerful rhythm over which vocals are hollered in the manner of slogans. It is hard but never too hostile for the dance floor. Singles like this and their other 1987 release, 'Join In The Chant', bridged the gap between the post punk sounds of Killing Joke, Siouxsie and the Banshees et al and the house sounds emanating in Chicago.

86
RYUICHI SAKAMOTO
Risky (Featuring Iggy Pop)
After All
NO CHART PLACING
CBS

Ryuichi Sakamoto melded traditional Eastern music with modern Western sounds. Bill Laswell produced his album *Neo Geo* that featured heavyweight talents such as Sly Dunbar and Bootsy Collins in supporting roles. Also participating on the track 'Risky' was Iggy Pop, casting aside his wild man persona to contribute a lyric that seems to suggest we should learn to accept the risk to our emotions as we embark upon love affairs. It also confusingly takes swipes at consumerism and the corporate world. Delivered in a sonorous croon by Iggy, it intrigues rather than infuriates and sits perfectly amidst the light, oriental-tinged funk backing track, creating a whole that is as emotional as it is quiet and undemonstrative.

85
SEVERED HEADS
Hot With Fleas (Extended)/
(Album Version)/
Canine (Extended)
NO CHART PLACING
Nettwerk

Jerky electronic rhythms abound. Strange voices sing lyrics of highly disturbing imagery. Devo had, as a recording entity, ceased to be relevant. Severed Heads had picked up the baton from the Ohio band and were running amok with it, twisting minds with dark humour and wild sounds.

84
TOM WAITS
Hang On St. Christopher (Extended Remixed Version)/
(Instrumental)
NO CHART PLACING
Island Records

The wilfully reckless subject matter of throwing caution to the wind and heading into the night on a wild foot-to-the-floor, all-guns-blazing ride is given appropriate backing by hard driving rhythms played as funk-fuelled, drug-addled, jazz-tinged rock & rhumba, with a harsh, clanging, industrial edge. It is a relentless barrage of glorious noise, and Tom Waits, seemingly more gravel-voiced with each passing year, and with megaphone in hand, reels off a cascading litany of images describing the hell-on-wheels road trip being undertaken. Breathtaking!

83
ON THE HOUSE
Give Me Back The Love (Club Mix)/(Radio Mix)/(Dub Mix)
NO CHART PLACING
Trax Records

Another Marshall Jefferson recording of supreme quality, 'Give Me Back The Love' is the epitome of classic deep house. With its synthesised backing that suggests strings and horns, the sound created by Jefferson obliquely references soul and funk records without mimicking them. Curtis McClain sings magnificently, with one foot seemingly in the church and the other in the nightclub.

82
TERENCE TRENT D'ARBY
Sign Your Name/Greasy Chicken
2
Columbia

The outrageous bragging that Terence Trent D'Arby engaged in during interviews perhaps worked against him as his musical gifts became overshadowed by an image of rampant ego mania. However the fact was he emerged in 1987 with a debut album that spawned four major hits and it seemed he would become an enduring star. He apparently had it all: he was a handsome, nattily-dressed dandy, with a smokey, soulful voice full of character, and on top of that he was a dab hand on the song-writing front. Evidence includes 'Sign Your Name', which is an elegant, melodic slow-burner that finds D'Arby declaring his love and devotion to a woman who he realises he needs to keep in his life.

81
BLOOD UNCLES
Crash/Caravan/
Never Happy Man
NO CHART PACING
Virgin

Scotland's answer to The Birthday Party, or perhaps Gun Club, Blood Uncles played a powder keg-dangerous, punk-blues hybrid, with drums clattering and overloaded guitars humming and screeching. It was exciting stuff. The band's previous single - a version of Prince's 'Let's Go Crazy' - had attracted some attention. But it was 'Crash' that caught them at their finest. It leaves scorch marks, and features a lyric heavily-influenced by J.G. Ballard's extremely provocative novel of the same name, screamed out on the edge of hysteria.

80
ERIC B AND RAKIM
I Know You Got Soul/
(Acapella)/(Dub)
76
Cooltempo

Taking its title from the Bobby Byrd single of the same name and using extensive samples from it too, 'I Know You Got Soul' ignited the trend of using James Brown samples in hip-hop. The track is superbly constructed, with a chattering rhythm and rock-steady bass meaning it is practically impossible to stop your head from nodding to it. Meanwhile, Rakim proves himself to be an extraordinary rapper, sounding effortless as he nonchalantly drawls his lines, flowing smoothly with icy cool aplomb.

79
GUNS N' ROSES
Welcome To The Jungle
Whole Lotta Rosie (Live)
24
Geffen Records

Not since AC/DC had hit the UK ten years before had anybody in their right mind cared about a hard-rocking metal band. The genre was moribund until Guns N' Roses hurtled onto the scene. They possessed a vitality that a decade's worth of rock bands had lacked. They had a feral quality, a delinquency that was real. They were from the streets and had punk rock style aggression in their DNA. 'Welcome To The Jungle' was their second single, and was about the underbelly of big cities and the danger posed to innocents in the urban jungle. It broke no new ground, and was traditional in its construction but what made it great was its "couldn't give a damn" swagger.

78
FRANKIE KNUCKLES
It's A Cold World/Bad Boy
NO CHART PLACING
Trax Records

Frankie Knuckles has his name on the label, but the suspicion is that this is the work of the uncredited Jamie Principle who is the unmistakable featured singer, or at least a collaborative effort from the pair.

'It's A Cold World' has a very strong European feel to it. It combines a synth-pop feel with Italo-disco, whilst retaining a dark Chicago house vibe. The lyrics are about feeling unloved and alienated and Jamie Principle sings it with the conviction of somebody completely lost. 'Bad Boys' is equally strong and melodic, more up-tempo. Principle here sounds like *Lodger*-era David Bowie as he sings his hymn to outsiderdom.

77
HÜSKER DÜ
Could You Be The One?
Everytime
NO CHART PLACING
Warner Bros. Records

Hüsker Dü would wind themselves up and then let rip, but behind the ensuing wall of noise they were armed with killer melodies. 'Could You Be The One?' ticks all the boxes as a great single. It sits both chronologically and musically between Buzzcocks and Nirvana, by dint of being punk enough for purists while unashamedly displaying its pop heart. Written by Bob Mould, he cleverly essays the emotional fall-out from a fractured relationship as the narrator calls time on his own grief and self-pity. 'Could You Be The One?' proved to be the last-gasp sound of a band who were fast unravelling. Soon they would crash head on into a wall, and cease to exist as functioning unit.

76
JULIAN COPE
Trampoline/Disaster
31
Island Records

Julian Cope was no music snob, and although he was capable of producing long, wigged-out, psychedelic pieces, he was always adept at conjuring up wonderful pop singles. He clearly had a deep love of the form. He had put together a group informally known as the Two Car Garage Band and they gave him a harder, punchy sound as Julian's fondness for Alice Cooper and other Detroit rockers was allowed to influence proceedings. 'Trampoline' is - if you will pardon the pun – bouncy! It is up-tempo and repetitive, and its driving beat hardly falters. It doesn't require great lyrics but receives ones that are more than adequate. Julian is a brilliant singer of reflective material and less great on rock pieces. Still, he pulls a good performance out of the bag, and 'Trampoline' proved to be a successful musical detour along the zig-zagging road travelled by Mr. Cope.

75
THE JUSTIFIED
ANCIENTS OF MU MU
All You Need Is Love/
Îvum Nayâ (Ibo Version)
Rap, Rhyme And Scratch Yourself
NO CHART PLACING
KLF Communications

The JAMs - or Justified Ancients of Mu Mu, to give them their full title - were Bill Drummond, a.k.a.

Kingboy D and Jimmy Cauty a.k.a. Rockman Rock. 'All You Need Is Love' was their first single. Released as a promo white label, it astonished and affronted many listeners with audacious and blatant usage of other people's music. There, however, lay the point. It questioned ownership and what constituted "proper music". It was using guerilla tactics to launch a subversive assault upon the music industry. The record opened with a 15-second sample of The Beatles, before using samples from MC5 and Samantha Fox. Distributors wouldn't touch it, fearful of prosecution, but DJs and journalists had been sent copies and it became a must-hear release. The purpose of all of this was to comment on media coverage of HIV/AIDS which was prejudicial and hypocritical. To that end, we have samples of John Hurt, speaking from the public information film *Don't Die Of Ignorance*. Rhythmic panting, plague-era nursery rhyme 'Ring o' Roses' and Drummond's patented Clydeside Rap. It was staggering - an important release on several levels.

74
THE GODFATHERS
Birth, School, Work, Death/S.T.B.
80
Epic

Brothers Peter and Chris Coyne formed The Godfathers after the demise of The Sid Presley Experience. They adopted a pseudo-Kray Twins image of sixties hairstyles, suits and tough guy machismo. Pathetic? It most certainly was. Musically they peddled second-hand Dr Feelgood riffs with added aggression that also wasn't particularly appealing. Somehow though they created this minor classic of sharp-edged, big-riffing polemic. Its gloriously dumb title acting as a spat-out chorus of disenchantment that nailed the helpless existence we are thrust towards.

73
MICHAEL JACKSON
Bad/I Can't Help It
3
Epic

Written by Michael Jackson and originally conceived as a duet with Prince that failed to materialise when the purple maestro refused to sing the opening line - "your butt is mine"- to Jackson or have it sung by Jackson to him. 'Bad' is written about a ghetto youth who seeks escape from his situation through education. He returns home on a school vacation and is murdered by a gang, jealous of what he has made of himself. The track is a snappy electro-melding of funk, with a punk edge. It finds Jackson adopting a harder-edged, more streetwise persona than had been seen before and delivering a vocal eschewing many of his trademark squeals and hiccups. Overall, while not one of his greatest ever singles, this was nonetheless excellent, and revealed facets of Jackson's talents we had previously been unaware of.

72
HOODOO GURUS

What's My Scene
Heart Of Darkness
NO CHART PLACING
Big Time/Chrysalis

Hoodoo Gurus were, up to this point, a kind of quirky, witty outfit with a thin 60s-influenced sound. Their American record label wanted something more mainstream, and put them into the studio with Mark Opitz, who had worked with AC/DC and INXS. He knocked them into a more orthodox shape and toughened up their sound, which made them a lot less interesting, but worked a treat for this fizz bomb of a single. It is fabulously catchy and likeable and has two choruses, though in truth, the whole song feels like one joyous long chorus, with a guitar solo thrown in for good measure.

71
NEW ORDER
Touched By The Hand Of God/
(Dub)
20
Factory

Recorded for the soundtrack of the film *Salvation* and remixed by Arthur Baker this was released as a standalone single. It illustrated the fact that when they applied themselves, New Order were brilliant purveyors of charming dance pop. If they could occasionally come across as po-faced, there was not a hint of that here, just glorious melodicism combined with a floor-filling rhythm. A fabulous bass part from Peter Hook is uplifting, and Bernard Sumner sings as well here as he ever did.

70
THESE IMMORTAL SOULS
Marry Me (Lie! Lie!)/
Open Up And Bleed/"Blood And Sand" She Said (Early Version)
NO CHART PLACING
Mute

Brothers Rowland S. and Harry Howard, along with drummer Epic Soundtracks, had been members of Crime and the City Solution. They were joined by Rowland's long-term girlfriend, Genevieve McGuckin, who played keyboards, to form These Immortal Souls, a band where Rowland would be able to sing his own songs. They made music that sounded like it came from a 1920s Berlin cabaret, infected by the ghosts of Charlie Patton and Robert Johnson.

'Marry Me' was their debut release and showcased their style, startling in its looseness in an age when slick performance and shiny production were perceived as being important. Rowland's drawled, unlovely vocal tones added to the sincerity of the songs, while alienating casual listeners. It's the price outsider artists must pay to retain self-respect and integrity in their work.

69
TOM VERLAINE
The Scientist Writes A Letter/
(Paris Version)
NO CHART PLACING
Fontana

Fontana issued a slew of singles from Tom Verlaine's back-to-basics album *Flashlight,* even gaining a number 99 chart hit with 'Cry Mercy Judge'. The best of the batch though was this, an ingenious piece written as a letter from a scientist locked away in a wilderness to a woman named Julia. Played largely on synthesiser, with hard-hit drums high in the mix, Verlaine sing-speaks the lyrics with a mounting feel of unravelling, before finally peeling off some trademark beautiful, unhinged flurries of guitar.

68
SLY & ROBBIE
Boops (Here To Go)/Don't Stop
The Music/Boops (Instrumental)
12
4th & Broadway

Sly & Robbie were moving away from the reggae sound that established them. Here they team up with Bill Laswell, Shinehead, and funk maestro Bootsy Collins, to create this playful electro groove which takes as its lyrical subject matter Boops who, in Jamaican slang, were the equivalent of English sugar daddies. Multiple elements are thrown into the mix without it ever appearing cluttered, and its meandering pace is perfect for Shinehead's easy-on-the-ear raps.

67
GEORGE MICHAEL
I Want Your Sex (Rhythm 1 Lust)/
I Want Your Sex (Rhythm 2 Brass
In Love)
3
Epic

Recorded just two months after Wham! had ended, this was created in the studio very much as a dance orientated piece. It succeeds admirably, and contains a filthy, squelching bass sound which was an embraced mistake. If there was a criticism to be made - as George Michael later realised and admitted - he was in such a thrall to the sounds and styles used by Prince that on 'I Want Your Sex', the influence was stretched too far and became an imitation.

66
PET SHOP BOYS
Always On My Mind
Do I Have To?
1
Parlophone

'Always On My Mind' had originally been recorded by Gwen McCrae. The strength of the song attracted cover versions from heavyweights such as Willie Nelson and Brenda Lee, but it was the stellar success that Elvis Presley had with the song that made it iconic and forever associated with The King. Ten years on from his death Pet Shop Boys appeared on a TV tribute to Presley called *Love Me Tender*. Their performance of 'Always On My Mind' drew high praise, and the decision was made to record it.

Theirs was a masterful version that took the song into the synth-pop era and helped in the re-evaluation of Presley who, at the time of his death, had been considered a deeply uncool anachronism.

65
SUBURBAN KNIGHT
The Groove (Pan Mix)/(Hot Mix)/(Late Mix)
NO CHART PLACING
Transmat

James Pennington is the birth name of Detroit techno wizard Suburban Knight. He moved in influential circles - Kevin Saunderson co-produces, and label Transmat was run by Derrick May. The track is darkly futuristic and atmospheric, with a vocal that simply repeats "house groove makes you move", alongside another indistinct whispered voice. It is simplistic but utterly compelling.

64
NOMEANSNO
Dad/Revenge
NO CHART PLACING
Alternative Tentacles

Nomeansno had existed since 1979, as a two-piece comprising brothers Rob and John Wright, playing bass and drums respectively. 'Dad' and 'Revenge' were the first tracks we heard from them following the addition of guitarist Andy Kerr. Their sound had always been a punishing mixture of jazz and progressive rock, played with hardcore punk ferocity. Kerr upped the ante even further. Sonically, both sides are hard and uncompromising.

'Dad' has a lyric from a teenager's point of view about the domestic violence inflicted upon his mother by his out-of-control father, it paints a harrowing picture that seems frighteningly real. 'Revenge' is slower and more wide-screen - it stops and starts, changing time and style throughout. It's a challenging piece of music with a chorus that seems to emerge from the deepest darkest depths.

63
KRAFTWERK
The Telephone Call (Remix)/House Phone/Der Telefon Anruf (German Version)
89
EMI

Notable for being the only Kraftwerk song sung by Karl Bartos, 'The Telephone Call' was taken from the album *Electric Cafe* and remixed by Francois Kevorkian. After a decade-and-a-half of being out on their own as forerunners in electronic innovation 'The Telephone Call' finds them in amongst a pack of synth-led artistes who have caught them up. That doesn't mean that this is a bad record, of course - it is a combination of beautiful, strong synth lines, ingenious beats, social comment on the impact of technology upon our lives, and deadpan humour. There had never been a 'bad' Kraftwerk record and 'The Telephone Call' was a welcome addition to their catalogue.

62
THE LA's
Way Out/Endless
86
Go! Discs

This was the debut release from Liverpool's The La's. Their recording career would prove to be short, but it was truly sweet and 'Way Out' was a perfect introduction to their brand of tuneful, rootsy, 60s-influenced pop, with dark expressive lyrics that are disarmingly sung with an almost jolly quality. It is mostly a mid-tempo, acoustic strum but as an electric guitar enters at the mid-point, things take a psychedelic twist, revealing another ingredient in the band's fascinating and exotic mix.

61
MODEL 500
Make Some Noise
Sound of Stereo
NO CHART PLACING
Metroplex

Juan Atkins once again served up the sound of tomorrow, today. Two sides of daring techno-funk that set a template for music makers to follow into the next decade. Cool and spacey sounds over triggered beats that make your pulse race and feet itch to move.

60
MARC ALMOND
Mother Fist/
Two Sailors On The Beach/
The Hustler
93
Some Bizzare

Never afraid to plunge headlong into sleaze, 'Mother Fist' sees Marc Almond dragging his band, The Willing Sinners, into the cesspool along with him, to perform this joyous ode to masturbation in delightful chanson style. As Marc points out, even locked in a cell, a man cannot be denied this sensual pleasure. Imagine *Jean Genet: The Musical*, 'Mother Fist' would undoubtedly feature.

59
IGGY POP
Shades/Baby, It Can't Fall
87
A&M Records

Having not released a record in four years, Iggy had reunited with David Bowie to record his *Blah Blah Blah* album. It was heralded at the time as a hugely successful return to form. In truth, it was lacklustre and pretty dismal: an Iggy Pop record should contain spirit and excitement yet this was poor to average. It was anodyne, just American rock with a high-gloss production sheen. And yet, among the dross was 'Shades', which was his best song since the 70s and his best and most romantic love song ever. Written with Bowie it is a simmering gem which Iggy sings in his rich and warm crooning voice. The lyrics involve the narrator receiving a gift of sunglasses from a girlfriend. He offers his thanks and expresses his love and gratitude to her for understanding that he is a man of simple needs. It is subtle, intelligent and very tender - a wonderful record.

58
EAZY E
The Boyz-N-The Hood/Fat Girl/
L.A. Is The Place/L.A. Capella
NO CHART PLACING
Ruthless Records

Eazy E had been born Eric Wright. He dealt drugs in Compton, Los Angeles. Aged 22, he thought it might be safer and more lucrative to get into the hip-hop scene, so with his drug money he founded Ruthless Records. A group came together including Dr Dre and Ice Cube, who would become NWA. They crafted 'The Boys-N-The Hood' track and offered it to New Yorkers, Home Boys Only, who rejected the chance to record it. Eazy was encouraged to rap it himself, and line-by-line, over two days, that was done. It stretched the boundaries of what was permissible as lyrical content including gun violence, sex, misogyny and drug dealing. Eazy's voice gave it a uniquely authentic flavour. Gangsta rap had just been born and hip-hop became the music of middle-class white boys' wet dreams. Don't blame Eazy and the crew though - they were just telling it as it was.

57
MADONNA
Who's That Girl/White Heat
1
Sire

Madonna was shooting the film *Slammer*, in which she had the lead role when she asked her song-writing partner, Patrick Leonard, to supply an up-tempo track that would capture the essence of her film character. He recorded a demo, and between filming Madonna wrote the lyrics and developed the song. It became 'Who's That Girl' and the film was re-titled with the same name. It used strings, trumpet, a drum machine rhythm, and a synth bass line. Vocally, it reflected Madonna's interest in Hispanic culture, dropping Spanish phrases at various points. In truth, the song relied heavily on its chorus for impact - it was memorable, and its haunting quality pushed all the right buttons.

56
JOE SMOOTH
Promised Land (Club Mix)/
(Underground Mix)/(Freestyle Mix)
56 (1989)
D.J. International Records

Taking inspiration from classic Motown songs, Joe Smooth attempted to write a song that would be a spiritual descendant of them. He wanted a universal message of positivity and inclusivity in his lyrics to combine with a house music sound. It was ambitious but he succeeded in his quest. 'Promised Land' spoke of hope and unity amongst people - it was soulful, emotionally charged and mightily uplifting. Already a huge club hit, the song came to more people's attention via a cover version by The Style Council, which propelled Joe Smooth into the UK charts.

55
MIAOW
When It All Comes Down/Did She
NO CHART PLACING
Factory

Factory always seemed to be something of a boys' club, and it was therefore odd that the female-fronted Miaow found a home there. It didn't quite feel right. The label's other acts mostly had a cold bloodedness about their music and image. Miaow were softer, lighter and brighter. They played a brand of sunny, jangling pop with a hint of Bossa nova just below the surface. It was sensuous, and Cath Carroll's vocals often felt like whispered secrets. 'When It All Comes Down', and the equally strong 'Did She', combined to create a beautiful single that deserved a wider hearing than it received.

54
PUBLIC ENEMY
Public Enemy No. 1/Timebomb
NO CHART PLACING
Def Jam Recordings

This was Public Enemy's first single and it landed like a bomb. No other hip-hop record had been as loud and aggressive. These guys sounded serious and scary. They seemed to seek confrontation and demanded attention. 'Public Enemy No. 1' was quite an introduction. Although famed for their politicised lyrics, that approach is eschewed here in favour of throwing down the gauntlet to their peers. Witheringly dismissive of easy-on-the-ear careerist rappers and declaring the pre-eminence of Public Enemy, the sound is minimal. The beats are brutal, and the raps are hard. It's all wound up tight as a nut, highly impressive and very smart indeed.

53
ADMIRAL BAILEY
Kill Them With It/ (Version)
NO CHART PLACING
Jammy's Records

At this juncture, Admiral Bailey was the hottest dancehall performer in Jamaica. Several of his tracks had become anthems, such as 'Politician' and 'Chatty Mouth People'. 1987 saw the release of his first album, and 'Kill Them With It' was the title track and single. It was an effervescent, tongue-twisting marvel, with more energy captured in its grooves than a box full of Stars On 45 records!

52
DANIELLE DAX
Big Hollow Man/Muzzles/
The Passing Of The Third Floor Back
NO CHART PLACING
Awesome Records

Big Hollow Man was taken from the masterful Dax album, *Inky Bloaters*. It is funky and rocking - somewhere betwixt Prince and Marc Bolan. The versatility of her voice serves Dax well as she sings a fascinating lyric in a constantly evolving style, ranging from kittenish purr to tigerish growl.

51
SINÉAD O'CONNOR
Mandinka/Drink Before The War
17
Ensign/Chrysalis

Over a hard rock guitar riff, Sinéad O'Connor fiercely lets rip, referencing the African Mandinka tribe and their coming-of-age rituals. She passionately rejects subjecting herself to mutilation of body or soul, rejects being bound to any type of slavery. Her supple voice is powerful, passionate and soars.

50
ULTRAMAGNETIC MC'S
Travelling At The Speed Of Thought/Travelling Dub/ M.C.'s Ultra (Part II)/ B-Boy Bonus Break
NO CHART PLACING
City Beat

'Louie Louie'-sampling, hard-hitting futuristic hip-hop from the Ultramagnetic MC's. They took hip-hop to places no other acts were going. Totally wigged out and unorthodox, owing diddly squat to the preoccupations of their peers, they were children of P-funk. 'Travelling At The Speed Of Thought' was scalpel-sharp and freakishly fresh as a daisy.

49
P.I.L.
Seattle/Selfish Rubbish
47
Virgin

John Lydon had assembled a wonderful group of musicians for this version of P.I.L. They composed this chiming, bubbly piece of pop, over which Lydon wrote an entertaining, if ambiguous, lyric that was taken to be a rebuke delivered to a Seattle audience who had given the band a hard and hostile time. This was an interpretation never given credence by Lydon himself. Whatever its providence, he certainly delivered it with gleeful relish. 'Seattle' was so nearly a great record, but it ended up as merely a good one, spoilt by a horrible, squeaky clean and shiny 80s production.

48
PHUTURE
Acid Tracks/Phuture Jacks/ Your Only Friend
NO CHART PLACING
Trax Records

The use of the word "acid" in this song's title launched a whole subculture of ravers and a sub-genre of the house music form. Its sound was massively influential, especially its fat and filthy, squelching bass in combination with crisp beats. By all accounts, that sound was created by accident, as the three-strong Phuture crew struggled to master the technology at their hands. Their genius was to embrace the mistake and stretch it out as part of a dark, minimal, 11-minute instrumental groove that drove dancers to ecstatic heights.

47
THE THE
Sweet Bird Of Truth
Harbour Lights/Sleeping Juice
55
Epic / Some Bizarre

Matt Johnson's opprobrium was aimed firmly at Ronald Reagan's meddling in the Middle East, and although this record pre-dated the Gulf Wars, it coincided with the U.S. bombing of Libya. The narrator of the song is the pilot of a plane on a mission to kill and destroy. His own plane has been hit, he knows he is going to crash and die, and we are privy to his final thoughts. It is a harrowing track - the music is jarring and dramatic and voices are used accordingly, carrying a charged desperation. This was a thought-provoking and vicious record, launched towards a mainstream that wanted shiny bright pop full of hedonism rather than ugly truth.

46
R.E.M.
It's The End Of The World As We Know It (And I Feel Fine)/
This One Goes Out (Live)
NO CHART PLACING
(1991 – 39)
I.R.S. Records

This was a frenetic rocker, pushed by pounding drums with a seemingly stream of consciousness lyric in the style of Bob Dylan's 'Subterranean Homesick Blues', topped off with a chorus announcing the apocalypse is imminent. Michael Stipe's voice is a thing of wonder, adding another rhythmic element. Guitars are mixed low to emphasise the vocal gymnastics. It was an attention-grabbing single that raised the group's profile considerably. They had broken into the mainstream in their native America, and it was only a matter of time before the UK would succumb to their musical charm.

45
ROXANNE SHANTÉ
Have A Nice Day/
(Instrumental Dub)
58
Breakout

Roxanne Shanté was from Queens, New York, part of the Juice Crew and releasing her first single aged 14 in 1984, making her one of the first female MCs to gain a foothold in the extremely macho world of hip-hop. Three years on from that first release, she released 'Have A Nice Day' with Marley Marl producing. It was raw and funky, with Shanté flowing freely as she asserts herself in the face of those who dismiss her because of her sex. "Just like Diana Ross, I'm the boss" is one choice line. Also in the firing line are Boogie Down Productions who had previously put her down as a mere appendage of male rappers.

44
U2
Where The Streets Have No Name/
Race Against Time/
Silver and Gold/Sweetest Thing
3
Island Records

'Where The Streets Have No Name' was the third single extracted from U2's album *The Joshua Tree.* It followed the excellent 'With Or Without You' and 'I Still Haven't Found What I'm Looking For'. This is a superb song with a lyric about how people are identified in terms of income and religion or by their postal address, specifically the divided city of Belfast. Music was devised by The Edge in demo form after challenging himself to create the ultimate U2 live song. The band struggled to record the track in the studio, but the finished result, pieced together by Brian Eno, sounds seamless and magnificent. Guitars breathe fire, and Bono's vocal alternates between quiet introspection and roaring passion.

43
FLEETWOOD MAC
Big Love/You And I, Part I
9
Warner Bros. Records

Written by Lindsey Buckingham for a solo album before Fleetwood Mac reunited to record the *Tango in the Night* album, 'Big Love' was the first single and it was outstanding. It had a cool, Mediterranean vibe and propulsive rhythm that made it a favourite on the Balearic dance scene, and in Arthur Baker's remixed form, a U.S. dance hit. Sung by Buckingham, who sampled and altered his own voice to simulate a female vocal, it was an exceptional record.

42
CHRIS + COSEY
Obsession (12" Mix)/(Short Mix)/
47 Sound/Metroeme
NO CHART PLACING
Play It Again Sam Records

Chris + Cosey, as 50% of Throbbing Gristle, had often indulged in what amounted to musical terrorism, but they hadn't been afraid to move on. Here, they display a mastery of synth-pop that, whilst not exactly in the radio-friendly style of Depeche Mode or Pet Shop Boys, is nonetheless easy on the ear. It proceeds at a stately pace with a strident reading of an intriguing lyric by Cosey, further enhancing the listener's enjoyment.

41
PRINCE
I Could Never Take The Place Of
Your Man (Fade)/Hot Thing (Edit)
29
Paisley Park

Originally recorded in 1979, this version of 'I Could Never Take The Place Of Your Man' was the fourth single taken from the *Sign o'The Times* album. It concerns a woman who has been deserted by her lover and who is looking for a replacement. Prince, in the role of narrator, is not keen on stepping into the shoes of her ex. It is played at an up-tempo pace and given a full-on treatment of a double drum track, horns, synthesiser and guitar solos. The tune is never lost amidst the blitz of instrumentation - it is a fabulously poppy piece.

40
THE TRIFFIDS
Bury Me Deep In Love
Baby Can I Walk You Home
97
Island Records

From their earliest recordings it was clear that The Triffids were a very special group, but by this point they had hit an undeniable peak. David McComb's writing was wonderful, his lyrics fascinating evocations of places and emotions. His tunes were glorious and his voice rich and soulful. With so much going for them they were granted a bigger studio budget and a big-name producer in Gil Norton, who gives 'Bury Me Deep In Love' a sumptuous sound whereby it takes on epic qualities. Violins soar and McComb's voice tugs at heartstrings. It is a superb record but was only a hit in Australia, where it featured in the soap opera *Neighbours*.

39
GEORGE MICHAEL
Faith/Hand To Mouth
2
Epic

It was suggested that George Michael write fifties pastiche. Embracing the idea, he composed 'Faith' which was built upon a borrowed Bo Diddley beat played on acoustic guitar, and a simple drum pattern. Styling the vocal in the manner of Prince, he had a two-minute short album track. People enthused about the song to him and he revised his opinion of its worth and realised if it was longer it would make a great single. To that end it was stretched by a fabulously eccentric guitar solo. Bingo! A much-loved signature song, and a huge hit into the bargain.

38
N.W.A.
Panic Zone/Dope Man (Radio Edit)/8-Ball (Radio Edit)/
Dope Man/8-Ball
NO CHART PLACING
Ruthless Records

N.W.A. were political and confrontational in all aspects of their grouping, from their name, an abbreviation of Niggaz Wit Attitudes, to the subject matter of their raps. They were determined to say something to create an impact, and from the off they did just that. 'Panic Zone' was the first single release by the group, and it displays their electro roots in a banging track produced by Dr Dre, while Arabian Prince and Eazy E provide the raps that mark out their desire and ambition to make their mark and maintain self-respect. "You're not only in dimension of sight and sound, but of mind" proclaims Arabian Prince. It is a signifier of N.W.A.'s intent.

37
ERASURE
Victim Of Love/
The Soldier's Return
7
Mute

Erasure's earliest songs had been fine, but in truth they lacked a little in individuality. They seemed like an extension of Vince Clarke's previous band Yazoo. By this point, however, Erasure had come into their own. They had developed a signature sound of acoustic guitar combined with synthesiser and insistent rhythms. Their sound was highly melodic, and Andy Bell had grown into his role as singer, quickly establishing himself as both a flamboyant personality and a singer armed with warm soulfulness and impressive power. All these elements are combined on 'Victim of Love', which is concerned with feelings of apprehension before committing to a new relationship. It was near perfect pop and cemented Erasure's status as purveyors of feel-good dance pop and chart regulars.

36
THE JESUS AND MARY CHAIN
April Skies/Kill Surf City
8
Blanco Y Negro

The initial shock of hearing The Jesus and Mary Chain's feedback-drenched melodicism was past - plenty of copycat bands were mining that seam now, and so JAMC neatly sidestepped any thoughts that they may be one trick ponies and dropped the noisy accompaniment to their sound. With 'April Skies', their sound is lean and clean. These classicists now proved they didn't need gimmicks or controversy to sell records - the quality of their songs and performance would suffice.

35
KENNY "JAMMIN" JASON
with "FAST" EDDIE SMITH
Can U Dance/Can U Drum /
Skratch-A-Pella/Bonus Jack/
Can U Jack
67
Champion

This is pure excitement: brilliant, emotional Chicago house, aligned to the kind of beat Giorgio Morodor had used in his mid-70s transformation of the disco genre. Guaranteed to receive a euphoric reaction from dancers, beats hit the feet and the brilliant sounds spin the head and touch the heart.

34
THE GO-BETWEENS
Bye Bye Pride/The House That
Jack Kerouac Built
NO CHART PLACING
Beggars Banquet

Grant McLennan writes about a sense of lost love and yearning as he wanders around Brisbane. 'Bye Bye Pride' is an irresistible epic - all our senses are heightened as we listen and are tugged by our heartstrings into McLennan's world of aching naïve wonderment. The sheer beauty of the song's melody and lyrics are stunning. Lindy Morrison anchors the piece with a rock steady drum, while Amanda Brown provides the most arresting oboe part in the history of rock 'n' roll.

33
YELLO
Oh Yeah (Dance Mix)/
La Habanera/
Oh Yeah (Indian Summer Version)
NO CHART PLACING
Mercury

Dieter Meier and Boris Blank were in complete disagreement regarding the development of 'Oh Yeah'. Dieter had recorded the deeply, darkly funky musical track, and Boris wrote lyrics. Dieter disagreed saying there were too many words, it needed to be simple. Boris was flabbergasted, and only reluctantly stripped away his input to its core phrase of 'Oh Yeah'. When he heard the finished product, he loved it. Dieter added a bizarre, ultra-deep voice, mouthing phrases, and the track was done. Released as a single in the U.S. in 1985, its European release came only after the success of the film *Ferris Bueller's Day Off* which featured 'Oh Yeah' as an integral part of the soundtrack. This striking mini masterpiece became synonymous with the film, and consequently Yello's most famous song, although the great British public were not persuaded to purchase it.

32
BOMB THE BASS
Beat Dis (Extended Dis)/
(Radio Edit)/Bonus Beats
2
Mister-Ron Records

Samplers were getting cheaper and that enabled young DJ Tim Simenon and producer Pascal Gabriel to combine their talents in the studio to create 'Beat Dis', massively influenced by American hip-hop, house and funk. Simenon literally took a selection of his records into the studio with him, where the pair took edits and spliced them together into a mind-melding collage to be placed on top of the rhythm track. 'Bombing' was a graffiti art term for spray painting a surface, and what Simenon and Gabriel were doing was a bombardment of the bass line by samples. From this, the name Bomb the Bass emerged. For the record's centre label, Simenon lifted a smiley face from *Watchmen* comics, and this gave the acid house scene its iconic symbol. The spirit of the age was captured by this record. It was hugely exciting and appealing to a generation finding new sounds and styles that represented the way they felt.

31
MADONNA
La Isla Bonita (Remix)/
(Instrumental Edit)
1
Sire

'La Isla Bonita' translates into English as 'The Beautiful Island'. It was the first occasion that Madonna had used Latin rhythms in her music, describing it as a tribute to the "beauty and mystery of Latin American people". The song is full of Spanish motifs, including some Spanish lyrics. Castanets, maracas, and Spanish guitar are used alongside more traditionally western instruments. The rhythms are played at an upbeat tempo, while the melody is sweet. Madonna sings with a lightness that recalls The Drifters, at the time they sound-tracked carefree, sunny days and passionate romance.

30
R.E.M
The One I Love/Last Date
NO CHART PLACING
(1991 - 16)
I.R.S. Records

Widely perceived as being a love song, 'The One I Love' has a darkness at its heart. Its chiming guitars and sing-along quality provide a prettiness that is at odds with the lyrics that suggest unashamed manipulation and abuse of others is the protagonist's preferred way of conducting relationships. "Fire!" cries Michael Stipe insistently and repeatedly throughout the song as if to warn he cannot control the flames within him that will burn those who get too close.

29
MARK STEWART + MAFFIA
Stranger Than Love/(Dub)/
Survival
NO CHART PLACING
Mute

Eric Satie is sampled and looped and 'Somewhere' from *West Side Story* is quoted and a mellow and subdued groove follows. As unlikely as it seems, Mark Stewart croons. One waits for the inevitable explosion of terror and violent noise. The tension is palpable. The track seems to simmer beneath its calm exterior. "When will the explosion happen?", we ask ourselves. It doesn't come. It doesn't happen. It is disorientating and yet it's also a wonderful highly effective piece of music.

28
KING SUN - D MOËT
Hey Love/(Radio Version)/
(The Music)
66
Flame Records / Rhythm King

This debut single from Harlem-based rapper King Sun and DJ D Moët sampled the elegant Art of Noise track 'Moments In Love', added beats and created a platform for King Sun to rap in a cool, unhurried, conversational style about the complicated three-way relationship he is embroiled in. Snippets of telephone calls, and excerpts from letters to the female at the centre of this ménage a trois display the hurt and emotional damage being inflicted, as it is revealed that the 'other guy' is in fact the narrator's brother.

27
PET SHOP BOYS with DUSTY SPRINGFIELD
What Have I Done To Deserve This?/A New Life
2
Parlophone

Brilliantly capturing and caricaturing the Thatcherite 'greed is good' philosophy, and displaying the vacuous and loveless lives that its embrace could lead to, this genius single displayed all the strengths of the Pet Shop Boys. Their knack for producing near-perfect, highly memorable pop of substance was unquestionable. On what was their first collaborative release, they proved their choice in who they wished to perform with was just as well-judged. They had to fight to get Dusty Springfield to record with them - she was initially uninterested and equally, the record label did not want her as she was considered to be washed up, having not had a hit in nearly two decades. The label pushed for Tina Turner, but the Pet Shop Boys eventually got the woman they wanted. Dusty's voice was as husky, warm and soulful as it had been in her sixties heyday - she was magnificent, and the record reignited interest in her, restoring her reputation as perhaps the greatest British pop singer of all.

26
THAT PETROL EMOTION
Big Decision/Soul Deep
43
Polydor

That Petrol Emotion featured brothers John and Damien O'Neill formerly of The Undertones, and was fronted by highly-assured American Steve Mack. They mixed up Undertones-like pop nous with wider influences such as Captain Beefheart, Can, and contemporary dance music and hip-hop - That Petrol Emotion were a rock band who genuinely grooved. 'Big Decision' was a magnificent record which proved to be the band's greatest success. It combined brilliant guitar riffs, hooks galore, a crafty rhythm, and an angry, urgent vocal containing a chanted/rapped section that felt like a rallying cry for those at the bottom of the pile to rise up.

25
ALEXANDER O'NEAL
Criticize/
A Broken Heart Can Mend
4
Tabu Records

Alexander O'Neal had been a member of a band called Flyte Time, which also included the redoubtable pairing of Jimmy Jam and Terry Lewis, who were red hot after the success of Janet Jackson's album *Control*, which they had written and produced. That duo produced O'Neal's album *Hearsay*, which had already yielded a hit single in 'Fake' before 'Criticize' was released.

The song is a commentary on the persistent nagging of a girlfriend who finds fault with all aspects of her lover's lifestyle. It is performed mid-tempo with female vocals contrasting with O'Neal's tough and gritty delivery, harking back to old-style soul men, as he raises the intensity levels on what was a classic of modern R&B.

24
PAUL SIMON
Diamonds On The Soles Of Her Shoes/All Around The World Or The Myth Of Fingerprints
77
Warner Bros. Records

Amid accusations about breaking the cultural sanctions against the evil apartheid regime in South Africa, and of exploiting and underpaying black South African musicians, Paul Simon had undoubtedly created a brilliant album in *Graceland*. The fourth single release from it saw no decline in quality. 'Diamonds On The Soles Of Her Shoes' was an amazing aural feast for the ears as the talents of musicians of the quality of Youssou N'Dour and Chikapa "Ray" Phiri combined with Simon to create a vibrant and exciting piece. With the astonishing voices of Ladysmith Black Mambazo harmonising in the Zulu language, Using colourful and intriguing metaphors, Simon sings a story about the love between a rich girl and a poor boy that emphasizes the huge divide in terms of wealth and opportunities in the unjust and brutalist system of South Africa.

23
BEASTIE BOYS
No Sleep Till Brooklyn/Posse in Effect
14
Def Jam Recordings

Producer Rick Rubin had produced *Reign in Blood* for heavy metal band Slayer, and for 'No Sleep Till Brooklyn' - named as a tribute to Motorhead's *No Sleep Till Hammersmith*, he fetched in Slayer guitarist Kerry King to hammer out the song's heavy riff and flash solo. There is no subtlety to 'No Sleep Till Brooklyn' but it is a delicious, joyful racket - rock and rap are combined like squabbling siblings, each element trying to be loudest and command attention. Lyrically, it is a rap on travelling home from gigs, tired to the point of exhaustion but determined to get back to home turf in Brooklyn.

22
LEE "SCRATCH" PERRY & THE DUB SYNDICATE
Jungle (Disco Plate)/
Jungle (Urban Breakdown)
NO CHART PLACING
Syncopate

Lee Perry's post-Black Ark Studios work was wildly erratic, which was hardly surprising for someone whose output was prodigious. There were, however, always jewels being produced, and his mid-80s hook up with British dub explorer Adrian Sherwood, resulted in more than one gem. This single, made with Sherwood's On-U Sound stalwarts Dub Syndicate, was a fine example.

Together they produce a loping reggae rhythm. Female voices chime "Lee Scratch Perry on the wire" and Scratch himself magically nursery rhymes and ruminates through a vocal of wonderful playful charm. I danced to it, I sang along, and I felt happier every time I played this record.

21
LAIBACH
Geburt Einer Nation (One Vision)/
Leben Heißt Leben (Live Is Life)
NO CHART PLACING
Mute

Queen were a brilliant pop group, of that there is no doubt. But behind the pomp and theatricality there was also something dislikeable. Pre-Live Aid, they were pariahs because of their willingness to play Sun City in return for a sackful of cash and help foist an impression of 'business as usual' in apartheid-riven South Africa. At Live Aid, they stole the show, playing a crowd-pleasing set of hits that saw a huge boost in record sales and profits. They then wrote and recorded the sickly, neo-utopian piece of empty posturing that was 'One Vision', a cynical tapping into the feelings and emotions stirred up by the Ethiopian humanitarian crisis but this was no philanthropic gesture - it was purely aimed at displaying fake compassion for the public whilst earning lots of money.

Laibach may not have had answers for the questions they posed, but the questions they asked were pointed and thought-provoking. They took 'One Vision', replaced the rock guitars with fanfares of horns, turned the beat into the sound of a column of marching stormtroopers, and without altering a single word but growling and roaring them in German, they displayed the flip side of lyrics about "one race, one true religion". It sounded like a terrifying manifesto and totalitarian nightmare. It was a piece of genius akin to the Charlie Chaplin film *The Great Dictator*. Laibach inspired strong emotions – loved, but also hated enough for an attempt on their lives by car bomb in Sarajevo. Some critics saw them as trivial, novelty pranksters. The pranksters took aim here and hit a bullseye, exposing the hypocritical self-serving, Messiah complex, not just of Queen, but of the whole corporate rock industry.

20
SALT 'N' PEPA
Push It/Tramp
2 (1988)
Next Plateau Records Inc.

Salt 'N' Pepa were a pair of young females from New York who took hip-hop into an area of female sexual self-confidence and empowerment. Originally the Lowell Fulson written, Otis Redding and Carla Thomas sampling 'Tramp' was the A-side of this record, but 'Push It' was so infectious that it received a remix by San Francisco DJ Cameron Paul. It couldn't be repressed and was soon made the featured track, despite its risqué content. Its hookiness and joyous sound made the record a radio and jukebox favourite. It originally peaked at 41 on the UK hit parade but it kept selling and in 1988 hit number 2.

19
HAPPY MONDAYS
24 Hour Party People/
Yahoo/Wah Wah (Think Tank)
NO CHART PLACING
(2002 - 96)
Factory

Nobody who saw the Mondays before their recording career began could possibly have imagined how good, nor how influential, they would become. They seemed nondescript, unfocused, with their songs no more than muffled, vaguely funky, unstructured and shapeless jams. '24 Hour Party People' was therefore a jolt to my preconceptions - a surrealist mangling of 'Come Together'-era Beatles and Chicago house music, with a detour into Funkadelic territory, an ode to hedonism and excess. It was completely anti-authoritarian and very welcome. When Captain Beefheart wrote 'Floppy Boot Stomp' he might well have been imagining music as strangely joyous as this.

18
PRINCE
U Got The Look/
Housequake (Edit)
11
Paisley Park

'U Got The Look' displayed Prince at his funkiest. Live drums and percussion from Sheila E combined with programmed beats, are at the base of the track. Above them are layers of extremely distorted guitars. Prince adopts the voice used for his female alter ego, Camille, and duets with Scottish singer Sheena Easton. On the flip of the single is 'Housequake', a nod to the influence of George Clinton. It is of interest not just for its high quality and funk quotient, but also because it was extracted from sessions for a Camille album that ultimately remained unreleased.

17
WIRE
Ahead/Feed Me
NO CHART PLACING
Mute

Having somehow missed out on the previous year's release, 'Snakedrill', I was surprised but highly delighted to find that the most fascinating, cryptic, enigmatic band Wire had regrouped, following a half-decade hiatus. 'Ahead' was a single that could have been, and should have been, a bona fide hit. The group had embraced synthesisers, drum machines and sequencers to create a track with an upfront, highly propulsive bass sound that wasn't very far removed New Order's sound. The lyrics were intriguing, though unfathomable, and led into a glorious sing-a-long chorus. It was a great pop record. "What were Wire doing and why were Wire doing it?" one was forced to ask oneself. There could have been a layer of cynicism attached as they were almost certainly making some kind of point. But in the end it didn't really matter – taken at face value, the record was superb.

16
ERIC B AND RAKIM
Paid In Full (Seven Minutes Of Madness – The Coldcut Remix)/ Paid In Full (Album Mix)/ Eric B. Is On The Cut
15
4th & Broadway

The original mix of 'Paid In Full' was a brilliant piece of work. Eric B provided a superb musical backdrop for Rakim to unleash his flow of words and quick-witted imagery in superb style. Despite the speed in which the creative process was undertaken, the track was a fully formed classic. And then, for a fee of £700, Coldcut remixed the track. They added parts, notably a sample of Israeli singer Ofra Haza from her track 'Im Nin Alu' and British actor Geoffrey Sumner speaking the opening line, "This is a journey into sound", as well as samples from Eric B and Rakim's own 'I Know You Got Soul'. They stripped away other parts, and the result was astonishing. Eric B was not impressed describing the track as "girly disco music". However, Rakim claimed it was the best remix he had ever heard. I err more towards that appraisal.

15
PET SHOP BOYS
Rent/I Want A Dog
8
Parlophone

'Rent' is such an excellent song, yet its subject matter made it a risky single release. Of course, the fact that it is extremely pleasing in terms of tunefulness negated some of that risk. The song is about somebody who is kept by another affluent and powerful person. They are safe and secure in the knowledge that they are being taken care of financially. The trade off is that they have sacrificed their personal freedom and their dreams in accepting this arrangement. It is indeed bitter-sweet.

14
THE THREE JOHNS
Never And Always/Turn Up Those Down-Hearted Blues
NO CHART PLACING
Abstract Sounds

Adrian Sherwood produced the always exciting and incendiary The Three Johns and their combined talents provided us with a sound that was razor sharp and dangerous. Guitars buzz like sci-fi spaceships invading the earth and at certain points the bass simply drops over the edge into cavernous pits while the drum machine rhythms are alternately fat and full or needle thin and sharp. Singing John engages his vocal chords at full-throttle and flings his Dadaist lyrics upwards towards the stratosphere.

13
MICHAEL JACKSON
The Way You Make Me Feel/
(Instrumental)
3
Epic

'The Way You Make Me Feel' is built around a loping rhythm that stops and starts. Horns and keyboards sit beneath the beat. The track has a great feel to it and rocks, though it remains steadfastly mid-tempo. Lyrically, it is no more than an adequate piece in praise of a desirable woman, but what Jackson does with his voice is extraordinary - he feels the rhythm and his vocal dances around it, improvising as he goes. He doesn't merely perform - he seems to inhabit the piece investing his flesh, blood and beating heart into the track.

12
THE GO-BETWEENS
Right Here/
When People Are Dead
82
Beggars Banquet

Grant McLennan had begun a relationship with band-mate Amanda Brown, and was inspired to write this wry, philosophical tale of love in which he declares himself willing to give anything she requires, but also cautions that she must accept some responsibility herself. The track is celebratory and sprightly. Its melody is gorgeous and once heard remembered forever. Phrases from the lyrics resonate and stick, while its simple, repetitive chorus, which finds McLennan expressing himself with heartfelt sincerity, is enhanced by lovely backing vocals and fizzing reels from the violin.

11
PUBLIC ENEMY
Rebel Without A Pause/
Terminator X Speaks With His Hands/Rebel Without A Pause (Instrumental)/Sophisticated Bitch
37
Def Jam Recordings

In the space of a year, musical technology had hugely advanced and Public Enemy got on board with it to give their sound a superior sonic wallop. They had been experimenting with higher tempos during live performance and noted a tangible increase in energy from the audience as the BPMs climbed higher. For 'Rebel Without A Pause', they put together these elements, so while Chuck D delivered a breathtaking accusatory rap about the mainstream allowing no access to Public Enemy, Hank Shocklee introduced a distinctive, piercing, whistling effect taken from a saxophone sample from James Brown's 'The Grunt'. Electronic drums were played live by Flavor Flav, rather than sampled, and Terminator X provided scratches that added to the musical tension. Chuck D was heard to declare "I could die tomorrow", so happy was he with this mighty piece of rhythm and rhyme.

Here with a Dylan Thomas album, people kept comparing me with him.

A homeowner with a Pere Ubu LP, 1988

10
NEW ORDER
True Faith
1963
4 (1994 - 9)
Factory

The gloomy reputation that had hung over the music of New Order was completely exorcised by the time 'True Faith' was created. It is replaced by a lighter, brighter, dance-pop sound. It was good that they refused to stand still and stagnate, but it also caused tensions about musical differences. One thing that didn't change was Bernard Sumner's singsong approach to his vocals, nor his nursery rhyme type of lyricism. However, for 'True Faith', the often-nonsensical wordplay was abandoned for an explicit imagining of heroin addiction, of starting each day with the sole intention of securing drugs, much to the dismay of friends from the innocent days of childhood.

9
THE POGUES featuring
KIRSTY MacCOLL
Fairytale Of New York
The Battle March Medley
2 (1991 - 36 /2005 - 3/2006 - 6/2007 - 4/ 2008 - 12/2009 - 12/2010 - 17/ 2011 - 13/ 2012 - 12/ 2013 - 14/ 2014 - 11/2015 - 13/ 2016 - 15/2017 - 5/2018 - 4/ 2019 - 4/ 2020 - 4)
Pogue Mahone Records

This mighty Christmas perennial had a long gestation period before finally being released. Hampered by the fall out with the band's original producer, Elvis Costello, who departed, taking bass player and prospective singer of the female part of the song Cait O'Riordan with him. The song originated with banjo player Jem Finer, who passed the idea onto Shane McGowan, who introduced its Broadway narrative and musical feel. New producer Steve Lillywhite had his wife Kirsty MacColl record a vocal for a demo of the song, and hearing the result the group realised she was the perfect vocal foil for McGowan. The song - set in a cell on Christmas Eve - finds a pair of drunken lovers bickering, reminiscing, and accusing each other of the fault for their miserable predicament. The emotions are spilled, ranging from tender to vitriolic. Sentimentality is laced with spitefulness but ends with an expression of love and hope that always opens up the tear ducts. It is a remarkable song.

8
FRANKIE KNUCKLES
Baby Wants To Ride
Your Love
NO CHART PLACING
Trax Records

Although it was most unethical and almost certainly illegal for him to do it, Frankie Knuckles allegedly took this pair of tracks that he had worked on for their composer Jamie Principle, and without consent or contract, had them released under his own name without crediting the artist who had released 'Your Love' himself the previous year. What is important, musically speaking, is that they are two of the greatest tracks that came from the Chicago house scene. Principle had a spacey, other-worldly vibe and his vocals were erotically charged enough to be X-rated. In combination with Frankie Knuckles' mixing skills, they made a peerless, though perhaps ultimately reluctant, pairing.

7
THE SUGARCUBES
Birthday/
Birthday (Icelandic)
65
One Little Indian

Although this was not her first appearance on record (she had released an album aged 11 and also been a member of Kuki who released music through Crass Records), this single gave most of us our first experience of hearing Björk sing and being drawn into her world of abstract expressionism. The Sugarcubes had formed in 1986 and reputably took their name from the way they ingested LSD. 'Birthday' was a magical single. The band sounded like nothing on earth. The music drifted from the grooves of the record as if being dampened by thick fog. A simple drum pattern gives structure while bass, guitar and keyboards are all used imaginatively in an unorthodox manner. Björk's vocal astonished us as she transmitted the confusing feelings of a five-year-old for her adult next-door neighbour. She captures the innocence of the child feeling this strange yearning. It is uncomfortable listening in that sense, although I do not agree with those who read into the lyric a dark tale of paedophilia. I rather think Björk is reaching inside herself and examining troubling emotional memories rather than a physical event.

6
ULTRA MAGNETIC M.C.'S
Funky/(Instrumental)
Mentally Mad /(Instrumental)
NO CHART PLACING
Next Plateau Records Inc.

Ultra Magnetic M.C.'s had a sound superior to every other hip-hop crew. This was down to Ced Gee who, as well as rapping, produced in such a way that he pushed sampling techniques to their limits. If The Beatles had pushed the sonic envelope in the sixties, their mantle had been taken up by Ultra Magnetic M.C.'s in the eighties. Their influence was immense. 'Funky' is a brilliant single - a celebration of creativity where Ced Gee and Kool Keith let rip with rhymes that are quick and clever. Ced keeps them earthbound while Keith aims towards space. The sound keeps bumping - it is expressive, it is free flowing, and it is supremely funky.

5
THE FALL
Hit The North Part 1/Australians in Europe
Hit The North Part 3/Northerns In Europe
57
Beggars Banquet

Originating from Simon Rogers' experiments with a sampler, upon hearing it Mark Smith seized control and claimed the punchy rhythm, with its distinctive, distorted horn hook, for lyrics concerned with the North/South divide. Its constantly repeated titular slogan is deliberately ambiguous. Was it meant to mean that the North was being hit, as in receiving punishment? Or was it a case of 'Hit The North' signifying the arrival of the man on home territory where he felt more at ease than in the southern flatlands? We will never know, and it doesn't matter. The intrigue of guessing what Smith was on about was a large part of the appeal of being a Fall fan. And although 'Hit The North' was big, bright, very brash pop music - and

unashamedly so - it contained enough of Mark's gnomic utterances to keep the hardcore audience happy.

4
M|A|R|R|S
Pump Up The Volume
Anitina (The First Time I See She Dance)
1
4AD

The massively influential, and equally successful, 'Pump Up The Volume' came into being when the band A. R. Kane approached *4AD* label boss, Ivo Watts, about the idea of recording a purely dance single, similar to what they were hearing coming out of the U.S. They wished to work with Adrian Sherwood but were steered towards a collaboration with the similarly-inclined band Colourbox. The collaborative approach suited neither party, who had clashing personalities and differing working methods. A compromise was reached whereby each outfit would record a track separately and then turn it over to the other for additional work. 'Pump Up The Volume' originated with Colourbox, and Anitina with A.R. Kane. The tracks were completed and, following further disagreement, the single was issued on a white label where 'Pump Up The Volume' generated significant interest. A remixed version was readied and released and stormed the charts, inspiring the likes of Bomb the Bass and S'Express to record similar records. 'Pump Up The Volume' was essentially a skillfully pieced together collage of samples, with the title phrase lifted from Eric B and Rakim's 'I Know You Got Soul', providing a prominent hook, while snippets of contemporary records, alongside 70s funk workouts, filled the track. It captured the imagination of a tidal wave of people out to have a good time on the mushrooming acid house scene. Colourbox were left embittered and disillusioned and never released another record. A.R. Kane were marginally happier and continued without ever recording in this vein afterwards.

3

RHYTHIM IS RHYTHIM

Strings Of Life (Flam-Boy-Ant Mix)/ Strings Of Life/Move It (Remix)/ Kaos (Juice Bar Mix)/Untitled

NO CHART PLACING (1989 - 74)

Transmat

Michael James dropped in at the house of his friend Derrick May and played him a piano ballad he was working on called 'Lighting Strikes Twice'. The piece went into Derrick May's sequencer and sometime later he returned to listen to the piece. He chopped it up, increased the tempo, introduced string samples and placed a rhythm right at the front of the track. It was given its title by Frankie Knuckles, who spoke fulsomely about the power and the energy of the track. He was not wrong. Despite the complete absence of bass on the record, it grooves and moves people acting like a fizzing rush to the head. Euphoria captured on vinyl, lauded by both the house and techno fraternities, it is a genius moment and amongst the greatest records to have come out of the dance music scene.

2

PET SHOP BOYS

It's A Sin

You Know Where You Went Wrong

1

Parlophone

'It's a Sin' was one of the Pet Shop Boys' earliest songs, recorded in demo form during the group's association with Bobby Orlando. That early version is a skeleton of this official release. Emboldened by success and highly confident, the updated version of the song is given a highly dramatic and theatrical reading. Opening and closing with the sounds of a rocket launch, nothing is understated - it is full of orchestral flourishes alongside a barrage of synthesisers. Neil Tennant's vocal is as neutral as ever and his unemotional approach adds power to his words which are crystal clear and unadorned with baggage. He sings about his childhood, being educated in a Catholic school where the parish priest would condemn his thoughts and actions as sinful and abhorrent. Although the song was written as nothing more than a petulant, jokey, sticking-out-his tongue in mock defiance of the ridiculous ladling of guilt onto impressionable children, the truth of

the words struck a chord with many of their audience.

1
PRINCE
Sign o' the Times
La, La, La, He, He, Hee
10
Paisley Park

Prince supposedly wrote his most introspective songs on a Sunday and 'Sign o' the Times' was one of his Sunday songs. At its heart it is a blues shuffle, with a lyric that addresses, among other topics, poverty, drug addiction, AIDS, gang violence, and the impending nuclear holocaust. Of course, this is Prince, and this blues shuffle comes heavily disguised and twisted into a new shape and form. Prince plays all the instruments on the track and sculpts a sound from a simple drum machine beat and a minimal recurring synth pattern. A dash of funk guitar adds colour. His phrasing and vocal delivery is absolutely impeccable. The record was timely, in capturing the prevailing mood of spooked fear in a world fractured and on the brink of disaster. It was prescient, political and also brilliant pop - it takes some kind of genius to achieve that feat.

1988

I was hardly rolling in it but relatively speaking I was well off. I was earning a wage considerably higher than I'd earned before and I had negotiated into my job the strict dispensation that I would not be required to work weekends. I was free to roam with money in my pocket and took advantage by frequently weekending in London taking in clubs and gigs. Also, after a decade of intermittent attempts, I passed a driving test at the ninth time of asking. I was given a transit van by my employer as it helped considerably with my job, it was only a matter of weeks before I had my first bump and several years until I truly got the hang of things. These bumps were a fairly frequent event!

In terms of creating music I had hit a wall and was inactive. It frustrated me and I drank too much and musicians at the Boardwalk often had to endure my negative vitriol if I felt their performance was in any way substandard. I was bitter and resentful that they were doing what I could not. Jealousy is an ugly emotion and I was quite plainly jealous. My behaviour was unattractive and I hated myself for my nastiness. Bizzarely I got my comeuppance at the hands of ex-Bay City Roller Eric Faulkner who responded to my goading by punching me, hard! I had only myself to blame and was in fact grateful to him for forcibly pointing out the error of my ways. I did keep my hand in doing occasional bits of DJing, usually at the request of friends and from this the opportunity to do a regular spot with my good friend Bob cropped up.

The gig was in our home town of Denton, only eight miles outside town geographically but in terms of culture it was a million light years. His was an offer I couldn't refuse. It was a popular night when the place was packed and we were paid £100 for our troubles, we turned up playing a set of hip-hop, house, early Happy Mondays and Stone Roses releases and other exotic fare. One night we scratched and looped Johnny Cash singing 'A Boy Named Sue' for 20 minutes. It was great fun, we were having a brilliant time but our audience hated it. They wanted the most saccharine pop hits and instead were getting weird shit, they began to vote with their feet and take their custom elsewhere. Others were more extreme - a slab of concrete was thrown through my house window after one session and by the sixth week of our residency we were spinning Suicides' immortal 'Frankie Teardrop' and there was a run for the exits, only ourselves and the bar staff remained. The licensee was a nice chap called George and he sadly shook his head, said 'I love it, but I think it's time for a change'. We couldn't complain, it was the most polite and civilised dismissal imaginable.

In among the chaos that often engulfed me Mark Smith of The Fall reappeared in my life. He had always been supportive of my musical endeavours and now he asked me if I would consent to be a part of The Fall's live performances. He wrote a spoken word piece that I would perform with the band before he appeared on stage to replace me at the mic. I was flattered to be asked but perhaps didn't show the required enthusiasm for the floated idea to be made real. His other proposal was that he release a four-track Hamsters EP from tracks we recorded with Grant Showbiz in 1980. I was delighted at this and wheels were set in motion , Mark later contacted me to tell me that reluctantly the EP was to be shelved through lack of funds but that he would like to release a pair of our tracks on a compilation LP and this came to pass so eight years after their demise The Hamsters were finally immortalised in vinyl on the disparate *cogscienti* album.

NOTABLE EVENTS 1988

In The Soviet Union the process of economic reconstruction known as *Perestroika* is initiated by premier Mikhail Gorbachev

The Phantom of the Opera opens on Broadway, it becomes the longest running show of all time.

Saddam Hussein orders a genocidal operation against the Kurdish population of Iraq. An estimated 180,000 people are believe to have died.

After eight years fighting in the Soviet-Afghan War, Soviet troops are withdrawn following US backing for the same Afghan mujahideen insurgents that would later attack the World Trade Centre and lead to an allied invasion of Afghanistan.

Wembley Stadium hosts a concert to mark the 70th birthday of Nelson Mandela

A NASA scientist testifies to the US senate that man-made global warming has begun.

Thousands of anti-government protesters in Burma are killed by troops

Al-Qaida is formed by Osama Bin Laden

The Iran-Iraq war ends with an estimated half a million lives lost, the majority being Iranian. The end of the conflict resulted in neither reparations nor border changes.

Benazir Bhutu becomes prime minister of Pakistan, the first female head of state in a Muslim country

The 'Singing Revolution' begins in Estonia as a protest against Soviet plans to begin Phosphorite mining in the country but later morphs into an independence movement. Estonians sing patriotic songs openly in Talinn and an independence party is formed.

Canadian Ben Johnson wins the Olympic 100 metres in a new world record time but is quickly disqualified for taking steroids and Carl Lewis is awarded gold. It is later revealed that of the first 5 across the line in that race only American Calvin Smith had never failed a drug test.

Alex Ferguson's first full season at Old Trafford sees Manchester United finish second in the league nine points behind Liverpool who fail to win the double, losing 1-0 to Wimbledon in the FA Cup final. United sign former Aberdeen goalkeeper Jim Leighton in the summer but early performances are not encouraging and a fanzine publishes a skit advertising 'The Jim Leighton Condom' that guaranteed 'you caught nothing'!

NOTABLE BIRTHS

Jonny Evans; Rihanna; Juan Mata; Adele; Tyson Fury; Robert Lewandowski; James Blake.

NOTABLE DEATHS

Trevor Howard; Emeric Pressburger; Divine; Andy Gibb; Kim Philby; Chet Baker; Nico; Raymond Carver; Jean-Michel Basquiat; Enzo Ferrari; Son House; Roy Orbison; Hal Ashby.

NOTABLE FILMS

Die Hard; Beetlejuice; Who Framed Roger Rabbit; Mississippi Burning; A Fish Called Wanda; Hairspray; The Unbearable Lightness of Being; The Last Temptation of Christ; Tetsuo The Iron Man.

NOTABLE BOOKS

The Silence of the Lambs - Thomas Harris
The Alchemist - Paulo Coelho
The Satanic Verses - Salman Rushdie
Oscar and Lucinda - Peter Carey
A Far Cry From Kensington - Muriel Spark
Empire of the Senseless -Kathy Acker
The Swimming Pool Library - Alan Hollinghurst
The Lives of John Lennon - Albert Goldman
Watchman - Ian Rankin Ian Rankin

100
BABY FORD
Oochy Koochy
(F.u Baby Yeh Yeh)/Flowers
58
Rhythm King

Influenced by the sounds he was hearing on Chicago House records, Peter 'Baby' Ford from Wigan set about doing something in a similar style and created 'Oochy Koochy' which is regarded as being the first British acid house record. It is a great listen; piano runs, stabs of synth, a quick-fire programmed drum pattern and a nonsensical repeated phrase (Oochy Koochy - Oochy Koochy) it is relentless it swells and rises, it keeps going up and up.

99
EPMD'
Strictly Business'(Vocal Mix)/
Radio Mix/Instrumental/Acapella
No Chart Placing
Sleeping Bag

The title track and choice cut from their classic album *Strictly Business* sampled Bob Marley's, 'I Shot the Sheriff' as performed by Eric Clapton. It has a pronounced R&B groove over which Erick Sermon adds his lazy sounding but precise lyrical flow. Try and stop your head bobbing as this plays - impossible.

98
INXS
Need You Tonight (Ben Liebrand Mix)/New Sensation/Move On
2
Mercury

This bunch enjoyed a success that mystified me. They were a decidedly dull proposition. They played perfunctory pub rock given a production that added an unthreatening new wave sheen and then they dropped this track. It was irresistible - a huge stylistic departure, confounding expectations.

Using more electronics than was customary for the group, it fizzed and whirred between an unforgettable staccato guitar riff with sequencers added to the mechanical rhythm. Singer Michael Hutchence's vocal mixed vulnerability with up-front wanton desire. It was funk rock comparable with tracks released by Prince or Cameo. INXS now had their signature sound and song.

97
KEVIN SAUNDERSON
The Groove That Won't Stop/
The Sound (Power Remix)
No Chart Placing
Kms

The third of the triumvirate known as the 'Belleville Three', along with Derrick May and Juan Atkins, this was a record that displayed Saunderson's prowess. It crosses lines of genre classification, it is a collision of Acid House and Detroit Techno that contains hi-hat sounds that could possibly slice the top of your head off and loose rubbery grooves alternately pushing and pulling frenetically.

96
NIRVANA
Love Buzz /Big Cheese
No Chart Placing
Sub Pop

Legendary Seattle label Sub Pop had released their first singles by Green River and Soundgarden in 1987, now they launched their singles club, a series of releases limited to 1000 copies. The first single issued was 'Love Buzz' by an unknown to group called Nirvana, who selected a cover version of a song by Dutch psychedelic rock band Shocking Blue famous for their hit 'Venus' later successfully covered by Bananarama. It was a fabulous record, described in the blurb as being Heavy pop sludge. Kurt Cobain excels both as a guitar player and vocalist but the star of the show is bassist Krist Novoselic whose playing is outstanding, it picked up great reviews in *Sounds* and *Melody Maker* by John Robb and Everett True who deserve great credit for their foresight.

95
PHUTURE'
We Are The Phuture/
Slam!/ Spank-Spank
No Chart Placing
Trax

Having defined the sound of Acid House with their first release, Phuture released another dance-floor gem with 'We are the Phuture'. Where 'Acid Trax' had been instrumental and quite minimal this one slammed hard and was heavily vocalised, it sounded as if they had somehow melded elements of Funkadelic and Sun Ra into their House Sound. This was seriously freaky music, an absolutely punishing dance track that features some instrumental drops that are like dizzying leaps between rooftops. Not one for the faint-hearted this was highly impressive music that felt like it arrived from outer space.

94
FELT
Space Blues/Be Still/
Female Star/Tuesdays Secret
No Chart Placing
Creation

From the first day of group's formation Lawrence had claimed Felt would release ten LPs and ten singles in 10 years and then split up. 'Space Blues' was the tenth Felt single and indeed the last. It offers up a tantalising glimpse of what might have been if they had continued. Drummerless here, keyboardist Martin Duffy provides what is surprisingly for Felt a seriously funky rhythm, violins add grandiose musical seasoning and Lawrence adopts a 'Lou Reed ' type sing- speak vocal style to draw a kind of homage to an uncompromising artiste (himself?). He had wanted Felt to become pop stars and in that aim he failed but Lawrence and the constantly changing line ups of his group had always remained relevant and interesting and that was a more worthwhile achievement.

93
LOOP
Collision/Crawling Heart/
Thief Of Fire/
Thief (Motherfucker)
No Chart Placing
Chapter 22

Loop were from Croydon and in thrall to the purity of scuzzy rock outcasts The Stooges and Suicide. They mixed a murky, churning sonic attack with the repetition found in early 70s German music. They didn't do songs as such, just riffs that droned and hammered their way into the subconscious. On 'Collision' they are at their most focused and power through its stoner space boogie as though they were the bastard offspring of Hawkwind which of course is a huge compliment. This is best listened to at extremely high volume and in a chemically-enhanced state, although of course those choices are optional!

92
PERE UBU
We Have The Technology
/We Have The Technology
No Chart Placing
Fontana

Pere Ubu returned after a six-year hiatus and made a conscious effort to make lighter sounding pop music. They succeed up to a point; the overall sound was sweet and palatable enough to encroach upon the mainstream but David Thomas's cerebral science-fiction tinged lyric about freezing moments delivered as a whine interspersed with yelps was inevitably going to frighten radio programmers and drummer Scott Krauss adds to the strangeness with his idiosyncratic rhythms .

91
A.R KANE
Baby Milk Snatcher /W.O.G.S
No Chart Placing
Rough Trade

Beating a retreat from the success of 'Pump up the Volume', there was a move away from dance music towards something more difficult to classify. 'Baby Milk Snatcher' referenced the evil PM Margaret Hilda Thatcher in its title but nothing else so it was easy to read. The sound is clearly influenced by a spacious dub combined with a jazz-leaning sensibility akin to 'Rock Bottom'-era Robert Wyatt. Lyrics are open to interpretation although there is a suggestion of oral sex taking place, they are sung quietly without histrionics. The effect is dreamy but not at all bland or twee, perhaps dark hued and mysterious is a more fitting description.

90
GREGORY ISAACS
Rumours /Pure Rumours
No Chart Placing
Music Works

Gregory Isaacs talent meant that his career endured, though the international spotlight had ceased to shine his way. In Jamaica he remained at the top even as musical styles came and went, he truly was 'the cool ruler'. This dancehall style slice of militancy and dub was recorded with producer Gussie Clark and a seriously hot band provide a perfect platform for that distinctive, wonderful voice. 'Rumours' is quite a sparse rhythm that is filled by deep reverberating bass, Issacs had that innate gift of finding space, akin to footballers of the calibre of Eric Cantona and Dennis Bergkamp but displayed in another field. Isaacs is never hurried in his delivery, he makes singing seem effortless as each phrase, no matter how difficult, is performed to perfection. Gregory Isaacs was a highly-prolific artist and as such quality could suffer but this was not one of those occasions, 'Rumours' was a fabulous addition to his bulging portfolio of work .

89
THE BARMY ARMY
Sharp As A Needle/
England 2 Yugoslavia 0
No Chart Placing
On-U Sound

Dub adventurer Adrian Sherwood' was not just a musical scholar, he was also a student of the beautiful game or the working man's ballet. He was a proper football supporter, a West Ham fan and unashamedly so. In this period football was something that was sniffily dismissed by a large percentage of the overtly sensitive elitists in the music industry. Football themed records were even lower down the totem pole than the actual game and to be fair only Don Farden's prescient plea to George Best to focus on what he did beautifully on the pitch with 'Belfast Boy' and 1987s Tackhead release 'The Game' had ever transcended Kitsch novelty

On 'Sharp as a Needle' alchemy was achieved between the polar opposites of credible music and football. It had at its base a rolling industrial funk rhythm that was combined with samples notably of a crowd singing 'Abide With Me' and TV commentary from Brian Moore eulogising about a goal scored by ' Liverpool and Scotland legend Kenny Dalglish. He describes the formidable and efficient Scot as 'Sharp as a Needle', the fact that Dalglish plied his trade at the wrong end of the East Lancs road was unfortunate, although begrudgingly I had to acknowledge his brilliant technical ability, and was therefore able to enjoy this great homage on vinyl to the full.

88
MARC ALMOND
Tears Run Rings/
Everything I Wanted Love To Be 26
Parlophone

'Tears Run Rings' found Marc Almond incorporating a brighter leaner sound than had been the case in recent years , the space allowed him to showcase his brilliant always emotionally charged voice to the full , the lack of clutter suits the song which is full of hurt and heartache, also unusually for Almond , it comments overtly and angrily in regard of the hateful and hurtful politics of the day, as Thatcher's shock troops attacked the very notion of community , the content it has to be said does not make the song a dour listen , the tempo is brisk , the chorus dramatic and the outro of fanfaring horns is terrifically stirring .

87
THE POGUES
Fiesta/Sketches Of Spain
24
Pogue Mahone

The Pogues found themselves in the Spanish town of Almeria for the filming of low budget Alex Cox film *Straight to Hell* and were inspired to write 'Fiesta' after Jem Finer developed the riff from a traditional fairground tune. Sean McGowan provides a nonsensical 'spanglish' vocal, ostensibly about hedonistic high jinks, and the band let rip through the tune with gusto and punk rock energy - it is insanely catchy and hugely celebratory.

86
JULIAN COPE
Charlotte Anne/
Christmas Mourning
35
Island

His touring band having fallen apart, Cope recorded an album using session musicians called *My Nation Underground* but it proved to be the most uninspired and least interesting album from his considerable discography. However, as is often the case that dog of a record contained one shimmering classic which was 'Charlotte Anne' the title being a pun on the word Charlatan. The song is achingly beautiful, quite fragile in fact, with a drum beat that sounds like a mechanical toy and there is a bafflingly strange middle eight featuring a spoken word section and a haunting pan pipe - wonderful.

85
ULTRA VIVID SCENE
She Screamed/
Walkin' After Midnight
Not In Love (Hit By A Truck)
No Chart Placing
4AD

Ultra Vivid Scene was essentially Kurt Ralske who wrote, produced and performed the music. His core influence of the Velvet Underground by way of The Jesus and Mary Chain is unhidden.

'She Screamed' comes though riding a Wurlitzer Organ riff and Kurt's vocal is fey and mannered. He stays therefore on the right side of the line betwixt being influenced by and being an imitation of his heroes and with that point settled satisfactorily I have to say the record is a true delight .

84
BAM BAM
Where's Your Child?
Where's Your Child? (Suck Mix)
No Chart Placing
Desire

Bam Bam was American musician Chris Westbrook - this is three parts wigged-out Acid House and one part Hammer Horror as a slowed down and deepened voice asks 'where's your child?' and laughs in a sinister knowing manner as we hear crockery smashing and a baby crying. The music rises and falls and rises again to the point of mayhem. The answer to the question seems to be in the grooves - the child is growing up and doing things that parents don't understand or approve of, the child is immersed in Acid House culture and is in the parlance of the day 'having it large'.

83
CRIME AND
THE CITY SOLUTION
On Every Train (Grain Will Bear Grain)/All Must Be Love
No Chart Placing
Mute

The Howard brothers, Rowland and Harry, were gone but Simon Bonney and Mick Harvey remained - Australian mavericks self-exiled in Berlin. Despite their physical dislocation the band played in a style rooted in old time American country blues, 'On Every Train' displays their formidable talents, they draw the listener into their orbit of spooky atmospherics and creepy unease, they are rough around the edges, dangerous sounding and Bonney delivers his lyrics slowly, they seem to crawl from his soul. Harvey tinkles ivories as though he is playing in 1920s burlesque whilst Bronwyn Adams' violin playing switches from mournful drones to frenzied over the course of the song .

82
CARDIACS
Is This The Life/I'm Eating In Bed
80
Torso/Alphabet Business Concern

Tim Smith started The Cardiacs in 1977 and ironically only a heart attack in 2008, which debilitated him until his death in 2020, halted his flow of startling, unique creativity. 'Is this the life' was the band's biggest, indeed only, hit single. In truth number 80 hardly counts, but still The Cardiacs deserved hits so this will have to do.

This was clearly a song Tim Smith liked as he returned to it frequently, this was the third version of it released. Starting off as a taut, typically idiosyncratic piece with yelped vocals and instrumental choruses, the guitar surges and a titanic solo ensues, it is akin to one of Neil Young's flights of fretboard fantasy. Suddenly a rhythmic element, redolent of early Genesis, comes into play before a breathless finale halts the juggernaut.

81
TIMELORDS
Doctorin' The Tardis (Extended)/(Radio Version)/(Minimal Version)
1
Klf Communications

Jimmy Cauty and Bill Drummond reappeared under a new guise as The Timelords and this time their intention was to release a House record that celebrated the trashiness of British Pop. To that end they travelled back to 1974 where they sampled 'The Dr Who theme' and mixed it up with the Glitter-stomp of 'Rock and Roll part 2' added a dash of 'Blockbuster' sirens and chanted along in the mindless manner of The Rollers. Succeeding probably beyond even *their* wildest dreams, their conceptual joke was embraced by the public at large who loved it in the way we all loved *The Morecambe and Wise* Christmas Day specials.

80
BY GEORGE
No Clause 28/No Clause 28 (Beats)
57
Virgin

Thatcher didn't only despise Trade Unions, the working class and foreigners, she hated gays too! Clause 28 was a proposed piece of legislation aimed at the suppression and undermining of the homosexual community by outlawing any mention of homosexuality in any but the most bigoted, negative manner. What would come next? Book burning? Pink stars sewn on clothing to identify queers? Concentration camps?

Nothing seemed too excessive for this nasty Conservative government which had drifted further right with every passing year. There was a backlash and politicising of gay groups already under heavy attack due to blame for H.I.V/AIDS epidemic being placed at their door with the tabloid press quick to blame deviant sexual practices. The finest musical response came from Boy George with this single wrapped inside a brilliant sleeve with artwork by Jamie Reed depicting George as Enid Blyton's Noddy. The record was agit-pop polemic done dance style, with a rousing declamatory chorus and samples of the Prime Minister spouting her vile, idiotic rhetoric.

79
DANIELLE DAX
Cat House/Touch Piggy Eyes/
House Cat
No Chart Placing
Awesome

Dax was so absurdly glamorous that the fact seemed to hinder her musical career. Her talent was immense but it seemed to be less important to most people than her striking appearance. 'Cat House' deserved to be a genuine chart hit, it is as bright as a button, its rich warm sound practically embraces the listener and it has a riff so good that The Damned have been known to power through this song on stage. As for Dax's vocals, they are as cool as can be with a knowing humorous edge, she purrs in the manner of a prowling panther - think Nancy Sinatra on ' Boots' or ' Some Velvet Morning' and you are close.

78
GAVIN FRIDAY
& THE MAN SEEZER
Each Man Kills The Thing He Loves/
An Extract From The Ballad Of Reading Gaol
No Chart Placing Island

Here we have the first post-Virgin Prunes' release from Gavin Friday and his first collaborative effort with Maurice 'The Man' Seezer. Also gathered are the talents of some of New York's finest left-field musicians including Marc Ribot, Fernando Saunders, Michael Blair and Bill Frisell.

The lyric for 'Each Man Kills the Thing He Loves' is taken entirely from Oscar Wilde's poetic masterpiece 'The Ballad of Reading Gaol', where he reflects on the nature of guilt and innocence. It is given a suitably atmospheric reading in a style suggestive of decadent cabarets of the era' one imagines plush velvet, lace and flickering gas lamps; Gavin Friday's gift for dramatic interpretation remained undiminished and he treats each syllable with relish as he delivers with practiced flair each mouthwateringly delicious couplet extracting, as he proceeds, the maximum possible impact .

77
TOM WAITS
16 Shells From A Thirty-Ought-6/
Big Black Mariah
No Chart Placing
Island

The storytelling hobo schtick that characterized Waits early years was now dead and buried with the earth atop it well and truly stamped down. This version of '16 shells from a thirty-ought-6' came from his live performance album *Big Time.* It was a jerking, awkward, rhythmic thing using sparse instrumentation with deadly intent. It clangs and crashes while Waits throat-shreddingly howls out vivid abstract lines that carry hostile intent to the point of malevolent threat.

76
STETSASONIC
Talkin All That Jazz/
Talkin All That Jazz
(Dominoes Version)
No Chart Placing
Breakout / Tommy Boy

Stetsasonic' use 'All That Jazz' as an answer to critics who dismiss Hip-hop because of its use of sampling. It is well thought out and brilliantly articulate as it takes on narrow-minded thinking and prevails conclusively. They point out that it took Eric B and Rakim's 'I Know You Got Soul' to revive interest in the music of James Brown and compare their own approach to that of Sly and the Family Stone. Beneath the raps swing-era jazz provides a musical counterpoint of great style and the addition of a titanic grooving bass line makes the whole record irresistible .

75
THE FALL
Jerusalem/Acid Priest/
Big New Prinz/
Wrong Place Right Time No2
59
Beggars Banquet

Fall obsessives will consider this an act of heresy but 'Jerusalem' is a fairly lacklustre tune. In his lyrics Smith seems to be contrasting the sentiments of building something gloriously idealistic expressed by William Blake for the pitiful whining he hears from people who blame the government for all that is wrong. This record is included here because it came as a twin pack of 7 inch singles and the second featured 'Big New Prinz' - a glam rock cousin of previous Fall classic 'Hip Priest' which was pure gold with Smith chanting out the simplest of lyrics and the Hanley brothers providing a rhythmic groove of immense proportions.

74
HEAD
Cars Outside/
The Face (Is A Lonely Place)
No Chart Placing
Virgin

Since the demise of The Pop Group there had followed similarly free and unstructured experimental bands such as Rip Rig + Panic and Float Up CP. Gareth Sagar's musical career seemed set in an unorthodox but fairly settled path. He then formed a band that tore up the script called Head and they were a loud, drunken sounding, raucous rock 'n' roll group attempting to play sea shanties in the manner of Captain Beefheart's magic band. I saw them live and I can attest that they were peerless, the most wonderful fun imaginable. It was hard to capture the reckless energy they possessed on vinyl but they tried and nearly pulled it off. Early in the year they had released 'Sin Bin', a rowdy sing-along that drew plaudits. 'Cars Outside' was even better, it was revved up to the max, insanely catchy and kicked like a mule. They took all concepts of and shredded them which made 'Head' just about the coolest band around in my book .

73
TRAVELING WILBURYS
Handle With Care/Margarita
21
Wilbury

A common problem in gatherings of superstar talents is that egos tend to get in the way and the adage about 'too many cooks spoiling the broth' is shown to be true as each participant strives to display their own dominance over proceedings. That didn't happen in The Traveling Wilburys, perhaps because there was no grand plan for world domination. Instead it seemed to be about a group of admittedly very famous musicians coming together and having fun and displaying a mutual respect. The band members had originally colluded to record a bonus track for George Harrison's album *Cloud Nine* on a song they recorded called 'Handle with Care' which they decided was far too good to waste in so humble a fashion and so The Traveling Wilburys were born

'Handle With Care' was the supremely charming single that announced their existence. It was defiantly unfashionable, just a great song originating from Harrison, played with good natured gusto and sung open-heartedly by the voices of the former Beatles alongside Jeff Lynne, Tom Petty and Bob Dylan - all fine and high-spirited with the secret weapon of Roy Orbison's incredible tenor raising the roof .

72
LAIBACH
Sympathy For The Devil
(6 Versions)
No Chart Placing Mute

Having released an album of deconstructions called *Let it Be* consisting of Beatles songs from their 1970 album which aimed at debunking the sacred cow status of the mop tops, Laibach next turned their attention to The Rolling Stones with a series of versions of that band's much-mythologised 60s counter-culture anthem 'Sympathy for the Devil'. The original's shimmer and shake is replaced by pummelling industrial rhythms and where Mick Jagger delivers the original vocal as a sensuous purr, here the lyrics are delivered as a ferocious guttural bark. The song is reconstructed in different ways emphasising different aspects of the piece. Laughingly for instance playing up the psychedelic psycho-babble engaged in by the Stones in one version and concentrating on the deaths of the Kennedy's in another.

71
ERASURE
Ship Of Fools
When I Needed You
6
Mute

Erasure's artistic growth didn't impinge on the commerciality of their material and 'Ship Of Fools' almost enters ballad territory. Sung by Andy Bell in a lower register than usual, he sings about the world of uncertainties facing a sensitive and vulnerable young man on the cusp of adulthood. It is a powerfully perceptive song that benefits greatly from the genius touch of Vince Clarke's melodic mastery .

70
JOHN HIATT
Slow Turning/Already Loved/
Your Dad Did
No Chart Placing
A&M

John Hiatt is a high quality songwriter and performer but commercially speaking he was niche. He garnered respect but not huge record sales, as an American he is perceived as being similar in a musical vein to Bruce Springsteen but a closer parallel from a UK perspective might be Graham Parker. He has that knack of melding rootsy influences into his rock 'n' roll and sings with a gritty, authentic rasp. 'Slow Turning' raised his profile without providing a hit. It was a crackling upper mid-tempo rocker with a wonderful guitar sound and, as in so much of Hiatt's work, there is a clever lyric, this one referencing Buddy Holly via The Rolling Stones and specifically giving a nod to Charlie Watts.

69
MICHAEL JACKSON
Smooth Criminal/Instrumental
8 (2009 - 13)
Sony

'Smooth Criminal ' was the seventh single release from Jackson's album *Bad* which indicates both the depth of quality on that album but also how his label underrated this outstanding track. It is one of the most satisfying rock-flavoured songs that Jackson used to portray himself as being harder edged than popular perception had it. Taking the phrase 'Annie are you ok?' from cardiopulmonary training where trainees are taught to say the phrase as they practice resuscitation on a dummy, he adds disturbing lyrics about discovering a bloodstained body to build a thrilling psychodrama. Jackson sounds perfectly natural and totally at ease with the material, other commentators have described the song and performance of it as being exhilarating - I can think of no better word to sum up this record .

68
YELLO
The Race (Video Mix)/
(Sporting Mix)/Another Race
7
Fontana

The Race opens with motor engine sound effects and a bossa nova style beat before taking a sharp left turn and morphing into a dance-based neo-jazz swing tune that is part Benny Goodman and Marshall Jefferson. It is as infectious as hell as Dieter Meier and Boris Blank shoot lines using racing track metaphors about competitiveness in exaggerated mock angsty fashion .

67
MARLEY MARL featuring
BIG DADDY KANE, CRAIG G,
KOOL G RAP, MASTER ACE
The Symphony (Remix)/
Wack It (Remix)
Featuring Roxanne Shante
No Chart Placing
Cold Chillin / Warner Brothers

Marley Marl was working as a DJ for WBLS and while there created ' The Symphony' using the distinctive piano hook from Otis Redding's, 'Hard To Handle' and seasoning it with spaghetti western stylings. It was then turned over to a bunch of Juice Crew affiliates to vocalise the track. The four rappers cut loose, each in a distinctive style which shifts the mood of the track from playful to aggressive, hard to smooth. The rhythm keeps rolling but the track remains compulsive listening as the words keep tumbling like wave upon wave .

66
BLACK RIOT
A Day In The Life/Warlock
68
Champion

This was a busy year for Todd Terry. Barely out of his teens he issued a barrage of singles under different aliases. 'A Day In The Life' was simple genius - a raw, energetic near instrumental track with stabs of synths used as a hook and guaranteeing a euphoric reaction from ravers high on adrenaline. Add in a classic House piano break and rhythms that are absolutely relentless, with tom tom percussion acting like pistons, this one set pulses racing .

65
STONE ROSES
Elephant Stone/
The Hardest Thing In The World
No Chart Placing (1990 - 8)
Silvertone

Previously an unremarkable goth band more famous for one of their supporters defacing the cenotaph in St Peters' Square, the addition of new bass player Mani transformed them. Together with brilliant drummer Reni they formed a killer rhythm section and the Stone Roses became a much more interesting proposition. Chiming guitars and a shift towards strong melodic structures were increasingly evident - now they grooved, their sound sinuous and fluid.

'Elephant Stone', produced by Peter Hook, was the first record by the band's classic line up. It elevated them away from the also rans, they were now contenders. On the face of it they were just one of many bands mining twee sixties jangling guitar pop as a primary influence, lyrically there was still considerable room for improvement, and yet the dance-infused rhythms added zip, the melodies soared, wings were sprouting and the Roses were heading from the gutter to the stars.

64
CBI
Big Tears/Braid On My Shoulder/
Good Thing
No Chart Placing
Radio Active

Concrete Bulletproof Invisible, to give them their full title, contained ex-Sex Pistol Glen Matlock along with Jo Shaw and Jackie Leven, formally of Doll by Doll. They joined together at a benefit for the family of the deceased ex-Heavy Metal Kids front man Gary Holton, encouraged by Robbie Coltrane who witnessed their performance. They formalised the arrangement and this was their sole release despite it being a cut above a large percentage of the guitar rock being peddled by stadium filling superstars and cult favourites. It was a tough but melodious song written by Matlock and sung with grace and power by Leven who was just recovering his voice following a serious assault. They played a few gigs and then nothing else happened, CBI were done and dusted.

63
CLOCK DVA
The Hacker/Correction Machine
No Chart Placing
Big Sex

Adi Newton was a Sheffield contemporary of Cabaret Voltaire and The Human League and had launched Clock DVA in the late 70s but they truly found their place here in the late 80s, categorised as an Industrial act. On 'The Hacker' they enter Cyberpunk territory, the music they create is hard, cold and dramatic, it echoes the soundtrack work of John Carpenter and has a similar cinematic quality. The vocal part of the song is a menacing spoken word piece that suggests authoritarian oppression and surveillance - the overall effect is genuinely edgy and unnerving.

62
NEW ORDER
Fine Time/Don't Do It/Fine Line
11
Factory

Invigorated by the Acid House scene of which their co-owned club The Hacienda was key, New Order released 'Fine Time' written and partly recorded in Ibiza and it's outgoing, up-tempo vibe reflects the fact. Every component part is outstanding and it is beautifully constructed, the beats are monumental, the bass monstrous, the keyboards sparkle, and contained within the track is a melodica solo that is so cheeky it almost winks.

61
GO BETWEENS'
Was There Anything I Could Do?/
Rock And Roll Friend
No Chart Placing
Beggars Banquet

Here the Go Betweens put their foot on the pedal and allow the music to drive. 'Is There Anything I Can Do?' is punchy and upbeat, its also bright and tuneful and has a refreshing openness in its simple construction. Grant McLennan sings lead engagingly, Lindy Morrison powers the song from the drums and Amanda Brown's violin breathes fire on another brilliant Go Betweens' single .

60
ERIC B AND RAKIM
Follow The Leader/Acapella/Dub
21
MCA

Eric B provides a soundscape from jazz and funk samples that is absolutely jaw-droppingly outstanding and acts as a launchpad for Rakim to aim for space and lead us on a lyrical journey that goes way beyond the realms of the concerns of most rappers; he philosophises and gets metaphysical, his vocal gymnastics are stunning, so quickly does one startling phrase follow the previous one that it resembles a high wire act that leaves nobody with doubts as to his lyrical dexterity and verbal agility.

59
FAST EDDIE
Hip House(LP Version)/
(Deep Mix)/I Can Dance (LP)/
Hip House (Nightmare Mix)
No Chart Placing
DJ International

Fast Eddie was a radio DJ in Chicago spinning the latest in House sounds who had recorded 'Can You Dance' in 1986 but in 1988 he decided to give up the radio to become a full-time music producer. He was highly prolific and his 'Acid Thunder' EP was a fine release. 'Hip House' however was a truly exciting and pivotal record; over an Acid House backing, a rap track was laid down. It is disputed whether Fast Eddie was the originator of the form or Beatmasters, whose 'Rok da House' had been released in 1986. A line from Merlin, who rapped on that track is 'Beatmasters stand to attention, hip house is your invention'. Nonetheless Fast Eddie made explicit what he was doing with the title of this release but more importantly it was a thrilling sound that displayed the possibilities of melding the two forces together to create something fresh and different.

58
THE LA's
There She Goes/
Come In Come Out
59 (1990 - 13)
Go Discs

From its opening notes 'There She Goes ' is recognisable, it has a simple but brilliant melody and a structure of equal simplicity and economy, it doesn't have to try too hard, it is a genuine pop nugget from first to last. The lyrics are ostensibly about unrequited love but in the manner of Lou Reed's 'Perfect Day' it could equally be an ode to the seductive effects of heroin.

57
DINOSAUR JR
Freak Scene/Keep The Glove
No Chart Placing
Blast First

Dinosaur Jr front man J Mascis had become so controlling and dictatorial within the band that he controlled every bass note or drum beat contributed by Lou Barlow and Murph respectively. They had zero musical wiggle room to express themselves and as a consequence tensions were unpleasantly high. 'Freak Scene' reflected the band's inner turmoil via a lyric about a messy love-hate relationship that Mascis drawls out over a track that reflected his love for both Black Sabbath heavy riffage and Byrd's like tunefulness. At under 4 minutes long it was a template for a new kind of pop that would inform the work of bands including Nirvana and Radiohead and remarkably inside that brief time two skull-battering guitar solos were inserted .

56
TRACY CHAPMAN
Fast Car/For You
4
Elektra

Tracy Chapman was a young American singer-guitarist operating in the Folk tradition, she exploded onto the world stage via an appearance at The Nelson Mandela birthday concert where she performed her debut single 'Fast Car'. It is a slender musical piece resting on a repeated guitar phrase played in a picking style. However the words paint a vivid picture and the manner of Chapman's performing them as she goes through a range of emotions, ranging from sadness to optimism, pulls at the heartstrings. It is set in a homeless shelter and is a first person narrative about the circumstances that caused the rootlessness of the narrator whose humble aspirations are to be driven in the titular Fast Car into a town where some unskilled work can be found that would enable a permanent abode to be rented. Above all she wishes for a feeling of security and belonging.

55
PHASE II
Reachin' (Brotherhood Mix)/ (Radio)/(Stand Firm Mix)/ (Redemption Mix)
No Chart Placing
Republic

This is a Rolls Royce-standard Garage House track - the beats and rhythms are top notch, the classic House piano chords are present but it is an organ part gives the track a distinct flavour of New York where disco music never really died. A gritty, deeply soulful vocal adds oomph and warmth but what makes this so great is the fact that it's lyric of positivity that is joyful and absolutely uplifting .

54
BRIAN WILSON
Love And Mercy/He Couldn't Get His Poor Old Body To Move
No Chart Placing
Sire

One of the most improbable musical events of the year was the release of a very good solo album by Brian Wilson of Beach Boys fame, Improbable because since the late sixties reports of his deteriorating mental health had surfaced so repeatedly that when he fell off the musical map in the early 70s it was widely assumed he was gone for good.

'Love and Mercy' was the lead single release and was genuinely excellent, it found Brian helming a rich sound that was an update of his mid-60s classics; full of choral flourishes and rich harmony surrounding his voice at the centre of the piece observing people clearly unhappy and struggling, he wishes them not just love to sooth their soul but mercy as he recognises that we all, at times, need people to show us enough compassion to help us be restored .

53
THE KLF
What Time Is Love (Pure Trance 1)
What Time Is Love
No Chart Placing (1990 - 5)
Klf Communications

A whole book could be devoted to 'What Time is Love'. It was a track reworked constantly by Messrs Drummond and Cauty and in radical re-recordings was twice a top 5 hit but this original instrumental acid/ techno/instrumental version was a low key release that became a club staple across Europe. Based on three repeated descending chords, along with whooping sounds, this may have been simple and repetitive but it was dance-floor dynamite in its exciting and energetic beats and constantly shifting emphasis.

52
THE MEKONS
Ghosts Of American Astronauts/
1967 (Revisited)/Revenge
No Chart Placing
Sin

Having over the previous two releases established an alt-country sound that proved to be highly influential and much imitated, The Mekons simply dropped it here and released what at first listen sounds like a beautiful ethereal dream pop single sung fabulously with wonderful purity by Sally Timms. It would be easy to simply enjoy the loveliness of the song, the restraint in the group's playing is most relaxing, the words however take root and at that point the anger and cynicism of the lyric is revealed. Conspiracy theories pertaining to the authenticity of the moon landing footage are brought up and it is noted that the image of American triumph in the space race sat well with a public and a government suffering the pain of its doomed war in Vietnam.

51
ELECTRA
Jibaro (English Version)/
Jibaro (Spanish Version)/
The Future (Edition 2)
54
FFRR

The Balearic sunshine island of Ibiza had become party central and what was dubbed the 'Second Summer of Love' was well and truly underway. One of the most beloved tunes that turned on the hedonistic revellers was 'Jibaro' which was originally recorded in the 1970s by a Columbian act called Elkin & Nelson. Paul Oakenfold and Steve Osborne put together a studio-based band and a cover of 'Jibaro' was their first release. It hit like a bomb going off when it landed in British clubs; its Latin percussion, chants and rhythms aligned to an Acid-techno style made it stand out amidst a deluge of dance records. This was a keeper, it was special, very special.

50
R.E.M
Finest Worksong/Time After Time
50
I.R.S

With a horn section added to add extra punch, 'Finest Worksong' looked at the issue of people doing thankless, useless jobs simply because that is what is expected of them. It observes the ways society is set up so that these small, interchangeable disposable cogs ultimately serve the rich and powerful and advocates alternative thought. If this sounds like a slog through a joyless polemic that is most certainly not the case, the song has all R.E.M's customary musicality; tunefulness, hooks aplenty and fabulous harmonies .

49
PET SHOP BOYS
Domino Dancing/Don Juan
7
Parlophone

The Pet Shop Boys went to Miami to record 'Domino Dancing' with producer Lewis A Martinee with the express purpose of incorporating a Latin pop influence into their sound. Artistically it was a successful collaboration, despite many more musicians being used on the track than was customary for The Pet Shop Boys, their individuality was not swamped and the incorporation of additional instrumentation showed their song craft remained strong enough for it to move into new areas. Even so, the song didn't quite catch the public imagination in the way that was expected, their imperial phase of being number 1 hit-makers had ended.

48
S'Express
Theme From S'Express/
The Trip (Microdot House Mix)
1
Rhythm King

Sample-heavy, UK-produced Acid House tracks were not simply club staples anymore and, following the huge chart successes of Bomb da Bass and M.A.R.R.S came this from the minds of Mark Moore and Pascal Gabriel. 'Theme from S'Express' was a collision of grooves and vocals taken from a highly eclectic mix of tracks and vocal soundtracks. It was cool in a wild way, it was exotic and fresh, it wasn't the cynically produced garbage that people were used to being spooned fed from the power players who believed they knew better than the audience. In sales terms this new breed were rolling roughshod over the taste makers that had dominated the industry since the beginning of the sixties. What punk had tried and failed to do was to make the old fashioned orthodox music scene redundant and bring change and these new innovators, born from club culture, were blowing over the houses of cards with ease. They invited us to enjoy the trip and millions of us were happy to accept.

47
SUICIDE
Surrender/Rain Of Ruin
No Chart Placing
Chapter 22

After a near decade-long hiatus Suicide reconvened. Alan Vega and Marty Rev may no longer have had shock value but they still had the capacity to thrill. With long-time admirer Ric Ocasek of The Cars producing, giving the group's electronics a luxurious sheen. 'Surrender' was the perfect follow up single to the timelessly beautiful 'Dream Baby Dream' released in 1979, it is a dreamy-sounding declaration of love. Marty controls his instrument masterfully providing a warm pulse, Alan croons sweetly, female vocalists back him in vintage style, it is curiously modern and yet at the same time evocative of a time that perhaps never truly existed except in the minds of auteurs such as film director David Lynch who coincidentally used music very similar sounding to 'Surrender' as the soundtrack to his *Twin Peaks* TV series a few years later .

46
ROXANNE SHANTE
Go On Girl/(Dub)
55 (1990 (remix) - 74)
Breakout

Produced by Marley Marl, with Big Daddy Kane providing scratching, the track leans heavily on a sample of Lyn Collins version of James Brown's 'Think'. However it is Roxanne Shante who is the undoubted star here; she sounds so fresh, so real, and so close to present in the room as I listen. Her raps are sharp and she has the confidence and chops to pull them off with aplomb.

45
PREFAB SPROUT
Cars And Girls/Vendetta
44
Kitchenware

Written not as an overt criticism of Bruce Springsteen's approach to song-writing in which he continually utilised imagery of cars and girls as metaphors. It also a wry observation of how a large part of Springsteen's audience misrepresented their hero's songs as being patriotic, making him a symbol he never intended to become. Paddy McAloon writes here from the perspective of one of the legion of Springsteen fans who has an epiphany and is saying you don't represent me, my life is not like the life you portray in your songs. It is a clever song, delivered in a very straightforward manner as a reaction to the way Prefab Sprout's work was perceived as being delicate and too precious.

44
JAMIE PRINCIPLE
Bad Boy (The Movie)/
(Radio Mix)/(House Of Trix Mix)/
(Mini Series)
No Chart Placing
DJ World

This was yet another Jamie Principle single released by 'Trax' records crediting Frankie Knuckles as the featured artist with Jamie Principle as a guest on his own record. An overtly poppy track, with an edge of carnality attached to it, it owed an equal amount to the electro-pop sounds of British acts and Italo-disco as to the House scene that claimed it. Jamie Principle's vocals are delivered lazily at points in what is a measured and nuanced performance that hints at tension as it winds its way towards the sounds of the kind of gratification that can only come from sexual release.

43
LEONARD COHEN
First We Take Manhattan/
Sisters Of Mercy
No Chart Placing
Sony

Leonard Cohen was 54 years old, he was considered by a lot of people an irrelevance - a relic of sixties folk who made music for people to feel miserable to. It was nonsensical of course but it was the general consensus - a convenient pigeon-hole. His album *I'm Your Man* and this attendant single tore up those lazy preconceptions. Cohen emerged with a new sound dominated by synths and drum machines, his music had a euro disco feel to it, his voice was as deep and resonant as ever but it betrayed a playful chuckle too, and 'First We Take Manhattan' was mysterious, ominous and prescient, powerful and staggeringly good. Each lyric painted a picture that was abstract but fascinating, it seemed to relay a warning of sorts whilst simultaneously being impossibly chic to the point of detachment. It confounded audiences and critics alike and announced once and for all that Leonard Cohen was looking toward the future rather than the past .

42
PUBLIC ENEMY
Bring The Noise/Sophisticated
32
Def Jam

Not since the Sex Pistols had gatecrashed the music industry had a group caused such an exciting frisson. Public Enemy split the public into a definite for or against lobby - to their supporters they displayed intelligence, strength and integrity, they told it how they saw it and told it straight. They were an emotional lightning rod to the feelings of alienated people sickened by the system and on top of that they sounded, by virtue of their in-house DJs ' The Bomb Squad', vital and explosive. For those lined up against them their use of Black Power symbolism and uniforms, their anti-authoritarianism and pro-Nation of Islam stance saw them cast in the role of dangerous subversives. These people tended not to like Hip-hop as a whole it is true to say and 'Bring the Noise' was a superb clarion call to those who cared to listen and frightening for those already critical of the group's aims.

It acts as a retort to the group's critics and a declaration of the group's belief in its inherent power. Shout outs are delivered to Louis Farrakhan and a number of Hip-hop artists as well as Sonny Bono and Yoko Ono. The music is created from samples, most prominently James Brown and Funkadelic. It is an abrasive, orgiastic feast of dissonant noise with beats.

41
INNER CITY
Good Life (Magic Juans Mix)/
(Mayday Club Mix)/
Big Fun (LA Big Fun Mix)
4
10 Records

Detroit techno innovator Kevin Saunderson teamed up with vocalist Paris Grey and the musical stars were immediately in close alignment. They quickly wrote and recorded and the result was 'Good Life', a veritable club anthem that managed to combine a sensational melody with street-smart smouldering funkiness and upbeat, uplifting lyrics. Flawless production and an authoritative exultant vocal steeped in soul were the icing on the cake of a record that appealed to ravers and dance-around-the-handbags traditionalists in equal measure. Mixes by

Saunderson's Belleville 3 associates Juan Atkins and Derrick May were further reasons to be cheerful.

40
STEVE EARLE
Copperhead Road/Little Sister
45
MCA

Steve Earle was a rootsy rocker whose songs encapsulated the outlaw, country music sound. 'Copperhead Road ' is the kind of taut storytelling song that the likes of Bruce Springsteen have tried to master without success. It is a mongrel of a track incorporating celtic instrumentation and pounding rock drums to colour the tale. It has a wilful ,near feral quality and is told in the first person in the character of John Lee Pettimore a third generation producer and smuggler of moonshine in Tennessee. This outlaw life brings problems from the authorities and his father is killed in a crash following a police pursuit, 'you could smell the whiskey burnin on Copperhead Road' Earle notes. In the aftermath the narrator enlists as a marine and serves two tours of duty in Vietnam. He returns to a place with few honest prospects and fetches marijuana seeds from Columbia and Mexico which he hopes to turn into a cash crop. Overhead the Drug Enforcement Agency helicopters search for his crop and the dance begins again .

39
SONIC YOUTH
Teenage Riot/Silver Rocket/
Kissability
No Chart Placing
Blast First

From the opening sounds of unorthodoxly-tuned guitars, this is trippy and odd. Beneath the guitars Kim Gordon incants some kind of ritualistic invocation and then the drums crack and the song moves up several gears. The guitars sound even stranger, like duelling lawnmowers, as Thurston Moore takes up the vocal which seems to come from a dream where J Mascis of Dinosaur Jr is elected president of the United States! The song seems to rattle like a trolley bus but it is truly compelling and the traditional pop structure of verse and chorus feels charming here in the manner of a beloved half-remembered children's nursery rhyme.

38
ROYAL HOUSE
Can You Party (Club Mix)/
(Instrumental Dub Mix)/
(Original Mix)
14
Champion

Todd Terry, here under the moniker Royal House, created this rave-era classic pulling together a selection of samples, most notably Marshall Jefferson's 'Move Your Body'. His use of hard-hitting, lean percussion sounds make the track as propulsive as if it were powered by pistons. The music created is electronic and the track's atmospherics are alive with electrical currents - it is euphoria captured on vinyl. The chanted question of 'Can you feel it ?' refers to both the power of the music and chemical stimulation.

37
YAZZ AND
THE PLASTIC POPULATION
The Only Way Is Up/Bad House
1
Big Life

Yazz had co-written and sung on the top 10 hit 'Doctorin' The House' with Jonathan Moore and Matt Black but credited to Coldcut. The same team reassembled for what would be the debut Yazz single. They took a song recorded by Otis Clay that was big on the eighties Northern Soul scene and gave it a Hi-NRG/House makeover. Yazz added a vocal full of enthusiasm and positivity that chimed perfectly with the songs message of uplifting self-empowerment to create an era defining mini classic .

36
WORLD DOMINATION
ENTERPRISES
I Can't Live Without My Radio/
(Original Style)
No Chart Placing
Product

LL Cool J's hit written with Rick Rubin is dragged through the backstreet and beaten up brutally. Remixed by Robert Gordon, who would found the seminal Warp Records label. At this time there was huge acclaim for Big Black who were doing similar work to this. Perhaps because they were American they seemed cooler however the truth was this unholy-sounding bunch of low-life Londoners who espoused anti-authoritarian free thought, were even more thrilling and visceral in their reshaping of musical forms.

35
KEVIN ROWLAND
Tonight/Kevin Rowland's Band
81
Mercury

I'd loved Dexys Midnight Runners but it was no surprise when they simply ceased to be. Their 1986 album *Don't Stand Me Down* was universally panned at the time, as were the individuals responsible for it. Dexys were ridiculed and abused by the music press to the point that they were the target of a feeding frenzy. Helen O'Hara and Billy Adams could take no more and quit in 1987, Kevin Rowland now recorded a solo album named *The Wanderer* and improbably recruited Eumir Deodarto of the jazz-disco hit 'Also Sprach Zarathustra'-fame to produce and pedal steel guitarist Eric Weissberg who had found fame with 'Dueling Banjos'. The album was excellent and this single taken from it was superb. It found Rowland in fine conversational voice melding seemingly incompatible influences from country, jazz, disco and soul with his distinctive bold song craft and knack for conjuring memorable choruses with potentially huge appeal. Sadly a lack of radio support saw 'Tonight' slip through the cracks

34
PRINCE
Glam Slam/Escape
29
Paisley Park

Not one of Prince's most outstanding and remarkable singles but equally a record I cannot sniffily dismiss. This is denser sounding and more complex than much of his work of the era although that doesn't equate to an absence of melody but it is a demonstration of the artist being at the height of his powers as he ponders the relationship between sexuality and spirituality and injects a massive irrepressible chorus into proceedings. The B side is also of note, 'Escape' is a kind of musical cousin of Glam Slam but is given a stripped-back dance rhythm and a lyric that is anti-gang , anti-violence and anti-drugs .

33
MORRISSEY
Everyday Is Like Sunday/
Disappointed
9 (2010 - 4)
HMV

Johnny Marr's courageous decision to walk away from The Smiths, just as they seemed poised for world domination, broke the hearts of poetry reading, cardigan-wearing, pseudo-sensitive types across the world. Fortunately their hero in horn-rimmed spectacles dusted himself off and embarked upon a lucrative solo career. Morrissey hooked up with producer Stephen Street, brought in Durutti Column guitarist Vini Reilly as a musical foil and with his first solo single 'Suedehead' even a cynic such as I had to concede that, taken purely on its musical merits, it was very good.

Moreover this proved not to be a flash in the pan as for this second single I found, much to my chagrin, that I enjoyed it enormously. Inspired by Neville Shute's 1959 novel *On the Beach* Morrissey penned a beautiful lyric about a tatty seaside resort that had somehow survived a nuclear holocaust. It was aching and tender as well as being blessed with sensitive musical performances and production, while a strong vocal full of melancholic sentiment captured the bleak scene to perfection.

32
JUNGLE BROTHERS
I'll House You (Gee Street
Reconstruction Mix)/(Instrumental)
22 (1998 - 26)
Gee Street

Jungle Brothers were a New York Hip-hop outfit fusing their raps with jazz grooves when they took the bold step of working with House producer Todd Terry on the track ' 'll House You' and in doing so emerged with a bristling livewire sound that bounced. It took the Hip-House sound into the charts as well as being a dance-floor classic and although Hip-hop purists dissed The Jungle Brothers for their supposed treachery, this vibrant record spoke for itself - it rocked.

31
THE WILD BUNCH
Friends And Countrymen/
Machine Gun (Down By Law)
No Chart Placing
4th & Broadway

Bristol Hip-hop collective the Wild Bunch were on the cusp of a musical revolution. Among their number were Robert Del Naja, Grant Marshall and Andrew Vowles who would go on to form Massive Attack. Also in their number was a very young Tricky and future Soul to Soul leader Nellee Hooper. Utilising a love of literature, graffiti art, punk, reggae, soul and politics, here on their second and final single release they quote Julius Caesar in the title. They slow the beats to a crawl, allow lots of space with a bass that hints at dub reggae. Del Naja's voice is prominent and very un-American as he spits out lyrics that are aimed at provoking thought rather than starting a party.

30
THE POGUES
Yeah Yeah Yeah/
The Limerick Rake
43
Pogue Mahone

The Pogues made a stylistic U-turn with 'Yeah Yeah Yeah', this was a straightforward good time number that dispensed with the bows and fiddles in favour of a huge crunching drum-powered sound with horns and guitars to the fore. Lest it be forgotten, The Pogues roots were in punk and this is full of wild punk energy although stylistically it harks further back to the sound of sixties beat groups such as Them and The Pretty Things .

29
DUB SEX
The Underneath/
Every Secret (That I Ever Made)/
Caved In/Instead Of Flowers
No Chart Placing
Cut Deep

I would see Dub Sex often and found them compelling. They were a unique proposition and quite out of step with perceived cool, indeed Dub Sex were not cool, they were too vividly real and without airs and graces to be cool. They were wound up so tightly, it felt like they were struggling to contain their emotions, as if they were holding on by their fingernails. As a front man Mark Hoyle was extraordinary, his passions boiling over, he twitched and jerked as words leapt from his seemingly parched throat. Their sound was taut and hard, it had the sharpness of razor blades, I was most impressed.

They shouldn't have been able to capture these qualities on record, it is notoriously difficult to accomplish that feat, thankfully they did here and sparks fly as this record plays.

28
JESUS AND MARY CHAIN
Sidewalking/Taste Of Cindy
30
Blanco Y Negro

This was a major deviation from the sound of the early JAMC singles, here they play to an enormous bass throb over drums sampled from a Hip-hop record (Roxanne's Revenge by Roxanne Shanté) , the vocal is delivered nonchalantly with a cool disdain for showbiz show-off orthodoxy and Duane Eddy like rock 'n' roll guitars add yet another flavour of sonic seasoning .

27
SMITH & MIGHTY
Walk On (Vocals)/(Mellow Mix)/ Traveling/Different Chapter
80
Three Stripe

Pioneers of the Bristol sound, Smith & Mighty released this debut single in 1988 as well as producing 'Any Love', the first Massive Attack single. Here they serve up the Bacharach and David classic 'Walk On By' in a slow and low style mixing dub elements and dance beats with a smouldering vocal from Jackie Jackson. 'Traveling' and it's dubbed part 2 'Different Chapter' were even more impressive on the flip side.

26
N.W.A
Fuck Tha Police/Fuck Tha Police
No Chart Pacing
Not On Any Named Label

I don't know how legitimate this release was but it certainly existed as a single and was every bit as brilliantly incendiary as its title suggests. It is presented as a court hearing with the LA Police department on trial. Dr Dre acts as the magistrate and Ice Cube, MC Ren and Easy E offer testimony against the force detailing examples of racial prejudice and brutality. No punches are pulled and the rhythm is popping and pumping. There is no let up from start to finish and when the police defendant is found guilty of being a 'redneck, white bread, chickenshit motherfucker', he yells obscenities and protests his innocence as he is led from the court.

25
FAITH NO MORE
We Care A Lot/Spirit/ Chinese Arithmetic
53
Slash/London American Recordings

With its killer bass line demanding attention, this hybrid of punk, rap, funk and metal introduced Americans Faith No More to a European audience and made us grin as we digested the lyrical content shouted out by the group's original singer Chuck Moseley deliciously satirising the fake compassion of multi-millionaire pop stars crying crocodile tears and asking their audience to cough up to appease their social conscience. Smug pomposity was skewered as a whole list of causes were listed that the pampered namby-pamby A-Listers professed to care a lot about from floods and fires to disease and drugs the list ran with perhaps the most pertinent line being 'we care a lot about starvation and the food that Live Aid bought' oh yes they cared a lot.

24
PET SHOP BOYS
Heart/I Get Excited
(You Get Excited Too)
1
Parlophone

As straightforward a love song as The Pet Shop Boys ever released 'Heart' is nonetheless utterly fabulous. An up-tempo dance track that was originally conceived to be offered to Hazel Dean, or audaciously Madonna, ultimately it proved to be a keeper and though not one of the Pet Shop Boys' greatest songs it is, because the two things are different, one of their best records .

23
NEIL YOUNG
& THE BLUENOTES
This Notes For You (Edited Live Version)/(LP Version)
No Chart Placing
Reprise

The ever-restless Neil Young had put together a large R&B band replete with a horn section and he was invigorated by the change of style. The band swaggered, strutted and grooved hard, Neil hit striking guitar licks and from his tongue came this acid-flecked condemnation of the money-obsessed music scene was delivered. "I ain't singing for Pepsi, I ain't singing for Coke" is the opening lyric and scorn is poured on those who sell their music for the corporate dollar as his own refusal to follow suit is avowed. It is a spine-tingling performance and caused quite a furore. A video that accompanied the single that parodied Michael Jackson being set on fire whilst shooting a commercial saw threats of legal action and MTV impose a ban on it. Neil, the old sixties hippy, was once again displaying his rebel spirit and ability to provoke debate .

22
WOMACK AND WOMACK
Teardrops/
Conscious Of My Conscious
3
Island

'Teardrops' is a song about the regret being felt by its narrator at the end of a relationship. Everything that had been a shared pleasure is now a painful memory that brings tears to the eyes, even music holds no consolation because it has too many associations with the feeling of loss. The musical arrangement of the song is fabulous, there is a real lightness of touch displayed, it is as if there is a dislocation between each note, a gap filled by the plaintive vocal supplied by Linda Womack that pulls the heartstrings as beneath her the superlative percussion track gives the track a delicate but highly funky buoyancy.

21
PRINCE
I Wish U Heaven/Scarlett Pussy
24
Paisley Park

Running at over ten minutes 'I Wish U Heaven' is a suite consisting of three distinct parts. It is lyrically very slight and is a spiritual tribute to a profound celestial love, all kinds of flavours are included in the track from psychedelic-tinged ornate pop to Avant Garde funk. Prince sermonises atop a stabbed keyboard and heavily treated horns and in lesser hands a track this ambitious might well have seemed ludicrous or just plain boring but the purple one pulls it off with considerable ease and this is a sumptuous pleasure. The B side 'Scarlet Pussy ' is credited to Prince's female alter-ego Camille and is a snaking funk piece full of cat related sexual metaphors .

20
PATTI SMITH
People Have The Power
Where Duty Calls/Wild Leaves
97
Arista

Written with her husband Fred 'Sonic' Smith, 'People have the Power' was Patti Smith's first single following the 9 year gap she took raising her children in Detroit. It is an uncynical, open-hearted and optimistic rallying cry for people to band together against oppressors and use the strength of unity to elicit change. It is possessed of great positivity and compassion no doubt inspired by the desire and hope that the world could be made a better place for her children and other people's children, It was good to have Patti Smith's strong voice returned to us and, as she correctly states, 'people have the power, to dream'.

19
NENEH CHERRY
Buffalo Stance/(Scratchapella)/(Instrumental)/(Electro Ski Mix)
3
Virgin

'Buffalo Stance' was the first solo single by Neneh Cherry who I'd seen, enjoyed, and admired when she had been the vocalist for Rip Rig + Panic. It was a striking single with a great soundscape created by producers Tim Simenon of Bomb the Bass and Mark Saunders. Existing somewhere between hip-hop and the kind of electro that had presaged it, this had a highly confident swagger and Cherry's vocal performance was electrifying. She playfully danced across the rhythms with nonchalant ease singing a lyric that spoke of having the confidence to be expressive right down to the way a person stands. It was a manifesto concerned with personal empowerment and street smarts and its rising chorus encapsulated the feeling. I saw her perform this song while heavily pregnant at The Ritz as part of an On-U-Sound revue and she was strong at ease and an inspiration.

18
PUBLIC ENEMY
Night Of The Living Baseheads (Anti High Blood Pressure Encounter Mix) / (Terminator X Meets Dst & Chuck Chillout Instrumental Mix) / Terminator X To The Edge Of Panic (No Need To Panic Radio Version)/ The Edge Of Panic
No Chart Placing
Def Jam

Public Enemy had the power, they had the fury and ferocity, they seemingly had a surfeit of energy but they could never be accused of being a blunt instrument. In their music there were high levels of intelligence, humour and art and even here, in a song of grim depressing reality, that fact is evident. 'Night of the Living Baseheads' is constructed using a total of twenty samples, most notably from James Brown's' 'The Grunt' which provides its propulsive riff. It opens with Nation of Islam spokesman Khalid Muhammad speaking about the black communities ancestors being brought to America as slaves, being robbed of their language, culture, religion and in some cases their minds and Chuck D follows up addressing the effects the crack cocaine epidemic is having on black communities. A chorus of 'how low can you go?' is arrived at and on this occasion it is not equated to dancing but instead to the levels of degradation that addiction reduces people to. The songs title reflects the sadness of the situation, twisting the title of the horror film *Night Of the Living Dead* and substituting the crack addicts, known as baseheads, for zombies.

17
WIRE
Kidney Bingos/Over Theirs/ Drill/Pieta
88
Mute

A repeated chiming guitar figure and a chunky rhythmical structure gives 'Kidney Bingos' a pleasant, if peculiar, poppy bounce. This is countered by a stream of consciousness lyric sung with an air of sadness and introspection by Colin Newman which is arresting and atmospheric. Wire remained as intriguing as they had ever been even as they grew to be ever more melodic and accessible.

16
COWBOY JUNKIES
Sweet Jane/200 More Miles
No Chart Placing
Cooking Vinyl

'Sweet Jane' had attracted plenty of cover versions that used the classic riffing evident on The Velvet Underground's studio take of the song however Cowboy Junkies opted to base their recording on the live version that pre-dates it. As a consequence their arrangement dispenses with the famous riff, it is slower, quieter and more delicate, it is treated as a sacred tract, almost hymn like and country tinged. Sung with empathy for the song's characters, it is beautiful, little wonder that the song's author Lou Reed stated on several occasions that this was his favourite version of the song .

15
BOOGIE DOWN PRODUCTIONS
Stop The Violence/(Instrumental)
No Chart Placing
Jive

DJ Scott La Rock had been murdered in 1987 an event that had a profound effect on his BDP cohort KRS1 who henceforth would incorporate socially-conscious themes with a message of positivity into his lyrics. 'Stop The Violence' was an eloquent take on the negativity that had been allowed to take a hold in the Hip-hop community and offered a wider perspective on the way minority groups are pitted against each other by the powerful as a way to maintain control.

14
MY BLOODY VALENTINE
You Made Me Realise/Slow
No Chart Placing
Creation

Raw and dissonant: a wall of noise is created without sacrificing melody and the verse/chorus structure of the song. Nevertheless there is a middle eight consisting of pure noise which is openly hostile in its intent and execution. What is for sure is, the manner in which the song is approached is most certainly not traditional; the guitars are drenched in reverb and other sonic effects are used as a weapon to express a non-conformist attitude, the effect is absolutely thrilling.

13
HAPPY MONDAYS
Wrote For Luck/Boom
68
Factory

Musically speaking The Happy Mondays had travelled a long way in not much time and from initially seeming a little lumpen and plodding now, under the tutelage of genius producer Martin Hannett, they began to funk. What had always been a component in their sound now began to sound like a Mancunian version of Chicago House. Here too Shaun Ryder comes into his own - his voice is unlovely by any conventional understanding of singing but it is delightfully real and absolutely authentic and is perfect for the aesthetic values of the Mondays. His lyricism is splendid too, its meaning is not clear, nothing is blatant but the implication is that 'Wrote For Luck' is a song connected to drug usage and dealing. The Mondays were capturing the Zeitgeist, as surely as The Beatles and Stones provided the soundtrack to the first summer of Love, this second coming cast The Mondays in the role of Satanic Majesties and Merry Pranksters .

12
A GUY CALLED GERALD
Voodoo Ray/Escape/Rhapsody In Acid / Blow Your House Down
12
Rham

Gerald Simpson was a music obsessive who immersed himself in Black music culture firstly through his father's reggae record collection and later through the Manchester clubs and specialist record shops that schooled him in electro-funk, Hip-hop, and Techno. He was an important early member of 808 State before leaving to concentrate on his own music and in his bedroom studio he created 'Voodoo Ray' credited as being the first UK Acid House record. It was hypnotic, strange, spacey and very compelling. It received its first plays at The Hacienda and began a long slow rise in sales as it was spoken about in awed tones until it hit the charts in 1989.

11
ERASURE
A Little Respect/
Like Zsa Zsa Gabor
4
Mute

Erasure's brand of dance-pop reached its zenith with 'A Little Respect'. Here they perfected the formula for a kind of pop that touches people's soul and moves them so that they can't help but react to the song in joyous communion with the band, bellowing the chorus out with passion at the top of their voice. Vince Clarke's fusion of synthesisers, programmed drums and acoustic guitar is close to perfection and Andy Bell's singing is inspired, nuanced during the verses before he unleashes his magnificent falsetto during the choruses ,

10
TALKING HEADS
(Nothing But) Flowers
Ruby Dear (Bush Mix)
79
EMI

Talking Heads would split up soon, ending a remarkably fertile decade of music that managed to be both cerebral and highly entertaining. With former Smiths guitarist Johnny Marr roped into the fold there was still time for this cheerful almost tropical sounding single that brought the curtain down. David Byrne sings from the viewpoint of a man in a post-apocalyptic landscape yearning for all the harmful things that brought about an ecological disaster: cars, factories, shopping malls and even lawn mowers are pined for and lovingly recalled. The irony is deliberately heavy and the absurdity would be funny if the scenario wasn't even more pertinent and worrying in the here and now thirty-odd years later.

9
BOOGIE DOWN PRODUCTIONS
My Philosophy (Extended) / (LP Version) / (Single Edit) / (Instrumental)
No Chart Placing
Jive

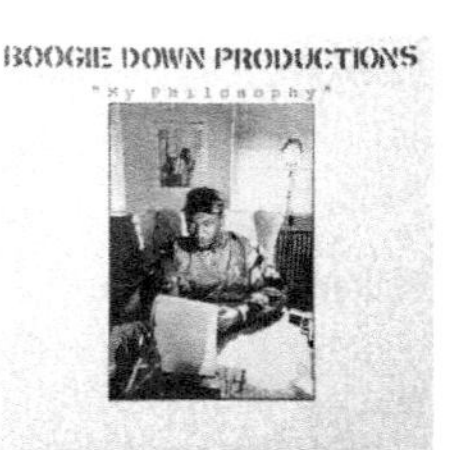

Challenging stereotypes and encouraging fellow Hip-hop artists to do some thinking to reflect and consider using the form to express themselves in ways outside dissing each other and glorifying violence, this track is stark apart from samples taken from Milt Jackson and Stanley Turrentine. All KRS1 requires is a hard-hitting drum loop over which he calmly and smoothly lays his rap to devastating effect .

8
PET SHOP BOYS
Left To My Own Devices
The Sound Of The Atom Splitting
4
Parlophone

With Trevor Horn producing, 'Left to my own Devices' is given a luscious orchestrated soundscape; strings sweep over the pulsing synth rhythm in a dramatic fashion whilst Neil Tennant takes us on a semi-autobiographical tour of a day in his life from inside his head. He muses over his options and daydreams, his thoughts becoming evermore colourful and abstract, name checking Debussy and Che Guevara who at some point drinks tea with him. Yet again Pet Shop Boys deliver a chorus that is absolutely irresistible and demands the listener's participation.

7
PRINCE
Alphabet Street
(This Is Not Music This Is A Trip)
9
Paisley Park

'Alphabet Street' was conceived initially as a guitar blues song and it retains its warped Bo Diddley rhythm. Along the way it took on a dance sensibility and samples are used as Prince incorporates new styles into his music. There are fevered gospel-infused backing vocals and a vamp that features a rap section performed by Cat Glover. Prince himself positively struts and swaggers through his own vocal performance, he is completely assured as he sets out to seduce and spread his message of spiritual love springing from the acting upon of carnal desire.

6
THE PIXIES
Gigantic (New Version)
River Euphrates (New Version) / Vamos /
In Heaven (The Lady In The Radiator Song)
No Chart Placing
4AD

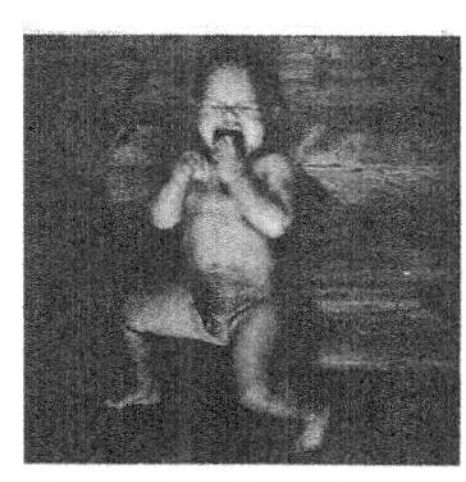

Oh boy! How I loved the Pixies at this point in time, their mix of seemingly unhinged strangeness and their gentle and then explosive dynamics had me well and truly hooked. Also fascinating was the interplay between lead voice Black Francis and Kim Deal or as we knew her then Mrs John Murphy. There was something discernibly volatile in the chemistry between them. 'Gigantic' was the first single release by the group. It was a song that had been on the album *Surfer Rosa* produced by Steve Albini, now it was re-recorded with Gil Norton producing specifically for release as a single. Written by Deal and Francis it is sung by the former and is a creepy, voyeuristic tale of a woman watching a black man making love to a white woman that crawls through its repetitive verses on the back of a simple but completely compelling bass line before all hell breaks loose on the chorus which is, of course, absolutely gigantic.

5
BEATNIGS
Television (Extended Mix) (Dub Mix)/(Radio Mix)/ Jazzy Beats
No Chart Placing
Alternative Tentacles

The Beatnigs were a San Francisco band who operated as an abstract industrial jazz and poetry collective yet combined hardcore punk and hip-hop as sonic elements in their work. 'Television' was their most famous track with a lyric written by Michael Franti for this single release. It was beefed up with a mix by Adrian Sherwood, Mark Stewart, and Gary Clail and released on former Dead Kennedy Jello Biafra's Alternative Tentacles label. It is an intelligent, articulate and accurate condemnation of thought-control through the medium of television and has all the socially conscious anger of The Last Poets combined with the sonics of Cabaret Voltaire and the experimental industrial noise of early Faust.

4
GO BETWEENS
Streets Of Your Town
Wait Until June
80 (1989 - 82)
Beggars Banquet

'Surely this one will get the Go Betweens a hit and the recognition they deserve,' I thought and although it got radio exposure and has become their best-known song, it failed to give the band the lift in fortunes they needed and they remained in a ghetto populated by also rans, marginal and irrelevant to the wider world. This song, and the recording of it is wonderful, was essentially one big circular chorus that was shimmering and sunny. Amanda Brown provided a glorious backing vocal to compliment and bolster Grant McLennan's lead, bassist John Willsteed offered a Spanish-styled acoustic guitar solo that sat beautifully in the songs midst, meanwhile McLennan sang about Brisbane though his imagery evoking the kind of town recognisable the world over - one that is mundane, humdrum and stifling but also a place of real and repressed violence. "Watch the butcher sharpen his knives, and this town is full of battered wives" is one lyrical couplet that displays the unpleasant underbelly of seemingly ordered civilised suburbia .

3
MUDHONEY
Touch Me I'm Sick
Sweet Young Thing Ain't Sweet No More
No Chart Placing
Sub Pop

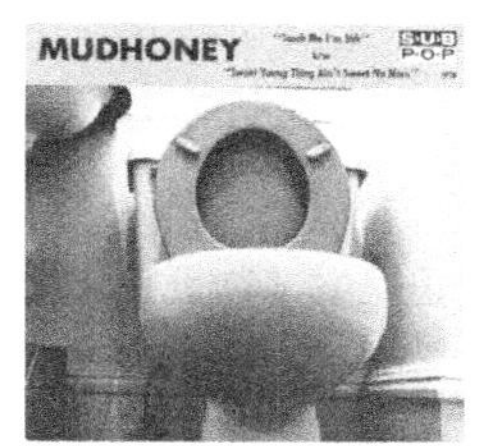

This record may not have been the first of a new breed of bands playing what came to be known as grunge but without a doubt this was the record that gave inspiration to many of those bands, it raised the bar and set the standard. 'Touch me I'm Sick' was the first classic of grunge, it turned eyes and ears towards the city of Seattle and towards the little independent label it was released on, Sub Pop, would soon become the hippest, most happening label in the world.

'Touch me I'm Sick ' was never supposed to be the A side of this record and possibly that fact lent the recording an off the cuff spontaneity and subversive mischievousness. It is a song built around the catchphrase that gives the song its title - its verses are about seduction, sex and disease. The narrator is contagious and intent on pollution of one person in particular and possibly of society as a whole. The structure of the song is basically that of sixties garage rock but it is played with astonishing power - it is fuzzy, distorted and dirty. Singer Mark Arm meanwhile performs with complete irreverence in a wild, pushing-everything-to-the-limits style. He parodies and mocks a series of rock music stereotypes and the result is two minutes of mayhem that is terrifically exciting and explosive.

2
PUBLIC ENEMY
Don't Believe The Hype
Prophets Of Rage & The Rhythm The Rebel
18
Def Jam

'Don't Believe the Hype' is a riposte to media manipulation and thought control. It rebukes the lies, distortions, and agendas of those who control the channels of communication and information. James Brown is again heavily sampled by the Bomb Squad to create a whistling, funky backing for Chuck D to lay bare his grievances in powerful style and Flavor Flav to add unpredictability and a measure of surrealism into the mix. Public Enemy were truly at the height of their considerable powers, they knew their history and learned lessons from it. They evoked the spirits of John Coltrane and James Brown to give their sound rhythm, fire, and fearless creativity. They took inspiration from Nation of Islam figures such as Malcolm X and Louis Farrakhan and transferred the ideas and principles of these teachers into lyrics aimed at inspiring and empowering their audience and community in a positive, constructive manner. They operated in the field of popular culture where so much that is served up is merely a disposable commodity yet Public Enemy were creating music that genuinely mattered - they were at this point the most essential group of musicians on the planet .

1
NICK CAVE AND THE BAD SEEDS
The Mercy Seat
New Day
86
Mute

This is a towering epic of a song. Written by Cave himself it goes to the heart of the relationship between the rule of law and Christian forgiveness set to a sonic musical juggernaut that amplifies the lyrical content written by Mick Harvey. 'The Mercy Seat 'of the title is both a nickname for the electric chair and in the Old Testament was the throne of God over the Ark of the Covenant. The song juxtaposes the two and is set in a condemned man's cell in the hours before his execution. As he contemplates his impending death there are numerous allusions to scripture and repeated use of the lines "an eye for an eye and a tooth for a tooth, and anyway I told the truth, and I'm not afraid to die". Cave sings with compelling conviction and the levels of intensity rise to feverish proportions as the music matches him in an unhinged frenzy of violin and drums. It is an exhausting performance and an exhausting listen, akin to being hit repeatedly with a tidal wave of emotion, it is ultimately a staggering and brilliant record .

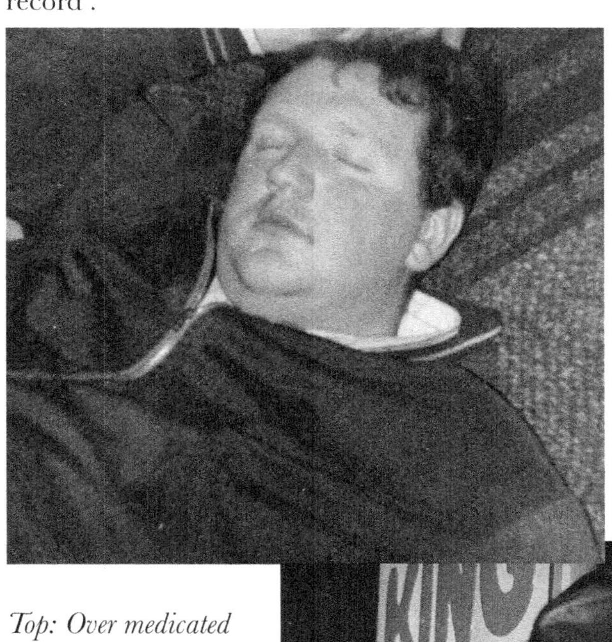

Top: Over medicated and crashed out mid 80s

Right: In Paris with the hangover from hell

1989

This was a year that pulled at the heartstrings. Huge political and social changes took place across Europe as people power toppled the old order in the Eastern Bloc. Overnight the news became the most compelling programme on television as we viewed footage from Poland and Hungary that showed that the repression imposed upon them by the Soviet Union was coming to an end. How I rejoiced at the Velvet Revolution in Czechoslovakia and the overthrow of the brutal dictatorship of Nicolae Ceaușescu in Romania. Yet the most visible sign that this was a seismic change was the collapse of the state apparatus in East Germany and the euphoria when the vile and evil symbol of repression, The Berlin Wall, was toppled among highly emotional scenes of euphoric celebration. Change was also on its way in South Africa where the government of the newly elected F.W. de Klerk began dismantling the apartheid system.

Not all protests went smoothly as the world watched peaceful protests in Tiananmen Square, Beijing, put down by the Communist government by troops and tanks. They massacred thousands of innocent people, impervious to the watching world. That, along with the terror attacks on the twin towers of the world trade centre, have been the most horrible and terrifying atrocities I have witnessed in my lifetime. I sobbed uncontrollably at the pain and suffering inflicted and the realisation that man's inhumanity towards others was more than a catchphrase, it was a bitter truth. We had been taught a harsh lesson in reality .

In my personal life I found myself liked and respected at work and enjoyed relative stability on the home front. I travelled to Yugoslavia, which was an awe-inspiring place to visit - beautiful and largely unspoilt. Its racial and cultural diversity appeared to be an asset but of course that superficial outsider's view would prove to be horribly inaccurate as tensions were already boiling over that a few years later they would escalate into full scale civil war. I also visited New York for the first time. To go to America for a holiday had seemed a remote fantasy but my friend Gene persuaded me of the feasibility of the trip and it was everything that I ever imagined. I loved it and felt very at home, the place was like a giant adult adventure playground and I had few inhibitions and a voracious appetite for new experiences. I wasn't always on my best behaviour but as always the only person I ever hurt was myself. It helped that The Mekons, who I was friendly with and who were one of my favourite bands, were in town playing a series of shows and I hung out with them; they were great fun to be around, I even got to join them onstage in Philadelphia adding my voice to the classic 'Where Were You'!

NOTABLE EVENTS

George H W Bush becomes the 41st president of the United States

Murderer Ted Bundy is executed using the Electric Chair

Eurosport begins broadcasting from France

Ayatollah Khomeini, the supreme leader of Iran, issues a *fatwa* calling for the death of author Salman Rushdie for the supposed blasphemy of his novel *The Satanic Verses.*

Super Tanker Exxon Valdez spills 240,000 barrels of crude oil on the coast of Alaska

Thatcher's vile government introduce the Poll Tax which spark riots in central London and lead to protest movements across the country. It is the beginning of the end for Mrs T.

The Hillsborough disaster at the FA Cup semi final in Sheffield claims the lives of 94 Liverpool supporters. Three more die later. The police and elements in the media collude to wrongly place the entire blame on Liverpool supporters.

In June the Chinese state murders thousands of its young for the treasonable act of peacefully protesting in Tiananmen Square Beijing.

In Tel Aviv, the first Palestinian suicide bombing against Israel takes place

Nintendo releases the Game Boy

51 people aboard the *Marchioness* pleasure cruiser lose their lives as it collides with a dredger on the River Thames in central London

2 million people from Latvia, Estonia and Lithuania join hands to form an unbroken 600km human chain as they seek independence from the Soviet Union

Hungary removes border restrictions with Austria. It is the first crack in the Iron Curtain

Tadeusz Mazowiecki of the trade union movement Solidarity is elected prime minister of Poland.

The Dalai Lama is awarded the Nobel Peace Prize

The Guildford Four, wrongly convicted of the IRA bombing of five pubs in the Surrey town, are released from prison after a miscarriage of justice that has lasted 14 years.

In Bhagalpur, India, religious fuelled violence leaves nearly 1000 people dead

In November the hard-line East German communist party topples and checkpoints at the Berlin wall are opened. As people flood out to the west, the hated wall is torn down by Berliners.

That same month the communist government of Czechoslovakia is overthrown in a non-violent revolution.

In Romania the army join mass protests and dictators Nicolae and Elana Ceaușescu attempt to flee but are captured , tried and executed on Christmas Day.

Riots break out in Hong Kong as the government begins forcible repatriation of Vietnamese refugees.

Arsenal win the 1988-89 First Division title in the final minute of the season, beating Liverpool 2-0 at Anfield. Liverpool win an emotional cup final 3-2 against local rivals Everton.

Manchester United finish 13th in the league and start the new season in confident mood beating champions Arsenal 4-1 at Old Trafford but results quickly subside and by December a banner is seen on the K Stand that states '3 years and it's still crap - Ta-ra Fergie'. United sit one place above the relegation zone.

NOTABLE BIRTHS

Shinji Kagawa; Daniel Radcliffe; Anthony Joshua; Thomas Muller; Gareth Bale

NOTABLE DEATHS

Emperor Hirohito of Japan; Salvador Dali; John Cassavetes; Vincent Crane; Robert Mapplethorpe; Abbie Hoffman; Sugar Ray Robinson; Lucille Ball; Sergio Leone; Don Revie; John Cipollina; Laurence Olivier; Laurie Cunningham; Irving Berlin; Graham Chapman; Bette Davis; Ewan McColl; Lee Van Cleef; Samuel Beckett

NOTABLE FILMS

Monsieur Hire; Indiana Jones and the last Crusade; The Cook the Thief his Wife & her Lover; Heathers; Drugstore Cowboy; Batman; Tie me up! Tie me down!; Sex Lies And Videotape; Do The Right Thing; My Left Foot; Dead Poets Society

NOTABLE BOOKS

The Remains of the Day - Kazuo Ishiguro

Sexing The Cherry - Jeanette Winterson

The General In His Labyrinth - Gabriel Garcia Marquez

London Fields - Martin Amis

The Innocent - Ian McEwan

Canal Dreams - Iain Banks

Girls Night Out - Kathy Lette

An Awfully Big Adventure - Beryl Bainbridge

The Neon Bible - John Kennedy

Toole Killshot - Elmore Leonard

100
KING OF THE SLUMS
Bombs Away In Harpurhey/
Big Girls Blouse
No Chart Placing
Play Hard

Violin is the lead instrument, it is used malevolently and its tone is on the edge of unpleasantness. The rhythm section is clickety-clackety and make a rickety racket. The flat-voiced vocals are sarcastic in their reading of a lyric that reflects the stultifying mundanity that is undercut with a get-rich quick mentality of the working class Tories who voted like turkeys for Christmas. It encapsulates the sickness and squalor of Thatcher's little England and this is the thrilling noise of non-conformity and simmering anger about the grim and grimy state of the nation .

99
TELEVISION PERSONALITIES
Salvador Dali's Garden Party/
The Room At The Top Of The Stairs
No Chart Placing
Fire

Dan Treacy takes us firstly on a shopping trip to Kensington Market to buy a paisley shirt and Chelsea boots to wear at a party. He's welcomed by the host and realises that this is special, it is some kind of happening, an exciting glamorous affair as one would expect, this being Salvador Dali's garden party. Dennis Hopper, Jack Nicholson and Peter Fonda are all fellow attendees, as is Debbie Harry - it's all magical fun and that's exactly what it sounds like .

98
A GUY CALLED GERALD
Fx (Elevation Mix)
Eyes Of Sorrow /
Emotions Electric 2
52
Subscape

FX was the fictional name of a drug in Trevor Miller's novel *Trip City* and this track formed part of the cassette soundtrack that accompanied the book. This was another slice of high quality UK acid House from Gerald Simpson. Hear this blasting through a club sized sound system and the effect is devastating; bleeps and beats twist and turn, the track has the feel of high speed motion, the dislocated though unmistakable voice of Jocelyn Brown adds the human element that gives FX it's deep soulfulness.

97
UPTOWN
Dope On Plastic (Vocal)/
(Plastipella)/It's My Turn (Vocal)/
(Acapella)/
Dope On Plastic (Dubstramental)/
It's My Turn (Dubstramental)
No Chart Placing
Tommy Boy

Uptown was a Brooklyn rapper christened Raie Dacosta and 'Dope on Plastic' was his only ever solo release. It is though, quite rightfully, regarded as a Hip-hop classic. It is rough and tough, explosive, aggressive and genuinely funky, utilising samples from Kool and the Gang and Parliament's 'Chocolate

City'. Dope on Plastic was in turn heavily sampled itself most famously by The Prodigy for their track ' 'Weather Experience'.

96
SHELLEYAN ORPHAN
Shatter/Tar Baby
No Chart Placing
Rough Trade

Shellyan Orphan were formed by Caroline Crawley and Jemaur Tayle in Bournemouth after bonding over a mutual fondness for the music of Nick Drake and poetry of Percy Shelley. Their style was a kind of postmodern folk often utilising exotic instrumentation that lent a psychedelic pop edge to their sound. They toured with The Cure and were served by members of Kate Bush's band as auxiliary musicians on occasion and stylistically they sat between those two acts.

Caroline Crawley possessed a voice that was crystal clear and though unshowy, her range and power was evident. Here on 'Shatter' she sings of dark emotions against a theatrical sounding musical piece taken at an up-tempo pace powered by violin, oboe and prominent saxophone played by ex-Dexys man Geof Blyth. It could be categorised as a neo-Gothic rave up.

95
FORGEMASTERS
Track With No Name/Shall We
No Chart Placing
Warp

This was the first release on the seminal Warp label. Forgemasters were a trio from Sheffield, a city with a history of embracing and innovating in the field of electronic music and this release, and others that followed showed the city as a credible rival to Detroit and Chicago in terms of experimenting and pushing the sonic boundaries within dance music. What was served up with the release of 'Track With No Name' was a dark, deep and at points bleak kind of techno-house that incorporates into its futuristic sound nods to Sheffield's heavy industrialised past. It is easy to hear the ghosts of mechanical presses, hammers and anvils buried inside the groove. What came to be called trance is evident too in its bobbing, weaving and bleeping journey through space and time.

94
FATIMA MANSIONS
Only Losers Take The Bus/
(Hail And Flames)/ (Hail And Adios
Non Stop
Pumpin Party Mix)/What?
No Chart Placing
Kitchenware

For anyone who had enjoyed the melodic pop of Microdisney, the band that Cathal Coughlan had been one half of along with Sean O'Hagan, this debut single from his new band, Fatima Mansions came as an almighty shock, this was an angry howling record where the drums were hammered with gusto and guitars were wrangled like steers in a coral. Then there is Coughlan's voice - it is no exaggeration to state that it could rival that of Scott Walker in its magnificence, but here it comes with a sneer attached, as even through a lyric of colourful abstraction his point is not lost, as he sinks his teeth into the hideous snobbery and arrogance of Margaret Thatcher .

93
BOOGIE DOWN PRODUCTIONS
You Must Learn/
And You Don't Stop
No Chart Placing
Jive

Over a distinctive 70s style backing that is bright and dancer friendly, KRS1 spreads the word with clarity and deadly precision. He talks about the way the powerful like to keep the marginalized black minority uneducated and ignorant because that ignorance keeps them in their place and stops them rising and challenging the status quo. He declaims that lessons can be learnt from black history and history in general and points out the evil of the belief in racial superiority. He discusses slavery and the Nazis holocaust as they tried to wipe out the whole Jewish race and states with conviction that knowledge brings enlightenment and power. He concludes the path to self-respect and self-improvement comes from the accumulation of knowledge. In his hands Hip-hop was an intelligent and inspiring weapon in the daily war against prejudice and oppression.

92
ADRIAN BORLAND
& THE CITIZENS
Beneath The Big Wheel/
Crystalline
No Chart Placing
Play It Again Sam

Adrian Borland had led the highly touted band The Sound who were a highly intense proposition and expected to become a commercial success. When that didn't happen it became apparent that Borland was suffering a depressive mental disorder and in 1988 they split. Borland went to the Netherlands to rest and decided to stay and form a band where expectations weren't a burden. The sound he created with The Citizens was lighter and brighter, he sounded more relaxed and 'Beneath The Big Wheel' is a beautiful song - the darkness of it's lyric offset by its warmth and gentility.

91
TOM TOM CLUB
Suboceana (Boom Boom Chi
Boom Boom)/ (Instrumental)
No Chart Placing
Fontana

Haunting and hypnotic, yet gently funky with an eerie organ prominent in the mix, Chris Frantz displays all his percussion prowess whilst

Tina Weymouth shows what an underrated vocalist she is sounding spookily sensual and other worldly.

90
PUBLIC IMAGE LTD
Disappointed/Same Old Story
38
Virgin

Generally speaking P.I.L had become part of the commercial rock scene. They were somewhat over polished, opting for safe predictability rather than the wild experimentation of their original incarnation, but 'Disappointed' was an excellent return to form. John Lydon takes venomous aim at unnamed people who he regards as friends who have betrayed him, and it doesn't take Sherlock Holmes to figure out the objects of his derision are old band-mates Keith Levine and Jah Wobble. The spicy invective of the lyric is matched instrumentally by John McGeoch who, as inventive as ever, provides a master-class of chiming guitar riffs while the rock solid and powerful Bruce Smith adds beef to the track. We find Lydon adopting a quasi-operatic vocal style, supported by female gospel singers who sweeten the song and help make it very catchy.

89
S'XPRESS
Hey Music Lover (G-Oo-D Vibration Mix)/Have A Nice Day/
(Music Is My Life Mix)
6
Rhythm King

Sly Stone's ' Music Lover' is retooled in Acid style with 'Stepford Wives' sampled for the pivotal line 'yes yes, this, it's wonderful'. Billie Ray Martin of Electribe 101 lends her voice which is helium-drenched - the track is bold, brash and unapologetically poppy.

88
THE NEW AGE ORCHESTRA
Let's Dream Together
No Chart Placing
Coma

Recorded in Copenhagen, this single sided nine minutes of bliss was released in an edition of 50 and before you ask, no, I don't own a copy. Massive on the Balearic House scene it has a pleasing simplicity that doesn't in any way diminish the impact of its floating melodies aligned to a dance-orientated rhythm. One could do without the irritating simulated sex noises dubbed onto the track but if you are able to swap them in your mind for whale song for instance this is a cleansing and calming beautiful record.

87
LIZA MINNELLI
Don't Drop Bombs/(Instrumental)
46
Epic

This single combined the talents of the legendary Liza Minnelli with those of The Pet Shop Boys who are the songwriters and producers in conjunction with Julian Mendelsohn. It is a strident, up-tempo disco track that pitches Ms Minnelli in the role of a woman whose unfaithful husband, either out of guilt or malice, drops the bombshells of his infidelities upon her, leaving her to deal with the emotional fallout and consequences of his actions. Minnelli gives a strident performance over the explosive backing of The Pet Shop Boys suggesting a woman who has had enough and who is not prepared to surrender any more of her dignity to her selfish man .

86
GOODBYE MR MACKENZIE
The Rattler/
Here Comes Deacon Brodie
37
Capitol

'The Rattler' had been Edinburgh-based Goodbye Mr Mackenzie's debut single release on the independent Precious Organisation label in 1986. Now, with a major label pushing the group, what was undoubtedly their strongest song was re-recorded and this time took them just inside the top 40. The group contained guitarist John Duncan, who had once been a member of The Exploited and the excellent Blood Uncles, and keyboardist/ singer Shirley Manson, later to find fame with Garbage. Country & western sounds that have long been popular in Scotland infuse this track, it is sung by Martin Metcalf with an urgency that helps put across the lyric about taking flight, abandoning ties that bind, conveying a compulsion to move forward and not allow feet to be caught in clay. It is a song about personal freedom and its sound is suitably wide-screen and upbeat to match that concept .

85
SPACEMEN 3
Hypnotized/
Just To See You Smile (Honey Pt 2)
85
Fire

Stupendously ambitious as befits a group of sonic adventurers, Spacemen 3 take aim for the stars. They drift blissfully exploring the epic proportions of the cosmos and seem able to stretch and bend time. As they groove unhurriedly they add a prominent saxophone part into the mix that acts as a fanfare and simultaneously aligns them to the wisdom, spirituality and soul of figures such as Al Greene or The Staples singers.

84
UMO DETIC
Farenheit/Farenheit
No Chart Placing
New Zone

We had grown used to the brand of Techno that had originated in Detroit; that contained sinuous and soulful elements that displayed the heavy influence of funk in its creation. The other element in the sound originated in Europe via Kraftwerk, Neu, Cabaret Voltaire et al and now a European brand of techno began to emerge from Berlin and this track was an example. It was stripped of the funk element which made it harder, leaner, more brazen and aggressive sounding than its American cousin. The difference was striking and the result was a fresh and exciting variant of the established form.

83
VAN MORRISON
Have I Told You Lately/
Contacting My Angel
76
Mercury

Van Morrison wrote 'Have I Told You Lately' as a prayer and although his spiritual love song is more often equated with earthly love, there is no doubting its simple, heartfelt and sentimental theme of learning to express the emotions of deep love and gratitude have resonated with many of us through our lives. This, after all, is the mark of a great song and hearing it delivered in Van's inimitable style is an added pleasure.

82
SKINNY PUPPY
Testure (12" Mix)/ (S.F. Mix)/
The Second Opinion/Serpents
No Chart Placing
Capitol

Skinny Puppy were a US industrial dance rock outfit and 'Testure' is a single that finds them at their most accessible. The track is notable for the prominent use of fret-less bass and the heavy use of samples from the film *Plague Dogs*. Its subject matter is the barbarity of vivisection as animals are tortured, often pointlessly, for the ultimate aim of improving profitability for the drugs and cosmetics industries.

81
TERRENCE TRENT D'ARBY
This Side Of Love/
Sad Song For Sister Sarah Serenade
83
Columbia

Destined never to become the superstar he aspired to be, Terrence Trent D'Arby nevertheless continued to progress as a musician and writer as this single admirably demonstrated. It is a skeletal guitar funk track reminiscent of Sly and the Family Stone at the time of 'There's a Riot Goin' On'. The subject matter is of loving but being unloved and the lyricism used to express this is florid and expansive. T.T.D. of course had a magnificent and attention-grabbing vocal style and he performed this song with a swagger and complete assurance .

80
FLAMING LIPS
Drug Machine/Strychnine/
(What's So Funny About) Peace
Love & Understanding
No Chart Placing
Glitter House/Sub Pop

Flaming Lips would in time morph into a band who were melodic enough, and not so frightening, that for a while they became genuine pop stars. Here however, on the band's first single 'Drug Machine' (originally an album track titled 'Drug Machine in Heaven') the sound is extreme; guitars squeal and feedback noise fills any spaces, the drums are pulverised to create an incessant but entertaining cacophony.

Wayne Coyne is at this point yet to hit upon his style of singing in a distinctive high register and here he performs a throat shredding shouted vocal that is effective for this type of material. Soon Flaming Lips would fall in love with the wonderfully strange Butthole Surfers whose influence would lead them to embrace a more eccentric style. Once honed it bore fruit for the group both artistically and commercially.

79
RHYTHM IS RHYTHM
Beyond The Dance (Cult Mix)/
(Bizzarro Mix)/
Sinister (Trolley Mix)
No Chart Placing Transmat

Here Derrick May produced a near-flawless techno masterpiece full of depth and expressiveness. On top of functioning as brilliant dance music, this is techno as art that delves into the heart of its Detroit birthplace , taking the listener on an aural journey through the city's dark streets as unmistakeably and vivid as any movie.

78
LIGHTNING SEEDS
Pure/Fools
16
Ghetto

Ian Broudie had been a member of Big In Japan alongside both Bill Drummond and Holly Johnson and he had followed that with a stint in Original Mirrors as well as producing the likes of The Fall and Echo and the Bunnymen. Reluctant to begin a solo career through a lack of confidence, he hid behind the band name Lightning Seeds and issued his first self-penned single. 'Pure' was bright, sixties influenced, had elements of eighties sounding synth pop with a romantic lyric that featured an insanely catchy keyboard riff, it was well sung and expertly played and produced. In other words it was a perfect, high quality pop that sounded great whether it came out of transistor radios, blasted from nightclub sound systems or as an accompaniment to a ride on the waltzers at the fairground - wherever you heard it, it was guaranteed to lift spirits and lighten the mood .

77
DOG FACED HERMANS
Too Much For The Red Ticker/
Timebomb
No Chart Placing
Konkurrent

Dog Faced Hermans rose phoenix-like from the ashes of funk-punk outfit Volunteer Slavery, they maintained those twin components and added a dash of ska and global folk styles while the whole intensity level was ramped up. They played with passion and ferocity that mirrored their commitment to their art where ideas and the transference of information was more important than technical virtuosity. Singer Marion Coutts' idiosyncratic vocals were perfectly in sync with the whirlwind of sound she performed to. 'Too Much For The Red Ticker' captures the group at their non-conformist, whole hearted, free-spirited, noisy best.

76
KILLDOZER - YOW !
Lupus/Nasty
No Chart Placing
Touch And Go

I saw Killdozer play at The Boardwalk in this period and was mightily impressed; the growling the bass that hit the audience at gut level was the most prominent instrument, the music was grinding and at points so slow that it felt like it was being filtered through a thick layer of treacle, the singer growled at high volume, it was a style of singing that was at that point alien and unique. Darkly humorous and inscrutably deadpan, few bands completely commanded my attention in performance but Killdozer certainly did.

'Lupus' was the group's first single, it is well produced and displays a lighter touch than one might imagine. Taking as its subject matter the racist and bigoted author Flannery O'Connor who died of lupus, she is parodied to the point of ridicule, The B side is a cover of Janet Jackson's, 'Nasty'. Killdozer were masterful in their reinterpretations of other people's songs and this is no exception, it is hilarious.

75
SHAKESPEARE'S SISTER
Your History/Dirty Mind
7
Ffrr

'Your History' was the second Shakespeare's Sister release but the first that projected Siobhan Fahey and Marcella Detroit as a duo rather than being promoted as ex-Bananarama singer Fahey's solo project. It is a highly distinctive and somewhat eccentric slice of clever pop, absolutely full to the brim with irresistible hooks. The pair share lead vocals perfectly and seem to bounce off each other with their Gothic image to the fore. Fahey and Detroit became perceived as perfect a pairing as comediennes French and Saunders who, as Shakespeare's Sisters fame grew, would include a deliciously funny and wicked parody of the group in their TV series.

74
YELLO
Of Course I'm Lying\Oh Yeah
23
Mercury

By this stage, Yello were master craftsmen and functioned with the precision of a Swiss watch. Their electronic sounds were melded exquisitely and their songs remained divinely strange and contained a humorous streak, it was as if they were recorded under the influence of laughing gas. 'Of Course I'm Lying' is an offbeat love song performed at a languid pace with a luxurious splendour to its sound. It concerns a couple who are living within a fantasy created by the female partner. The male is spellbound and fascinated by her imaginative creation of an alternate reality. She is confident enough to admit her deception as she knows it adds layers of intrigue to their relationship and that intrigue keeps the relationship alive and at fever pitch.

73
JUNGLE BROTHERS
Black Is Black (Ultimatum Mix)/
Ultrablack/
Straight Out The Jungle/In Time
72
Gee Street

This pioneering slice of consciousness Hip-hop was dropped by Jungle Brothers with Q-Tip from A Tribe Called Quest adding his voice in brilliant style. Musically they pave the way for the emergence of De La Soul, the sound is bright and upbeat with James Brown and Gil Scott Heron being sampled. The raps embrace a message of Afro-centric pride, unity and equality and they are delivered in a measured, almost light-hearted tone rather than with anger. It was a wholly different approach to the likes of Public Enemy or N.W.A for instance, but the message was fundamentally the same .

72
TAD/PUSSY GALORE (2)
Damaged 1/Damaged 2
No Chart Placing
Sub Pop

Although Black Flag never recorded for Sub Pop, their influence ran right through the attitude and sound of the label. On this split single Tad and Pussy Galore pay tribute and put their own individual stamp on Black Flags 'Damaged 1 ' and 'Damaged 2' from their album named, almost inevitably, *Damaged*.

Tad present us with a slow, heavy, grinding take with a vocal pitched somewhere between David Thomas of Pere Ubu and Ozzie Osborne. Pussy Galore play a speedier, reedier, deranged blues that fizzes and crackles. Pussy Galore would split in 1990 and the leader, Jon Spencer, would eventually form Blues Explosion while Neil Hagerty and Jennifer Herrema would found the seminal Royal Trux whose brand of scuzzy noise and lo-fi blues rock was one of the most distinctive and influential sounds of the 90s.

71
R.E.M
Stand/Memphis Train Blues
48
Warner Brothers

'Stand' was consciously written in the style of sixties bubblegum acts such as The Archies and Banana Splits, and this was no bad thing as acting on a "first thought, best thought" principle gives the song a sense of spontaneity rarely found elsewhere in R.E.M's oeuvre. The lyrics are absurd and thrown together, yet they are gleefully sung with a hint of unhinged menace by Michael Stipe. The rest of the band play with unrestrained abandon, throwing themselves into the role of pop puppets and abandoning notions of taste and subtlety. Toward the end of the song the verses are progressively played in a higher key making the listener feel as if they are spinning out of control on a fairground ride. We are on a giddy carousel of pop! It is wonderful fun.

70
THE ORB
A Huge Ever Growing Pulsating Brain That Rules From The Centre Of The Ultraworld/
Alternate Mixes
78
Big Life

What actually constituted a single was being challenged and changed here, with the A side running to over 19 minutes in length and the total package at over 30 minutes it had a running time longer than some albums. Yet that wasn't a case of "never mind the quality feel the width", this was a fascinating and stimulating trip of a record pieced together with samples taken from science fiction sound effects albums, nature, and initially, before lawyers intervened, the voice of Minnie Riperton taken from her single 'Loving You'. This felt futuristic, space aged, it birthed Ambient House and chilling out became a part of the raving experience.

69
THE BANGLES
Eternal Flame/
What I Meant To Say
1
CBS

'Eternal Flame' was written by Bangles member Susanna Hoffs along with the song-writing team of Billy Steinberg and Tom Kelly and took inspiration from a visit to 'Graceland', the former home and resting place of Elvis Presley. There, in the garden of memories, was a small box which was supposed to contain a flame which always burned - an eternal flame. As it took shape this song bore no resemblance to other Bangles releases. Instead of bright guitar pop this was a romantic ballad. Initially rejected at a band meeting it was ultimately recorded and with the addition of a chiming keyboard part and a quirky vocal recorded by Hoffs naked in the studio, as she tried to convey a feeling of vulnerability, the track was completed. There was no doubt it was slushy and a touch maudlin yet it had an undeniable charm and loveliness and brought to mind the hits of The Carpenters. It struck a chord with people in the way only great pop music can do.

68
WOLFGANG PRESS
Assassination K-Kanserous/
Kansas/Scratch/Twister
No Chart Placing
4AD

Wolfgang Press had evolved from 70s post-punk outfits The Models through Rema Rema and The Mass. They favoured experimental noise with an industrial feel but at this point they began to incorporate friendlier dance rhythms into their music. This release came under the umbrella title of 'Kansas' and the long form 'Assasination K-Kanserous' on side A consisted of an extended and sonically expanded version of 'Kansas' which is on the flip side. It is a snaking, grooving piece with the addition of dissonant noise, meanwhile the vocal expresses nervousness and anxiety as in jumbled imagery and with a geographical juxtaposition between Dallas and Kansas the assassination of John Kennedy is imagined from the shooter's perspective.

67
FINGERS INC
Never No More Lonely/
Music Take Me Up/
Distant Planet (Club Mix)
No Chart Placing
Jack Trax

Fingers Inc was the brainchild of House Music producer Larry Heard, the group consisted of himself and singers Robert Owens and Ron Wilson. Here the track is kept simple but elegant - it is a masterful example of Heard's exemplary good taste and musical prowess. Gradually the sound builds layer upon layer, its intensity riding through natural, unforced musical progressions, meanwhile Robert Owens vocal verges on the sublime - it is emotional and deeply soulful .

66
BEASTIE BOYS
Shadrach/And What You Give Is What You Get
No Chart Placing
Capitol

The Beastie Boys earlier success had come from them adopting the roles of comic book juvenile delinquents; the brash sound of heavy beats and rock guitars that producer Rick Rubin had given them had suited the style superbly, but it was time to move on, to carry on in the same manner would be to trap themselves as caricatures forever. They moved from Brooklyn to L.A., signed to a new label and most crucially hooked up with producers The Dust Brothers. Their new material was constructed with great attention to detail and almost exclusively from samples. It was a great leap forward in terms of sophistication and experimentation and the lyrical themes followed suit. 'Shadrach' was built on a drum loop taken from rock dinosaurs Black Oak Arkansas, also prominent was a vocal sample from Sly And The Family Stone's, 'Loose Booty'. The lyric concerns the biblical story of Shadrach Meshach from the book of Daniel, but finds time to include a nod to AC/DC and an annual Brooklyn Street festival. The excitement level stayed at a fever pitch on this release and its energy was supercharged .

65
DAVID SYLVAIN
Pop Song/A Brief Conversation Ending In Divorce/
The Stigma Of Childhood (Kin)
83
Virgin

'Pop Song' was a stand-alone single that saw David Sylvian playing with the pop music form to make a point about the shallow nature of pop and pop stars. He was subverting from within as he suggested what a boring waste of life it was to buy into the pop industry's propaganda and sales pitches for vacuous facsimiles of emotional content from a procession of pretty puppets. To that end Sylvian archly performs over a bright piano accompaniment and, although he doesn't go as far as introducing a chorus into the song, it does knowingly and fiendishly contain hooks and vocal refrains to seduce and grip any casual listeners, only later will they realise the nature and intent of the song is to encourage them to think and question rather than blindly consume .

64
CARTER THE UNSTOPPABLE SEX MACHINE
Sheriff Fatman/R.S.P.C.E/
Twin Tub With Guitar/
Everybody's Happy Nowadays
23
Big Cat

Recorded in a shed in producer Simon Painter's garden, this was the moment in the proverbial sun for Jim Bob and Fruitbat aka Carter USM. They had a large street-level audience but were for a moment propelled into the national consciousness by 'Sheriff Fatman', which was big and bright and uber-catchy. It was also an unambiguous condemnation of slum landlords and their unethical modes of business practice, Nicholas Van Hoogstraten and Peter Rachman are targeted and compared to Nazi war criminal Klaus Barbie. Prince Charles and the TV program *Crossroads* get mentions too .

63
A TRIBE CALLED QUEST
Description Of A Fool (Talkie)/
(Silent)/Instrumentalism Of Fools
No Chart Placing
Jive

A Tribe Called Quest were the third part of a collective called Native Tongues along with De La Soul and Jungle Brothers. Between them they created alternative Hip-hop and though Tribe were the last of the trio to record and release music, they had listened and learned and arguably were the most influential of the three acts.

'Description of a Fool' was their debut release and immediately displayed their agenda and unique brand of progressive Hip-hop. Q-Tip created a soundscape that was deep and endlessly fascinating using a sample of Roy Ayers 'Running Away' as its core. Over the flowing rhythm the rhymes concern themselves with destructive modes of behaviour that can be defined as foolish: dealing drugs, violence against women, indeed violence of all kinds are condemned, and though the subject matter is dark the words are delivered in a calm and measured tone. This is not music that kicks in fury, it is music for the mind that sticks.

62
WIRE
Eardrum Buzz/
The Offer/It's A Boy
68
Mute

Without doubt 'Eardrum Buzz' is the single most incessantly nagging and poppy song recorded by Wire, it is as catchy as measles. Its fanfare opening heralds a delightful and full to the brim track replete with scraped guitar noises to simulate the horrible sounds that are afflicting the song's narrator, a stream of Dadaist non sequiturs form verses that each lead into the chorus that goes around and around in dizzying giddy abandon as the suffering being endured makes the vocalist grow increasingly frantic in his protestations about the endless and irritating buzzing in his eardrum.

61
THE POGUES
Misty Morning Albert Bridge/
Cotton Fields
41
Pogue Mahone

Written by Jem Finer, this was the last Pogues single to chart before Shane McGowan quit the group the following year. Here, over a stirring, majestic track, McGowan captures all the hurt and longing in Finer's painterly lyric about a man in exile missing home and a loved one. He describes himself as being in hell, that description is never expanded upon but one surmises that the subject is possibly incarcerated abroad. A simpler explanation could of course be that Finer is writing autobiographically and is describing the pressure of constant touring keeping him apart from loved ones .

60
N.W.A.
Express Yourself (Extended Mix)/
(Bonus Beats)/Straight Outta
Compton/Bitch Iz A Bitch
26
4th & Broadway

Although this track was written by Ice Cube it is performed solo by Dr Dre using a sample of Charles Wright & The Watts 103rd Rhythm Band's 1970s funk masterpiece of the same name over which he raps about free expression in opposition of radio censorship of rap music, he pointedly criticises other rap acts for recording tracks without any expletives as a way to gain radio play. It's a fair point but then on the other hand 'Express Yourself' contains no expletives either and was deemed suitable for broadcast. Maybe that irony was deliberate and pointed, either way 'Express Yourself' still managed to hit the sweet spot .

59
CHRIS ISAAK
Wicked Game/
Don't Make Me Dream About You
No Chart Placing (1991 - 10)
Reprise

This brooding ballad about fighting the impulse to fall in love with somebody who will cause hurt and damage reeks of emotional conflict has sentiments echoed by a magnificently desolate and devastating guitar part from James Calvin Wilsey. His Stratocaster seemingly wails and moans in sorrow as Isaak croons in the manner of the great Roy Orbison and to his credit lives up to the comparison. The record passed by the radio programmers and public without being noticed but after being prominently used in the David Lynch film *Wild at Heart* it gained a new lease of life and became the success it deserved to be.

58
PET SHOP BOYS
It's Alright/One Of The Crowd/
Your Funny Face
5
Parlophone

Originally recorded by Sterling Void & Paris Brightledge, produced by Marshall Jefferson and released by DJ International, the song came to the attention of The Pet Shop Boys who included a nine-minute version of it on their album *Introspective*. When it came to be released as a single it was significantly remixed with additional synthesiser parts added and an extra verse concerning environmental issues added to the lyric that already made reference to global political concerns. Where the original version of the song had ultimately been hopeful and optimistic in its message, The Pet Shop Boys here sound less sure and more cautionary. Beyond its message this was another example of the group's mastery of the pop form, it is a near perfect construction of dance rhythms and musicality with a vocal from Neil Tennant that carries emotion along with timing of impeccable precision .

57
THE BATS
Smoking Her Wings/Mastery/
Passed By
No Chart Placing
Flying Nun

Hailin from Christchurch, New Zealand, The Bats have been a consistently excellent band with a stable line up from their early eighties inception to the present day. 'Smoking Her Wings' was a highpoint single for them - it is both infectious in its neo-folk jangling and yet it has a darker, mysterious quality too. Its lyrics are oblique and sung with a touching earnestness that verges on the unsettling. Violin passages add more atmospherics and a hint of psychedelia to this strange little gem .

56
WIN
Love Units /Scary Scary
No Chart Placing
Virgin

Davey Henderson had formed Win after the demise of previous band Fire Engines. Where that band were too incendiary to achieve commercial success Win aimed to play the game (up to a point) and hopefully reap the rewards. It didn't quite work out but 'Love Units' was such a frothy eccentric concoction that feasibly it could have become a hit. The 'Love Units' in the title I imagine to be coins to insert into the slots of public telephone boxes and though the lyric is slight the sound is anything but - it marries the coke-fuelled bombast of mid-seventies T. Rex with the sleak funkiness of Sly and the Family Stone and the modernity of Prince. Hooks abound, the lead vocal is put through a strange effect and sounds like it is being bounced from a satellite and the backing vocals are wildly expansive to the point of being over the top. It is saccharin sweet and as excessive as rich chocolate sauce poured over brandy-soaked plum pudding - naughty but rather nice.

55
FRANKIE KNUCKLES
PRESENTS SATOSHI TOMILE
Tears (Vocal Edit)/
(Classical Instrumental Edit)
50
Frrr

This combination of Frankie Knuckles and New York-based Japanese producer Satoshi Tomile created a track of seamless, sophisticated, subtlety utilising piano and vibes. Add to that a lyric and vocal from Robert Owens who pours out emotion yet unyielding pride, this was House as deep and other worldly as it could go.

54
R.E.M
Get Up/Funtime
No Chart Placing
Warner Brothers

This was a single taken from the album *Green* and only available in the UK as an import from the U.S. It's a bright poppy piece with a growling guitar part, the backing vocals are inspired and lift the song and there is a breakdown where the only sound we hear are several music boxes playing - it is a magical moment. Michael Stipe is on fine singing form and his lyric is a half-serious rebuke of bassist Mike Mills for his reluctance to get out of bed and get to work. The B side is a jolly romp through Iggy Pop and David Bowie's 'Funtime' that doesn't add anything to the original but sounds like a band having fun together.

53
PRINCE
Partyman/Feel U Up
14
Paisley Park

Prince supplied the soundtrack for Tim Burton's blockbuster *Batman* movie and 'Partyman' accompanied a scene where The Joker and his henchmen deface priceless exhibits at the Gotham Art Museum. The music is suitably maniacal with humorous lyrics; it crackles with unrestrained energy and rides on a funk riff that doffs it's cap to James Brown. The showman inside Prince's personality is given free reign and he clearly enjoys himself inhabiting the role of the twisted charismatic villain.

52
JESUS AND MARY CHAIN
Head On/In The Black/
Terminal Beach
57
Blanco Y Negro

The J.A.M.C. here mixed the mechanics of a drum machine and synth bass with their more organic sound to create an absolutely driving piece of music with big fifties-flavoured guitar riffs to the fore. Their gift for melodicism had not deserted them and somehow, due to the contrasting stylistic elements existing within the same song, they sound like an unholy mash up between The Beach Boys and Joy Division - very interesting, indeed.

51
THE B52s
Love Shack
2
Reprise

The B-52s had suffered since the start of the decade. Founder member Ricky Wilson had succumbed to a H.I.V.-related illness and the band's commercial decline had been dramatic. 'Love Shack' emphatically changed that. It was given a robust sound by producer Don Was and although the eccentricity and quirky flavour of their early records was sacrificed energy and contagious fun remained. 'Love Shack' was hugely celebratory, it depicts a place where people get together, where good times bond its patrons, it is more a state of mind than a physical place. It was a bold statement of intent from the group who needed to prove to themselves, as much as anybody else, that there was a light at the end of the darkness they had been struggling through and with 'Love Shack' they did themselves justice and deserved the accolades that followed .

50
JOE STRUMMER
Gangsterville/Jewellers & Bums
91
Epic

Since The Clash had finished Strummer had produced and co-written some songs with Mick Jones for Big Audio Dynamite's second album and done some soundtrack work for the Alex Cox' movie *Walker*. Now, his confidence seemingly restored, he went to L.A., put together an American band who he dubbed The Latino Rockabilly War and recorded an album called *Earthquake Weather* that was a lot better than the final Clash album, although it was far from flawless. One of the strongest cuts was 'Gangsterville' on which Strummer delves into world music styles purposefully rather than as a voyeur. It is an up-tempo rocker for the most part with a typically impassioned vocal. The choruses take on a distinctly tropical flavour featuring steel drums incorporated into a reggae groove and it works superbly. Another added ingredient is a guitar solo that is closer in style to Aerosmith than The Clash, that works too and indicated Mr Strummer was tearing up the rule book.

49
MUDHONEY
You Got It (Keep It Outta My Face)/ Burn It Clean
No Chart Placing
Sub Pop

The whole Seattle Grunge scene was still regional at this point but the sound was taking shape and there was raw power and vitality aplenty in this Mudhoney single. There was also, it has to be said, a noticeable melodicism introduced along with a traditional verse-chorus pop music structure. The song is a blast - it's lyric is a rebuttal of those who push religion, sex or consumer goods; whatever they're selling isn't wanted or required.

48.
JUNIOR REID
One Blood/Fast Car
No Chart Placing
Big Life

Junior Reid had been recording since the age of 13. In the intervening years he had served as lead singer for Black Uhuru , collaborated with Coldplay and begun producing a number of artists. 'One Blood' was a mighty record with a message of unity. Reid is concerned we do not emphasise our differences in nationality or skin colouring, that course is dangerous and divisive, he advocates instead universal brother and sisterhood. The song is voiced full of passion and rings true and sincere, he rides above a wicked dancehall rhythm to create a record that of power and positivity.

47
THE THE
Armageddon Days Are Here (Again)/Perfect
70
Epic/Some Bizarre

Now with a fixed band in situ, including Johnny Marr on guitar, Matt Johnson was able to move The The's music forward in terms of sonic complexity. Layers of sound shift like sand on a beach making the music here fascinating and cinematic in its scope while Johnson explores themes of politics and religion. He views governments (particularly the US Government) and clashing religious ideologies with fear and loathing. His vocal sounds like reportage from the brink of the apocalypse that he imagines to be imminent.

46
KATE BUSH
The Sensual World/
Walk Straight Down The Middle 12
EMI

Wuthering Heights had been the spark that ignited Kate Bush's remarkable rise. On that song she inhabited the novel's character Cathy as a device to narrate the song. She returns to the same device here as she adopts the persona of Molly Bloom who has stepped from the pages of James Joyce's novel *Ulysses* and is revelling in the three dimensional modern world that she finds full of sensuality. Featuring Davy Spillane on Uilleann pipes, this was another completely absorbing and original single from Kate Bush who proved once again that she was operating in a field of just one.

45
STONE ROSES
Fools Gold/
What The World Is Waiting For
8 (1990 - 22/1995 - 25/1999- 25/ 2005 - 93/2009 - 95)
Silvertone

Drummer Reni learned the James Brown 'Funky Drummer' beat, Mani played a bass part that was derived by Isaac Hayes for 'Theme from Shaft' and with this killer rhythm in place further building blocks were put in place. John Squire went heavy on the wah wah pedal and other effects as he sprayed guitar over the track and Ian Brown performed a whispered vocal as he delivered a lyric inspired by John Huston's film *The Treasure of the Sierra Madre* which was a morality play about the destructive nature of greed and its effect on the soul. This was an ambitious sounding record that moved The Roses away from their more usual rock sound into the world of funk. They were taking a chance, their audience could have rejected this left turn, thankfully they didn't, in fact their numbers swelled and the band were rewarded with their highest charting single .

44
JAMES
Sit Down/Goin' Away/
Sound Investment/Sky Is Falling 77 (1991 - 2)
Rough Trade

Here, in its eight-minute plus original form, was the single that announced James to the world, albeit on a word of mouth basis. It had a fantastic melody, mostly carried by a great piano part, flourishes of guitar from my old school chum Larry Gott, and a bass solo from Jim Glennie, but mostly it had a lyric about finding time for , and showing consideration to, those who are struggling. It was compassionate and humane, its emotion found release in its insanely catchy surging chorus, there was a nice piece of silliness attached to its outro too, the band showing self awareness in puncturing any perceived pomposity as they chirrup about the jockey Lester Piggot.

43
SOUL 2 SOUL FEATURING CARON WHEELER
Keep On Movin (Club Mix)/
(Big Beat Acapella)/ (Pianophella) / (Instrumental)
5
10 Records

Soul 2 Soul were initially a collective led by Jazzie B and Nellie Hooper. In the mid 80s they had run a seminal night at The Africa Centre in London's Covent Garden. They fused elements of soul, funk, jazz, dub reggae, hip-hop beats and house. Singles featuring Doreen Waddell and Rose Windross had been released and been very minor hits before Caron Wheeler added a turbo charged R&B vocal on 'Keep on Movin' to give them their breakthrough into the mainstream. The lyric was an uplifting message to those in need of motivation, its musical element was breathtaking in the broadness of its scope; slow and sensuous it grooved, this was elegance personified in its use of piano with strings inspired by the late 60s psychedelic soul of The Temptations. Soul 2 Soul had arrived and in mixing up genres and stylistic elements created a brand new sound.

42
LIL LOUIS
French Kiss/Wargames
2
Ffrr

Lil Louis hailed from Chicago and 'French Kiss' was a record that expanded the parameters of the House sound. It experimented with tempo changes when such a thing in dance music was a virtual no-no. Its unhurried, blissful climb to a conclusion meant it entered into the world of trance, with a length of 10 minutes the record was an unrelenting build up towards an eventual orgasmic release. Banned by the BBC on grounds of public indecency, 'French Kiss' nonetheless reached an audience more thrilled by its musical innovation than its heavy breathing sex noise titillation.

41
DE LA SOUL
Me Myself And I (Radio Version) / (Richie Rich Remix)/Ain't Hip To Be Labeled A Hippy/What's More /Brain Washed Follower
22
Tommy Boy

New Yorkers De La Soul came at us with this slice of consciousness Hip-hop that wore a smiling face. It was bright and breezy carrying a message of non-conformist attitude and a dig at people who lazily accused them of being hippies. There's a salute to The Jungle Brothers track 'Black is Black' to which 'Me Myself and I' is structurally similar. De La Soul were armed though with more bounce to the ounce and this track was an irrepressible force of nature.

40
JAMES
Come Home/Promised Land
No Chart Placing (2008 - 32) Rough Trade

The streets of Manchester were awash with people bedecked in James T-shirts. There was clearly an audience waiting for them, for the follow up to 'Sit Down' they had an eye catching record sleeve designed by Central Station Design who were associated with Happy Mondays. Graham Massey of 808 State mixed the B side, and A side 'Come Home' was, if not quite as anthemic as 'Sit Down' cut from the same cloth. It was another crowd pleaser and communal sing along, its mighty chorus rang out and lodged in the head, it was tighter than its predecessor, more driving. Larry Gotts guitar riffs were melodic yet spiky, the rhythm section were sure footed and grooving, and singer Tim Booth performed with the conviction of a star in the making, it had all the ingredients of a hit and the band had huge momentum yet it failed dismally and that can only be attributed to incompetence from the record label. James certainly thought so, and upped sticks to sign to Fontana where their commercial potential was soon realised.

39
MOMUS
Hairstyle Of The Devil/
Monsters Of Love/
Amongst Women Only
96
Creation

Nick Currie, known to the wider world as Momus, was and remains a highly literate, spectacularly good songwriter whose stock in trade is to trawl through the damned and seedy underbelly of human behaviour in the manner of Jacques Brel or Serge Gainsborough. At this juncture of his prolific career his sound moved into synth-pop territory while the lyric, delivered with dramatic inflection, purports to be channelled through a third party in an uncomfortable ménage à trois; his rival constantly seeks intimate information about him, his looks, his stature and his sexual prowess. This track delves into dark obsessional behaviour and is highly original and delightfully perverse.

38
KLF
3am Eternal (Pure Trance Original)
/(Break For Love)
1 (1991-12)
KLF Communications

This is another baffling release from the KLF in that it came in multiple mixes and indeed was re-released twice in the next few years in radically differently recorded forms. What is beyond doubt is that by this stage they were complete masters at the manipulation of sound and made brilliant club records that easily transferred onto daytime radio. This pure trance version of '3am Eternal' is sumptuous, at its base is a hard-kicking beat but above that is layer upon layer of blissful techno loveliness and floating ethereal backing voices assisting a soulful female lead. Also blended seamlessly into the mix is a super smooth Saxophone solo that is as sweet as chocolate.

37
MARY MARGARET O'HARA
Body's In Trouble/Year In Song
No Chart Placing
Virgin

Mary Margaret O'Hara hailed from Toronto and was touched by genius. Her 1988 album Miss America was easily one of the most original and startling and best albums of the decade. One of the outstanding tracks was 'Body's in Trouble' which was released as a single. It is determinedly non conformist musically, it is razor sharp and angular, all the pieces of the jigsaw puzzle are in place but not necessarily in the most conventional places. Her voice too is unclassifiable, her phrasing awkward, she goes from conversational to abstract wailing within a heartbeat. I confess I didn't really relate to the lyric at the time, but these days, having undergone several bouts of invasive surgery, I understand only too well the sentiments she brilliantly conveys. I was one of the fortunate few who attended her candlelit show at The International Club one Friday evening, she ignored the sparsity of the audience and thrilled with the audacity and invention of her music. She left the hairs on the back of my neck standing on end at her stunning voice and presence.

36
MANTRONIX
Got To Have Your Love (Club With Bonus Beats)/(Hard To Get Rap)/(Luv Dub)/(Club Edit)/(Instrumental)/(Radio Edit)
4
Capitol

Mantronix adapted their style here fetching in a female singer named Wondress who has a blistering R&B style. They cloaked her voice in sumptuous sampled strings that could have graced a Philadelphia International soul classic, the electro hip-hop beats remained and were as riveting as ever but this was deliberately aimed towards attracting radio play and arresting a slump in fortunes. It succeeded handsomely in its ambitions, and gave Mantronix the commercial boost they desired as well as an artistic shot in the arm.

35
MELVINS/
STEEL POLE BATH TUB
Sweet Young Thing Ain't Sweet No More/I Dreamed I Dream
No Chart Placing
Tupelo

There's only so much sophistication a man can take before he needs something crude, noisy and very loud as an antidote. This split single sees the Melvin's tackling Mudhoney's 'Sweet Young Thing Ain't Sweet No More' and Steel Pole Bath Tub getting to grips with Sonic Youth's 'I Dreamed I Dream'. The Melvin's don't try to emulate Mudhoney's brand of garage rock but sound more solid, dark, and dangerous with a wild vocal from female singer Lorax which changes the song's sexual emphasis. Steel Pole Bath Tub meanwhile take their art punk approach to 'I Dreamed I Dream' they dismantle it, only to piece it back together in their own image, it is a shrieking noise horror show with creepy vocals .

34
HAPPY MONDAYS
Hallelujah/Holy Ghost/
Clap Your Hands/Rave On
19
Factory

These 4 tracks were released under the umbrella title *The Madchester Rave On E.P.* which was a way of announcing to the rest of the world that something was afoot in our grimy northern enclave. 'Hallelujah' captured the radio plays, the

Mondays hit the charts and appeared on Top of The Pops alongside The Stone Roses playing 'Fools Gold' and the next day the world went 'baggy'. 'Hallelujah' was truly outstanding, it caught the Mondays at their most acid-drenched as the guitars make noises that one doesn't equate with guitars. The rhythm lurches dangerously and Shaun Ryder is the deranged rabble rousing ringmaster - it is a swaggering and lairy track that bristles with up to no good attitude, how could any teenager resist .

33
NENEH CHERRY
Manchild/(Original Mix)
5
Virgin

'Manchild' had been the first song the young Neneh Cherry had written, it was a bitter-sweet ballad with a sting in its tail aimed at a man with plenty of growing up left to do. Robert Del Naja, en route to Massive Attack, wrote a rap section and Cameron 'Booga Bear' McVey, tidied up the songs rough edges to make it flow. Cherry is superb in her vocalising of the song, even as she accuses her subject she expresses compassion and frustration, rather than anger. McVey surrounds her with a lush string sound and gives the track tough hip-hop beats, it is an arresting combination not dissimilar to Massive Attack's epic breakthrough single 'Unfinished Sympathy'.

32
DIVINE STYLER FEATURING
The Scheme Team Ain't Saying Nothing/Tongue Of Labyrinth
No Chart Placing
Rhyme $Yndicate

Divine Styler took Hip-hop into left-field here, displaying an abstract jazz sensibility. He had been part of Scheme Team who were Ice T's dance crew. Ice produced and released this record on his own label. The sound is spare and sprightly and features the horn stabs that House of Pain would later make famous on their hit record 'Jump Around'. Both sides of this release display an other worldliness and a defined vision that was a little too advanced for the time. There would be no compromise as the next Divine Styler record was an homage to his Muslim faith and very strange indeed.

31
SKULLFLOWER
I Live In The Bottomless Pit/
Bo Diddleys Shitpump
No Chart Placing
Shock

Skullflower were a psychedelic tinged noise rock band from London, their stock in trade was sludgy riffs drenched in fuzz guitar noise and feedback that was best listened to at exceedingly high volume and that's exactly what is served up here along with a pummelling rhythm and wordless screaming.

30
TECHNOTRONIC
Pump Up The Jam/(Instrumental) 2
Swanyard

House music may have been created in the U.S. but the American mainstream remained resistant to the form until Belgian act Technotric crashed into the chart with the gigantic beats of 'Pump up the Jam'. Dancers required no additional invitation than to hear the opening chords of this irrepressible monster, they swamped the floor in unison to party hard. Radio too could not resist the record's effervescence and its hooks, both musical and lyrical - it is a great pop record with boundless energy.

29
DEPECHE MODE
Personal Jesus/Dangerous
13
Mute

Martin Gore was inspired to write 'Personal Jesus' after reading Priscilla Presley's book *Elvis and Me* where she writes about her devotion to the God-like figure who she believed in unquestionably. The biggest shock for Depeche Mode fans though was not evoking The King Of Rock & Roll, but the blasphemous use of guitar rather than synthesiser as the primary instrument, for these synth pop pioneers this was a risky strategy. The monumental riff is unrelenting and has a nagging quality, the rhythmic thrust of the song is its match, see-sawing urgently while Dave Gahan sings with a sneering contempt making the invitation to "reach out and touch me" sound cruel and cynical rather than a sexual come on. These Basildon boys had seemed like twee and innocent waifs at the start of the decade were now heading towards the nineties as a highly confident unit unshackling themselves from an image they had outgrown, Depeche Mode had truly come of age.

28
PUBLIC ENEMY
Black Steel In The Hour Of Chaos
/B Side Wins Again
No Chart Placing
Def Jam

Heretical though it may seem, I must confess I prefer the later full on assault of Tricky's version of this song to this original. Of course dealing with absolutely genius material and Public Enemy had genius material pouring out of them at this point. The spare but incessant rhythm track comes from a high-pitched sample from Isaac Hayes' 'Hyperbolicsyllabic-sequedalymistic' from his Hot Buttered Soul album. The lyric is a story concerning a black conscientious objector who understands that the U.S. army simply uses and abuses its black recruits and then spits them out with no thanks or fanfare. He is jailed for his beliefs and stages a prison breakout. Chuck D performs the main rap and in-between verses the slightly dislocated voice of Flavor Flav purportedly speaking over a telephone is heard. The track is raw and the imagery used is harsh and vivid, it is a highly exciting listen that delivers a powerful thought-provoking point of view from a minority position.

27
STONE ROSES
She Bangs The Drums/
Standing Here
34 (1990- 32)
Silvertone

"The past was yours, the future's mine" sang Ian Brown, it was a highly prescient lyric. This single was remixed from the group's album and was their most accomplished track at this point, it took them out of the indie-ghetto where they could have languished, and delivered them like a gift to the wider world as an antidote to manufactured pop dross. The rhythm section that set them apart from their peers perform superlatively, the guitar is choppy with a wicked chunky sound, the singer too performs admirably, the whole world knew that when he was in a live situation Ian Brown's voice would sound as flat as a pancake but that problem was addressed and surmounted in the recording studio where the whole band gelled and alchemy occurred.

26
GO BETWEENS
Love Goes On/Clouds
No Chart Placing
Beggars Banquet

We didn't know it at the time but 'Love Goes On' would be the last released single by this consummate singles band for 11 years. Produced by legendary Bowie-Bolan collaborator Tony Visconti, this swansong captured all the beautiful mystery of The Go Betweens. The songs is principally played on acoustic guitar, but discreet brass is added, subtle strings too and there is a Spanish guitar solo that adds further colour, the drums give the song a driving energy despite the unobtrusiveness of Lindy Morrison's performance. Grant McLennan's vocal express hurt, bewilderment and vulnerability, the backing vocals counter these emotions with their brightness and brilliance, overall it's yet another gem from The Go Betweens and its commercial failure proved to be the final straw.

25
THE FALL
Cab It Up/Dead Beat Descendent/
Kurious Oranj/Hit The North
81
Beggars Banquet

'Cab it Up' was a slice of outré rock 'n' roll decorated with a keyboard part that is a cousin of 'Hot Butter' by Popcorn, it teasingly mocks a group of hedonists as they flit like gadflies around London. Mark Smith claimed the song was initially intended to be about William of Orange for the ballet *I am Kurios Oranj* which was a collaboration between The Fall, and Michael Clark's dance troupe, who ultimately provided inspiration for the lyrics. They are lampooned mercilessly and in Smith's vocal there is a degree of mirth. Heavyweight additions on the record are the excellent 'Dead Beat Descendent' and live versions of 'Kurious Oranj' and 'Hit The North' which made this package yet another splendid Fall single in a long run of splendid Fall singles.

24
BOB DYLAN
Everything Is Broken/
Death Is Not The End
98
Columbia

Bob Dylan's output this decade had been patchy at best in terms of quality. Often mediocre work was heralded as a return to form by people whose idolatry negated their critical faculties. 'Everything is Broken' however was genuinely very good indeed, it is basically an up-tempo rocking blues played with great gusto by Bob and his band who locate the groove from the opening bars of the tune and ride it splendidly finding space for some fluid guitar licks and a harmonica part. It is a 'list' song in the manner of his own iconic sixties hit 'Subterranean Homesick Blues'. Here the lyric that rolls off his tongue concerns life in general viewed from the point of view of a deeply despondent man who sees all manner of things from the trivial to the deadly serious falling apart.

23
DOUBLE TROUBLE
AND REBEL MC
Street Tuff (Scar Mix) / Street Tuff (Club Mix) Uk Chart-3
Desire

For Street Tuff the production pair Double Trouble utilise the sped-up bass rhythm of Harry J's All-stars 'Liquidator', its effervescent bounce is absolutely irresistible, it is practically impossible to sit still once the needle hits the groove, such is the raw vitality of the record. Added to the reggae rhythm are House music beats, then factor in the energetic toasting of Londoner Rebel MC who acts as rabble rouser and cheerleader and this mash-up of hip-house and dancehall equates to a party on plastic - it's a party not to miss.

22
LANDLORD FEATURING
DEX DANCLAIR
I Like It (Club Mix)/(Blow Out Dub)/(Groovy House Mix)/
(Deep Garage Mix)/(Cosmic Dub)
No Chart Placing
Bigshot

Simplicity and brilliance combined here to create the ultimate raver's record. It has a wonderful rolling groove, piano stabs that strike like ice picks in the cranium and a rhythm similar to 'Good Life' by Inner City. The difference is that where Inner City combined their sound with pop elements, here the opposite is true - this is an exploration into the depths and darkness of sound where the grooves anchor the listener to prevent them being sucked forever into the enticing sonic whirlpool.

21
ICE T
Lethal Weapon/Heartbeat/
This One's For Me
98
Sire

'Lethal Weapon' showcases Ice T at his most abrasive and confrontational. Although the song is full of violent imagery and could easily be perceived as Gangsta Rap, the inferred violence is here used as metaphor, the crucial oft-repeated hook line is "the lethal weapon is the mind" and the targets are fellow Hip-hop acts who chase the dollar through comprising their music. The moral watchdogs and censors who try to silence him too are in his sights. Produced by Afrika Islam, this track is gritty and claustrophobic and a sample from the funk track 'Razor Blade' by Little Royal is used extensively.

20
TRIFFIDS
Goodbye Little Boy/
Go Home Eddie
No Chart Placing
Island

Working with the hot producer of the day, Steven Street, The Triffids widened the parameters of their sound and incorporated digital technology alongside traditional instrumentation. 'Goodbye Little Boy' was the band's finest pop moment, it was written by band leader David McComb and Adam Peters and given to keyboardist Jill Birt to sing, she gives a brilliant performance where sweetness is combined with steel, her voice rides over a driving beat and bright chiming instrumentation as she delivers a break up song with a twist in its tail. Here the female narrator is hurt by the cruel manner in which she is deserted by her beau only for him soon to change his mind and state he is coming back. By then she has different ideas and delivers her kiss off goodbye to him with apparent relish.

19
ULTRA VIVID SCENE
Mercy Seat/Codeine /
H Like In Heaven/
Mercy Seat (LP Version)
No Chart Placing
4AD

Not to be confused with the brilliant Nick Cave song which shares its title, this is nevertheless a great song and great record in its own right. The Velvet Underground were the principal source of inspiration for Kurt Ralske' who was to all intents Ultra Vivid Scene: a one man band who chose not to maintain a regular group of musicians. Here he sings a risqué homage to the joys of sado-masochism with all the innocence, clarity and purity of a choir boy. He sounds reminiscent of a young John Cale, around his voice is a beautiful throb of distorted ascending guitar chords which are like waves crashing against a rock; tireless, relentless and merciless, it is a cousin to the V.U.

classic 'Venus in Furs'. I saw these play at The International Club and hearing this song and feeling its power was a transportive moment, it was bliss.

18
JANET JACKSON
Rhythm Nation (House Nation Mix)/(United Mix)/(United Dub)
23
A&M

Opening with a bold guitar riff that is a variant of Sly and the Family Stone's 'Thank you (Falettinmebemiceelfagain') the track moves through the gears to morph into a startling, mechanised industrial funk that conveys a militaristic feel. Jimmy Jam and Terry Lewis had used all their production skills to pull this out of the hat and Jackson matches their achievements with a well measured vocal for a lyric that projects a utopian vision of a colour-blind world without division, a world that marches together in unity to the beat of dance music. Its first pumping chorus is as good as it gets, if people felt her sentiments were naïve or glib they needed to be reminded of similar messages from acts as diverse as Bob Dylan, Bob Marley and Funkadelic - there was certainly room for her optimism inside my heart anyway, in combination with the seriously rocking sound that delivered, it this was outstanding.

17
MODEL 500
The Chase (Mayday's Version)/(Natural Version)/(Juans Version)/(Smooth Mix)
No Chart Placing
Metroplex

Richly textured, layer upon layer of electronic sounds combine to make this an incredible listen, whilst its frenetic rhythm remains at the song's heart and is of course what captivates dancers, Juan Atkins provides enough melodic flourishes to ensure 'The Chase' remains a memorable listening experience as well as being a wild ride. He may well have invented the whole genre of Techno music and released a staggering amount of excellent music but if we were to compile a best of Juan Atkins mix then The Chase would be track 1.

16
MADONNA
Express Yourself/
The Look Of Love
5
Sire

Madonna co-wrote and co- produced 'Express Yourself' with Stephen Bray and it was the second single extracted from her *Like a Prayer* album. It is an upbeat dance funk track intended as a tribute to Sly and the Family Stone , the song is a call for female empowerment, it calls for a rejection of passive acceptance and an embrace of an assertive manner and asks women not to accept second class roles but to express their desires and inner feelings. Heavy on hand clap percussion and bubbling synth that build to the horn-backed choruses that mirror turn of the seventies funk and soul singles in their fervour and intensity.

15
THE MEKONS
Memphis Egypt/
Heaven And Back/Cocaine Lil
No Chart Placing
A&M/Twin Tone

Somehow The Mekons had wound up on A&M records, that bastion of good taste and easy listening helmed by Herb Albert and Jerry Moss. They'd had the Sex Pistols of course but the Pistols offered no real threat, they were simply too rude and badly behaved for the company. The Mekons on the other hand were not seduced by their opulent surroundings, they did not dream of stardom and hits, they were too wise, too intelligent and had too much genuine integrity to fall into that trap. The Mekons sought to agitate from within, they were the spanner in the works, the fly in the ointment.

They released an album *The Mekons Rock 'n' Roll* which was an assault on a sick and sickening industry. Track 1, 'Memphis Egypt', it was an obvious single and it absolutely slams - it is ferocious practically from beginning to end, it has the power and crunch of The Who or The Clash, although because this is The Mekons and they do not sing from a classic rock hymn sheet, it also has a sawing violin high in the mix which, like an angry wasp, feels dangerously malevolent. Jon Langford begins to sing with deadly intent beginning with, "Destroy your safe and happy lives..." and then goes on to attack the corporate nature of the rock 'n' Roll business, tying it into a policy of dumbing down and enslaving those consumed by its fake glamour and manufactured image. This was an essential release from an essential band who were an antidote to the masses of careerist fakes. unsurprisingly A&M soon washed their hands of The Mekons.

14
CINDI LAUPER
I Drove All Night/
Maybe He'll Know
7
Epic

This was yet another hit song written by Billy Steinberg and Tom Kelly tailored and intended for Roy Orbison who recorded it 1987 but it was only released posthumously in 1992, in the meantime Cindi Lauper claimed the song. It is a breathless emotional drama about a man alone, he is bereft and so consumed by love and lust that he drives through the long dark night to be with his lover. Cindi Lauper is of course not a man , she explained that she liked the idea of "a woman driving , a woman in control" and she more than does the song justice, she sings in a strong low register only unleashing her thrilling falsetto towards the songs epic climax.

13
THE PIXIES
Here Comes Your Man/
Wave Of Mutilation/
Into The White/Bailey's Walk
54
4AD

Black Francis claimed he had written this song aged 14 inspired by the use of the word 'boxcars' in the R.E.M song 'Carnival Of Sorts (Boxcar)' but he was now embarrassed by it considering it too straight and poppy. The band referred to it disdainfully as 'the Tom Petty Song' but producer Gil Norton thought differently and so, as Black Francis put it, he thought it polite to "throw him a bone" and record the accursed tune.

The arrangement was spruced up and an additional verse composed. It opens with what guitarist Joey Santiago called his "Hendrix chord" and then proceeds, lyrics concern hobos waiting for a California earthquake to hit, they have sensed it coming due to an atmospheric change and by Pixies standards it is a straightforward song on which Black Francis sings sweetly without histrionics backed by Kim Deal during the choruses. This is however The Pixies in their peak period, so the word straightforward is very relative, they still sound strange, edgy and vital.

12
DINOSAUR JR
Just Like Heaven/Throw Down/
Chunks (A Last Rights Tune)
No Chart Placing
Blast First

If one is going to record a cover version the intention surely should be to transform the source material and that is what Dinosaur Jr do to this Cure song. Where the British band played the song with a lightness of touch and wistfulness, Dinosaur Jr take the opposite approach. All the melody of the original is maintained but the playing is hard, the rhythm section is taut and tough, the guitar is a combination of noise and well chosen notes and J Mascis sings in as unorthodox a manner as Robert Smith but his voice carries a scornful note while bassist Lou Barlow provides backing vocals by yelling a throat shredding noise, this was an electric performance.

11
MAURICE
This Is Acid (A New Dance Craze)
/(Deep Dub)/(K&T Mix)
No Chart Placing
Trax

The original 'This is Acid' was recorded using just a drum machine and bass synth and released in 1988 as the B side to the 'Maurice Joshua with Hot Hands Hula' single 'I Gotta Big Dick'. In 1989 it was revisited as the Acid House scene boomed, the track retained the spoken word vocal by (Hot Hands) Hula Mahone and acts as an introduction to the delights of the Chicago Acid sound. Next, the instantly recognisable synth lead from Black Riots 'A Day in The Life' is incorporated alongside the synth rhythm from Inner City's 'Big Fun', euphoric screams echo, sirens wail, more samples are added, it is a wild celebration that heralds the pleasure seekers who in their droves are rejecting conformist society and seeking illicit pleasure in fields and warehouses. It is a gesture from the people in the margins towards the conservative mainstream, it says "fuck you".

10
PERE UBU
Waiting For Mary
(What Are We Doing Here?) /
Wine Dark Sparks
No Chart Placing
Fontana

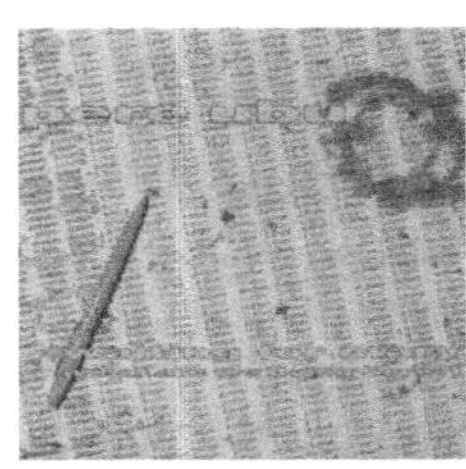

The world seemed to be going increasingly mad so what were arch-contrarians Pere Ubu to do? They reigned in their abstract concepts, the 'noise for noise's sake' sonic warfare was relegated to the background in the mix and worked with a big shot hit-making record producer who gave them a crisp and clean sound and put out this ridiculously catchy pop single that, in a fairer alternate universe, would have put them into the hit parade.

'Waiting for Mary' was, on the face of it, nothing like a Pere Ubu record, it obeyed the rules of song structure, it went - verse, chorus, middle eight, verse, chorus, outro, end - but it was still too weird for the kids! It was a tad too urgent in its tempo, it had a nervous energy that could discomfort nice folks, as for the vocals they were tackled with a near maniacal glee by David Thomas who sounded like he was singing atop a bucking bronco while the backing vocals could have come from a Hammer horror film. However one looked at this record one had to conclude that it was touched by genius .

9
WIRE
In Vivo
Illustrate
Finest Drops
No Chart Placing
Mute

Not as immediate as preceding singles but all the more satisfying for that fact, 'In Vivo' is sweeping and majestic, it is propelled by a bass line pushed high into the mix, the vocal is crystal clear and beautifully enunciated as a cryptic lyric that appears to be concerned with uprisings and revolution, although I suspect that would be too literal an interpretation. Wire exist in a self-contained musical universe, they are a unique proposition in that they betray little in the way of their influences and consequently their music sounds fresh and timeless.

8
808 STATE
Pacific 202/Pacific State - Origin/
Pacific State 303 /Cobra Bora Shortcut
10
ZTT

There are so many remixes of 'Pacific State' ("42", quipped Graham Massey) that no single one is definitive. The track was originally released on the album *Quadrostate* where Gerald Simpson (A Guy Called Gerald) who had been a member of the band was credited as co-writer and co-producer, although he claims to have written the whole track, a claim that is disputed elsewhere, what is not in dispute is that, with its bird song sample and yearning soprano sax part played by Massey, this is an incandescent beauty. Even though it grooves and the beat remains insistent it is the record that introduced to ravers the value of music that was mellow, and would later be labelled 'chill out'. It made its mark in clubs immediately and was heard in Ibiza by holidaying BBC DJ Gary Davies who gave it daytime radio play and it's commercial rise began.

7
MADONNA
Like A Prayer
Act Of Contrition
1
Sire

1988 had been a bad year for Madonna: two big budget film flops and a Broadway acting role that was panned by critics were compounded by the end of her marriage to Sean Penn. She was 30, the same age as her mother when she had died and her feelings needed to be addressed through her music. A conscious decision was made to make a more serious and adult-themed record than she had done previously which culminated in her album *Like a Prayer*. The title track was the first completed and set the template for the rest, and inevitably was the first song released as a single - it was bold and brilliant.

Opening with Madonna's voice unaccompanied except for an organ as if in prayer, a gospel choir add their voices and drums kick adding power and emphasis to her words where she portrays a girl so consumed by religious fervour that the male figure of God dominates all her thoughts; the sacred and the lustfully profane. The sound swells, guitar noises contributed by Prince are added as the song moves towards its final conclusion - mission accomplished for Madonna!

6
DE LA SOUL
Eye Know (I Know It All Mix)
Eye Know (The Kiss Mix)
The Mack Daddy On The Left
14
Tommy Boy

In much the same way as the great jazz saxophonist John Coltrane had taken standards apart and reshaped them for a new era on his classic My Favourite Things album, so did hip-hop producers who blended sampled phrases into new forms. Prince Paul, De La Soul's producer in residence, creates a masterpiece, his collage of found sounds on 'Eye Know' is stupendous, he uses a pallet of wide-ranging source material; the drums come from Lee Dorsey, guitar and horns courtesy of The Mad Lads, the vocals on the chorus are extracted from 'Peg' by Steely Dan while the great Otis Redding's iconic whistling from 'Sittin' on the Dock of a Bay' provides a melodic hook. The sound is bright and upbeat, what's more it swings and wears a party hat. The vocals that complete the track are cool and relaxed and convey friendliness and promise fun, the slightly surreal hipster jive lyric boils down to a plain old declaration of love, this is music that makes people smile inside.

5
THE PIXIES
Monkeys Gone To Heaven
Manta Ray
60
4AD

'Monkeys Gone to Heaven' is the epitome of Pixies loud-quiet-loud approach to music construction but it is also much more than that. For the first time they use outside instrumentalists adding cello and violin parts, the song was written as usual by Black Francis and alludes strongly to ecological problems caused by man. He opens by describing the destruction of Neptune the God of the Sea who is buried under 10 million pounds of human generated sludge. Later the creature in the sky, 'God', is trapped in a hole that has formed in the ozone layer. Man is depicted as a monkey, a vandal, obsessed with religious mumbo jumbo and numerology, descending into a figurative and literal hell. The band are at the top of their game, they are alternately lean in their performance and next conjuring up what sounds like thermo-nuclear power as they unleash their sonic arsenal. Kim Deal sings choruses in a bored monotone while Black Francis adopts the role of detached commentator, his voice laced with contempt at the stupidity he is witnessing before taking on the role of demented fire and brimstone preacher counting out time before the end of the world,

4
LOU REED
Dirty Blvd
Last Great American Whale
The Room
No Chart Placing
Sire

New York gave Lou Reed all the inspiration he needed to fuel a 40-plus year career as songsmith and alternate poet laureate to the city he loved. Lou certainly cherished much of what New York offered but that did not blind him from seeing the city's harsh iniquities. 'Dirty Blvd' is a piece of reportage laced with anger, he sings with a snarl never far from his lip of the city's inequalities and compares the lives of the high-flying rich and the desperate poor co-existing in close proximity to each other geographically but worlds apart in terms of wealth and opportunities. His band at this point were highly proficient and precise players who displayed no flamboyant tendencies, which is exactly what is required here - it is spare and simple based around a repetitive chord sequence, the job of the music is to support the message which it does admirably .

1989

3
SOUL 2 SOUL
Back To Life (However Do You Want Me)
1
Virgin

With its shuffling rhythm, House style piano, strings that swoon (courtesy of the Reggae Philharmonic Orchestra), and a heart-stoppingly beautiful slow burning vocal performance from Caron Wheeler 'Back to Life' became the most ubiquitous sound of the summer. Originally recorded acapella and used somewhat wastefully as an album track it took time for the song's possibilities to be realised and instrumentation added. The lyric is simple and repetitive, it is a request for clarification of the narrator's romantic status, "however do you want me/however do you need me?" hook line was insistent and inescapable. The sound which predated what came to be known as Trip Hop was revolutionary. This was music that veered away from the template offered up by America - it was homogeneous, home grown, black British club music that could stand proudly, toe to toe, with any imported sound

2
PUBLIC ENEMY
Fight The Power
Fight The Power
(Flavor Flav Meets Spike Lee)
29
Motown

Film producer Spike Lee needed a musical theme for his movie *Do The Right Thing* and so, at his behest, Public Enemy created and delivered 'Fight The Power'. It is an incendiary piece which is highly political. It was a call for black people to revolutionise their thoughts, to look at facts rather than believe propaganda and oppose the white oppressors, the system and its injustices. The musical track was constructed using samples from the music of James Brown intercut with pieces that allude to Afro-American culture - the sounds of Black church services are heard alongside exhortations from civil rights speeches. Chuck D's lyric is persuasive and provocative, his delivery of the words is awe-inspiring in its power, Flavor Flav's interjections add even more juice, white American icons used to symbolise the nation's supposed greatness such as Elvis Presley and John Wayne are held up to be inspected and ridiculed, torn down, and dismissed with the line "most of my heroes don't appear on no stamps" and we understand the pernicious nature behind that truthful observation. If my synopsis makes this record sound like heavy going I apologize because it is a joyous sound, a celebration of the black culture that spawned the soundtrack to many of our lives.

1
NEIL YOUNG
Rockin' In The Free World (Acoustic)
Rockin' In The Free World (Electric)
83
Reprise

The title of 'Rockin in the Free World' was gifted to Neil Young by way of a chance remark made by his guitarist Frank 'Poncho' Sampedro who, on hearing a planned tour of the Soviet Union had been cancelled, supposedly said "we'll just have to keep rockin' in the free world", Young completed the song hours later. It was recorded in the manner of the earlier 'Tonight's the Night' and 'Hey Hey My My, into the black/out of the blue' in two versions - one primarily acoustic, the other all electric. In terms of power it made little difference because both versions surged through every word and Neil Young's impassioned performance. For the lyric Young casts his eye around the globe to talk about the deprivations put upon citizens by harsh administrations in this time of global turmoil as nations faced off against each other and divisions in ideological belief were becoming increasingly fraught. He searches for hope in the same manner as 'man of the people' Jesse Jackson as he refers implicitly to Ayatollah Khomeini's inflammatory proclamation that the U.S. was 'The Great Satan'. The outgoing American president, Ronald Reagan, is castigated for his economic policies that victimised the poor and fuelled the iniquity of drug addiction and the crack epidemic, while his successor George H W Bush is satirised for his perceived hollow promises of a "kinder gentler nation". The song pulls off the trick of being angry and passionate and yet sounding jubilant and celebratory, it is a song that has spoken to people in the decades since its release, a song that continues to speak as it carries a message that opposes tyranny and injustice. It carries the flame of freedom .

Top: My first time in NYC 1989

Left: At my worst, far drunker than Bestie!

Afterword

I approached the writing of this book with a degree of trepidation. My superficial memories of the eighties were of its tastelessness, and artificiality. In my mind I pictured Reagan and Thatcher, pastel-coloured knitwear, shiny tracksuits, Noel Edmonds and Phil Collins. Fortunately, this trepidation proved groundless once I'd done some research and awakened dormant memories. The decade was one of marvellous musical innovation and experimentation and this book has been a joy to write. I hope that this joy has been transmitted and the reader takes a degree of pleasure from my words.

Stevie B and I taking the DJing too seriously

Printed in Great Britain
by Amazon

21283698R00233